*Social Studies
in the United States*

A Critical Appraisal

Contributors

MARK CHESLER
The University of Michigan

JACK E. COUSINS
Ball State University

C. BENJAMIN COX
University of Illinois

EMILY S. GIRAULT
The University of Michigan

PETER V. GRECO
Syracuse University

PAUL D. HINES
Indiana University

M. KENT JENNINGS
The University of Michigan

BRUCE R. JOYCE
Teachers College, Columbia University

BYRON G. MASSIALAS
The University of Michigan

LAWRENCE E. METCALF
University of Illinois

JOHN R. PALMER
The University of Wisconsin

JOHN J. PATRICK
Indiana University

WILLIAM D. RADER
The University of Chicago

FREDERICK R. SMITH
Indiana University

Social Studies in the United States

A Critical Appraisal

Edited by

C. BENJAMIN COX
University of Illinois

BYRON G. MASSIALAS
The University of Michigan

HARCOURT, BRACE & WORLD, INC.
New York / Chicago / San Francisco / Atlanta

Preface

Books are the products of vision, toil, and compromise. In creating this volume we have tried to maximize the visionary factor and minimize compromise; we were unable to regulate the toil factor. We began with a group of fourteen experienced educators and social scientists who shared a similar vision of the social studies curriculum and the central role of inquiry in it. Nevertheless, what looked like a relatively easy task two years ago has turned out to be a major undertaking.

Our central purpose has been to assess critically the quality and content of elementary, junior high, and senior high school social studies instruction in the United States today. We have tried to provide both the experienced teacher and the prospective teacher with creative suggestions on how to use and evaluate existing social studies materials and instructional procedures. We have also tried to suggest some guidelines for future developments in social studies teaching.

This book makes two basic assumptions. First, an accurate picture of the content, methods, and goals of social studies courses is best obtained by analyzing a representative sample of widely used textbooks. Second, the most important function of social studies courses is to develop skills of critical inquiry among students. The Introduction suggests several specific criteria for evaluating how well textbooks help to perform this function. Each author then applies these criteria to existing textbooks in his field and offers suggestions for improving future textbook materials.

Social Studies in the United States presents a definite point of view which may be embraced or questioned; in either case it serves as a point of departure for the inquiring college instructor and his students. We hope too that this book will be a useful reference for elementary and secondary social studies teachers and school administrators who must deal with the perennial problems of textbook selection, course and curriculum planning, and program development.

As most readers know, the social studies curriculum presents a remarkably consistent face throughout most of the United States. The elementary school has traditionally dealt with social phenomena by means of the "expanding horizons" approach. The junior high school stresses civics, American and state history, and world geography. In the senior high school sophomores can ordinarily study world history; juniors, American history; and seniors, government or civics, often economics and sociology, and occasionally psychology.

We have accepted the traditional social studies curriculum pattern as the framework for this book for several reasons: First, this pattern is reflected in the titles and scope of most social studies courses and published school materials. Second, each author claims special competency—through academic preparation and teaching experience in elementary or secondary school social studies—in the area he is writing about. Finally, grade-level organization on a discipline-by-discipline basis seems the clearest way to designate each area.

The organization of the book along these lines, however, should not be interpreted as an acceptance of this traditional curriculum pattern. The authors have recommended a number of alternatives in their chapters, and the Conclusion suggests certain curriculum changes that reflect many of these recommendations. We sincerely hope that as we engage in this dialogue we will be joined by the thousands of other elementary, secondary, and college teachers and researchers who are concerned about the future of the profession.

C. Benjamin Cox
Byron G. Massialas

Contents

*Social Studies
in the United States*

A Critical Appraisal

CHAPTER I

Introduction

The Inquiry Potential of Social Studies

C. BENJAMIN COX
BYRON G. MASSIALAS

Demands and Promise

It is increasingly clear that there are changes afoot in social studies.
Not the least of these was heralded a decade ago by Hunt and
Metcalf's *Teaching High School Social Studies* (10). Perhaps more
than any other single publication, this text in social studies education
clearly predicted future trends in the field. Hunt and Metcalf (10)
asserted in 1955 that social education in a democracy demands a
"much greater emphasis on developing higher thought processes,
with all that this implies for reflective examination of critical social
issues." They predicted that the social studies curriculum would
"eventually rely heavily on data supplied by social scientists, particularly in the fields of sociology, anthropology, psychology, and
psychiatry." The demand, they hypothesized, was for a more systematic means of social judgment in a democracy; the curriculum
trend would necessarily be toward a wider spectrum of social knowledge, emphasizing the disciplines of social analysis.

Both the demand and the trend have displayed continuous, if not vigorous, existence in the literature since the 1955 statement. In 1960, for example, Engle (6) pithily stated, "in teaching social studies, we should emphasize decision-making as against mere remembering." Like Hunt and Metcalf he went on to show that data and appropriate learning content are synonymous only when data converge in reflective judgment, that is, when facts are used to support or negate ideas. All of these authors went far in describing a new framework for social studies that entailed social analysis, systematic inquiry, multidisciplinary sources of data, and a focus on social issues and judgments.

Formerly, except for certain often abortive efforts with problem solving, social studies had emphasized selected closed systems of knowledge to be taught as truths. That is, the limited areas of knowledge dealt with at all were treated as the finished products of social and historical research. As Wesley and Wronski (22) describe it, the task of social studies was to simplify and adapt these factual packages for student consumption without systematically devising models that students could use to confirm or modify ideas presented to them. As Joseph Schwab delicately phrased it, social studies students were to be taught a "rhetoric of conclusions" (21). Particularly after the Woods Hole Conference in 1959 the social studies field began in earnest to take stock of itself and to reexamine its direction and focus. The Engle statement cited above, made first at the convention of the Indiana Council for the Social Studies in 1959 and subsequently published and reprinted, pinpointed the issue. The plea was for a new center of interest—the decision—and a new strategy— reflective inquiry. This proposed reconstitution of social studies amounted, in effect, to an inversion of the area of study, asking both students and teachers to begin to invent new frames of knowledge that would be based on their own social attitudes and judgments.

A revolution must, in the end, be judged by its products, not by its promises. While it is too early to see the final products, at least two major factors appear to differentiate the present reform movement from abortive past ones. One is the willingness of educators and social scientists to carry on a dialogue. Another is the amount of financial support presently available from foundations and the federal government for program development and research.

Social Studies, Social Scientists, and Grants

One of the major consequences of the revolution in social studies was that the social scientists themselves began to listen and to preach the emerging gospel! Franklin Patterson (18), for example, took a careful look at the field and said categorically, "For the most part, the present social studies curriculum is simply obsolescent." He noted the "curious irony" that for forty years had kept social studies protected from the incursions of the social sciences and described society's urgent need as follows: "The social studies are needed to impart a body of factual knowledge, a theoretical apparatus for supplying this knowledge with order and significance, a methodology of inquiry and verification, and an appreciation of the range of values reflected in the study of man."

The task thus identified for social studies was an imposing one: to present to the students the broadest possible spectrum of knowledge about human behavior and to teach them the techniques of systematic inquiry and the process of evaluation. This task, according to Patterson, must be carried out within some unifying framework based on such emphases as causation, citizenship, social self-perception, and social science methodologies.

Robert Feldmesser (8), another social scientist, also viewed the social studies curriculum as reflecting, for the most part, the spirit of 1916, the date of the National Education Association's famous curriculum report. As a means of updating the curriculum, he envisioned the formidable task of developing for the public school "a single course in the social or 'behavioral' sciences." But he saw as the major obstacle to such social studies reform "the mutual suspicion of social scientists in various disciplines and their inhibiting disdain of their estranged colleagues of lower status, the social studies teachers."

A measure of rapprochement between some social scientists and teacher-educators has been developed through a few of the social studies curriculum centers funded through Project Social Studies of the U.S. Office of Education. But for the most part the responses to the need cited by Patterson and Feldmesser have consisted of extending the influence of particular social sciences in the public school or updating existing social studies courses. For example, the American Anthropological Association's Curriculum Study Project, supported by the National Science Foundation, has been preparing special anthropology units for inclusion in the world history course, and the curriculum center at the University of Georgia has recently begun to prepare a separate anthropology course of study for the elementary school. Economists, sociologists, geographers, political scientists, and historians—each group reacting to self-perceived needs and the availability of funds—are beginning in diverse ways to refurbish their public school offerings. Some studies aim at incorporating the major concepts from all the social sciences into an interdisciplinary structure stretching from kindergarten through the twelfth grade. Others plan to develop curriculum and materials for a single course. Developmental programs in history look to building two- or three-year sequences; for example, a recent effort by Leften Stavrianos and associates produced a two-year course in world history. At least one Project Social Studies curriculum center will examine the public school offerings in United States history in the fifth, eighth, and eleventh grades.

Flux and Ferment

In the long run probably nothing but good will emerge from what Donald Robinson (19) has characterized as "flux and ferment" in social studies. Certainly the penetrating light of research and scholarship will produce remarkable resource materials in quantities never before available to the social studies teacher. Units like Robert Hanvey's *The Idea of Liberty in American Culture* (9) are already earning plaudits by teachers and scholars alike. The social studies curriculum has seldom been courted and wooed by so determined an array of scholars and educators.

But the ferment in social studies represents a curious mixture of revolution and counterrevolution. The predictions made a decade ago by Hunt and Metcalf, Engle, and others anticipated only the positive developments in social studies. But it is not surprising that suggestions that would, in effect, revolutionize an entire area of study could not be made without encountering pitfalls and fomenting counterrevolutionary responses. Precious few of the present proposals in social studies give promise of pressing forward the thrust initiated by Hunt and Metcalf and Engle. A notable exception is the research carried out by Donald Oliver and associates (17) at Harvard, focusing on the examination of political controversy in social studies. In the

main, present curricular developments seem to be exercises in retrench-
ment—albeit at a more sophisticated level than is common in such
activities. Witness, for example, the Indiana historians who rather
successfully blocked a relatively innocuous curricular innovation
embodied in a statewide proposal to change the emphasis on United
States history (1).[1] Further attempts at countermoves by the "establishment" (mainly narrative historians) are seen in articles such as
those by Walter Rundell (20) and Mark Krug (13), who have continued to stress the centrality of the historical method and historical
knowledge in finding meaning in most human pursuits. In a more
recent article (12) Krug, presenting himself as the spokesman for the
status quo and conveniently disregarding the relevant evidence produced by Piaget, Bruner, Guilford, Torrance, Getzels, Bloom, Such-
man, and others, attacked the new curriculum orientation expressed
in such concepts as the inductive method, analytical and intuitive
thinking, the spiral curriculum, knowledge structure, and learning to learn. Furthermore, he severely criticized the movement to
develop a social studies program based on concepts, generalizations,
and the methods of investigation of the social and behavioral sciences
rather than on historical information describing unique and "dramatic" events. His proposal is no more than an emotional plea to
return to the "good old days" when the storytelling historians reigned
supreme, when teaching was characterized by didactic rather than
dialectic practices, and when learning was synonymous with memorization of information rather than genuine exploration and validation of ideas. To prove their point traditionalist historians like Krug
have disregarded the growing segment in their profession who want
to escape from the study of the unique to develop broad principles
and generalizations about human affairs to be tested systematically
through both social science and historical methods.[2]

    Notwithstanding the diversity and improved scholarly content

[1]In fact this volume grew out of the increased interest in history courses en-
gendered by the supposed threat to them.
[2]Some prominent historians of the modern persuasion and their works are David
M. Potter, *People of Plenty: Economic Abundance and the American Character,*
University of Chicago Press, Chicago, 1954; Louis Gottschalk (ed.), *Generalization
in the Writing of History,* University of Chicago Press, Chicago, 1963; Crane
Brinton, *The Anatomy of Revolution,* Vintage, New York, 1958; H. Stuart Hughes,
History as Art and as Science, Harper & Row, New York, 1964; William H.
McNeil, *The Rise of the West,* University of Chicago Press, Chicago, 1963. Also,
some sociologists study history to develop explanatory principles; for example, see
the superb work of Seymour Martin Lipset, *The First New Nation: The United
States in Historical and Comparative Perspective,* Basic Books, New York, 1963.

of social studies offerings that may result, we suggest that several present efforts at curriculum development may be more of a sophisticated counteraction than a revolution. In the guise of giving curricular sinew to the ideas of structure and discovery popularized by Bruner (3, 4), these efforts may well represent a modern means of resisting the radical change called for by Hunt and Metcalf, Engle, Oliver, and others by perpetuating the influence of isolated disciplines. Thus new centers of interest and new social realities are sacrificed in order to identify the structures of *old* disciplines, now given a new lease on life in the public school program. To identify the logical structure of a discipline that is "out there" may imply a separation of the known and knowable from the knower. Recent psychological and behavioral research, however, suggests that the personality and the social milieu of the learner shape his perception of his environment. There is something to be said for Carl Becker's dictum (2) that "every man is his own historian." In commenting on certain apparent weaknesses in social studies projects, Massialas (14) has suggested that "the Centers have placed a disproportionate amount of emphasis on the 'structure of the disciplines' " rather than on human values and social concerns. He proposed that social studies programs be built on an interdisciplinary basis and provide defensible models to analyze social controversy.

That many of our present efforts in teaching social studies and many of our attempts at curricular revision may be missing the point is suggested by Engle (7), who asserted that "the application of valid ideas to important social problems" is "the ultimate purpose" of social studies instruction. Concepts, problems, facts, or general ideas presented without a contextual interrelationship are "merely academic; their learning quickly becomes a bore." Massialas (15), too, appeared to reflect this same contextual orientation when he stated the social studies program is acceptable insofar as it meets these requisites: (1) "It emphasizes principles and generalizations that explain human interactions"; and (2) "It incorporates within itself models of search, verifiability, and invention, which the learner employs in his quest to find dependable knowledge."

A New Assessment

In this context the authors of this volume began to ask some basic questions about social studies: What is the present status of public school social studies? Is it possible to identify the good and bad aspects of the curricula or courses ordinarily offered, the prevailing teaching practices, and the classroom use of materials? Is there a way to arrive at such a description, short of visiting every class or reading every curriculum guide? Does the "revisionist" literature suggest tenable criteria by which the practices, if describable, could be judged? Given an imaginative license, could the requisites of an acceptable social studies curriculum be designed?

In order to respond positively to these questions we made a number of assumptions about curriculum and instruction, textbooks and materials, and future developments in social studies. We have assumed, for example, that the most promising route of development for social studies is that identified in the literature cited earlier in this chapter—a route best described as the inquiry process. We accept Dewey's general definition (5) of this process as "the active, persistent, and careful consideration of any belief or supposed form of knowledge in the light of the grounds that support it and the further conclusions to which it tends." Furthermore, we have assumed that social studies content, practices, and purposes are reflected in large measure in textbooks, the basic material source of most courses. These assumptions form the basic framework of this study, which assesses current elementary, junior high, and high school texts, curriculum patterns, and instructional methods in social studies. Each chapter tries to answer the following general questions:

1. To what extent do current texts and instructional programs employ critical inquiry?

2. To what extent do they promote further critical inquiry among students?

3. What immediate strategies can the teacher employ to enhance the inquiry method using available materials?

4. What future developments will be likely to produce the greatest development of inquiry as goal and method in public school social studies?

In order to maintain some consistency of judgment among ourselves in evaluating the content, organization, and approach of textbooks according to the above questions, each author applied the following specific criteria, at least in part, to selected textbooks in his area of specialization. These criteria, with minor modifications, are those suggested by Massialas (16) for teachers selecting a textbook, and they reflect the focal consideration of this book: To what extent do social studies texts and various other materials now available contribute to critical inquiry in the social studies curriculum?

1. Does the text have a conceptual framework that gives it direction and purpose? Does it present and adhere to a consistent theory about social phenomena? Are the basic assumptions identified?

2. Is the content based on stated or clearly implied principles and generalizations? Does the author offer only relevant information and relate it clearly to these major ideas? Does the text provide hypotheses that can be tested by student inquiry?

3. Is the student encouraged to question various observations and related interpretations of reported social phenomena?

4. Is the text "inductively" oriented in order to promote the creative discovery of relationships by pupils? Does it provide "creative encounters" in the form of cases, episodes, or dilemmas?

5. Has the author used a defensible scheme for the selection of his material? Does the author make a conscious effort to apply the scientific method to his work? Does he show how his conclusions are supported? Does the book identify the existing gaps in human knowledge?

6. Does the book focus on or identify broad problems of social import that can serve as "springboards" for student inquiry?

7. Is the author consistent in his meanings or ideas? Is he careful to avoid ambiguities and vague terms? Does he make his meanings clear?

8. Does the author present information appropriately and freely from other cultures to support broad generalizations and ideas? Does he guard against an ethnocentric, Western bias?

9. Does the book reflect the most recent developments in scholarly research? Does it employ data from all the social sciences, and are these data reliable? Does it show the interrelatedness of all social knowledge?

10. Does the book attempt to interpret the methods of research

in the social sciences as they apply to the statements of fact and the relationships reported?

11. Does the author identify value issues? Does he differentiate between value judgments and descriptive propositions? Does he pose a systematic and defensible means for dealing with value issues?

12. Does the text deal freely with controversial social issues? Does the text identify all points of view where feasible? If it takes a point of view, does the text make clear on what grounds the conclusion was reached?

13. Are definitive, detailed, and annotated bibliographies provided? Are paperbacks included? Are statistical data sources identified? Are primary and secondary sources presented?

14. Does the author tailor his discussion to the age level of his student readers?

15. Do the end-of-chapter questions and exercises promote reflective thinking? Are they inquiry oriented?

16. Does the publisher provide a manual for the teacher that states the objectives and criteria of the textbook? Is the teacher provided with an additional, scholarly, annotated bibliography? Do the tests provided measure higher cognitive processes? Are suggestions given for the creative use of the text? Is further inquiry encouraged?

These criteria are not necessarily identical for all subjects and all grade levels. A criterion may apply to an elementary text or program somewhat less rigorously than to a senior text or program, and some criteria may be less applicable in one case than in another. Each author has exercised his judgment in applying the above criteria to his area of specialization. Some authors have also applied additional criteria that seem appropriate to their subjects and grade levels. Finally, each author has used his textbook analysis as a springboard for developing his own ideas about curriculum and instruction and his own suggestions for more effective use of texts and other materials. The resultant variety of interpretation, however, occurs within a common frame of reference: the assumption that inquiry in social studies is a process applicable to all levels of instruction and to the several subject areas and learning activities.

Selected Bibliography

1. BAXTER, MAURICE G., FERRELL, ROBERT H., AND WILTZ, JOHN E., *The Teaching of American History in High Schools,* Indiana University Press, Bloomington, 1964.

2. BECKER, CARL, "Every Man His Own Historian," *American Historical Review,* 37 (Jan., 1932), 221–36.

3. BRUNER, JEROME, *On Knowing,* Harvard University Press, Cambridge, Mass., 1963.

4. ———, *The Process of Education,* Harvard University Press, Cambridge, Mass., 1961.

5. DEWEY, JOHN, *How We Think,* Heath, Boston, 1933.

6. ENGLE, SHIRLEY H., "Decision-Making: The Heart of Social Studies Instruction," *Social Education,* 24 (Nov. 1960), 301–04, 306.

7. ———, "Thoughts in Regard to Revision," *Social Education,* 27 (Apr., 1963), 185–89.

8. FELDMESSER, ROBERT A., "Sociology and the Social Studies Curriculum of the American High School," speech delivered at a meeting of the American Sociological Association, Washington, D.C., Aug. 31, 1962.

9. HANVEY, ROBERT, *The Idea of Liberty in American Culture,* Anthropology Curriculum Study Project, 5632 Kimbark Avenue, Chicago, 1963.

10. HUNT, MAURICE, AND METCALF, LAWRENCE E., *Teaching High School Social Studies,* Harper, New York, 1955.

11. KRUG, EDWARD A., *The Shaping of the American High School,* Harper & Row, New York, 1964.

12. KRUG, MARK M., "Bruner's New Social Studies: A Critique," *Social Education,* 30 (Oct., 1966), 400–06.

13. ———, "History and the Social Sciences: The Narrowing Gap," *Social Education,* 29 (Dec., 1965), 515–20.

14. MASSIALAS, BYRON G., "Reaction to the Reports on Project Social Studies," *Social Education,* 29 (Oct., 1965), 356–57.

15. ———, "Revising the Social Studies: An Inquiry-Centered Approach," *Social Education,* 27 (Apr., 1963), 185–89.

16. ———, "Selecting a Social Studies Textbook," *Social Education,* 25 (May, 1961), 237–38.

17. OLIVER, DONALD W., AND SHAVER, JAMES P., *The Analysis of Public Controversy: A Study in Citizenship Education,* Cooperative Research Project, 8145 U.S. Office of Education, Harvard University, Cambridge, Mass., 1962.

18. PATTERSON, FRANKLIN, "Social Science and the New Curriculum," *The American Behavioral Scientist,* 6 (Nov., 1962), 28–31.

19. ROBINSON, DONALD, "Ferment in the Social Studies," *Social Education*, 27 (Nov., 1963), 360–64, 410.

20. RUNDELL, WALTER, "History Teaching: A Legitimate Concern," *Social Education*, 29 (Dec., 1965), 521–24, 528.

21. SCHWAB, JOSEPH J., "Inquiry, the Science Teacher, and the Educator," *The School Review*, 68 (Summer, 1960), 176–95. Also published in *The Science Teacher*, 27 (Oct., 1960), 6–11.

22. WESLEY, EDGAR B., AND WRONSKI, STANLEY P., *Teaching Social Studies in High Schools*, Heath, Boston, 1958.

PART I

The Elementary School

CHAPTER 2

The Primary Grades

A Review of Textbook Materials

BRUCE R. JOYCE

Until very recently the production of instructional materials for public schools in the United States has been left almost entirely to commercial firms, and the commercially produced textbook has become the chief material used in the school.

It is reasonable to expect that no publisher will embark on the publication of anything as expensive as a textbook series unless he has a reasonable chance to sell his product. Consequently the publisher tries to produce textbooks that will fit into the curricular patterns that prevail in the schools. In an effort to predict what kind of textbooks will be salable, the publisher examines curriculum guides published by school districts, consults with educational theorists, and examines recommendations made by national organizations of educators. Where the publishers find that several curricular and instructional patterns are used in schools or recommended by theorists, we are likely to find variety in textbook content and approach, as some publishers cater to one pattern, and others prepare their material to fit another pattern.

Where a single curricular pattern or approach to teaching has preempted attention within a curriculum area, all the textbooks can be expected to adhere to that pattern. Such was the case for nearly thirty years in the primary social studies field. The expanding-horizons approach to the selection of topics, which dictated that the young child should study things physically and psychologically close to him and gradually extend the study to his "expanding world," has dominated primary social studies textbooks. The titles of the six books that comprise the Scott, Foresman & Company Basic Social Studies Program (11), edited by Paul R. Hanna, illustrate how the series begins with the learner's nearby environs and then spirals out to include the wider world. The first four titles are aimed at the primary-grade market. (These titles and annotations are taken from promotional materials for the 1963 edition of this series.)

> *At Home* (Primer) and *At School*
> The Family and School Communities
>
> *In the Neighborhood*
> The Neighborhood Community
>
> *In City, Town, and Country*
> The local, metropolitan area, and county communities
>
> *In All Our States*
> The state community and regions of states
>
> *In the Americas*
> The national and inter-American communities
>
> *Beyond the Americas*
> Nations and regions of nations across the Atlantic
> and across the Pacific

As we will see, nearly all social studies textbook series in the last quarter century have had a similar pattern of titles. The expanding-horizons approach, of course, did not confine itself to the placement of content. The child, exploring his nearby milieu and social relations, was to develop the social knowledge and skills that would prepare him for cooperative, democratic life. He would also begin to study fundamental ideas, such as the interdependence of all men, that would serve him as he met his fellow citizens and world neighbors. In addition, through the study of national holidays and heroes the child would begin to develop a sense of his heritage. However, during the primary school years the places and people he would study would be those that were close to him and therefore easily studied directly.

In the last few years alternatives to the expanding-horizons approach have begun to appear. These emerging patterns will not succeed, however, unless they can replace the dominant scheme or unless a pluralistic approach to social studies curriculum patterns can be developed. Hence we will organize this chapter around the rationalizations for the expanding-horizons approach, the criticisms of it, and the attempts to develop new patterns.

A Period of Harmony

Considering the breadth of the social studies, the period from about 1920 to 1960 was, for the primary grades at least, a period of remarkable harmony among social studies curriculum theorists, teachers, supervisors of instruction, and publishers of textbooks. The expanding-horizons approach was rationalized by psychology ("We learn best those things with which we have experience"). Educational psychologists emphasized the distinction between the rote learning of symbols and slogans and the building of meaningful concepts from the children's own experience. The expanding-horizons approach also lent itself to the cooperative-unit method that expressed so well the spirit of the Progressive Era. Children and teachers working together could study their homes, schools, and neighborhoods and learn to practice democratic behavior as they studied. Curriculum guides across the country, in cities large and small, echoed the expanding-horizons approach. In the great experimental schools of the 1920's, units on "toys" and "ships" led children from their personal interests and life spaces into vigorous analysis of the world.[1] The desire for integration among subjects resulted in the unification of social studies with art, music, and reading. Children sang about the community helpers, drew pictures of their school, and learned to read from experience charts developed during the study of the bakery, the home, and the landing of the Pilgrims.

To meet the demand for curricular materials, all the leading publishers geared their textbooks to the expanding-horizon ap-

[1]As in the social studies units carried out at the Horace Mann Lincoln Institute at Teachers College, Columbia University. See, for example, Baxter and Young (2).

proach.² These textbooks are carefully synchronized with the curriculum guides. For example, the manual for one series informs us that 150 state and city courses of study were consulted and that questionnaires were sent to curriculum directors to seek their advice.

To facilitate the integration of curricular areas, social studies texts increasingly assumed the character of reading books, offering many poems, dramatizations, and opportunities for projects. The texts are, in fact, closely coordinated with reading books. The manual for one first-grade social studies book (12) reports that it "can appropriately be introduced when most of the children are prepared to begin the reading of Book One of their basic reading program." Many of the manuals state explicitly that the books are written to be "in tune with current trends in the social studies." These manuals are often written by the leading theoreticians of the day. They exhort teachers to use the cooperative-unit method; to provide rich experiences through field trips, motion pictures, and dramatization; to define objectives carefully; and to lead the children to discover significant issues, values, and concepts.

The agreement among teachers, theoreticians, and publishers has led to relative homogeneity both in curricula and materials. This state has been so well documented elsewhere (for example, see Joyce, 14) that we can avoid spelling it out here.

The chapter titles of the American Book Company series (10) illustrate in more detail the approach that we observed earlier in the book titles of the Scott, Foresman series.

[Book 1] *Our Home and Our School*
      At School
      Safe Work and Safe Play
      Family Work and Family Play
      Family Plans
      A Party at Home
      School Plans
      The School Pet Show

[Book 2] *Our Neighborhood*
      Fire! Fire!
      How the Doctor Helps Us

2Scott, Foresman; Silver Burdett; Ginn; American Book; Rand McNally; Follett; Heath; Holt, Rinehart and Winston; Allyn and Bacon; and Macmillan. To some extent Allyn and Bacon and Macmillan have introduced the "Wider World" a little earlier than the others.

People Who Help Us Get Food
A Long Bus Ride
The Work of the Post Office
The Men Who Work on Our Houses
The Playground Worker

[Book 3] *Our Community*
Clothes for the People of Riverside
Food for the People of Riverside
The Buildings of Riverside
Getting to and from Riverside
How People in Riverside Get the News
The Schools of Riverside
How Riverside Protects Its Citizens
Enjoying Free Time in Riverside

While there are some differences in approach, this pattern or a similar one has been followed very closely by nearly all the leading textbook publishers. An exception is the Allyn and Bacon series (32). For example, its third-grade book, *Learning About Our Country*, includes the following chapter titles:

The United States of America
New York—Our Largest City
Boston—One of Our Oldest Cities
Miami—The Sunshine City
Pittsburgh—City of Steel
The Mississippi—Our Largest River
Texas—The Lone Star State
Montana—The Treasure State
Tacoma—Where Tall Trees Grow
California—The Golden State
Washington, D.C.—Capital of Our Country
Your Part in Our Country

As might be suspected from the titles, this series includes material from regional economic geography earlier and in greater quantity than the others. The examination of specific cities is unusual, and there are advantages to treating a few cities in some depth rather than skimming over a region.

Nearly all the guidebooks or manuals that accompany the textbook series urge the same goals. The child is to develop democratic skills through the cooperative exploration of this expanding world, and he is to form democratic values and concepts through project-centered, inductive teaching. The textbooks are to be used only as a starting point.

This same approach is carefully spelled out in the standard textbooks on teaching the social studies in the elementary grades (for example, see Michaelis, 22). The harmony among theory, practice, and materials has resulted in a uniformity among the commercial textbook series that belies the potential diversity in this field and in this nation. Yet uniformity in social studies is no greater than we have had in the other curriculum areas. While maintaining a myth about local control of education, we have succeeded in creating what amounts to a national curriculum, modified only slightly to meet local conditions.

The Critics

Recently social studies curricula and materials have been under extremely heavy fire. Much of this is a part of the general criticism of the schools and teachers that has characterized the reform movement of the 1950's and 1960's. It is impossible to separate criticism directed at the social studies materials from criticism directed at the schools or the theoreticians. Frequently the expanding-horizons–centered materials are simply regarded as the products of what is, to the critics, the hated Education Establishment. The critics have been assiduous, if not always scholarly, and have attacked the materials and curricula from every conceivable angle. In this chapter we will briefly sketch seven common criticisms that are being voiced, for out of them is gradually emerging the shape of the future social studies materials.

TOOLS OF OTHER DIRECTION

Some critics have suggested that primary social studies curricula and materials are designed consciously or unconsciously to induct the young child into an other-directed society. In his social studies he meets the friendly milkman, the cheerful school principal, and the happy workers in the factories. He learns the virtues of cooperation (through the project method) and the values of interdependence.

Riesman (27) has stated that the progressive school has become corrupted by the purposes of other-direction. The very emphasis on social studies has lowered the intellectual purpose of the school, he claimed, and the teacher occupies himself by teaching the children to adapt to group life. "Thus the other-directed child is taught at school to take his place in a society where the concern of the group is less with what it produces than with its internal group relations, its morale." This criticism, in fact, is a general attack on the school and on social studies as a field. For a critic who fears that other-direction will produce acquiescent, empty people, it is easy to jump to the conclusion that cooperative inquiry into the neighborhood and the community is part of the general conspiracy in the home and school to deprive our children of their individualism.

A look at the first-grade materials provided by most commercial publishers provides some evidence to support these criticisms. Nearly all the textbook series begin with a unit on the school in which the reader-type materials take the child through the brand new suburban school, where he meets the smiling classmates and functionaries with whom he will work and where he is systematically taught to cooperate. For example, the manual to one of the first-grade books includes the following paragraph, which is intended to explain to the teacher the object of one of the book's sections:

Understandings Developed

Schools provide tools and materials that enable children to make things. By working cooperatively it is possible to build or make something that the whole group can enjoy. A successful classroom project requires cooperation and careful work on the part of each person. Some projects require adult help and supervision. People can provide shelter for birds. Everyone can learn new and interesting things through careful observation. Things we help create can be purposeful as well as personally satisfying.

Values and Behavior Traits Fostered

Working cooperatively to plan and carry out a classroom project; doing one's part on a group project in such a way that the group can take pride in the finished project.

(Hanna and Hoyt, 12, p. 65.)

LACK OF REALISM

The charge that textbooks are unrealistic is closely akin to the charge that the materials are other-directed. The school depicted in the primary social studies textbooks has generally been a place where everyone cooperates and no one fails. The neighborhood, even the city neighborhood, is not littered by garbage or threatened by air pollution or drought. The workers in the factories do not strike, nor are they afflicted by poverty. All races work harmoniously together—although in some texts certain races are conspicuous by their absence.

Presumably the child is simultaneously being introduced to his real school, classmates, and functionaries. It should be *unnecessary* to create a fictional cast of characters, but the textbooks do so, and moreover, they select a suburban school with what the critics describe as a bland environment. This world is antiseptic, say these critics. The city should look like a city, the factory should be a noisy, discordant struggle between workers and employer, and the slums should smell like slums. The world of the textbook should be mussed up so that children form realistic concepts about a real world. On the one hand, lower-class and rural children think these books are fairy tales, according to these critics, and on the other, these texts do not ruffle the cloistered world of the bedroom suburb in which the middle-class child lives. (It is intriguing to think that these books may fail *both* middle- and lower-class children simultaneously, and for much the same reason—being unrealistic.)

We can look at any third-grade social studies textbook and find evidence to support these critics. "Race relations" are not found in the index, nor are "strike" or "air pollution" or "aid to dependent children." The language in these books does not include the language of the streets, and the people do not include prostitutes, drunkards, or dope addicts.

But should they? Just what kinds of realism *can* be developed in textbooks aimed at a mass audience? Parents in neat middle-class suburbs would no doubt react rather volcanically to a textbook that included a unit on "Minnie, the Friendly Prostitute," as one of the "community helpers."

A textbook *can* be constructed to teach children to think about human interaction, and a sophisticated social studies textbook *can* be used to teach them how to use the strategies of social science to analyze human relations. Even without the textbook, a skillful teacher can teach the children to apply social science strategies to the analysis of the *real* world. But that the society is really ready for *realistic* textbooks at the primary level is a proposition I doubt.

Gradually, however, reading and social studies texts for the primary grades are responding to these critics. Pictures show intermingled brown and white faces. Some really lovely photographic essays, such as those the John Day Company has produced recently on American cities (33), show more aspects of the world, more people, and, in the case of the Day materials, more realistic scenes of life. The Day materials also have the advantage for inner-city schools of being nonverbal. As someone put it recently, "Most social studies materials would be irrelevant to city kids—*if* they could read them!"

Some of the Allyn and Bacon materials mentioned previously (32) also include some realistic descriptions of city life. Nearly all the textbooks contain realistic geographic and economic information.

The delightful Young Owl Books (21) from Holt, Rinehart and Winston include titles like:

> *City and Street Games*
> *My Turtle Died Today*
> *All Kinds of Neighbors*
> *The River*

These are supplementary books that explore a host of topics in an unusually realistic way. *The River* is an outstanding example of a content-filled wordless book that communicates nondiscursively for the most part. A passage from *My Turtle Died Today* (29) shows the unusual topics it opens up to exploration:

> Tommy said, "Leave food for Boxer."
> I said, "No, dead turtles don't eat."
> Billy said, "Leave water for Boxer."
> I said, "No, dead turtles don't drink."
> Tommy said, "Is Boxer in heaven?"
> Billy said, "My mother's in heaven."
> I said, "But now you have a new mother."
> Billy said, "Yes, now I have two mothers."

Actually, much of the problem of realism involves topic selection. Once a topic like death is opened, as in the case of *My Turtle Died Today*, the treatment in textbooks is often very fair.

RACIAL AND ETHNIC BIAS

Over the years quite a few critics have noticed that primary-grade social studies materials have dealt chiefly with middle-class Caucasian society. There have been formal studies of secondary school textbooks demonstrating that some races and religions frequently receive less than fair treatment (20). (The coming of the Pilgrims, it is claimed, is told in glorious detail, but the bringing of slaves in chains is told somewhat less explicitly.) On the whole the texts and curricula have found themselves unable to deal with the unpleasant aspects of race relations, and their effort to avoid this issue has resulted in the omission of much information about anyone except Caucasians, aside from occasional salutes to the melting-pot concept.

This is a difficult problem, linked as it is to our culture's general treatment of racial and ethnic problems. Few people are willing to expose seven-year-olds unnecessarily to the harsher aspects of racial and ethnic conflict. An alternative is to deal with diversity directly (as Kenworthy has been arguing for years) and to teach children the more delightful aspects of world cultures (Songs Around the World, Dances Around the World, Toys Around the World, Tales from Many Lands) as an entrée to diversity and the positive aspects of intercultural relations (15). Kenworthy's *Three Billion Neighbors* (16) is a charming potpourri of people, with serious undertones.

Holt, Rinehart and Winston has just brought out three books that will probably encourage most of the other publishers to treat race relations in primary-grade books:

> *William, Andy and Ramon* (6)
> *Five Friends at School* (4)
> *Living as Neighbors* (5)

William, Andy, and Ramon describes three city boys—Caucasian, Negro, and Latin-American—and their families. Photographs rather than pictures are used, adding to the impact of the inclusion. The stories are no more "realistic" than the materials of the past, but the racial inclusion is definitive.

OLD STUFF TO THE KIDS

One of the most serious charges made against the primary social studies is that they introduce children to facts and concepts *that most children have already mastered.* J. D. McAulay (18) approached this problem head-on by means of a series of interviews in which he demonstrated rather neatly that the children in his sample could manifest the behaviors that were the object of the units they were about to be taught. The study of the home frequently involves, for example, distinguishing "What Mommy and Daddy Do"—information that is already available to the children, to put it mildly.

For many years the purpose of "Home and Family" units has been the development of concepts and skills undergirding interdependence and cooperativeness, but McAulay's claim that the instruction often does not elevate the children above their previous knowledge has probably been true in many cases.

On the other hand, as we will see later, two of the newly developed subject-centered approaches to curriculum materials, the University of Georgia Anthropology Curriculum Project and Senesh's approach to economics for primary graders, use the familiar content of home, school, and neighborhood as vehicles for learning concepts in the subject fields.

SUPERFICIALITY

Ralph Preston (24) has made a similar complaint in somewhat different terms. His view is that the elementary social studies have skimmed the surface of many topics with indifferent results. He has advocated deeper study of fewer topics in order to allow for greater exploration of significant concepts and more time for vigorous cooperative inquiry into the real problems of society. For example, one publisher provided an entire reading book on the school. Many aspects of school life are presented, but the following dialogue is a sample of the level:

> Jack said, "I like that umbrella.
> I would like to have an umbrella.
> I do not have one."
> "You may have this one," said Patty.
> "I do not like the old thing."
> "Oh, Patty," said Jack.
> "I cannot take your umbrella.
> Your mother would not like that."
> (Hanna and Hoyt, 12, p. 48.)

The directions to the teacher say, "After the children read the dialogue on this page, discuss the reasons for the actions of the characters." This kind of material is not likely to precipitate a free-wheeling inquiry into the dynamics of the society. The material is constructed to be handled as a reader is handled, with the reading of a few lines followed by a discussion that must necessarily lead to a superficial conclusion, since only a few items of stereotyped data are provided.

Also, as pointed out earlier, nearly all textbook materials are developed in the form of a reading book in which the child studies a mythical school, neighborhood, community, and so forth. This is a real paradox in the development of textbooks that conform to the expanding-horizons theme. Since the child has a real school, neighborhood, and community of his own to study, why should his textbook present him with an abstraction of these topics? He does not need a reader to give him data about a community; he *lives* in one. His text does not have to tell him about a family; he is *surrounded* by it. The disadvantage of the expanding-horizons approach is that, because topics have been selected that are familiar to the child, the textbooks are likely to be redundant to the child's experience if they are constructed to present information about the home, the family, etc., rather than leading him to probe more deeply into life. But if social studies materials are developed to help the child develop new ideas about these homely topics, then we have something to think about.

When most of the textbook series are criticized for their lack of depth, what stands up against rebuttal is the criticism that the children are not led by primary-grade materials to probe deeply into an understanding of their society. Even the most meaty materials deal chiefly with economics or economic geography. Probing into the society and poking its soft spots is something textbooks do not do much. In fact, of course, very few people know how to do this with young children. There is a rich theoretical literature bearing on the cognitive development of the child, but bringing this cognitive capacity of the six- to nine-year-old to bear on serious social studies is another problem altogether.

ANTI-INTELLECTUALISM

Everyone feels safe when he assails American schools for being anti-intellectual, and one will never be safer than when he points to the sections of primary social studies materials that deal with "The Dairy Farm" or "We Salute the Flag" or "The Corner Store." When I take a Professor of Not-Education into a second-grade classroom where children are drawing pictures of their Community Helper, the Friendly Mailman, I want to hide under the table in the SCIENCE CORNER. We all know that the study of literally anything *can* be intellectual. However, many elementary school principals will admit that they give top priority to the teaching of reading, writing, and arithmetic in the primary years, and they do not want to devote much time to science or the social studies. (Even children's literature, an area much closer to reading, has never been decently developed as a curriculum area for primary-grade children; there is simply not enough time and energy left for this area once the "skill" subjects have preempted their share.) In the view of many school administrators (and teachers) *primary social studies are not intended to be intellectual.* Textbooks in social studies and science are expected to reinforce the reading curriculum and not to interfere with the skill subjects by introducing too many difficult ideas from the social sciences. Truly intellectual inquiry in social studies would actually be subversive to the purposes of the primary grades as seen by many school administrators.

Whatever the causes, the charge of anti-intellectualism seems to me to have some merit. Many textbooks and many teachers begin with what the child is familiar with, in accordance with the expanding-horizons approach, but they leave him right there, rather than leading him to a more sophisticated level of understanding. For example, one of the two main objectives listed in the manual of a leading second-grade text is to understand that "all workers contribute to community well-being." No doubt the idea behind this is to condition the children to recognize the worth of low- and high-status jobs and to be aware of the ways in which we all need each other. Note, however, that admen who work for tobacco companies, featherbedders on railroads, and union officials who practice segregation, to name a few, are *workers!* The child who learns the objective is led one step toward gullibility or Pollyannaism, or at least one step away from reality, rather than being helped to develop more adequate ideas that describe and explain this aspect of reality.

Too often passages in textbooks lend themselves only to petty moralizing. For example:

> Lee went to look for a book.
> He did not see the toy.
> Down, down went Lee.

> Lee said, "Why is this toy here?
> I will put it away."
> Lee knows where to put toys.
>
> (Thomas, 30, p. 51.)

No doubt teachers need to discuss rules of cooperative behavior with children, but is it a good use of the textbook to provide excuses for moralism? One should value the printed page enough to use it artfully and compellingly. Otherwise the child may come to believe that books are *not* places of stimulation and ideas.

One serious attempt to provide more intellectual content for primary grades is being made by the Educational Research Council of Greater Cleveland (8). Its first-grade materials center on "Learning the Meaning of Love of Country—The Importance of School, the Child's Part of the World." The second-grade topic, "Living in Varied Communities," has much cross-cultural content, and the third grade's "Land and People of Anglo-America" and "Living in Anglo-America" emphasize economic geography. A thesis of the series is that the social sciences should be integrated in the primary grades and separated in the upper grades. I do not follow the rationale for this thesis: should we really have *seven* courses in the upper grades, one for each social science?

The Cleveland materials are packed with more facts and ideas than the usual textbooks. For example, the comparative approach in the second-grade materials provides much information about peoples around the world that can be used to build significant ideas. The first-grade materials, which are simply in picture-caption form, are intended to promote the study of the real world. For this they are much less adequate than the really excellent John Day materials mentioned earlier, but they still represent an independent deviation from the expanding-horizons approach and an attempt to elevate the intellectual level of primary-grade materials by drawing on the social sciences.

NOT HISTORY AND GEOGRAPHY

For many years, moved no doubt by nostalgic recollections of childhood years spent memorizing dates and capital cities, some adults have criticized any social studies materials that have not been devoted to history and geography. These courses, they say, are the "hard content" subjects, whereas the newer social sciences are not. This is one criticism of the social sciences that I attribute to nostalgia and little else. "*We* studied history and geography, hence our *children* should, or they won't be exactly like us when they grow up."

My own view is that the really new *and* appropriate social studies, when it emerges, will be an entirely new synthesis of the systematic study of the social sciences, child development, learning theory, and the requirements of society. If we are lucky, the dialogue on the reconstruction of the social studies will be vigorous enough to generate *several* competing syntheses. I fervently hope that we will *never* return to the agreement that has burdened primary social studies these last few decades.

The Beginning of the Future: The Teaching of Inquiry

The reform movement of the last dozen years has emphasized the teaching of inquiry, usually meaning that instruction should simulate scholarly activity, enabling the child to learn the "modes of inquiry" of the social sciences, and that instruction should proceed as a cooperative inquiry in which the learner and his companions develop a little scholarly community. In that community they attack common problems, develop and test hypotheses, seek accurate information, and learn how to handle themselves as inquirers and as members of an inquiring group. Whereas the reform movement of the Progressives tended to stress the development of the cooperative community of inquirers, the scholars who have provided the driving force for the present reforms have tended to emphasize the learning of scholarly modes of inquiry. Whether in mathematics, science, language, or social science, scholars have tried to find ways of helping even the youngest child practice the game of scholarship and, in so doing, not only develop knowledge of facts and scientific concepts, but also internalize the ways of thinking of scholars. In English, for example, the approaches to the teaching of grammar, spelling, and reading are based on an effort to teach linguistic principles—that is, the system of thinking that the linguist uses to analyze language.

The academic reform movement is slowly beginning to come to the primary-grade social studies. The University of Georgia Anthropology Curriculum Project (26) is experimenting with primary-grade materials aimed at teaching the young child the structure of anthropology, how the anthropologist works, and how to apply these to analysis of his own social life. Their materials for the first and fourth grades include a packet containing material for the teacher and source materials for the children. Many of the materials are deductive (that is, the concepts are introduced before the data that illustrate them), but some of the materials are inductive, permitting the child to generalize from his study of two primitive peoples (the Arunta and the Kozak) and his own society. The language of anthropology is given much stress, and the ways of thinking of the anthropologist are reiterated constantly. The background material for first-grade teachers says, "The first lesson in this series is designed to transmit an understanding of how the anthropologist applies the techniques of science to the study of people." According to the Teacher's Manual the suggested classroom activities, involving pupil discussion under teacher leadership, "will help the pupils grasp the meaning of scientific study before initiating the other lessons." This quote captures the spirit of the materials very well, reflecting both their scientific emphasis and their generally deductive teaching methods. The materials for children seem to be heavy on anthropological ideas and light on providing children with the data from which to form the concepts. The Georgia project, however, represents the most complete set of "social science" materials available for elementary school children and their teachers.

The much publicized work of Senesh in economics education (28) is now proceeding into print under the banner of a commercial publisher. His materials for the first grade include picture books, records, and workbooks. These take the child on the familiar tour of home, stores, and neighborhood, but what is different is that the materials are organized around the concepts of economics. Hence the concept "division of labor" is seen in the home, the bakery, the factory, etc. Saved income becomes invested as "capital." Such terms as "scarcity," "work," and "market," are developed and explored.

Senesh's *Our Working World* is bright, cheerful, and less straitlaced than most texts, and it illustrates how one can use the commonplace to introduce the ideas of a scholarly discipline. The materials are deductive, and much less emphasis is given to the methods of science than in the Georgia anthropology materials. Senesh uses less the modes of inquiry of the economist than he does the concepts of economics.

It is interesting to note that the anthropology and economics materials developed so far are not simply textbooks, although the translation to commercial form has given to Senesh's work some of the character of a textbook. I have real reservations about whether text-type materials *can* be developed that will lead primary children to scientific inquiry. A text is well suited to narration—it can tell the child how others inquire and suggest what he might inquire into. But for inquiry he needs a problem and a random universe in which to hunt for a solution. He must sort relevant from irrelevant data, make and discard hypotheses, and balance his ideas against the ideas of others. If he knows that the approved answer is planted in the text, he is unlikely to root around for a week in search of his own answer—especially if the text is his chief source of data.

The materials Fox and Lippitt (9) are developing for the fourth through sixth grades ought to help us break set on this problem. These materials teach the child how to collect behavior samples, make inferences about causation in social relations, and distinguish observation and inference from value judgments. He is then led to study characters in stories and, finally, to collect and analyze data about his own social world. Hence the materials set the child up to *inquire.* He has to find the data, organize it, come to conclusions, and check these against the conclusions of his peers. Fox and Lippitt, with their associates, are developing packets that do not look like textbooks.

Michaelis (23) is engaged in the development of materials on the Far East that may result in more data sources into which primary-grade children can delve. The books published by Day on the large cities lead us to hope that other publishers will join in bringing to young children more balanced data about the world. But despite some notable exceptions (see 13), many existing trade books for primary graders are not much different from the texts.

So far, we lack a fresh thesis for primary social studies that effectively integrates the social sciences and conceptions of the cognitive and affective development of the child. Consequently the promise in the Georgia materials, Senesh's work, and Michaelis' project are the only concrete representations of the future. Until some new general conceptions of primary social studies education emerge, text-type materials are likely to continue to reflect the expanding-horizons approach or the structures of the separate disciplines.

At present the best instructional material available for primary-grade social studies is a lively teacher who knows the social sciences and has the courage to organize her students to study significant aspects of human society. No matter that texts are biased, bland, other-directed, even anti-intellectual. No matter that many social issues involve harsh reality and shifting social values. The great, raw, lovely social world is there to be studied. Real families, real communities, real airports, real courts and legislatures, real slums, real factories and farms lie all around the school. Through television, letters, films, and pictures, children can study real Japanese families, the war in Southeast Asia, elections in England—in short, the very United Nations. Children do sing, dance, and play in all nations, and loving hands have collected their songs, dances, and games for primary-grade children to study. The teacher who knows her social science can experiment and will soon learn which issues are too complex for six-year-olds, which ones require more life experience, and which ones result in the electrifying combination that occurs when the child's concern leads him to explore significant problems and deal with important ideas.

John Dewey pictured a teacher with a map of knowledge in his head leading the inquiry of children over the important terrain. Today, however, too many people seem to hope that we can develop materials that will lead children to inquire in such a way that the process of inquiry will be proof against the inadequacies of the teacher. These people seem to have given up on the teacher. Is the problem, perhaps, that we ask too much of our teachers when we ask them to manage twenty-five, six- seven- or eight-year-olds and teach them to read, compute, write, and, now to introduce them to the ways of thinking of mathematicians, scientists, social scientists, linguists, and humanistic scholars?

The existing structure of the primary school evolved when reading, writing, arithmetic, and discipline were the functions of primary education. Now that inquiry, intelligent socialization, and the study of humanizing values are seen as legitimate processes in primary education, an entirely new structure will have to be developed. Publishers have long argued that teachers will use only workbook-type, read-and-recite text materials. Considering the training of teachers, their conception of their job, and the organization of the school, the publishers were probably correct. As we change these factors, however, materials can be construed less as systems for controlling children and purveying concepts in a foolproof program and more as sources of data for inquiring learners.

Alternatives for the Future

We will close this chapter with a package of dreams. These dreams are possible because in this huge nation we should be able to develop several viable approaches to the social studies—approaches requiring quite different types of materials.

We might begin by wondering whether the textbook is really a suitable medium for the social studies. The function of a textbook is to structure material for the student—to present a sequence of ideas and information. Now if one begins to help a student inquire into his world, one cannot tell exactly where that inquiry is likely to lead. Hence one does not need a textbook, one needs open-ended resources into which the student can dip as he needs to. The worst feature of the textbook built on the expanding-horizons thesis is that it is really not necessary at all. The basic wisdom of the expanding-horizons approach is that it helps the student examine his familiar world, proceeds to enlarge his perspective, and gradually moves back the boundaries of his world. To construct a textbook to lead the child to study the community he is already living in is a contradiction. To design a textbook to structure personal inquiry is to design a neurosis. *People*, not textbooks, structure personal inquiry.

What is needed is a variety of materials that do not function as a textbook—to structure material *for* students—but serve as resources that the student structures or bring to him new strategies for inquiry. For example:

Resource Kits. "Pools" of instructional materials might be developed as resources for inquiry by children. These pools could utilize all media. Film clips, still pictures, film strips, records, models, plays, dances, maps, stories, and text-type materials could be packaged as "inquiry resource centers." Cities, villages, and farms from all over the world could be represented. A single airplane, steamship, or train journey could provide a topic. A social process, such as making friends, organizing a game, or resolving an argument, could be the focus for a resource center. These resource kits would not structure inquiry but could be used by the capable teacher who knows how to handle the children's social science inquiry without the aid of a text. The John Day materials are their forerunner.

Multimedia Idea Stimulators. Sets of films and readings could be developed to introduce new ways of looking at oneself, at group behavior, and at societal processes in general. For example, a sequence showing a newcomer looking for friends could introduce ways of looking at friendship and open that area to inquiry. A sequence showing the family as an economic unit would provide another frame of reference for investigation. Sequences could alternately show an individual as a breadwinner, a father, and a member of a team. This technique could be used to present social science concepts, such as the cultural universals, ideas from economics, and so on.

Self-Instructional Packets. Films, tapes, books, and programmed materials could be woven together to provide information or introduce social science concepts. These could be used flexibly to help children instruct themselves.

Problem-Posers. Multimedia packets could realistically introduce children to social problems and processes. Such topics as "A Water Supply for a Town," "Trouble in the Neighborhood," or "Working for Clean Air," could be experimented with. If such materials became available, with carefully worked out plans, they may encourage teachers to experiment with ways of studying social problems with children.

Nondiscursive Exploration of Feeding. Motion pictures of bridges, rivers, beachcombing, people reaching out to others, music, dancing, artists painting pictures—all can open up exploration of the world of feeling to children and expand the areas of legitimate inquiry in the classroom. The development of the child's aesthetic capacity can thereby become a major goal of the social studies.

Conclusion

We can dream of the day when the expanding horizons of the child will be the natural consequence of his inquiry into himself and the social world that stretches around him. That day, of course, presupposes teachers who know their social sciences and who are engaged in active inquiry into *their* social world. Those teachers will work in schools that are well staffed—they will not share the plight of the present inner-city teachers holding together a barely functioning school society against tangible odds of understanding, community unrest, and difficult-to-handle children. They will work where materials are flexible and imaginative and where there are adequate resources for all levels of ability and language development. That dream is what we work for. The slow evolution from the expanding-horizons approach will move past the concept-centered materials of the academic reform movement and bring us a scene of lively children, turning their free and cheerful minds to the old problems of the world, learning the ideas of the present only as stepping stones to a creative future.

Selected Bibliography

1. ANDERSON, E. V., *et al.*, Silver Burdett Primary Social Studies (series), Silver Burdett, Morristown, N.J., 1966.
2. BAXTER, TOMPSIE, AND YOUNG, BESS M., *Ships and Navigation,* Columbia University Press, New York, 1933.
3. BORCHERT, JOHN R., AND McGUIGAN, JANE, Elementary Geography Program (series), Rand McNally, Chicago, 1961.
4. BUCKLEY, PETER, AND JONES, HORTENSE, *Five Friends at School,* Holt, Rinehart and Winston, New York, 1966.
5. ———, *Living as Neighbors,* Holt, Rinehart and Winston, New York, 1966.
6. ———, *William, Andy, and Ramon,* Holt, Rinehart and Winston, New York, 1966.
7. CUTRIGHT, PRUDENCE, AND JAROLIMEK, JOHN (eds.), Macmillan Social Studies Series, Macmillan, New York, first book published in 1962.
8. EDUCATIONAL RESEARCH COUNCIL OF GREATER CLEVELAND, OHIO. Sample publications are "Learning the Meaning of Love of Country—The Importance of School, the Child's Part of the World" (first grade); "Living in Varied Communities" (second grade); and "Land and People of Anglo-America" and "Living in Anglo-America" (third grade).
9. FOX, ROBERT M., AND LIPPITT, RONALD (directors), Social Science in Elementary Schools, University of Michigan, Ann Arbor.
10. FRASER, DOROTHY M., AND HOY, HARRY E. (eds.), The ABC Social Studies Series, American Book, New York, 1961.
11. HANNA, PAUL R. (ed.), Basic Social Studies Program (series), Scott, Foresman, Chicago, first book published in 1963.
12. HANNA, PAUL R., AND HOYT, GENEVIEVE ANDERSON, *Guidebook to Accompany At School,* Scott, Foresman, Chicago, 1963.
13. HAUS, HELEN, *Children's Books to Enrich the Social Studies,* National Education Association, Washington, D.C., 1961.
14. JOYCE, BRUCE R., *Strategies for Elementary Social Science Education,* Science Research Associates, Chicago, 1965.
15. KENWORTHY, LEONARD S., *Introducing Children to the World,* Harper, New York, 1955.

16. KENWORTHY, LEONARD S., *Three Billion Neighbors,* Ginn, Boston, 1964.

17. ———, World Affairs Guide (series), Teachers College, Columbia University, New York, 1965.

18. MCAULAY, J. D., "Social Studies in the Primary Grades," *Social Education,* 18 (Dec., 1954), 357–58.

19. MCINTIRE, ALTA, *et al.,* Follett New Unified Social Studies Series, Follett, Chicago, Revised Edition published in 1965.

20. MARCUS, LLOYD, *The Treatment of Minorities in Secondary School Textbooks,* Anti-Defamation League of B'nai B'rith, New York, 1961.

21. MARTIN, BILL, JR. (ed.), Young Owl Books: Social Studies (series), Holt, Rinehart and Winston, New York, 1964.

22. MICHAELIS, JOHN U., *Social Studies for Children in a Democracy,* Prentice-Hall, Englewood Cliffs, N.J., 1963.

23. ——— (director), Teaching Guides and Materials on Asian Countries for Grades 1-12, Department of Education, University of California, Berkeley.

24. PRESTON, RALPH C., "Teaching for Depth," *Childhood Education,* 36 (Jan., 1960), 213ff.

25. PRESTON, RALPH C., *et al.,* Heath Social Studies Series, Heath, Boston, first book published in 1964.

26. RICE, MARION (director), Development of a Sequential Curriculum in Anthropology for Grades 1-7, Department of Sociology and Anthropology, University of Georgia, Athens.

27. RIESMAN, DAVID, *et al., The Lonely Crowd,* Yale University Press, New Haven, Conn., 1950.

28. SENESH, LAWRENCE, *Our Working World,* Science Research Associates, Chicago, 1965.

29. STULL, EDITH G., *My Turtle Died Today,* Holt, Rinehart and Winston, New York, 1964.

30. THOMAS, ELEANOR, *et al., Stories About Linda and Lee,* Ginn, Boston, 1963.

31. TIEGS, E. W., AND ADAMS, F., The Tiegs-Adams Social Studies Series, Ginn, Boston, Revised Edition published 1960–63.

32. WANN, KENNETH D. (senior author), Living in Our Times Series, Allyn and Bacon, Boston, first book published in 1962.

33. WRIGHT, BETTY ATWELL, Urban Education Studies (series), John Day, New York, 1965.

CHAPTER 3

The Intermediate Grades

Should Children Answer Their Own Questions?

WILLIAM D. RADER

Introduction

In the preface to a recent social studies methods book (13) the authors stated that "the fundamental problem of instruction is not to tell children facts, but to teach them how to pursue answers to their own questions." This statement represents one of the most dramatic developments in education in the 1960's. Perhaps we do want children to know that Columbus discovered America in 1492 or that July Fourth is a date that has a special meaning for us, but we expect our children to be able to do more than absorb mountains of factual information—much of which will be forgotten.

Children need to develop an understanding of fundamental principles and ideas in order to apply them to future action. We must help them to develop skills of questioning and analysis. Contemporary educators are responding to these needs by developing and retraining teachers. In social studies particularly, scholars from the social sciences are working with educators to develop new curriculum materials and courses of study. Better-trained teachers and improved curriculum materials will go a long way toward the development of constructive citizens in our democratic society. Since the major part of this chapter focuses upon curriculum and textbooks, it is appropriate to consider the pre-service and in-service education of teachers.

More and more demands are being placed upon elementary teachers to upgrade their own backgrounds in science and mathematics, language and reading. Now this burden is being increased by the addition of several social sciences. Elementary teachers should study economics, political science, sociology, and anthropology. What is more, they should increase their knowledge of history and geography. Under the sponsorship of the National Defense Education Act a multitude of summer institutes in these subjects has been held. Teachers have been encouraged to attend these institutes and have been rewarded with stipends and academic credit.

It will be several years before these attempts to improve the preparation of in-service teachers affect a significant number of elementary school teachers. Meanwhile we need to do more to prepare future teachers to use the new curricula that are being developed. Teacher-training institutions are responding to this challenge by reconstructing their courses of study to include larger doses of subject matter and by increasingly adopting Conant's recommendations. When the full impact of improved curricula and better-prepared teachers is felt in American elementary schools, the results will be reflected through improvements in many facets of our democratic society. The United States of the twenty-first century will be a much better place in which to live if we have carefully prepared today's children to assume their roles as citizens in our society.

The intermediate-grade classroom of the future will be an exciting one. The outside observer will notice that the teacher does not do his job the way he did when we were in school. The observer will notice that the teacher is not lecturing while thirty pairs of ears listen with varying degrees of attention. Instead, he may be sitting at his desk while a variety of activities are occurring simultaneously. Several children may be out of the room at the library doing research on a few questions the class has formulated. Another small group may be gathered in one corner of the room preparing a report to present to the rest of the class. Other students may be engaged in map-making or model-building activities. Students will move about freely, turning to the teacher for guidance. There will be times when the class draws on the teacher's experience and knowledge by asking him to explain something to them. They ask because they are interested or because the information will be useful to them in thinking critically about a problem. Since the students plan to make active use of this information, they listen carefully, asking for clarification when they do not understand. Discussion of the teacher's remarks is initiated by the students, not the teacher.

In the classroom of the future, teacher and students will have a well-marked destination. But they will move toward it via several alternative roads, and they will stop along the way to examine some areas more thoroughly. The objective will not be the completion of a 300-page textbook but rather the achievement of understanding through critical thinking and discovery on their own initiative. The teacher will be challenged to lead the class into new areas and to help it sustain the interests generated. If he succeeds in stimulating the intellectual curiosity that many children have, he will see many discipline problems vanish.

Admittedly it may be many years, even decades, before such a classroom becomes a significant reality in American elementary schools. However, classrooms such as this are already in existence; many teachers may take justifiable pride in the fact that their classrooms are similar to the ideal described here. But unfortunately the curriculum and materials that are currently provided for intermediate social studies make achievement of this ideal possible only where excellent teachers have risen above them. In the pages to follow, the curriculum and textbooks of the intermediate-grades—defined here as the fourth, fifth, and sixth grades—will be examined.

The Intermediate-Grade Curriculum

Diversity is the rule in the intermediate-grade social studies curriculum. Fraser (23) observed that in the fourth grade emphasis is on geographic content, with the study of the home state prevailing. However, regional geography is also popular, and the study of American history is sometimes begun in this grade. The 1964 *Curriculum Guide for Social Studies*, published by the Chicago Board of Education, is based on geography, introducing children to the study of Illinois and to a study of regions of the United States. A study of curriculum guides in selected communities was conducted by the Social Studies Project Staff of the Industrial Relations Center of the

University of Chicago in 1963. Seventy-eight school systems responded to Center requests for curriculum guides. The results of this survey tend to corroborate the findings of Preston and Hodgson, as reported by Fraser: most of the respondent school systems emphasize the history and geography of the home state.

Differing emphases also occur in the fifth grade, although evidence suggests that fifth-grade classes commonly study the history of the United States, its geography, or a combination of the two. Other parts of our hemisphere, that is, Canada and Latin America, are less often studied.

The sixth grade appears to be considerably more diverse than the fourth or fifth; geography, however, still seems to receive the greatest emphasis. Frequently the history and culture of the area are also studied. The Industrial Relations Center study indicated that the geography, history, and way of life in the Western Hemisphere are most frequently studied in the sixth-grade curriculum. Next in order are Europe, Asia, and Africa. The curriculum of the public schools of Chicago is entitled *World Cultures,* and it includes study of sub-Saharan Africa, North Africa and the Middle East, India and Southeastern Asia, Nationalist and Communist China, Japan and Korea, Australia and New Zealand, and the Soviet Union and Europe, in that order.

Social studies teachers and curriculum specialists in school systems are becoming increasingly concerned about the neglect of many of the social sciences in their curricula. History and geography, worthwhile as they may be, have had a disproportionate role in the intermediate social studies curriculum. McAulay (33), however, felt that the primary need of intermediate social studies is for uniformity of curriculum across the nation because of the mobility of our population. He recommended a historical base for the intermediate grades. "The time is ripe," concluded McAulay, "for the establishment of more integration and coordination in the nation's social studies programs for the elementary school. This is particularly true in regard to our historical background which each and every child should receive." A national social studies curriculum would be an advantage for children whose parents find it necessary to move to other school districts. The costs of such a curriculum, however, are loss of diversity and the increased difficulty of meeting the particular needs of a school district's residents.

Schmuck *et al.* (41) listed four major limitations of the social studies curriculum: (1) the social studies are viewed as information children must learn; (2) the social studies do not distinguish between inquiry into values and indoctrination of values; (3) the social studies make little use of the social sciences that deal with man in his social world, that is, psychology, social psychology, anthropology, and economics; and (4) too little has been expected of children; our assumptions about their learning potential have been erroneous. This last point was in a limited sense documented by Davis (14). The results of his study (conducted in Davidson County, Tennessee) of classes of fourth-, fifth-, and sixth-grade children, suggest that assumptions about the slow maturation of children's ability to understand concepts and about the misconceptions found in children's thinking are incorrect and that the "social studies curriculum theory which advocates deferment of certain concepts, such as those of time and space," may well need "radical revision."

Many social studies projects across the nation are concentrating on the enrichment of content in the elementary grades. Under a United States Office of Education grant the Anthropology Curriculum Project at the University of Georgia has been developing units of study in anthropology for the elementary grades. This project, directed by Wilfred C. Bailey, concentrates on the concept of culture in the first and fourth grades. Field-testing took place in the 1965–66 school year, while units for the second and fifth grades were undergoing development. Eventually teachers of the intermediate grades will have units in anthropology available to strengthen their social studies offerings.

The new University of Michigan Social Science Program consists of five units, which were field-tested during the 1965–66 school year and which will soon be available for classroom use. The materials are aimed at the intermediate grades and propose to teach children some of the social scientist's methods. Unit one introduces children to the world of the social scientist by means of a sound filmstrip. The unit then deals with behavior and systematically develops lessons on observation and its methods, cause and effect, and multiple-causation. Children are provided with a reader and a workbook.

This program offers a refreshing alternative to the traditional curriculum programs described above, but it is not a perfect substitute. It deals with the world surrounding the classroom rather than an inert body of facts that are soon forgotten. By the time children are exposed to Unit Five, presumably in the sixth grade, they are engaging in an active process of inquiry.

The intermediate grades are also being enriched by the development of curriculum in economics. The Elementary School Economics Program at the University of Chicago has field-tested its materials in the fourth, fifth, and sixth grades. Each year's work (actually about six weeks of classroom time) concentrates on a particular economic function. In the fourth grade the emphasis is on consumption, in grade five on production, and in the sixth grade on exchange. Wherever possible, these units are correlated to the existing social studies curriculum.

Other national projects currently under development will affect the intermediate curriculum, but we know little about them at this stage. One of the outstanding local efforts at improvement is that of the Contra Costa County Department of Education in California. The content of its curriculum is similar to that found elsewhere, but it is richer. Each unit has a set of main ideas, six each in the fourth and sixth grades, and eight in the fifth grade. However, the units emphasize critical thinking, as well as skills, attitudes, and feelings. Doubtless other school districts are engaged in curriculum revision that will lead to a greater emphasis on critical thinking and discovery.

Those Textbooks Again

Some of the favorite "whipping boys" of social studies teachers and scholars are the textbook publishers. Price (40) introduced an article on textbook evaluation with the statement that "the entire teaching profession is presently being assaulted by an avalanche of criticism particularly related to the quality of textbooks being used in the schools." He examined six common criticisms of social studies textbooks at the elementary level: (1) Textbooks are dull. (2) Textbooks are superficial. (3) Textbooks are too broad. (4) Textbooks are too simple. (5) Textbooks present an unrealistic picture of the world. (6) Textbooks do not stress the important or dominant nations of the world.

Price examined these charges and reported in favor of the textbooks on most counts. But the concern of textbook publishers with meeting these charges is precisely the problem. Certainly publishers are striving for appealing readable books, neither too short nor too long, too superficial nor too deep, too unrealistic nor too trivial. The store of knowledge is vast, and any text is necessarily selective. But most of the information presented in textbooks is descriptive rather than analytical, and the books do not give students an opportunity to review critically the information presented or to apply the techniques and concepts of the social scientist.

The textbook publisher may well argue that he tries to meet the demands of the market, and schools and teachers in fact seem to want books that meet the criteria of Price and are also up to date. In order to satisfy the demands of a diverse market, publishers have produced textbook series in history, geography, history and geography, and social studies. We recently examined two editions of a popular textbook. That the publisher had successfully met the demands of the market is evidenced by the fact that the 1965 edition was virtually the same as that of the 1960 edition. Some copy was rewritten, new pictures were added and some were deleted, and a few questions at the end of chapters were changed. But by and large one could not distinguish the earlier edition from the later one except that the later book was more attractive.

There are other criteria, however, by which elementary social studies textbooks may be evaluated, such as the criteria listed and discussed in this book's opening chapter. How do intermediate-grade social studies textbooks measure up against these criteria? Careful scrutiny of several series reveals that only the one by Hanna, Kohn, and Lively (27, 28, 29) makes use of a conceptual framework. This series lists nine basic human activities (28), which it fits into the "expanding-horizons" type of curriculum:

1. Producing, exchanging, distributing, and consuming goods and services
2. Transporting goods and people
3. Organizing and governing
4. Providing education
5. Expressing spiritual and esthetic feelings
6. Providing recreation
7. Protecting and conserving life, health, property, and resources
8. Communicating facts, ideas, and feelings
9. Creating new tools and techniques

(Hanna, Kohn, and Lively, 28, pp. 84–85.)

This approach has been the basis for social studies curriculum for decades. For the intermediate grades this means that the state is studied in the fourth grade, the nation in the fifth grade, and the world in the sixth grade. The fourth-grade book accordingly introduces a number of "significant historical concepts and understandings" under each basic human activity discussed for the state. These concepts are frequently generalizations drawn from a social science; for example, "the kind and distribution of factories in a state are related to raw materials, markets, and adequate transportation facilities" (28). However, these concepts also include facts that seem relatively trivial: "The state maintains a police department for the protection of its citizens" or "each star on the American flag represents a state in the United States" (28). The series pays too little attention to the fact that the concepts it lists represent different levels of abstraction and require different levels of comprehension.

A second criterion for evaluation is whether the books or series are based on a set of major ideas. Few of the elementary social studies textbooks examined list an overall set of themes for the series. Most contain long lists for particular units and shorter lists for chapters. At least one series, however, is a notable exception (31, 35, 36). The Teacher's Manual for *This Is Our Land* lists seven "basic concepts" and states that these are developed with "varying emphasis at different grade levels":

1. Peoples' ways of living are a product of interaction with their environment.
2. In search of progress people have built a constantly changing panorama of culture and civilization.
3. People work, invent, and build to satisfy their changing needs and desires.
4. People strive continually for justice and order through law and government.
5. Through sharing experiences people learn to live together.
6. People need enrichment for their daily existence.
7. People increasingly recognize their interdependence with all mankind and should take responsibility for the general welfare.

(Patterson *et al.*, 36, p. 4.)

Scholars might question whether these are the most significant themes to be introduced to intermediate-grade children, but it is commendable that at least an attempt has been made to choose meaningful themes. The authors evidently believed that no further explication of these seven "basic concepts" is necessary, for none is offered. Each unit develops one or more of these concepts in some way, but it is left to the teacher to deduce which of the seven concepts are being illustrated by the unit. Each book in the intermediate series has its own theme, which is superimposed on the basic seven; unfortunately the series does not explicitly reconcile the book themes with the seven themes listed above. (For example, "The Pledge of Allegiance" is the theme for *This Is Our Land*; Chapter 1 defines the meaning of the words in the pledge but does not relate it directly or indirectly to any of the seven themes.) Nonetheless, this series is one of the very few that are based on major ideas.

No intermediate-grade social studies textbook we examined satisfied the criterion of interrelating disciplines. A few textbooks unabashedly refer to their series as American history (18, 19, 20) or geography (2, 3, 4). Research indicates that these are among the leading sellers in the field. These texts for the most part ignore the illustrations of concepts from other social sciences that are inherent in most discussions of history and geography.

In order to see how well intermediate-grade textbooks interrelated disciplines, I checked to see how much use certain history and geography texts made of economics concepts. My findings confirm those of a special textbook study committee of the Committee on Economic Education of the American Economic Association in 1963. Their report, published as a supplement to the *American Economic Review*, criticized high school textbooks in economics, social problems, and United States history. I would agree in principle, if not in degree, with their statement (42) about textbooks in United States history: "Much of the history of the United States is to an appreciable degree economic in nature, and any substantial text in this area should include sound economic as well as social and political analysis."

Consider the following quotation from a leading American history textbook:

> Jackson found that groups of men were buying western land from the government for a dollar and a quarter an acre. They were paying for it with paper money that was not worth much. They were holding the land to sell later to people at higher prices. This did not seem right to the President, so he gave an order. "The government will sell land only for gold and silver," he said. Then he went further and said he would like to see government land given to people who would settle on it. (Eibling, King, and Harlow, 19, p. 220.)

It is interesting to read the annotation in the teacher's edition below this quotation: "Personality concept: Have pupils use reference books to learn the qualities that made Andrew Jackson a favorite on the frontier." Notwithstanding the implications of the above-mentioned "personality concept," the foregoing quotation aptly illustrates several economics concepts. The statement that "paper money . . . was not worth much" would suggest to a careful reader that the supply of money was increasing faster than production and reducing the value of the former, but neither the book nor the teacher's manual provides questions about why money was outdistancing production. Yet this problem of the nineteenth century has its counterpart today: economists theorizing about the money supply disagree as to whether the Federal Reserve is increasing the supply of money and credit too slowly or too rapidly. Obviously children cannot be expected to analyze this controversy and its ramifications fully. But an examination of the above quotation can help children begin to understand a complex issue. Other important economic concepts are contained in the statement that "they were holding the land to sell later to people at higher prices." It illustrates the concept of price as determined by the interaction of supply and demand, and it implies that changes in supply or demand will affect the equilibrium price.

A second example of a missed opportunity to illustrate economic concepts is found in a leading geography textbook (6). The "Guide Materials and Tests" section of this book lists this "general idea to emphasize" in a chapter on the South: "By working together, people can usually achieve more than by working alone." Yet the text, the end-of-chapter questions, and the notations to the teacher contain no references to specialization and division of labor.

Linn Orear of the Industrial Relations Center of the University of Chicago recently conducted a study of the quality and quantity of economics in sixth-grade social studies textbooks. She concluded that the books were replete with possibilities but that they assumed a good deal about children's understanding of economic concepts. Many conclusions were stated, and the children had little basis on which to question them.

A fourth criterion for intermediate-grade texts is whether they encourage student questioning. Few textbooks meet this criterion satisfactorily. While there are occasional exceptions, textbooks ask students mainly to answer questions such as the following:

1. New York is divided into five parts. What are these parts called? Name them.

2. Name at least five products used in your home or school that must be imported from other lands.

3. Which Southern states were among the first thirteen states in our nation?

For the most part the teacher's editions of these books encourage classroom teachers to ask specific factual questions. A delightful exception is found in a fifth-grade social studies text (36): "Why are governments and laws necessary? Why aren't people allowed to live just exactly as they please? Can we have both freedom and government? Tell what you think would happen if we did." These questions have much potential. Student discussions of them will generate other questions and expand the area of inquiry if the teacher permits this to happen.

Our intermediate textbooks do not appear to foster reflective thinking. They are a rhetoric of conclusions and facts to be digested. For the most part they do not even suggest to children that contemporary societal problems exist. Perhaps this explains why children prefer other fields of study to the social studies in our schools. They recognize social studies as being divorced from the real world, and they react accordingly.

A Proposal for Better Textbooks

Textbooks ought to present information that is not readily available from other sources and to contain problems that will challenge students to ask questions. Texts should utilize the research tools of social scientists whenever and wherever possible. Primary source data should be translated into the student's language. Textbooks and teachers should assist students in becoming investigators of problems past and present. Students need not always learn one right answer; their scientific approach and questioning attitude will assist them in formulating alternative solutions. And a student may find that his solution differs from that of his peer.

I suggest that a textbook series could meet these criteria by implementing the recommendation of Engle (21) that "the course of study should provide that every child will have the opportunity to study and understand thoroughly the important problems that confront the American people." In his article he discussed the ten to fifteen problems reported by the President's Commission on National Goals.

The proposed texts need not emphasize problems to the exclusion of the positive aspects of society, but texts should relate to the world the student actually sees. At least some of the problems should be real and contemporary, but hypothetical or past problems should not be disregarded.

The advantage of this approach is that a study of problems exploits the interrelationship of the social sciences. In investigating various aspects of a problem the student will usually need to utilize knowledge and techniques drawn from several disciplines, even though on a very low level. Let us consider how this approach might be used in a social studies textbook for the fourth grade. Since in the expanding-horizons curriculum the state is typically studied in this grade, it will be used as a case in point.

STATE PROBLEMS AND PROSPECTS

A textbook could select any state for study because method and not specific content is the concern in this approach. In fact several states could be studied, for the problems are common to nearly all. I tentatively propose the following ten problem areas: (1) government, (2) education, (3) health, (4) construction, (5) public safety, (6) taxation, (7) relations to its citizens, (8) relations with other states, (9) relations with the federal government, and (10) relations with its local communities. Students would probably have time to explore only one problem in each category. Each problem would have historical, political, economic, and social dimensions. The textbook should present some primary source data from various points of view, and it should serve as a point of departure. The problem could be real or hypothetical. No answer need be provided for the students, although if the state has taken action on the problem, the teacher's edition might note its decision.

For example, consider highway construction. What has been the history of road-building in the state? Have other means of transportation been developed? What were the reasons for building turnpikes or toll roads? What happens to communities when expressways or toll roads are built? What are the financial costs? What are the human costs in terms of dislocation, noise, and loss of privacy? What groups favor these roads? Who is opposed? Are there genuine differences of opinion as to whether new highways are the best solution to the problem of traffic congestion? What are the alternatives to road-building? Are any of the state's other problems related to this one?

Conclusion

In his now famous syllabus for Education 305, Ralph Tyler has identified four questions that must be answered in developing any curriculum:

1. What educational purposes should the school seek to attain?
2. What educational experiences can be provided that are likely to attain these purposes?
3. How can these educational experiences be effectively organized?
4. How can we determine whether these purposes are being attained?

(Tyler, 43, pp. 1–2.)

The social education of children is only one part of general education in the elementary grades, but it is a very important part. The challenge for all elementary school educators is to determine overall objectives. Then we may ascertain the role of the social studies in helping to attain these objectives. Lawrence Senesh has said that the most important objective of social studies education is the development of the problem-solving ability of children. This ability, he argued, is a result of the development of analytical faculties. Some years ago the Educational Policies Commission published a statement to the effect that the central purpose of American education is the development of rational thinking. Our task is to provide the means for accomplishing this goal. But the curriculum and textbooks that we have today are inadequate for doing so. The future holds great promise for us in social studies. We need and are getting more and better teacher training; we need and are getting better curriculum materials. However, we need and are *not* getting sufficient commitment on the part of teachers to inquiry-oriented teaching. And we need and are *not* yet getting a new type of textbook. It is difficult to determine whether the social studies curriculum has influenced the textbooks or vice versa. It is certain, however, that textbooks form the base for elementary social studies instruction. Relatively few school systems have been willing to discard them and rely solely on their own resources. Elementary school teachers are busy people who teach other subjects besides social studies. Let us help our school children and their teachers by revitalizing the textbooks to improve children's faculties of inquiry and to make the social studies more meaningful to these young scholars.

Selected Bibliography

1. ALILUNAS, LEO J., "An Analysis of Social Studies Content in the Middle Grades," *The Social Studies,* 52 (Nov., 1961), pp. 210–18.

2. ALLEN, JACK, AND HOWLAND, ADELENE E., *The Earth and Our States,* Prentice-Hall, Englewood Cliffs, N.J., 1966.

3. ———, *Nations Around the Globe,* Prentice-Hall, Englewood Cliffs, N.J., 1966.

4. ———, *The United States of America,* Prentice-Hall, Englewood Cliffs, N.J., 1966.

5. ANTHROPOLOGY CURRICULUM PROJECT, Teacher's Guide, Grade Four, *Concept of Culture,* University of Georgia, Athens, Apr., 1965.

6. BARROWS, HARLAN H., PARKER, EDITH P., AND SORENSON, CLARENCE W., *The American Continents,* Silver Burdette, Morristown, N.J., 1964.

7. ———, *Old World Lands,* Silver Burdette, Morristown, N.J., 1964.

8. ———, *Our Big World,* Silver Burdette, Morristown, N.J., 1964.

9. BROWN, GERTRUDE STEPHENS, *Your Country and Mine,* Ginn, Boston, 1965.

10. BRUNER, JEROME, *The Process of Education,* Harvard University Press, Cambridge, Mass., 1960.

11. CARLS, NORMAN, AND SORENSON, FRANK E., *Knowing Our Neighbors in Canada,* Holt, Rinehart and Winston, New York, 1964.

12. CHABE, ALEXANDER M., "Evaluating Elementary Social Studies Textbooks," *Education,* 86 (Jan., 1966), pp. 302–07.

13. CLEMENTS, H. MILLARD, FIELDER, WILLIAM R., AND TABACHNICK, B. ROBERT, *Social Study: Inquiry in Elementary Classrooms,* Bobbs-Merrill, Indianapolis, Ind., 1966.

14. DAVIS, O. L., JR., "Learning About Time Zones in Grades Four, Five, and Six," *The Journal of Experimental Education,* 31 (Summer, 1963), pp. 407–12.

15. DAWSON, GRACE S., *Your World and Mine,* Ginn, Boston, 1965.

16. DEDERICK, NELLE, AND MACKENZIE, JOSEPHINE, *Your People and Mine,* Ginn, Boston, 1965.

17. DIMITROFF, LILLIAN, "A Quantitative-qualitative Analysis of Selected Social Science Generalizations in Social Studies Textbooks in the Intermediate Grades," *The Journal of Educational Research*, 55 (Nov., 1961), pp. 135–37.

18. EIBLING, HAROLD H., KING, FRED M., AND HARLOW, JAMES, *Great Names in History*, Laidlaw Brothers, River Forest, Ill., 1965.

19. ——, *Our Country*, Laidlaw Brothers, River Forest, Ill., 1965.

20. ——, *World Background for American History*, Laidlaw Brothers, River Forest, Ill., 1965.

21. ENGLE, SHIRLEY H., "Thoughts in Regard to Revision," *Social Education*, 27 (Apr., 1963), pp. 182–84, 196.

22. FRASER, DOROTHY McCLURE, "Grade Level Themes in Elementary Social Studies," 1963 Yearbook of the New York Society for the Experimental Study of Education, *Critical Review of Education for Changing Times*, pp. 160–62.

23. ——, "The Organization of the Elementary School Social Studies Curriculum," *Social Studies in the Elementary School*, 56th Yearbook of the National Society for the Study of Education, University of Chicago Press, Chicago, 1957.

24. GROSS, HERBERT H., GABLER, ROBERT E., AND McINTIRE, ALTA, *Teacher's Guide for Exploring Regions Near and Far*, Follett, Chicago, 1961.

25. GROSS, HERBERT H., *et al.*, *Exploring Regions Near and Far*, Follett, Chicago, 1961.

26. HAGAMAN, ADALENE P., AND DURELL, THOMAS J., *People and Resources of the Earth*, Harper & Row, New York, 1964.

27. HANNA, PAUL R., KOHN, CLYDE F., AND LIVELY, ROBERT, *Beyond the Americas*, Scott, Foresman, Chicago, 1964.

28. ——, *In All Our States*, Scott, Foresman, Chicago, 1961.

29. ——, *In the Americas*, Scott, Foresman, Chicago, 1962.

30. HANNA, PAUL R., *et al.*, *Guidebook to Accompany In the Americas*, Scott, Foresman, Chicago, 1962.

31. HUNNICUT, C. W., AND GRAMBS, JEAN D., *The Great Adventure*, L. W. Singer, Syracuse, 1963.

32. JOYCE, BRUCE R., "Content for Elementary Social Studies," *Social Education*, 28 (Feb., 1964), pp. 84–87, 103.

33. McAULAY, J. D., "A Sequence for the American Heritage—Elementary Grades," *Peabody Journal of Education*, 42 (Jan., 1965), pp. 219–23.

34. NYSTROM, J. WARREN, JONES, EVELYN D., AND HARTER, HELEN, *Beyond Our Borders*, Rand McNally, Chicago, 1961.

35. PATTERSON, FRANKLIN, *et al.*, *Man Changes His World*, L. W. Singer, Syracuse, 1963.

36. PATTERSON, FRANKLIN, *et al., This Is Our Land,* L. W. Singer, Syracuse, N.Y., 1963.

37. PENIX, FINDLAY C., "Teaching Social Studies in Elementary Schools," in *New Challenges in the Social Studies,* B. G. Massialas and F. R. Smith (eds.), Wadsworth, Belmont, Calif., 1965, pp. 63–88.

38. POLANSKY, LUCY, WANN, KENNETH D., AND WARMAN, HENRY J., *The Changing Earth and Its People,* Allyn and Bacon, Boston, 1965.

39. POUNDS, NORMAN J. G., AND JONES, EVELYN D., *Beyond the Oceans,* Rand McNally, Chicago, 1961.

40. PRICE, ROBERT D., "Textbook Dilemma in the Social Studies," *The Social Studies,* 57 (Jan., 1966), pp. 21–23, 26–27.

41. SCHMUCK, PATRICIA, *et al.,* "Social Science Education: A Curriculum Frontier," *Educational Leadership,* 22 (Feb., 1965), pp. 300–05.

42. TEXTBOOK STUDY COMMITTEE, "Economics in the Schools," *American Economic Review* (Supplement), 53 (Mar., 1963).

43. TYLER, RALPH, *Basic Principles of Curriculum and Instruction,* University of Chicago Press, Chicago, 1950.

44. UNIVERSITY OF MICHIGAN SOCIAL SCIENCE EDUCATION STAFF, *Teacher's Guide for Social Science Unit One,* Science Research Associates, Chicago, unpublished field-test copy, 1965.

PART 2

The Junior High School

CHAPTER 4

American History

Chronology and the Inquiry Process

C. BENJAMIN COX

Objectives and Justifications for the Course

The teaching of American history at the junior high level is an established tradition, though few public school traditions in the United States go back further than a century. This particular tradition, dating from the famed curriculum report of 1916, has in fact contributed to the welfare of only two or three generations of our citizens. Even the term "junior high school" must be used symbolically, since it is not a universally accepted administrative unit.

Curriculum reports and evaluations usually perpetuate the belief that the history of the United States should be taught to our young citizens. Some of these studies give intrinsic reasons for studying history: for young students to know something of their antecedents is good in itself, and the very existence of history is justification for studying it. Others give extrinsic reasons for studying history: a knowledge of the history of one's country is instrumental in developing patriotism and good citizenship among young people.

There are at least two other kinds of justification for the teaching of United States history. It could be hypothesized that the history of one's country is an implicit and necessary part of a logical or operational system. That is, a person's role in society could be defined as having social, psychological, civic, economic, *and* historical dimensions, all of which define his system of interaction with society. Logically such a system could be invented. In a limited sense those who assume that historical knowledge promotes citizenship have already created this system. But there is no empirical evidence that historical knowledge is an aspect of such a system. In fact there is little enough evidence of the actual need for the other knowledge dimensions within such a system of social interaction.

INQUIRY AS A JUSTIFICATION

It is an implicit assumption of this book that promoting the inquiry process is the prime concern of social studies in the public school and that a course in the social studies curriculum can best be justified in terms of its ability to contribute to this process. This chapter assumes that United States history can make a contribution to inquiry. Moreover, this book assumes that the inquiry process, insofar as it is applicable to social affairs, has an historical dimension that is locked into the act of reflection.

But this is not to say that all kinds of history teaching contribute effectively to the inquiry process. For example, it appears from a number of classroom experiments that, for teaching to be effective, a development other than chronological must be used in the inquiry-centered history classroom. When history is conceived of as a linear development, when historical explanation relies mainly on *post hoc—propter hoc* causation, inquiry in the classroom is subverted. Chronology can provide a general framework for the practice of inquiry only if it is considered a convenient vehicle for moving the attention of the class from one episodic confrontation to another.

History as a discipline and United States history as a subject may serve the following purposes for inquiry-centered teaching:

1. History can provide episodes that concretely suggest relationships, concepts, rules of action, or principles. For example, the textual description of English colonization on the American eastern seaboard may suggest many hypotheses about cultural diffusion, social control, or social change.

2. History can offer cases in point in which further evidence relevant to a hypothesis can be sought, where special cases of a rela-

tionship are described, or where a hypothesis may be more precisely tested. For example, a hypothesis linking individual freedom and constitutional government can be more fully examined by comparing the histories of national states that have constitutions with those that do not.

3. History can provide a rhetoric of investigation appropriate to some inquiries. Historians, for example, make use of certain rules of evidence, internal and external criticism of documents, and modes of research that can offer valuable guidance to teachers and students at strategic points in their own inquiries. A class studying local history might well adopt the historian's procedures for searching for information and ensuring the authenticity of his primary sources and the accuracy of his secondary ones.

A Review of Textbooks in United States History

This section examines some of the major history textbooks available to the junior high United States history teacher. This review will explore the type of support the teacher may expect from available texts if he intends to emphasize inquiry-centered teaching. We will also identify exercises that are potentially subversive to this approach and indirectly suggest techniques for furthering inquiry in the classroom.

THE USE OF GENERALIZATIONS

As a point of departure for the analyses in this volume, the introduction states that social studies textbooks should base their content on stated or clearly implied generalizations. These can serve a number of purposes: (1) As predictive statements they show relationships among factors and events reported in the narration. (2) They comprise frameworks for presenting information. (3) They represent the focuses of an author's treatment of a subject and provide the bases for evaluating the relevance of the material presented. (4) They serve as hypotheses to be used for inquiry in the social studies classroom.

Most history textbooks, however, seem deliberately to avoid generalizations. And, when included, generalizations are ordinarily confined to a particular historical context. For example, in the story of American industrialization Winther and Cartwright in *The Story of Our Heritage* (18) say, "So, as Americans were moving West, inventions were changing their ways of living." The alert teacher, of course, would be quick to induce from this statement a broader hypothesis about cultural change that could then be applied to specific events reported by Winther and Cartwright and to other experiences read or remembered by the class. The inquiry-oriented teacher must learn to extract his own springboards and devise his own hypotheses from almost any descriptive material, historical or nonhistorical. The willingness to search for implied explanations and to test them is the basis of his teaching method. For example, he reads: "Many inventors continued to work on the problem. So many of them built model steamboats that no one man deserves credit for the invention." In response he hypothesizes, "Inventions emerge from the combined efforts of many who are working in similar situations toward similar goals," or "Important inventions are produced by disciplined attempts to apply known principles and processes in new ways to a recognized problem."

Any text that assiduously avoids general explanation and hypothesizing obviously offers the teacher little or no support in this task, except for those aspects of our national development where the social sciences have popularized general explanations. For example, the trends toward industrialization and urbanization have benefited from sociological interpretations that historians cannot easily ignore. Also, the efforts of the economists to develop dependable analyses of production, resources, and markets are widely accepted by historians and serve to identify the kind of historical events that will be reported. Some texts, however, are reluctant to demonstrate their dependence on social scientific analysis. In *The Story of Our Heritage* (18), for example, the authors restrict the review of the "Great Depression" largely to a narration of historical events in an apparent effort to protect the student from economic analysis. In answering the question of why "the greatest of all American depressions" came about, they suggest that a "look back into our history" reveals that "it was partly brought on by the tremendous changes" that followed the Civil War. In the review that follows, the economic analysis underlying the narrative is only implied.

Despite the fact that its first edition was in 1938 Moon and Cline's *Story of Our Land and People* (15) offers the teacher more opportunities for stimulating inquiry among his students because the authors do not avoid generalization. A good example of this style is seen at the conclusion of a chapter dealing with the French and Indian War:

> Nations that win wars usually want something besides the satisfaction of victory. So, nations that are the losers pay for their defeat in many ways. (Moon and Cline, 15, p. 142.)

In the same context Moon and Cline also say:

> National pride and ambition, greed for colonies and wealth, memories of past wars, religious differences—all of these helped plunge France and Great Britain into a series of four wars. (*Ibid.*, p. 134.)

The first generalization is in the present tense and attempts to offer a sweeping explanation for the demands and restitutions that "usually" follow a national victory and surrender. The second generalization limits its scope to one situation and two specified nations. However, it also makes use of general concepts (national pride, national ambition, greed, wealth, colonies, and religious differences) and a general idea (memory of wars). All these terms have wide application. Both kinds of generalizations can, with little change, serve as hypotheses to guide further explanation and inquiry.

Caughey, Franklin, and May's *Land of the Free* (4), on the other hand, does not contribute to this aspect of inquiry. The text patently refuses to generalize. While it reports events and historical developments as well or better than other junior high texts on the market, it does less well in explaining these events with well-placed generalizations. The authors know the facts and they report them clearly, but they do not use these facts to build concepts or to support generalizations. Facts are selected because they tell a story or detail an event that seems to be an important link in a chain of developments leading to a present situation. This linear concept of history is too simplistic and too delimiting, because it avoids the kind of multicausal and multidisciplinary analysis so necessary in the process of full inquiry.

On the other hand Drummond, Fraser, and Alweis's *Five Centuries in America* (8) offers much better support to teachers looking for generalizations. The promising aspects of this text are best seen in red marginal notes of the teacher's annotated edition (9) and the green-tinted section, *Teacher's Guide and Key for Five Centuries in America*. Both suggest a fair concern for generalizations as frameworks in organizing content. Under "Basic Generalizations" the *Teacher's Guide* explains:

The generalizations that have been given systematic cumulative development in this history series are grouped in six areas, as listed below. These generalizations are not presented as statements to be "learned" by pupils; indeed, they are stated here in adult language for consideration by the teacher. Girls and boys should be encouraged to use relevant facts to build these generalizations or understandings and express them at their own level of maturity, in their own terms. (Drummond, Fraser, and Alweis, 9, p. G3.)

The generalizations are organized under such categories as "The Nature and Meaning of History," "Change," "Culture," and "Interdependence." Although the generalizations identified are of varied quality and usefulness, here are two of the better statements: "All people express their religious feelings through worship of their own deities" and "The ability of a people to direct or adapt to basic changes is influenced by their level of education and their application of scientific knowledge." A selected group of generalizations is then used to introduce the teaching suggestions for each unit.

In addition the marginal notes in the teacher's edition emphasize the development of generalizations and the analysis of relationships. On a page devoted to questions and exercises on a chapter the text (8) points out that "the exercises emphasize the geographic factors which help influence the course of history" and elsewhere that "the activities listed under 'Thinking about this unit' stress important generalizations."

The *Teacher's Guide for Five Centuries in America* (9) contains the very productive suggestion that the relationship between poor transportation and diversity among regions be discussed. But even in this case the teacher must be able to transcend the particular context of the text discussion, for neither the text nor the *Teacher's Guide* openly asserts that isolation creates and maintains diversity. The *Guide* does not call for teachers and students to test this idea but merely to accept it as an explanation of the wide differences in the ways of life of Americans in 1750. This particular chapter has quite a broad discussion of the factors leading to cultural diffusion, especially geographic and environmental differences and social continuities among four regions in the eighteenth-century American continent. But the use of generalizations as hypotheses to be tested and the use of facts and general statements about life in the colonies as evidence to be related to the hypotheses are left to the teacher's discretion.

In sum *any* text can be used for inquiry. The teacher who

understands the strategies, phases, and skills entailed in inquiry can adapt a great variety of material to his needs. But he must work at a disadvantage if his textual materials do not contribute directly to these efforts. The text that explicitly generalizes, that consistently offers explanatory hypotheses for events, and that presents factual information and cases as evidence for these general assertions clearly encourages inquiry far more than the text that does not. A textbook that stimulates the student to raise questions, make analyses, or draw inferences, one that alerts him to general statements of causation, correlation, definition, or conceptualization, makes an appropriate contribution to inquiry. But the textbook that lulls the student into a lethargic attitude with a narrative depicting a linear sequence of events does not carry its own weight in the inquiry process.

THE DEVELOPMENT OF EXPLANATION AND UNDERSTANDING

Closely related to the statement and support of generalizations in history texts is the development of understanding and explanation. Palmer (16) has carefully dealt with this aspect of inquiry in history textbooks at the high school level and further emphasizes it in Chapter 7 of this book. The types of explanation most often utilized in history texts may be classified as subsumptive, genetic, and causal.

A subsumptive explanation classifies the event to be explained under a general principle that is purportedly valid in all times and places. This is the primary purpose of the generalization in history. For example, the generalization that "victorious nations exact retribution from their defeated enemies" explains the behavior of the allied powers at the peace conferences following World Wars I and II.

A genetic explanation traces trends and movements so that a phenomenon in one era is seen as the culmination of its antecedents in past eras. For example, the Bill of Rights in the United States Constitution may be "explained" by its antecedents in colonial and English history, such as the Magna Carta.

A causal explanation identifies a particular phenomenon that led to another phenomenon. Thus slavery is sometimes said to have "caused" the Civil War.

Complex logical and empirical questions can be raised about the validity and reliability of each type of explanation and the interrelationships among them. Nonetheless junior high texts do make some use of these models at various levels of sophistication.

A suggestion in Glovinsky's *Teacher's Manual and Answer*

Book (14) warrants some comment in this respect. The *Manual* states that "the study of American history takes on real meaning for your pupils only when they begin to think about cause-effect relationships." Only in this way, says the *Manual*, can history escape being "meaningless plodding through a maze of unrelated facts." The *Manual* then explains that American history is really "an inspiring narrative of people and forces that have shaped the past and the present and will influence all of their tomorrows." Without the final explanation the earlier suggestions are too vague to be meaningful, for the concept of cause and effect is a very complex one worthy of the most vigorous analysis. But the added explanation, entailing such extravagant notions as "narrative," "forces," "shaped," "past," "present," "influence," and "tomorrows" transforms vagueness into distortion. The comfortable implication is either that all that has happened in the past is the cause of all that is happening now or that each event is caused by the event preceding it. The teacher and student seduced by so imprecise a notion of causal relationships cannot engage in a rigorous and exact analysis of causal factors. That the study of history should deal with cause and effect relationships is indeed a rubric of inquiry. But this should not suggest that the relationships are easily accessible or that they emerge from narratives or even that history per se can produce them.

Some reference to the problems of explanation and understanding is made in Eibling *et al.* *Teacher's Manual for Use with the Story of America* (13). The *Teacher's Manual* includes "understandings to be developed" in the introductory information for each chapter. But the potential of this feature is not fully developed. The opportunity could have been used to indicate some important relationships, to point toward the development of concepts, or to state major generalizations that could contribute to explanation and understanding. Instead the statements are all the kind of historical summaries often used as topic sentences for paragraphs. As such, they do not comprise real understandings but abort inquiry. Their one virtue lies in alerting students to possible general relationships. Summary statements are truly useful only if they are approached as an initial entry to reflection. If the inquirer can see in the summary a generalizable relationship or a conceptual correlation or if he can push beyond the parameters of a unique time and place, then he can initiate reflective inquiry.

In *The Story of Our Heritage* Winther and Cartwright (18)

make use of a vague combination of causal and genetic explanations. At one point, under the heading "Things Happened!" they said, "History is about events in the past. Some events are so important that we cannot understand the story without knowing when they happened." Then in a following section entitled "Where Is It?" they add, "And things do not just happen. They happen some place. We do not really understand what happened unless we know where it happened." The notion that time is an important attribute of events suggests genetic explanation, while the identification of place—thus implying geographic factors—embraces an aspect of causal explanation. These devices, however, only begin to tap the possibilities of understanding, and identifying the time and place of an occurrence certainly does not explain its causes.

A purer form of genetic explanation is illustrated in Wilder, Ludlum, and Brown's *This Is America's Story* (17). One of the book's special features is a series of paragraphs entitled "Linking the Past and the Present." Each paragraph tries to establish a continuity between some item in a chapter and an event or characteristic in our present day. Most teachers refer to this practice as showing the contemporary relevance of history and demonstrating that history is not simply a dead image of the past. Such practices, of course, provide useful genetic explanations.

But often the links between the past and present focus on such "interesting" information as the origins of state names, the designing of Washington, D.C., the writing of "The Star Spangled Banner," and the genesis of historical monuments. The effect is deleterious in two ways. By highlighting this information the text gives the impression that these facts are not a legitimate part of history—that the real material is indeed dry and dead. The student may get the impression that these entertaining sidelights are designed to make the rest of the book palatable, and he may then view the major part of the text with even less concern. Or on the other hand the student may become convinced that these interesting linkages actually represent real history, in which case he will misunderstand the meaning of history itself. In fact the real meaning of history emerges from considering it (1) as a source of demonstrated relationships and hypotheses and (2) as a source of evidence to support hypotheses, to say nothing of its legitimate genetic function. Any practice that subverts these functions violates the real purpose of history in the process of inquiry.

Counterfactual Examples

Related to explanation and understanding in history is what Glovinsky calls in his *Teacher's Manual* (14) imaginative young people's "tendency to ask 'what if' questions." It is his impression that certain " 'what ifs' can be tremendously useful in challenging pupils to weigh alternatives, to examine historical facts, and to give intelligent opinions." He suggests that such excursions should be kept within limits, though he does not define these limits.

This idea warrants a more careful examination. Glovinsky's statement implies that a major reason for encouraging these counterfactual explorations is to increase student motivation. History, at times a dull labor, may fail to excite students. Invention and caprice offer a whimsical release from reality and in effect create added interest in the subject at hand. If this were the rationale of "what ifs," then one could justify the practice if kept within limits. There are obviously other areas of study where counterfactual suppositions are used to good effect. For example, in an enterprise involving fixed procedures and alternatives an operator could be asked, "What if the gear had not engaged? What would you have done?" The operator would be expected to demonstrate his knowledge of procedures by indicating the proper action to have been taken. Or in a system involving job functions and relationships a manager could be asked, "Now what if your typist had not come in?" The manager could then indicate his method of dealing with the situation in order to keep the system functioning. A general's understanding of strategy is tested and proved by means of "what if" contingencies. One's economic understanding might be sharpened by responding to "if" situations and then testing them with a hypothetical model. In fact the entire theory of simulation is based on the possibility of imposing different kinds of circumstances—the "ifs"—and watching or testing their effects on the model.

Three aspects are common to the above examples: (1) The situations occur in finite, closed systems. (2) The "if" contingency can be tested according to the known and observable functions of a model. (3) The response required is a limited one. Ordinarily only a single inference is called for.

The problem with counterfactual proposals in history is that few, if any, empirical or theoretical tests can be applied to them, because the questions cannot be asked within a limited and known (or hypothetical) system. Proposals such as "what if Lincoln had not been shot," "what if Hitler had been killed," "what if the Lusitania had not been sunk," and "what if the South had won the Civil War" open such an enormous range of possibilities that they escape the realm of rational analysis and represent little more than an introduction to fantasy.

Chronology and Historical Periodization

A major stumbling block to the development of explanation and understanding in junior high history texts is the unequivocal commitment to chronology and historical periodization. A perfect case in point is Casner and Gabriel's *Story of the American Nation* (3), a venerable text that has recently been revised and updated. Each section of the book is said to deal with "one idea . . . complete in itself." It seems somewhat strange that an *idea* should have as discrete a life span as the periods 1763–87, 1783–1823, or 1823–60, and it quickly becomes apparent that "idea" is really the old historical notion of periodization. Hence Unit 2, entitled "The English Colonies Win Their Independence (1763–1787)," is in reality a chronological treatment of the revolutionary period; and Unit 6, "A Strong Nation Arises from the Ruins of War (1860–1865)," is quite naturally the Civil War period. By skipping Units 5 and 7 the student can follow an unbroken sequence of events from 1450 to 1961. Since later chapters are merely compendiums of contemporary events, the book is easily updated in successive revisions by adding a chapter for each new presidential term, consisting of headline events over four years or so.

Development in Casner and Gabriel is by event and chronology. Questions asking for student explanations refer to the collection of facts contained in the preceding section as suggested in the *Teacher's Manual* (2). There is no attempt to make explicit principles or generalizations from psychology, sociology, economics, or biology that may have been operative in the events described. For example, students are asked, "Why did Europeans become interested in faraway lands?" Under the general direction to "discuss" they are told, "to answer it properly, you must use many of the facts that you have learned in reading the section."

The exercises in the text and the further suggestions for lesson development are all directed toward establishing a "sense of chronology" and a sequential story. In fact the book is unabashedly represented as a story, and its chief author is touted as "a pioneer in the use of story telling methods." The book leaves us with the impression that the development of the United States and American society has been a unilinear procession of events, each occurring logically after its predecessor. Seldom is further explanation or analysis elicited in such a story. The implication is that only events cause events.

The effect of this approach on explanation and inquiry is clear. Historical treatment that confines itself to chronology cannot easily escape the trap of simply reporting "one damn thing after another," in Toynbee's apt phrase. The extraction of meaningful experience is made precarious and difficult by the relatively undifferentiated listing of events. Also, the supposition that great ideas are confined to certain periods of time seriously hampers the development of both genetic explanation and generalizations and concepts that could be tested or applied in other times and places. The student is seduced into the indefensible position of inferring *post hoc, propter hoc.*

DOGMA VERSUS INQUIRY

There are other convergences in these texts that militate against understanding and the inquiry procedure in the history classroom. One of these tendencies is the viewpoint from which historical facts and events are consistently reported. A dogma of interpretation appears to embrace all American history textbooks in the public schools. If the teacher is looking for a divergent hypothesis to enliven his classroom discussions or to foment inquiry, he should not search for it in junior high history books. The traditional, the safe, and the shopworn are carefully protected under the guise of established scholarship.

The Importance of Divergent Hypotheses

This Is America's Story (17) can serve as the exemplary participant in this dogma. Take, for instance, this text's description of the Crusades, which are explained—as in all school texts—solely in terms of religious motives. The authors report that the Saracens were interfering with and sometimes stopping the pilgrimages to the Holy Lands: "Surely, the Christians thought, the blessing of God would be given to the people who helped recapture the Holy Land!" They continued, "Believing as they did about religion, the Christians responded eagerly when they were called upon to fight against the Saracens." This interpretation, emphasizing noble religious motives, is perpetuated with little adulteration in public school books. In examining this period, however, modern scholars have suggested that prospects of economic rewards, commerce, and raw conquest may have been stronger motives.

As a matter of fact the effects of the Crusades are ordinarily discussed later in textbooks mainly in the economic sphere with reference to trade, merchants, and urbanization. While the introduction of this two-century affair largely in religious terms and its later development in terms of economic and cultural effects may present the teacher with a historical disjunction that he can capitalize on for purposes of inquiry, they cause a certain loss of textual integrity. It would be more academically respectable to hypothesize a mixture of conquest, economic benefits, and religion as the acknowledged, if morally incompatible, motives for joining a Crusade.

In another instance *This Is America's Story* gives less attention to Leif Ericson and the Viking explorations to America than most of the junior high texts. This book refers to the Vikings only in a footnote and with a single picture and caption. With the dramatic new evidence provided by Yale University's *The Vinland Map and the Tartar Relation*,[1] however, future editions of history texts may well expand their treatment of the Vikings. The recognition of the relationships between the Norsemen and other Europeans, particularly Irish Catholic monks and in fact the Pope, may well spur further research in Vatican library sources. The unavoidable hypothesis is that Columbus and hence many other knowledgeable seamen of the fifteenth century were well aware of the existence of Vinland and its inhabitants, the Skraelings.

Now such a point may be a niggling one as far as a junior high text is concerned. Whether Columbus knew about America before he sailed hardly bears on the fact and effect of his discovery, and every schoolboy acknowledges Ericson's precedence in some manner. But the Yale University evidence may well support new generalizations about the processes of exploration and discovery. One such interesting hypothesis is that only what is already known or expected can be discovered. Not incompatible with this idea is Edmundo O'Gorman's philosophical interpretation that America was "invented" in 1492, not "discovered," since fifteenth-century Europe

[1] R. A. Skelton, Thomas E. Marston, and George D. Painter, *The Vinland Map and the Tartar Relation*, Yale University Press, New Haven, Conn., 1965.

was philosophically and theologically unprepared for the new world.[2]

The preceding examples illustrate two obligations of the social studies teacher. First, he should be familiar with scholarly sources other than the adopted text. Documentary discoveries as important as the Vinland map are uncommon occurrences in historical research, but changes in points of view and emphasis and the reinterpretation of known information occur in any area of human knowledge. Obviously a textbook cannot and should not reflect all this in the positions it assumes, since the assuming of a position precludes so broad a reflection. It is therefore an academic responsibility of the teacher to broaden the base of examination in his classroom by presenting the divergent ideas of historians and social scientists or, when possible, to make these hypotheses and their supporting evidence available in the study materials given to students.

In order to take full advantage of outside scholarly sources, a teacher must also be flexible enough in the management of his class to entertain a great many divergent ideas and explanations—particularly from students—about historical matters. The premature closure of discussions on the basis of one textbook's claims is deadly to creative thought processes. Critical thinking is stifled—especially in its early phases—if alternate hypotheses are not given an opportunity to compete with the "accepted" explanation or interpretation. This "open stance" on the part of the teacher is a very useful methodological strategy in countering a text's special pleading for one interpretation or explanation. This strategy can also encourage students to invent alternative positions as bases for their own testing procedures. Moreover, the statement and testing of more than one possible explanation or hypothesis may well demonstrate to students how a preponderance of evidence forces historians and social scientists to accept one conclusion over others.

A Hopeful Departure

A new text in this field that has departed somewhat from the traditional dogmas is Caughey, Franklin, and May's *Land of the Free* (4). These authors have accomplished this departure simply by selecting some events for greater emphasis and by abbreviating the treatment of others. Unfortunately their strategy produces both positive and negative effects. The notion of emphasis on the important

2Edmundo O'Gorman, *The Invention of America: An Inquiry into the Historical Nature of the New World and the Meaning of Its History*, Indiana University Press, Bloomington, 1961.

is commendable, but perhaps if an event is unworthy of emphasis it is best left unreported. In this respect the book is an uneven combination of useful and important historical information that provides evidence for understanding and oversimplified reporting of a chronology of events, which is more debilitating than helpful.

On the positive side, however, is the book's most exciting treatment of certain parts of the American experience. Among the most important differences between this book and its competitors are (1) its excellent and greatly expanded sections on minority peoples in American society, especially Negroes; (2) its liberal political and economic orientation—a welcome relief from the pseudoneutrality of most junior high histories; (3) its emphasis on "social history" and, in particular, conservation as a national policy; and (4) its extensive use of black and white and colored plates presenting contemporary photographs, etchings, and paintings illustrative of various periods, styles of life, and famous persons.

TEXTBOOK OBJECTIVES

Functionally related to the several aspects of inquiry dealt with in the foregoing sections, that is, generalization, understanding, explanation, interpretation, and selectivity of information, is the identification of goals and objectives. While the final product is not always consistent with the author's expectations, teacher's manuals accompanying textbooks, such as Eibling *et al. Teacher's Manual for Use with the Story of America* (13), are often the clearest representations of his intentions. Here authors often reveal their major goals in writing their books and most explicitly establish their orientation and philosophy. Thus Eibling *et al.* placed their text squarely in the utilitarian traditions of citizenship and patriotism. One studies American history principally to enhance his appreciation for his heritage, to instill a desire for cooperation and smooth human relationships, to learn to value justice and to respect others who are different, and to increase his willingness to accept the responsibilities of a citizen. Incidentally one may also learn certain skills, establish relationships—such as between geography and history—and gain social understandings (13). The list is not unusually long, as social studies objectives go, but it is nonetheless formidable.

What an imposing list of objectives requires of the teacher and his students is obviously an uncompromising acceptance of the authors' system of values. For example, history cannot teach that "human relations have priority over other considerations" (13) unless the historian decides that he will give priority to human relations in making his judgments about events. Certainly there are *realia* relationships in history, but the lessons of history are always *logical* constructs and must be extracted from the *realia*. They are never inherent. A major error of authors and teachers is the unwarranted supposition that lessons and values are self-revealing entities in events and episodes. As a matter of fact events and episodes reveal only certain kinds of relationships, and these vary according to the nature of the inquiry.

Moreover, there is little evidence that the study of any social studies course has much effect on citizenship or patriotism. These predispositions on the part of citizens have been shown to be largely the product of other factors, such as parental attitudes and personal involvement in citizenship activities. It is thus both unscholarly and impractical to continue to justify the study of history on these grounds.

ADAPTABILITY TO THE INQUIRY PROCESS

A question to be raised by the teacher bent on inquiry is how to choose or adapt textbook exercises and passages to promote a consistent pattern of inquiry in class. Unfortunately few of the exercises and questions in textbooks are usable in inquiry without some adaptations. Can all questions or exercises be changed to promote inquiry? Is there a formula to guide the teacher in recasting questions toward that end? The answer seems to be "no" on each count. Inquiry is patterned thinking and investigation. It is always hypothesis-focused, and its primary concern with facts and data is in their use as evidence. Furthermore, it consistently recognizes that explanation and understanding depend on concepts and generalizations that have wide application beyond any particular event or circumstance. To illustrate both the use of certain exercises provided in textbooks and the vitiating dangers inherent in many of them, this section essays examples from several texts.

Particularly valuable in *This Is America's Story* (17) is the feature entitled "Gaining Skill." It begins with helpful suggestions on the use of various aspects of the text, such as its chapter divisions, levels of headings, questions, and indexes. Other skills identified are "How to Read Maps and Pictures," "Making Reports," "How to

Prepare a Map," "How to Prepare Charts and Graphs," "Map Projections," and "How to Evaluate Information." Unfortunately these useful skills are only superficially examined. For example, the section on evaluation, stating criteria for judging the qualifications of a reporter of information, warrants extensive treatment in social studies. The paragraphs on differentiating fact from opinion in the discussion of evaluation techniques are especially misleading, partly because of the perfunctory treatment. A textbook could greatly support the process of inquiry in the classroom were it to emphasize the more important issues in decision-making, historiography, and social judgment. But the preoccupation with fact, story, and chronology in junior high history books relegates skill development to the level of incidental concern.

Eibling, King, and Harlow's *History of Our United States* (11) and Eibling *et al. The Story of America* (12) emphasize another study aid. Each book intersperses "at important points" within every chapter "Stop and Think" questions set off from the text by asterisks and italics. The authors claim that these questions will encourage the student to consider his thoughts on the reading or to recall other examples of a given phenomenon. These questions are not significantly different from the typical thought or discussion questions in texts, but their placement just after the related episode may have greater impact on students. At least these questions would be harder to avoid than those isolated at the ends of chapters. As is too often the case, however, the authors do very little with these questions except provide a stipulated correct answer or a vague "answers will vary" in the manual. This treatment simply does not assure the statement and testing of hypotheses that many of these questions would allow. Of course, the teacher could make such use of these questions if he so desired. But he would have to bring to his task all the required skills because the text offers him no supportive guidelines.

The end-of-chapter and unit exercises in Caughey, Franklin, and May's *Land of the Free* (4) reflect its overall orientation toward linear history and genetic development. Most of the questions require only the recall of facts from the preceding reading. In fact only a few of the questions "For Thought and Discussion" demand anything but the simplest level of thought. A few ask for the listing of contemporary phenomena that are similar to certain historical phenomena. Such a comparison makes use of the important critical skill of analogy, but the authors make no effort to help the student develop this skill or to show him how to test it. Other "thought questions" call for outlines of arguments and lists of facts from the chapter that relate to some event reported in it. In general the exercises are undistinguished even when compared to the prosaic collections of questions in the other texts.

The most flagrant abuse of inquiry procedures in commercial classroom materials is represented by the workbooks or exercise books that accompany many texts. Although the workbook potentially offers the easiest access to inquiry procedures for junior high history textbooks—or any text, for that matter—no publisher has taken advantage of this potential. A typical example of the traditional workbook is the *Exercise Book for History of Our United States* (10). This booklet contributes little to the development of a "sense of history," to analytic skills, or to the student's understanding. Its intent is merely "to fix in mind various phases of the subject matter in the text." The booklet provides some anecdotes not included in the text itself that are interesting and colorful but certainly not systematically instructive.

Occasionally the exercises in workbooks suggest a vague notion of programing, but there are only abortive attempts to establish or develop meaningful relationships. The exercises rely almost exclusively on the arbitrary association of facts as reflected in the tiresome use of matching, true-false, and fill-in-the-blank items.

The time-honored separation of thought questions from memory questions is ordinarily the closest approximation of inquiry made by most texts. The teacher who consistently emphasizes the thought exercises will be most likely to promote inquiry in his classroom. For example, Winther and Cartwright (18) occasionally pose problems or questions that could encourage reflective inquiry. Under the title "Think It Over!" they ask, "Sometimes we hear people say that what makes a country great is its many natural resources. What else does it take to make a country great? Why was America not a great country before Columbus's time?" Other questions under the heading "For Class Discussion" that could promote inquiry are: "Why did Europeans believe that a nation should sell more goods than it bought?" "Why were Americans different from people living in Europe?" "What is the purpose of a political party?" and "What could government regulation do for people that they could not do for themselves as individuals? Is too much government regulation also a danger? Why?" But what is lacking in this text, as in most junior high history texts, is a systematic method for helping students to develop the intellectual skills that differentiate facile and loose opinions from vigorous reflection.

Moon and Cline's *Story of Our Land and People*

Moon and Cline's textbook (15) offers several types of exercises for students that might be adapted to inquiry techniques. First, it offers "Study Questions" as part of its end-of-chapter exercises. But the teacher must exercise careful judgment in selecting from them. While some of the questions have fine potential for inquiry, others are either too limited or too vague to be of much help. The following questions appear in one list, for example:

> Describe the Wright Brothers' first airplane. How successful was their first flight at Kitty Hawk?
>
> How did World War II affect the coming of television?
>
> What benefits and what problems came with the automobile?
> (Moon and Cline, 15, p. 514.)

The first statement and question would serve only to spark the student's incidental interest. They are too particular to relate to broader questions. The second question is quite promising in that it could easily lead to a very productive investigation of the relationship between war and the development of technology. The third question obviously has some possibilities but is so general that the teacher would have to make it more specific to be useful. For example, does "came with the automobile" imply some notion of causation or does it merely suggest the era one is to consider? Also, in evaluating the "benefits" and "problems" are we to consider the economy, agriculture, the family, medical practice, adolescent car addiction, the disappearance of the domesticated horse, and the move to suburbia or just transportation?

The text's unit review, bearing the promising title "The History Laboratory," also merits attention. The introduction states: "People learn by doing. When you plan and carry through an activity or project, you improve your skills, learn new skills, and make use of facts and ideas that you then remember." The supposition is probably a valid one, and the activities and projects are on a fairly high level and of interesting variety. The teacher who draws upon this source would at least make his course more enjoyable. Creative writing, panel discussions, exhibits, book reports, notebook-keeping, and library research are certainly legitimate techniques to employ in social studies. But carrying out these suggested activities would not necessarily change the real nature of the classroom from an acquisitive one to an inquisitive one. It is the stance the teacher and his pupils assume toward knowledge and the intellectual strategies involved in carrying out activities that set the inquiring classroom apart from the acquiring one.

The activities most clearly designed to ensure reflective thinking in "The History Laboratory" are those entitled "Learn to Draw Conclusions" and "Learn to Reach Conclusions." In the first activity of this kind Moon and Cline wrote:

> Drawing conclusions requires very careful thinking and the use of logical and accurate information. There are some conclusions that might have been reached from the facts presented in this unit. Write one of your conclusions on the chalkboard. Then have your classmates list underneath it the facts that lead to your conclusion. Try one or more of the following:
> 1. To develop civilization, people must settle in a particular place for a long time and live in security.
> 2. Geography influences the life of man.
> 3. The invention of the printing press began a gradual replacement of superstition with knowledge.
> 4. Most of the Italian explorers claimed land for other countries.
>
> (Moon and Cline, 15, p. 63.)

The exercise is an excellent beginning, but it has a number of limitations. For instance, it is improbable that teachers and students are well enough acquainted with the procedures of hypothesizing, logical exploration, and seeking evidence to carry out the exercise without more guidance than is given. It is unrealistic to imply that conclusions proceed easily and full blown from a listing of facts. Hypotheses may bloom from sudden insights. But conclusions ought to be made of firmer stuff. One wishes that the perfunctory nod made to inquiry in this series of exercises could be expanded to show students further aspects of reflection.

In summary the quality of the exercises in Moon and Cline is not exceptional, but the book does offer several exercises from which to choose. Most of its study aids are typical of those appearing in junior high school texts—testing for the usual terms, names, and dates related to selected events in the chapter—but a few certainly broach the inquiry process. By exercising a very careful selection among these a teacher might encourage reflective thinking among students.

A point to be reemphasized is that any material that deals with a relationship between phenomena can be used by the knowledgeable teacher as a springboard for reflective appraisal. And, conversely, inquiry can be abrogated no matter how skillfully the material is put together if the teacher fails to capitalize on its potential. Nevertheless some materials present more challenges, more dilemmas, more issues, and more paradoxes than others. That is, some material is highly "inquiry-engaged" and some is comparatively "inquiry-flaccid." The degree of engagement is measured in part by the extent to which a book's exercises develop the potentialities of this approach.

DEPARTURES FROM THE TRADITIONAL TEXTBOOK STEREOTYPE

When a single conception dominates an area of study, as it apparently does in American history at the junior high level, a reviewer cannot expect to find anything new and fresh as he looks from book to book. He can only evaluate how well each book meets the traditional criteria—writing style, use of color and illustrations, appropriate language level, and placement of national documents. In truth no new concept of presentation, no improved accommodation of social knowledge, and no integrated point of view have been introduced into junior high history texts in two decades. Each text does some things better than its competing predecessors and contemporaries. Each does some things less well. But in most books the style is expository, the development is chronological, the basis of explanation is continuity, the theme is national growth, and the goal is national pride and citizenship. The continued prostitution of the junior high social studies course to this sacrosanct syndrome can only stifle the development of new approaches to the teaching of history.

There are, however, two or three textbooks that differ significantly from the majority. One of these is the new text by Caughey, Franklin, and May (4). Though great historians do not necessarily produce great school books, there is the mark of the historian in *Land of the Free*. This quite obviously lends a certain style to the material—a style that shows itself both in the selection of events and in the language of reporting. But this style does not, unfortunately, improve the readability of the book. Many junior high school students will struggle with their lessons in this book, though their teachers may find lesson-planning a bit more enjoyable.

Three points of emphasis in *Land of the Free* are certainly consistent with our criteria of good texts. First, it offers more balanced discussions of the relative contributions of anglowhites and our several minorities, which provide a much richer store of experiences as a basis for inquiry. It is often the paradoxes in human affairs that are the fountainheads of inquiry, and a teacher using this text simply cannot avoid dealing with the social and value contradiction represented by minority-group experiences in the development of our nation. Second, the fact that the book quite openly supports political and economic liberalism can sharpen the debates between those who approve of its explicitly stated judgments and those who disapprove. An identifiable point of view is a necessary component of the process of inquiry—particularly at its inception and conclusion. Third, the text's inclusion of many aspects of human affairs allows readers to confront other persistent problems of society besides political and military ones. Most texts comply with this emphasis. However, few do better than this one.

From a different point of view two other texts make a unique contribution to junior high school history literature. *The Story of America* (12) is an adaptation of *History of Our United States* (11) for low-level readers. The pagination is the same for the two editions. With one exception the maps and charts in the two books are identical, though the captions and information accompanying them in *The Story of America* often use easier words and phrases. Titles and subheadings are also simplified in the easier text. Most of the pictures and illustrations are the same in the two books, but there is one remarkable difference: the more difficult of the books carefully avoids pictures of Negroes and whites in integrated settings, while *The Story of America* makes an effort to show Negroes and whites in social situations in which they have equal status.

The provision of parallel text editions has several advantages. All junior high texts have made some accommodation to student reading ability, but few have dealt realistically with the fact that grade placement is not a precise indication of reading level for many students. Recent experiments in grouping and the special interest in exceptional children have demonstrated that interest and success are related phenomena among students. According to its *Teacher's Manual* (13) *The Story of America* provides readability for below-grade-level readers, high interest for seventh- and eighth-grade pupils, completeness, and multiple utility (stemming largely from the book's correspondence with *History of Our United States*). The *Manual* suggests the possibility of using both texts in classes that are ungrouped. Parallel reading assignments would be possible, though exercises and activities differ in the two editions.

The notion of parallel texts is an intriguing one, and its introduction is certainly to be applauded. But an enterprising publisher could apply this notion far more creatively to areas other than reading. Why not, for example, accept the chapter and unit organization of a traditional text and offer a parallel edition presenting a particular thesis or point of view? A truly geographic interpretation (many texts claim to relate geography and history, though they do so ineffectively) or an economic or sociological one could be the focus of the parallel edition. For the timid or traditional history teacher the primary text would offer the linear story of America. The purposely biased parallel text would then demonstrate the application of a frame of reference and the use of analytical hypotheses in determining meaning and creating understanding in human affairs.

The Need for a Focus on Issues

Still needed on the United States history textbook scene is a book that rejects the narrative chronological approach. Such a book would focus seriously on important and persistent issues and explore explanations for their recurrence in various historical contexts. This type of text would do more than tell a whimsical tale of America from birth to maturity, taking playful slaps at the behinds of concepts when they happened to be exposed. It would make full use of the vital concepts of human affairs and would discuss the historical context as a useful tool in explanation and understanding. It would present springboards for inquiry on every page. Many of its paragraphs would offer explanatory generalizations or generalizable explanations, and many of its questions and exercises would press the student into the reflective examination of issues. Its tenor would be interrogative and analytic; it would prod the student to infer, to induct, and to test; and it would encourage the teacher to question and to introduce doubt into student discussions.

Conclusion

Hopefully a consistent conception of inquiry in the junior high American history course has emerged in this chapter. I have examined several facets of this approach to rational closures to problems. Operationally inquiry is effected by confronting students with situations, problems, or paradoxes that encourage the identification of issues, call for a strategy of analysis, and give promise of feasible resolution or explanation. Logically inquiry demands the examination of propositions, assumptions, implications, and proofs for clarity, meaning, and logical validity. Empirically the process requires the marshaling of reliable evidence as support for solutions and generalizations. Affectively inquiry asks that the inquirer examine his own attitudes, beliefs, and values; if internalized, inquiry becomes a permanent prelude to action, a way of life.

I have assumed that the study of history can make a contribution to this important work. History can provide rich resources for events and confrontations that dramatize the real issues of life. It can provide hypotheses that are the fountainheads of inquiry. History offers an almost unlimited storehouse of evidence that can be logically gathered to support or refute propositions about human behavior. It presents an opportunity to investigate the longitudinal waxing and waning of many factors and trends and to examine threads of continuity. History can suggest analytic models or can present a variety of circumstances in which analytic models can be tested.

I have argued, however, that history alone can do few of these things well; United States history can do even fewer of them well; and history as represented in junior high courses and texts can hardly do them at all. To be an adjunct to inquiry, history must rely heavily on modes of analysis better developed in the social and behavioral sciences. It must emphasize the generalizable uniformities in events, rather than their uniqueness, and must search for patterns and consistent relationships. It must reject simplistic narration and linear chronology for a clearer focus on crucial issues in the life of the society and the individual.

Selected Bibliography

1. ANDERSON, HOWARD R., *Practice and Review Tests for This Is America's Story*, Houghton Mifflin, Boston, 1960.
2. BILLER, EDWARD L., *Teacher's Manual and Resource Guide for Use with Story of the American Nation*, Harcourt, Brace & World, New York, 1962.
3. CASNER, MABEL B., AND GABRIEL, RALPH H., *Story of the American Nation*, Harcourt, Brace & World, New York, 1962.
4. CAUGHEY, JOHN W., FRANKLIN, JOHN HOPE, AND MAY, ERNEST R., *Land of the Free, a History of the United States*, Benziger Brothers, New York, 1966.
5. CLINE, DON C., AND BAYNE, HELEN MAY, *Key to Tests for Story of Our Land and People by Moon and Cline*, Holt, Rinehart and Winston, New York, 1962.
6. ————, *Tests for Story of Our Land and People by Moon and Cline*, Holt, Rinehart and Winston, New York, 1962.
7. ————, *Workbook for Story of Our Land and People by Moon and Cline*, Holt, Rinehart and Winston, New York, 1963.
8. DRUMMOND, DONALD F., FRASER, DOROTHY M., AND ALWEIS, FRANK, *Five Centuries in America*, American Book, New York, 1964.
9. ————, *Teacher's Guide and Key for Five Centuries in America*, American Book, New York, 1964.
10. EIBLING, HAROLD H., KING, FRED M., AND HARLOW, JAMES, *Exercise Book for History of Our United States*, Laidlaw Brothers, River Forest, Ill., 1964.
11. ————, *History of Our United States*, Laidlaw Brothers, River Forest, Ill., 1964.
12. EIBLING, HAROLD H., *et al.*, *The Story of America*, Laidlaw Brothers, River Forest, Ill., 1965.
13. ————, *Teacher's Manual for Use with the Story of America*, Laidlaw Brothers, River Forest, Ill., no date.
14. GLOVINSKY, ARNOLD, *Teacher's Manual and Answer Book* for *Moon and Cline, Story of Our Land and People*, Holt, Rinehart and Winston, New York, 1961.
15. MOON, GLENN W., AND CLINE, DON C., *Story of Our Land and People*, Holt, Rinehart and Winston, New York, 1961.
16. PALMER, JOHN ROBERT, *The Treatment of Social Change in High School History Textbooks*, unpublished doctoral dissertation, University of Illinois, Urbana, 1961.
17. WILDER, HOWARD B., LUDLUM, ROBERT P., AND BROWN, HARRIETT MCCUNE, *This Is America's Story*, Houghton Mifflin, Boston, 1960.
18. WINTHER, OSCAR O., AND CARTWRIGHT, WILLIAM H., *The Story of Our Heritage*, Ginn, Boston, 1962.

CHAPTER 5

State History

The Reign of Provincialism

JACK E. COUSINS

State History and the Curriculum

If any one word decribes the curricula for social studies in the public schools, that word is "confusion!" This situation exists throughout the United States and is largely due to the fact that public schools still follow the general curricular patterns suggested by the 1916 Subcommittee on Social Studies in Secondary Schools (5). It is true that many schools are now experimenting with curricular designs, but history, stressed by the Subcommittee, still dominates social studies instruction throughout the United States. An examination of the actual course offerings indicates that the amount of time alloted to the study of history is much greater than the time devoted to all the other social sciences put together. Further examination indicates that most history courses are organized chronologically and that the goal is "to cover a certain amount of ground" by the end of the semester or year.

In spite of local control—a situation that could conceivably foster diversity—social studies programs appear to be remarkably similar throughout the United States. Lowe (24) summarized much of the criticism of present social studies curricula as follows:

1. [It] is repetitive and redundant.
2. It is provincial. It puts too much emphasis on the local, national, and Western cultures . . . .
3. It tries to cover too much ground. . . .
4. It produces economic and geographic illiterates . . . .
5. It fails to affect the social and political behavior of its students.
6. Its teachers are more unsure than teachers of other areas as to their basic purposes.

(Lowe, 24, p. 210.)

It thus appears that social studies programs do not help students to meet the fundamental requirements of thoughtful citizenship. This conclusion is supported by Kvaraceus (21), Oliver (26), and Starr (32) in addition to those mentioned in Chapter 1 of this book.

These criticisms, though aimed at social studies in general, apply particularly well to the junior high state history course, taught in the seventh, eighth, or ninth grade in practically every state. This course is such a traditional part of the curriculum that questions raised about it tend to deal with such issues as which grade it should be taught in, whether it should be correlated with geography and civics, and whether it should be taught separately rather than included in the course on United States history. Questions concerning the contribution of state history in achieving crucial goals are not often raised.

HISTORIANS VIEW STATE HISTORY

In order to analyze the teaching of state history, I examined statements by professional historians and teachers. Not all these statements were made specifically about state history, but all are applicable to it.

Henry Steele Commager (8) argued for the intrinsic pleasures to be derived from the study of history but criticized history that perpetuates provincialism. He pointed out that even the Founding Fathers were not trained in American history since there was none at that time. Commager also argued that facts should not be memorized but analyzed to develop concepts and generalizations. Draves (12) agreed with Commager when he complained that history teachers are bound by chronology, that they emphasize facts rather than concepts, and that they assume that facts speak for themselves.

J. H. Plumb (28), reader in English history at Cambridge, questioned the argument that a good memory, a sense of logic, and the ability to weigh evidence are best developed by examining historical problems. He stated that the examination of problems important to *modern* society is a better means of developing these faculties than is the study of largely dead issues. He attacked provincialism in these words:

> But the whole sickening deadening process of increasing specialization within history destroys half its value for education in its broadest sense; the major purpose of historical studies should not be to produce professional historians but to explain the past for our time and generation and by so doing deepen human experience and breed confidence in the capacity of man to master his environment. (Plumb, 28, p. 98.)

The implication of Plumb's argument is that the real value of history is lost when it is taught in patriotic enclaves.

Arthur Bolster (5) criticized the historians for requesting more and more history. If history involves the use of critical judgment, argued Bolster, then the historian must provide criteria for the selection of content that will develop this critical judgment. If social studies is designed to teach problem-solving, is it not practical to start with present rather than past problems? Bolster also criticized historians for establishing secondary school curricula without facing the problem of how to cover an enormous amount of ground in the limited time available, and he challenged them to define "the historical process." He also contended that one cannot argue for any discipline to be taught in the secondary school for its own sake; one must be able to defend courses for their contribution to identifiable goals of education, rather than for their ability to develop professionals in a given discipline.

Although Wesley (35) saw definite value in teaching state history, he listed the following liabilities of what he calls "state patriotism": (1) State patriotism promotes a romantic and distorted image of the relative importance of the state; (2) it alienates the citizens of other states and enables chauvinists to gain office by pledging loyalty to the state; (3) it promotes a romantic and distorted view of the state's history which emphasizes the unique, bizarre, and traditional while neglecting the demands of a changing society; (4)

it undermines and disrupts national unity; and (5) it is perpetuated by patriotic and genealogical societies that tend to glorify the past while ignoring present problems such as outdated constitutions.

Writing about state history in New York, Rollins (30) stated that "if the program strengthens provincialism and local prejudice and promotes the worship of some peoples' ancestors, we are open to the same sharp criticisms we ourselves level at the people who created the television West, with its noble cowboy-criminals and its ridiculous Indians."

One might argue that the statements of these historians were selected because they appear to oppose the provincialism that characterizes so much of state history. It is, however, very difficult to find statements by reputable historians who would defend the present status of state history either as good history or as desirable education.

TEACHERS VIEW STATE HISTORY

Furthermore, it is equally difficult to find articles by teachers that are favorable to the status of state history instruction.

On examining the literature published during the past five years, I found relatively few statements about teaching practices relevant to state history. Most of these articles were concerned about the local dimension of state history and about ways to make state and local history palatable to young students. The development of interest among students appears to be the only educational goal stressed by these articles. For example Delaney (11) and Gittus (16) suggested that students engage in writing a local history and in a sense become "junior" historians. This is undoubtedly an interesting deviation from the typical "read-and-recite" procedures, but those who advocate this approach have an obligation to show how it contributes to critical inquiry. The development of student interest is not a sufficient goal. In a world plagued by problems such as hunger, disease, conflicting ideologies, and the population explosion, a program designed to develop student interest in state history appears sterile and redundant.

In advocating more Texas history Grimm (17) and Hoeber (19) help to perpetuate some of the serious faults of state history courses, such as provincialism and tourism. Their zealous approach may actually encourage subtle prejudice toward Mexican Americans. Neither writer appeared to have any goal other than the development of interest in the history of Texas—one more indication that Wesley (35) was correct in questioning some of the reasons for which state history is taught.

Spangler (31) also suggested that history students should know more about their town, city, and state, but he did indicate the purposes of acquiring this type of knowledge. Like other writers, Spangler talked about the contributions of state and local history to education for citizenship, but he did not specify what these contributions are. Paul and Paul (27) assumed the same questionable position when they implied that state and local history can advance the goals of social studies teaching, but did not identify these goals. An interesting course encourages student learning, but the interesting course that also has definite long-range goals is far more desirable.

Contrasting with the ambiguity of the above articles is a substantial booklet published by the Anthropology Curriculum Study Project in Chicago entitled *An Anthropological Contribution to the Teaching of State History* (2). Using New York as an example, this group has developed an anthropological approach to the study of the cultural life and social and economic organization of the various tribes of the Iroquois. This approach to the study of Indians is radically different from that used in some texts. For example, consider this typical quotation from *The Story of Texas:*

> Until 1757 the Spanish had made no attempt to establish a mission among the Plains Indians. These Indians were much fiercer and more warlike than the Indians who lived in the timbered area. The Comanches and Apaches did not live in permanent villages. Their way of life was wholly dependent upon the buffalo, and they followed this animal as it wandered across the plains. They were expert horsemen and would ride hundreds of miles to kill their enemies or to steal horses. (Carroll, Nesmith, and Gentry, 6, p. 29.)

The anthropological approach can lead to the development of generalizations about family systems, the relative roles of men and women, education, political organizations, and religion. These generalizations would deal with basic human behavior and could be tested and revised as other groups are studied in similar fashion. This approach, although probably not what the architects of various state laws intended when they required the teaching of state history, seems preferable to present ones because it helps students formulate concepts that explain man's activities.

One other effort to improve the quality of state and local history should be mentioned. Clifford L. Lord has edited *Teaching History with Community Resources* (23), a book written in the traditional manner that sees much intrinsic value in historical studies. However, it criticizes the romanticized treatment of state and local studies and suggests the development of topics such as the importance of the individual, the diversity of the American scene, and the connections that historical studies can establish between the present generation and the past. Although Lord does not make explicit suggestions for developing problem-centered social studies, his ideas appear to be an improvement over most present practices.

If we accept the opinions of professional historians as one means of evaluating these classroom practices, it is obvious that state history is not making a particularly dynamic contribution to the fundamental goals of social studies. It is also evident that teachers are attempting to create interest in the study of state history by using techniques for glamorizing the subject that seem to become ends in themselves.

State Requirements for Teaching State History

Although it is generally assumed that states require the teaching of state history in public schools, it is difficult to systematically summarize the requirements available. In order to learn the extent to which state history is required or recommended, I wrote to each of the fifty state departments of public instruction, asking three questions: (1) Does state law specify or recommend that state history be taught? (2) If state history is required, are the grade levels at which it should be taught specified? and (3) What is the name (or names) of the most commonly used textbook(s)? In addition courses of study were requested, if the state had such publications.

Although replies were received from all states, it was fairly difficult to specify actual practices within any one state, let alone all fifty. One reason for this difficulty was the variety of uses for terms such as "elementary schools," "secondary schools," "requires," "recommends," "integrated with," and "correlated with." Moreover, many states extend to local school officials the authority to establish the particulars of curriculum organization and classroom instruction. For example, state law may "recommend that state history be taught in the elementary school," but local officials apparently interpret this statement to mean "requires." In practice this requirement is met in the eighth grade of the junior high school in one community and the sixth grade of the elementary school of another.

A similar survey was conducted by Dabbert (10), who was interested in how a required course in state history would affect high school graduation in a highly mobile society. He found that thirty states listed some type of requirement in the seventh through twelfth grades and that thirteen states made specific requirements for graduation to be completed during the ninth through twelfth grades. It is quite difficult, however, to be certain about requirements. Various states, such as Illinois, do not specify that state history be taught, but they do require students to study the constitution of Illinois in the seventh or eighth grade. An examination of popularly used textbooks indicates that this requirement is met by correlating government, geography, and history. Other states, such as Louisiana, require state history, but do not specify the particular grade in which it should be taught. In practice it is most frequently taught in the eighth grade.

Despite the lack of clarity, replies to my three questions and an examination of various states' curricula and textbooks made the following summary possible:

ALABAMA requires state history in the fourth and ninth grades.

ALASKA requires state history in the fourth and eighth grades.

ARIZONA requires state history in the fourth and eighth grades.

ARKANSAS requires state history in the fifth grade or above.

CALIFORNIA requires state history in one grade from the fourth to sixth or eighth in elementary school. State history is also required in one grade from the seventh to the twelfth. This requirement is often met by giving special attention to California within United States history courses.

COLORADO requires state history but does not specify the grade level at which it should be taught. In such states the course is frequently taught in the junior high school.

CONNECTICUT recommends that state history be included in the eighth-grade course, "The History of the Americas."

DELAWARE requires a study of the constitution and government of Delaware beginning no later than the opening of the eighth grade and continuing in high school courses. The materials examined indicate that this requirement is met through an historical study of the development of the state constitution and government.

FLORIDA requires state history in the elementary schools. It is usually included in the fourth-grade curriculum.

GEORGIA requires state history but does not specify the grade in which it should be taught. The course is usually taught in the seventh or eighth grade. In states where the law is so general the course varies with the school system.

HAWAII requires state history in the fourth and seventh grades.

IDAHO requires state history in the fourth and eighth grades.

ILLINOIS does not specify that state history be taught but does require that the constitution of Illinois be studied in the seventh or eighth grade. An examination of textbooks used in Illinois reveals that this requirement is met through a course that attempts to correlate history, government, and geography.

INDIANA requires state history in the fourth grade. In addition the course is usually included in the seventh or eighth grade as part of the United States history course. Many schools correlate state history with a study of Indiana government.

IOWA requires state history in one grade from the first to the sixth, and the course is often taught in the seventh and eighth grades as well.

KANSAS permits local jurisdiction in this matter, but the consensus is that the state "requires" the teaching of state history, while local authorities decide the grade in which it will be taught. It is most often taught in the sixth, seventh, or eighth grade.

KENTUCKY requires state history in the seventh grade.

LOUISIANA requires state history but does not specify the grade in which it should be taught. This course is most frequently taught in the eighth grade.

MAINE requires a course in state history in one grade from the seventh to the twelfth. The course is most frequently taught in the eighth grade.

MARYLAND requires state history in elementary school but does not specify the grade in which it should be taught. In practice the course appears in elementary school, junior high school, or high school.

MASSACHUSETTS requires state history in the elementary and secondary schools but does not specify the grade in which it should be taught. The state does not indicate whether the course is to be correlated with areas such as civics and geography or whether it is to be taught as a separate subject.

MICHIGAN does not require state history, but many elementary schools offer the course in the fourth grade.

MINNESOTA requires state history in the sixth grade and state and local government in the ninth grade.

MISSISSIPPI requires state history in the sixth and tenth grades. In such states history appears to be correlated with civics and geography.

MISSOURI requires state history in the fourth and eighth grades, and the subject is also correlated with a study of the state constitution and government in the eleventh and twelfth grades.

MONTANA requires state history in elementary school but does not specify the grade in which it should be taught. One textbook examined suggests that the course is taught in the upper elementary grades (probably in the sixth, seventh, or eighth grade).

NEBRASKA does not require state history but does require instruction about the state constitution in two years of secondary school. However, most schools in the state offer instruction in Nebraska history in the fourth and eighth grades.

NEVADA requires state history and recommends that it be taught in the seventh grade.

NEW HAMPSHIRE does not require state history but does require that the state constitution be studied beginning no later than the eighth grade.

NEW JERSEY requires state history in the fourth grade.

NEW MEXICO requires state history in the seventh or eighth grade.

NEW YORK requires state history to be taught before the end of the eighth grade. The subject is usually covered in a general study of the state that includes government, geography, and history. This course most frequently appears in the seventh grade.

NORTH CAROLINA requires state history in the seventh grade.

NORTH DAKOTA requires state history but does not specify the grade in which it is to be taught. The course is most frequently taught in the seventh or eighth grade.

OHIO requires state history and recommends that it be taught in the seventh or eighth grade.

OKLAHOMA requires state history in high school. The textbooks examined indicate that it is also taught in junior high school.

OREGON requires state history in the fourth and eighth grades.

PENNSYLVANIA requires state history in elementary and secondary school. The subject is correlated with civics and geography in junior high school and with the United States history course in high school.

RHODE ISLAND requires state history but does not specify the grade in which it is to be taught. The course is taught in elementary or junior high school.

SOUTH CAROLINA requires state history in the seventh grade.

SOUTH DAKOTA requires state history in the fourth grade.

TENNESSEE requires state history in one grade from the fourth to the eighth.

TEXAS requires state history in the seventh grade. The materials examined indicate that the approach is one of the most provincial in the nation.

UTAH requires state history in the seventh grade.

VERMONT does not require state history, but the subject is generally taught in the sixth and eighth grades.

VIRGINIA requires state history in the fourth, seventh, and eleventh grades. In the eleventh grade the subject is correlated with United States history.

WASHINGTON requires state history in elementary and secondary school.

WEST VIRGINIA requires that state history be taught prior to the completion of the eighth grade. One textbook examined indicates that it is probably taught in the sixth, seventh, or eighth grade.

WISCONSIN requires state history but does not specify the grade in which it is to be taught. Local schools have autonomy in selecting the grade or grades in which the course is taught. In elementary schools it appears most frequently in the fourth grade, and in junior high schools the course is offered in the seventh, eighth, or ninth grade.

WYOMING requires state history, but local districts may determine the grade in which it will be taught. Information from Wyoming did not indicate the grade or grades in which state history is most often taught.

In many instances state laws are not explicit about the minimum time to be devoted to teaching state history. Neither are these laws explicit as to what constitutes fulfillment of the requirements—that is, what period of time the course must cover and how much integration with other subjects is allowable. Such situations reflect the confusion created when politicians attempt to legislate school curricula. These men must answer to superpatriotic groups, zealous newspaper people, and various professional organizations, all of whom control votes and tax dollars. It may seem expedient or patriotic at a given moment to require a specific subject. As new conditions arise, however, these requirements become obsolete. The schools are then hampered by archaic legal requirements and must develop ways of "meeting the state law," even though these ways may be of questionable legality. Specific requirements, such as those governing the teaching of state history, appear to be more harmful than valuable, especially in a society characterized by extensive change and mobility.

In spite of somewhat ambiguous state laws or recommendations, it is safe to conclude that some form of state history is taught in junior high schools in practically every state. When a subject is offered so extensively, it is important for it to make a definite contribution to the students' education. One of the most basic objectives of any social studies course is to help the young become effective citizens in a democratic society. In order to become effective citizens our young people must learn to identify and analyze problems, gather and reflect upon information relevant to the problems, and participate in decision-making processes. To assess the educational value of any course, one must examine what is taught. Since it is impractical to visit a large number of classrooms in many states, we have examined textbooks currently used in state history courses in order to construct a description of the "typical" course. We are not concerned with the specific merits or faults of the texts we examined but rather with the general characteristics of the materials commonly employed to teach state history courses.

Content of State History Courses

Although it is perhaps dangerous to describe a "typical" course or unit in state history, the texts and courses of study I examined indicate that the following description is generally accurate. One must allow, however, for great differences in the abilities of those who teach.

State history often begins with a study of the geography of the state. This survey usually includes materials relating to climatic regions, vegetation zones, physical features, natural resources, and population distribution. This geographic survey will sometimes be preceded by materials on the first European explorers to enter the region or by information about the "original inhabitants" of the area. The order in which these three topics are taught varies, but they all appear very early in nearly every course in state history.

Next the texts describe the early European settlers, presenting considerable information about their leaders and the trials these people faced, with emphasis on the dangers from Indians. This type of discussion usually continues until the colony or territory becomes a state of the Union, when state history enters the mainstream of United States history. Do the texts then stress national history? No. Although national history provides the pivotal situations, events within each state are given such prominence that the nation appears to be following the lead of the various states, and the native state is made to seem more important than its neighbors. For example, consider the following quotations from a textbook on New York:

> The American Revolution began as a struggle to free the colonies from the control of the British government. New Yorkers and other colonists protested that the actions of Great Britain were not only unfair but also illegal because they imposed taxation without representation. During and after the Revolutionary War New Yorkers continued to think about their rights and how to protect them. (Ellis, Frost, and Fink, 14, p. 154.)

> New Yorkers took a leading role in the new federal government. President Washington relied for advice upon Hamilton, whom he had made Secretary of the Treasury, and he called on John Jay to settle our difficulties with Great Britain. (*Ibid.,* p. 165.)

The first excerpt implies that New Yorkers did more protesting and thinking than did other colonists, while the second ignores the fact that Alexander Hamilton was born and spent his earlier years in the British West Indies. Consider also this quotation: "The Charter of Privileges gave Pennsylvania the most democratic government of all the colonies (33)." This statement presents as a fact what is really a value judgment without defining what is democratic, more democratic, or most democratic. The selections cited above were taken from texts regarded as among the more desirable. Other texts include even more questionable material. For example, the following statement is made about Hood's Texas Brigade and its contribution to Confederate efforts during the Civil War: "These fearless men always considered themselves the best soldiers in either army, and they proved it on the battlefields from Virginia to Tennessee (6)." How does one prove that a particular group is more or less fearless than other groups, especially when various groups face so many different situations?

Junior high school students under instruction from an enthusiastic teacher could decide that states are really more important than the nation or that in times of past national crises an individual state was more important than all the others. Wesley's criticism that state history often promotes a romantic and distorted concept of the importance of individual states (35) is well taken. Furthermore, this romanticized approach tends to ignore the geographic, economic, political, and social interdependence of the states in the twentieth century. Even the more desirable texts discuss myths as though they were facts. This statement, for example, appears in *Exploring New York* (34): "In May, 1775, Ethan Allen with Benedict Arnold at his side captured Fort Ticonderoga. The British officer in command asked Allen by what right he demanded the surrender of the fort, and he replied, 'In the name of the great Jehovah and the Continental Congress.' " Yet there is no valid historical evidence on which to base this quotation.

After the colony or territory enters the Union, emphasis is placed upon the politics within the state, the development of a state government, and the social and political problems that evolve. The materials examined indicate that approximately half the state history courses stress the sensational and overromanticized episodes of the past. The following dialogue is taken from *Iowa, Beautiful Land:*

> One morning as the governor sat at his desk signing papers, he suddenly was surprised to see an Indian silently surveying him from the open door.
>
> The man was unkempt; his garments were badly soiled. The leather fringe on the sides of his breeches was nothing more than tattered shreds. Across his shoulders was a buffalo hide so large that it hung clear down to his moccasined feet.
>
> Briggs invited the visitor in but received a negative shake of the head.
>
> "You governor?" asked the Indian bluntly.
>
> "Yes," was Brigg's reply. "Governor of the state!" he exclaimed. "Iowa isn't a territory any more!"
>
> "I know," the Indian nodded. "White man at garrison told."

Briggs wondered what had brought the man to his office but didn't like to put the question directly so tried a roundabout way.

"Come far?" he inquired in his genial manner.

"Far," said the Indian. "From Big Muddy."

"Clear from the Missouri river!" exclaimed the governor in surprise.

There was a grunt of affirmation. "I, Half-Moon. I Sac."

Briggs waited expectantly, and the Indian went on to explain: "I want to shoot . . . buffalo . . . on . . . hunting ground again."

"But the buffaloes are gone!" declared the governor. "Been gone a long time!" he reminded in a kindly tone.

The Indian gave him a solemn look and continued: "Every night . . . I dream of buffalo. Every night . . . I cannot sleep. I come long way . . . on range. I wait by big rock . . . with bow and arrow. Last night . . . I see buffalo! . . . Not ten . . . not twenty . . . just one! He come slowly . . . he stop at waterbrook . . . he drink . . . he shake head . . . he bellow! Then . . . Half-Moon shoot!" The Indian's face lighted with unspeakable joy when he spoke of the killing. "Now . . . I go back to reservation by Big Muddy. I not homesick any more for hunting ground." The Indian slipped the buffalo hide from his shoulder, and it fell to the floor. "For governor," he said and pointed at the dark fur that lay in a heap on the threshold. "For governor of state!" he added, and with that Half-Moon was gone. (Dwelle, 13, pp. 128–30.)

It is quite doubtful that such an episode could be so accurately preserved or that the Sac were so tolerant of the loss of their land.

Or take this passage from a book on Texas state history:

The constitutional convention met in Austin on June 1, 1868; of the ninety delegates only twelve were Democrats; the rest were carpetbaggers, scalawags, and Negroes. The president, Edmund J. Davis, had been a cavalry brigadier in the Union Army. During 1864 he and his men had spread terror across the Rio Grande section of Texas until Rip Ford's Confederate cavalry drove them back to Brazos Island near Brownsville. After the war Davis entered politics and rose rapidly in the Republican Party. An ambitious man, he wanted to be governor. As president of the constitutional convention he stood a good chance of getting the support he needed. (Carroll, Nesmith, and Gentry, 6, p. 199.)

The paragraph implies that Democrats were desirable people, while all others, including Edmund J. Davis, were of questionable character. Similar materials are found in the texts for West Virginia (9),

Oklahoma (18), and Montana (1). The texts that emphasize such romanticized material are also characterized by a chronological narrative approach. If the text provides the basis for course organization, it must be assumed that teachers using such materials are perpetuating the same questionable ideas.

Examination of other text materials indicates that some courses are concerned with more substantial topics, such as the development of labor unions, the correction of corrupt city governments, and the development of valid conservation laws. For example, the following quotations raise some provocative questions about the support for and the quality of public school education in North Carolina:

> Even so late as the twenty years of Democratic [party] rule after Reconstruction, the progress of public education in North Carolina was very slow. State and local school taxes never produced enough money for the four-months' schools required by the state Constitution.
>
> . . .
>
> The public schools in 1890 were poorer than they had been in 1860. They were perhaps the poorest in the United States.
>
> . . .
>
> Although long before 1900 [North Carolina's] wealth had recovered from the losses of war and its property was increasing in value, it was not collecting enough money in taxes to spend on schools or any other great public services. An important reason for this was that most of the governors, legislators, and political leaders, as well as businessmen and common people, were more interested in low taxes than in building better public schools. Many of the wealthier people did not believe in public schools for all children, for they sent their own children to private schools and did not want to pay taxes to educate the children of other people.   (Lefler, 22, pp. 345–47.)

The next statement would probably be controversial, particularly in affluent communities:

> The long hours of heavy labor often wore out the workers and frequently injured their health. Many of the jobs were dangerous, and accidents commonly resulted. When workers were disabled by such accidents, they were given no assistance or help. Their low wages barely provided enough to pay for food, clothing, and rent, so they seldom had anything left to meet emergencies. When a factory shut down, the men were thrown out of work, and their families often went hungry.   (Stevens, Cordier, and Benjamin, 33, p. 318.)

The following quotation raises questions concerning the conduct of wealthy American planters in Hawaii during the reign of Queen Liliuokalani shortly before the islands were annexed by the United States:

> Some Hawaiians felt the republic was a police state. Because of their fear of informers, many large gatherings were broken up and people arrested on suspicion of treason. At one point large gatherings were prohibited. Many of the puritanical laws were revived. Dancing of the hula was forbidden, and Sunday concerts were stopped. Finally, when Sunday concerts were resumed, only European classical musical numbers could be played. Despite all this many balls were given by wealthy Caucasians, particularly when a naval vessel was in port. (Potter and Kasdon, 29, p. 219.)

Although teachers strongly influence the way in which controversial material is used, it can be safely assumed that if one uses such material, he is likely to develop inquiry-oriented classroom episodes. Similarly, if one utilizes materials characterized by romantic myths, it can be assumed that class encounters will probably perpetuate and reinforce unrealistic ideas.

Both of the above approaches give considerable coverage to authors, artists, state politicians, and heroes. In fact it is often implied that certain persons became famous primarily because they were born in a given state or lived there—an example of how courses oversimplify causal explanations of important historical developments.

There are two general ways of handling the relationships between state and national history. The most popular is to refer to national history only when necessary for the narration of state history. Although this approach is more noticeable in those materials designed to teach a rather provincial history, it is nevertheless used in practically all the books examined. This is one indication that it is extremely difficult to construct a course in state history—particularly one that meets a definite goal such as the development of reflective thinking—with the material available.

The second approach is to present the national episode—sometimes in a global setting—and then relate the events within the state to the national situation. This latter approach seems to exaggerate the importance of the state less than the former approach but is still repetitive.

Courses in state history are, for the most part, chronicles of events that took place in a given state. The materials vary in quality, and their value is likely to be determined by the ability of the teacher using them. Knowledge of state history is undoubtedly valuable for studying the government, geography, and problems of a given state; but when presented in a predominantly chronological fashion this subject adds greatly to the repetition that is already a major short-coming of social studies instruction. Furthermore it is difficult to develop inquiry- or concept-centered instruction with the text materials available. Some texts are preferable to others, of course, but even the best require skillful handling by the classroom teacher.

Analysis of State History Textbooks

On the assumption that the development of critical inquiry skills is the most important goal of social studies education, I examined fifteen state history textbooks representing thirteen states in order to evaluate the degree to which they help students attain this goal.

Although none of the books have an explicit conceptual framework, they reflect two general approaches to the selection of material. Descriptive chronology characterizes the material in seven of the books: Carroll, Nesmith, and Gentry's *The Story of Texas* (6), Moore's *Oklahoma—Our Home* (25), Dwelle's *Iowa, Beautiful Land* (13), Harlow's *Oklahoma History* (18), Clifford's *Maine and Her People* (7), Abbott's *Montana in the Making* (1), and Conley and Stutler's *West Virginia, Yesterday and Today* (9). These seven books describe events, men, and places without any conceptual organization but chronology. Barnhart's *Indiana: The Hoosier State* (3) is also chronologically organized, but it does describe the changes in a society that develops from an agricultural to an industrial economy.

A second organizational pattern in which civics, geography, and history are correlated is noticeable in six texts: Lefler's *North Carolina* (22), Stevens, Cordier, and Benjamin's *Exploring Pennsylvania* (33), Kilduff and Pygman's *Illinois* (20), Flierl and Urell's *Living in New York* (15), Ellis, Frost, and Fink's *New York: The Empire State* (14), and Wainger, Furman, and Oagley's *Exploring New York* (34). It must be noted that the correlation of the three areas in these texts is more apparent than real. Nonetheless, these books more nearly approach a conceptual organization than those organized chronologically.

The lack of emphasis on geography, particularly basic geographic concepts such as the region concept or spatial and economic interdependence, is perhaps the most noticeable shortcoming of all six books. The two texts in which the subject is most thoroughly correlated with state history are *North Carolina* (22) and *New York: The Empire State* (14). In the other four books geography and civics are "correlated with history" by including various chapters devoted to these areas. In terms of objectives none of these books contain criteria much more advanced than "Knowledge of Classifications and Categories," the most elementary level of educational objectives identified by Bloom (4). In other words the texts emphasize information without a framework, and they do not develop principles, concepts, and generalizations in an explicit manner.

Despite their lack of definite conceptual framework, however, these six texts do provide the raw material for critical analyses of management-labor relations, segregation, stream pollution, and corrupt political practices. Although these topics are not always presented as controversies, they are discussed at length, particularly in *Exploring Pennsylvania* (33) and *North Carolina* (22) and to a lesser degree in *Living in New York* (15). Descriptive passages on minority groups or conservation can be used effectively as springboards by inquiry-oriented teachers to lead classes into the analysis of social, political, and economic problems—even though the authors may not have intended such usage.

These books contrast significantly with *The Story of Texas* (6), which devotes two paragraphs in all to desegregation of the public schools, concluding with the implication that such matters are best solved by citizens themselves without coercion from the federal government. Even the superficial textbooks, however, can supply a clever teacher with more reflective material than the authors intended by making assumptions that need to be tested for their validity. For instance, an alert teacher might use the paragraph heading "The Problem of the Wild Indians" in *Oklahoma History* (18:149) as a springboard for an analysis of interpretation in historical writing and the effect a writer's frame of reference has upon his work.

One of the texts examined could not be classified with either of the two foregoing groups of books. Potter and Kasdon's *Hawaii: Our Island State* (29) emphasizes the cultural changes that took place as a technically skilled group imposed itself on a less complex society. Although they do not stress the conflict between the two groups, the authors do not deliberately avoid discussing controversial historical episodes, such as the role of the missionaries in suppressing much of the Hawaiian culture. The textbook also includes basic ideas from the field of anthropology. For example, the authors emphasize that the Hawaiians had an educational system long before the missionaries arrived and established a more formal system. This recognition deals with the concept that all societies have an educational system, whether it is formal or informal. Materials dealing with the conduct of sugar planters and missionaries can be developed into situations in which critical inquiry will characterize classroom activities and study. Thus current attitudes and policies toward peoples in Southeast Asia and Africa can be examined as well as group conflicts arising in a highly heterogeneous society such as that of Hawaii.

In terms of objectivity *North Carolina* (22) is remarkable, particularly in its treatment of the Civil War. One suspects that if racial problems were treated similarly in other state history textbooks, the racial situation would be less volatile. On the other hand *The Story of Texas* (6) implies that for Texas to be forced to remain in the Union in 1865 was a great tragedy, even though less than twenty years before, one of the precipitating causes of the war with Mexico was the admission of Texas to the United States. Six other books seem to be quite objective: *Exploring Pennsylvania* (33), *New York: The Empire State* (14), *Illinois* (20), *Hawaii: Our Island State* (29), *Indiana: The Hoosier State* (3), and *Montana in the Making* (1). Although *Montana in the Making* is written primarily as a chronological narrative, its treatment of such episodes as "Custer's Last Stand" and the Nez Percé under the leadership of Chief Joseph seems quite objective. Custer is not described as a martyr, and the Nez Percé are neither discussed pejoratively nor unduly romanticized. The content of this book will probably stimulate considerable interest among junior high school students.

Ten of the texts examined are poorly illustrated and are probably unappealing to junior high school students. Five books, however, make attractive use of color and have appealing and appropriate illustrations: *Illinois* (20), *Living in New York* (15), *New York: The Empire State* (14), *Exploring Pennsylvania* (33), and *North Carolina* (22). *Exploring Pennsylvania* (33) also includes many interesting biographical and explanatory anecdotes.

It must be emphasized that none of the texts examined deliberately promote controversy nor do they present material explicitly for critical inquiry, although the books previously categorized as more usable do present controversial topics in their descriptions of labor movements, conservation problems, racial relations, and corruption in government. The end-of-chapter exercises are consistent with each book's treatment or nontreatment of controversial situations. For example, the following question is found in *North Carolina* (22): "2. The author of a book condemned in the South was _____?_____." The correct answer is "Helper," who wrote *The Impending Crisis: How to Meet It*. Although this question deals with a controversial era in the history of North Carolina, it is structured merely as a recall item, as are most of the questions in this text. The following questions are taken from *Exploring Pennsylvania*, a text that presents more possibilities for inquiry than most of the others:

4. In what ways were working conditions in Pennsylvania factories improved?

7. Why did employers oppose labor unions?

8. What gains did industrial workers obtain by establishing labor unions?

(Stevens, Cordier, and Benjamin, 33, p. 331.)

Such questions can stimulate critical inquiry, for they seem to imply that the workers were "right" in supporting the union movement, a position unlikely to be supported by the families of all children in any given class.

Although the above-mentioned books (22 and 33) frequently present inquiry-oriented questions and exercises, most texts are characterized by exercises requiring students to remember material for its own sake. The following are characteristic questions from a book that stresses chronological, narrative history:

1. Who was Henry Morfit? What effect did he have on the history of Texas?

4. What foreign nation established a legation in Texas?

(Carroll, Nesmith, and Gentry, 6, p. 161.)

Under a category entitled "Who Said It and on What Occasion?" the book includes these questions:

1. The Father of Texas is no more. The first pioneer of the
wilderness has departed.

4. Well, boys, we have to draw, so let's be at it!

(Ibid.)

Such material requires the student to memorize a romantic version
of the past largely for its own sake. This is hardly an adequate diet
for nurturing citizens capable of making intelligent decisions.

To sum up, it must be stated that although there is great diversity in the state history textbooks examined, most of them do not
make explicit use of a conceptual approach to social studies. All but
one of the books fall into two general categories. Approximately
half the texts purport to correlate history with civics and geography,
but they fail to carry out this correlation successfully, and geography
receives the poorest treatment. The second group of texts emphasizes
chronologically organized narrative history and romantic interpretations of the past. It is very doubtful that such books can be used in
an inquiry-centered approach except as examples of how historians
write from a particular frame of reference.

Assuming that the content of state history courses can be predicted by examining the texts used, we can only conclude that most
junior high school students undergo an intellectually sterile experience when exposed to such materials. We must remember, however, that a good teacher can use such materials effectively if he
organizes his classes for inquiry.

Improving the Use of State History Textbooks

If teachers are to use state history textbooks for inquiry-oriented
instruction, they must have their goals firmly in mind before the
course begins. The better texts—those that correlate geography and
civics with history and discuss controversial topics—can be utilized
as sources of information on social problems. Teachers and students
can use text data to test assumptions, develop concepts, or analyze
generalizations about society and culture. Used in this manner, texts
become instruments of learning rather than ends in themselves. The
teacher must develop his own unit or course dealing with state history instead of accepting the text as the final authority about course
content. Textbooks might well be improved if states would cease
to make state history a compulsory course. This requirement has

been conducive to the writing of books filled with material of doubtful educational value—material included mainly to provide enough "content" to occupy a class for an entire semester.

Much has been written about the need for history to contribute to the development of good citizenship, but this requirement is ignored more often than it is recognized in the teaching of state history in junior high school. How can good citizenship be developed through textbooks that are romanticized, parochial, and of questionable scholarship? How can students believe that their state is "the best" when they are likely to live in more than one in the course of their schooling? Teachers must develop defensible definitions of good citizenship that apply to the local community, state, nation, and world. They must evaluate course content by these criteria and include only material that makes a positive contribution to the concept of good citizenship. Although the weaker state history textbooks would be of limited use here, the better books could provide valuable sources of information and springboards into controversial situations that require students to discuss the basic issues of our time.

Effective use, particularly of the better texts, depends upon the willingness of the teacher to develop his own writing assignments, tests, and evaluative devices. Textbook publishers require authors to write end-of-chapter exercises that have wide appeal and that are for the most part objective. It is therefore difficult to include a substantial proportion of inquiry-oriented exercises in such a text. Since the development of inquiry-centered exercises and situations is left to the classroom teacher, it is particularly important that he be fully cognizant of his own philosophy and psychology of education, especially the social studies.

State history textbooks could be effectively employed within a United States history course as a historical study of the people of a certain state. Studying about the various ethnic and linguistic groups that settled a given area may help students understand the stresses and adjustments of different cultural groups living in one community. Students may be surprised to learn that Jews, Negroes, Italians, and other cultural minority groups have made outstanding contributions to the development of every state. When examining social problems such as minority rights, legislative apportionment, malpractices in conservation, and the labor movements, the student can learn from historical information how these problems evolved. But historical data should *not* be used to justify the status quo.

Voting regulations stipulated in state constitutions and laws can be partially explained by knowledge of earlier eras, but one cannot justify denying Negroes the right to vote on the grounds that it was once a common practice. In short, if state history is to remain a valuable part of the junior high school curriculum, it should provide information about the questions, problems, and concepts that are relevant to education for citizenship in a democratic society.

Conclusion

State history is taught in junior high schools in every state of the Union. In some states history is correlated with studies of civics and geography, while in others the course is a chronological description of the exploration, settlement, and development of the state. The chronological approach emphasizes romanticized versions of the past, while the approach correlating history with civics and geography includes substantially more material dealing with social, economic, and political problems. Both approaches make considerable use of description of state politicians, artists, authors, and heroes, although the emphases upon these topics vary from state to state.

Textbooks vary considerably in schematic framework, scholarship, use of illustrations, and adaptability to critically oriented teaching. None of the texts explicitly develop controversial issues, but several do present material that can be used effectively by inquiry-oriented teachers. I believe that the quality of textbooks is a valid indicator of the quality of education in social studies classes. A teacher's effectiveness depends upon his ability to use textbook materials in conjunction with other reference materials rather than being a slave to the text.

Unfortunately, articles suggesting how to improve the teaching of state history do not emphasize any educational goals beyond kindling the interest and motivation of students. And statements by professional historians cast doubt upon both the substantive contributions and the educational goals of state history as it is now taught.

In conclusion most of the teaching of state history in junior high schools does not make an explicit contribution to the development of critical inquiry. This does not mean that everything taught under the name of state history should be ejected from the curriculum, but this course should be examined seriously by those who control public school curricula. If material on state history lends itself well to inquiry-centered teaching, it should by all means be utilized; but a course that is primarily concerned with isolated facts to be memorized must be drastically altered if social studies is to educate students for effective democratic citizenship.

Selected Bibliography

1. ABBOTT, CARL NEWTON, *Montana in the Making*, Gazette, Billings, Mont., 1964.

2. ANTHROPOLOGY CURRICULUM STUDY PROJECT, *An Anthropological Contribution to the Teaching of State History*, Chicago, no date.

3. BARNHART, JOHN D., *Indiana: The Hoosier State*, Harper & Row, New York, 1963.

4. BLOOM, BENJAMIN S. (ed.), *Taxonomy of Educational Objectives, Handbook I: Cognitive Domain*, David McKay, New York, 1956.

5. BOLSTER, ARTHUR S., "History, Historians, and the Secondary School Curriculum," *Harvard Education Review*, 32 (Winter, 1962), 39–65.

6. CARROLL, HORACE BAILEY, NESMITH, FRANCES, AND GENTRY, MAY JANE, *The Story of Texas*, Noble and Noble, New York, 1963.

7. CLIFFORD, HAROLD B., *Maine and Her People*, Bond Wheelwright, Freeport, Me., 1963.

8. COMMAGER, HENRY STEELE, "Why History?" *American Education*, 1 (June, 1965), 26–29.

9. CONLEY, PHIL, AND STUTLER, BOYD B., *West Virginia, Yesterday and Today*, Education Foundation, Charleston, W.Va., 1952.

10. DABBERT, CHARLES E., "State History Requirements and Our Mobile Population," *Social Education*, 30 (May, 1966), 338–40.

11. DELANEY, ARTHUR C., "Anatomy of Your Community," *Teachers College Journal*, 34 (Mar., 1963), 153–55.

12. DRAVES, D. D., "What's Wrong with the Teaching of History in High School?" *Social Studies*, 56 (Mar., 1965), 193–96.

13. DWELLE, JESSIE MERRILL, *Iowa, Beautiful Land*, Klipto Loose Leaf, Mason City, Iowa, no date.

14. ELLIS, DAVID M., FROST, JAMES A., AND FINK, WILLIAM B., *New York: The Empire State*, Prentice-Hall, Englewood Cliffs, N.J., 1964.

15. FLIERL, HOWARD H., AND URELL, CATHERINE, *Living in New York*, Follett, Chicago, 1965.

16. GITTUS, ARTHUR, "A Course in Local History," *Social Education*, 24 (Mar., 1963), 147.

17. GRIMM, AGNES G., "Texas History Comes Alive," *Texas Outlook*, 48 (Mar., 1964), 18–19.

18. HARLOW, VICTOR E., *Oklahoma History,* Harlow, Oklahoma City, 1961.

19. HOEBER, BETTY, "Let's Teach Texas," *Texas Outlook,* 48 (Mar., 1964), 20–21.

20. KILDUFF, DORRELL, AND PYGMAN, C. H., *Illinois,* Follett, Chicago, 1962.

21. KVARACEUS, WILLIAM C., "Tomorrow's Youth and Tomorrow's Citizens," *Citizenship and a Free Society: Education for the Future,* The Thirtieth Yearbook of the National Council for the Social Studies, Franklin Patterson (ed.), Washington, D.C., 1960, 16–32.

22. LEFLER, HUGH T., *North Carolina,* Harcourt, Brace & World, New York, 1959.

23. LORD, CLIFFORD L. (ed.), *Teaching History with Community Resources,* Teachers College, Columbia University, New York, 1964.

24. LOWE, WILLIAM T., "Where Should History Be Taught?" *Clearing House,* 39 (Dec., 1964), 210–13.

25. MOORE, DAISY L., *Oklahoma—Our Home,* Harr Wagner, San Francisco, Calif., 1955.

26. OLIVER, DONALD W., "Educating Citizens for Responsible Individualism, 1960–1980," *Citizenship and a Free Society: Education for the Future,* The Thirtieth Yearbook of the National Council for the Social Studies, Franklin Patterson (ed.), Washington, D.C., 1960.

27. PAUL, LOUIS, AND PAUL, JOAN, "Experiences in Teaching Local History," *School and Community,* 47 (Oct., 1960), 22–25.

28. PLUMB, J. H., "The Sorry State of History," *Horizon,* 5 (Sept., 1963), 97–100.

29. POTTER, NORRIS W., AND KASDON, LAWRENCE M., *Hawaii: Our Island State,* Charles E. Merrill, Columbus, Ohio, 1964.

30. ROLLINS, ALFRED B., "Why Teach 'New York'?" *New York State Education,* 49 (Feb., 1962), 11–13.

31. SPANGLER, EARL, "Teaching Local and State History," *Minnesota Journal of Education,* 45 (May, 1965), 14.

32. STARR, ISIDORE, "The Nature of Critical Thinking and Its Application in the Social Studies," *Skill Development in Social Studies,* The Thirty-third Yearbook of the National Council for the Social Studies, Helen McCracken Carpenter (ed.), Washington, D.C., 1963, 35–52.

33. STEVENS, SYLVESTER K., CORDIER, RALPH W., AND BENJAMIN, FLORENCE O., *Exploring Pennsylvania,* Harcourt, Brace & World, New York, 1963.

34. WAINGER, BERTRAND M., FURMAN, DOROTHY W., AND OAGLEY, EDITH BROOKS, *Exploring New York,* Harcourt, Brace & World, New York, 1963.

35. WESLEY, EDGAR B., "State Patriotism: Asset or Liability?" *Social Studies Texan,* 15 (May, 1963), 3–6.

CHAPTER 6

Civics

Relating Social Study to Social Reality

FREDERICK R. SMITH
JOHN J. PATRICK

The Equivocal Character of Civics

Civics in American schools has varied considerably since it first appeared in the 1790's. It has always focused on instruction in American government and political ideals for the purpose of promoting patriotism. But beyond this common concern civics has been a curious medley of purposes and practices. This diversity continues today: civics instruction ranges from vocational guidance to studies of family life and personality adjustment. The equivocal character of the course in itself does not represent a serious problem. Certainly variations in curricular offerings are necessary to meet the demands and peculiarities of different regions of the country. And variability in curricula is part of a long-standing and treasured American tradition of local control of public school programs. But today's variations in junior high school civics indicate that social studies educators have not been certain about the goals of civics courses, and because of this equivocation civics courses have come to include amorphous and unwieldy masses of loosely integrated content.

From the 1790's until the latter part of the nineteenth century most civics programs involved little more than intensive studies of the federal and state constitutions—the main purpose of which was to inspire patriotism. The catechetic teaching method was used widely. Pupils were required to memorize and repeat verbatim stock answers to standard questions (3).

Civics programs were expanded during the latter years of the nineteenth century to include studies of the structure and activities of local, state, and national government, but rote memorization and recitation of facts remained strongly entrenched. Pupils were required to know and regurgitate many dreary details about the structure of American government, while little attention was given to analysis that could lead to understanding of the American political process (3).

The modern era of civics instruction began during the decade 1910–20. It was heralded by committees of educators such as the Social Studies Committee of the National Education Association, which in 1916 recommended the teaching of civics in the eighth and ninth grades in a greatly revised form. The Social Studies Committee declared that the overriding goal of social studies instruction should be the development of good citizens, and civics courses were to be the keystone in the program. Thus civics became primarily the study of the many aspects of citizenship: the cultivation of loyalty to American institutions and interests manifested by a reasoned patriotism, constructive involvement in community affairs, vocational efficiency, and the ability to cope successfully with personal and societal problems.

In order to accomplish these lofty objectives, the scope of civics courses was broadened to include knowledge from several social sciences. Content from sociology, psychology, and economics was added, and attempts were made to relate instruction to the experiences and interests of students. Civics courses emphasized the function and process as well as the form of government and the teaching of democratic values as a necessary means to proper character formation and good civic behavior. Stress was placed on behavioral outcome rather than merely on acquisition of factual knowledge (3).

This new approach to civics was a bold attempt to reconstruct social studies instruction in terms of childhood interests and experiences. The goal was to relate social study to social reality; to bring the schoolroom into continuing contact with the functioning world;

to transform artificial and sterile academic pursuits into practical and vibrant experiences. But this audacious attempt at progressive reform never really materialized. Certainly it guided civics programs away from some anachronistic nineteenth-century practices; yet many unsatisfactory traditional teaching methods persisted. It widened and enlivened the range of instructional concerns; but in so doing its substance was often diluted and diffused. It obviously appealed to more pupils in more ways than had been conceivable previously; yet in its attempt to appeal to many interests it often appealed to none. The modern civics became a strange amalgam of traditional and progressive, manifesting uncertainties, inconsistencies, and imprecisions that continue to afflict civics instruction today.

For the most part junior high school civics courses in the 1960's remain within the framework established during the 1910–20 period; but they continue to be quite varied in their extensions and refinements of these earlier reforms, and uncertainty remains about the proper subject matter of civics and the proper function of the course within the social studies curriculum.

Despite the flurry of discussion about multimedial teaching the textbook remains the most widely used educational tool in the social studies. Cronbach (7) reported that in many cases the textbook is the entire course of study. Thus in order to describe and appraise current civics courses, it is necessary to examine the most widely used junior high school civics textbooks.

Examination of twelve widely used junior high school civics textbooks reveals two basic types of civics. The first type is concerned mainly with the theory of democracy and the form and functioning of politics and government at local, state, and national levels. Some attention is given to our nation's foreign policy and the United Nations. Economic activities and social problems are considered briefly and only as they relate to government. This type of civics is derived almost entirely from the academic discipline of government, with some reference to economics and history as they relate to government and citizenship. The first type of course is often only one semester long or is combined with American history or economics in a one-year program. Most of the textbooks designed for this course (27, 36) stress government and politics at the national level, but some (38) divide the coverage about evenly among national, local, and state governments.

A second type of civics gives less emphasis to the study of the form and function of government per se, especially local and state government, and more stress to the way in which governmental institutions relate to the society at large. The academic discipline of government remains central, but it is combined with history, sociology, economics, and psychology in studies of government and politics; the workings of the American economy; social problems such as conservation, social welfare, and crime prevention; and various social institutions such as the family, church, and school (14, 30, 31). A variation of the second type of text adds still another dimension to civics programs—that of vocational and educational guidance (6, 18, 22). Another variation combines studies of health and personality adjustment with vocational and educational guidance (9, 26, 34). Because of its extended scope this second type of civics course is intended to be a year-long program.

The ambiguity on the proper subject matter of civics is related to the perplexity about where to place civics within the range of social studies curriculum offerings and to whom civics should be taught. At present civics is the most widely offered social studies course at the ninth-grade level, although a few schools offer instruction in civics at the seventh- or eighth-grade levels (33), and world geography and world history or world cultures are increasingly being offered in place of civics at the ninth-grade level—especially for the better-than-average or college-bound student (5). Also there appears to be a definite trend toward moving civics entirely out of the junior high school and into the eleventh or twelfth grades (33). Some school systems offer junior high school civics only to less able or to the noncollege-bound pupils. Often this course is considered the last chance to offer potential dropouts some guidance on how to conform to the requisites of our society (8).

The prevailing uncertainties about course content and curriculum placement indicate considerable confusion regarding what civics courses are supposed to accomplish. Current efforts to reform the social studies curriculum have compounded this confusion. Widely used textbooks continue to proclaim basically the purposes for civics instruction that were formulated during the 1910–20 period; good citizenship, with its broad implications, is still the all-important goal. Current curriculum reformers, however, have forced the textmakers to acknowledge the need for encouraging formal methods of inquiry and the disciplined use of social science concepts. To this end, one teacher's manual (10) states that the text it accompanies is founded upon the basic idea that "understanding, generalizations, and structure of knowledge provide the framework for good teaching." Another (32) declares that its "study aids help students to master important concepts." Still a third manual says:

> skill in critical thinking is a major goal in the teaching of civics. . . .
> This skill involves the recognition, analysis, and definition of a problem; the gathering, organizing, and interpretation of data; the drawing of conclusions on the basis of the data; and, finally, the making of generalizations on the basis of the conclusions. (Babcock, 1, p. 8.)

One textbook (6) even includes a separate chapter entitled "The Importance of Clear Thinking," in which the steps of critical inquiry are outlined and discussed. This incongruous grafting of undigested modern curriculum reform ideas to a framework for civics instruction that was devised a half century ago and that was based upon presuppositions that differ significantly from the premises of today's reformers has produced a peculiar blend of inconsistencies in course content and teaching methods.

Civics Textbooks as Barometers of Civics Instruction

Certainly today's civics textbooks are vastly superior to earlier products. They are better designed, better written, and more helpful in suggesting sound teaching methods. They easily stand out as better than even the books of only ten years ago. However, they still do little to encourage critical inquiry, cited today by important social studies educators (including most text writers) as a central goal of instruction. Although the textmakers acknowledge the importance of teaching in terms of a structure of knowledge and of developing skills of inquiry, these criteria have not permeated the design and content of the textbooks that are examined in this study. A careful examination of widely used civics textbooks reveals that they do not implement their lofty objectives.

When measured against the criteria described in Chapter 1 of this book, civics texts for junior high schools exhibit four basic weaknesses. First, they do not effectively integrate disparate course content. Second, they fail to represent America as it really is. Third, they inculcate values through moralizing prescriptions. And fourth, they do not help students to attain skill in applying precise methods of inquiry.

THE FRAGMENTATION OF COURSE CONTENT

The civics textbooks examined are organized around points of interest rather than around basic social science concepts and principles. The structure and function of local, state, and national government; the workings of our economic system; vocational and educational guidance; international affairs; and physical and mental health are treated almost as separate entities. Important ideas developed in the sections about government are not effectively used to interpret information in the sections about economics, family life, or vocational and educational guidance. Similarly, discussions of personality adjustment or health and safety appear not to relate basically to the facts and ideas described in other parts of the book. The texts attempt to unify these topics by relating them to vague and superficial precepts of desirable democratic behavior and good citizenship; but these precepts do not integrate information in terms of fundamental relationships. Consequently, most civics textbooks are so fragmented that they comprise three or four distinct subjects rather than being integrated wholes.

Learning theorists contend that fragmentation of subject matter limits understanding and interferes seriously with the practice of critical inquiry. They claim that structuring knowledge into a meaningful pattern quickens the pace of comprehension, cuts down the rate of forgetting, and facilitates the application of facts and ideas learned in one context to related new situations. Understanding fundamentally related concepts and principles allows the inquirer to connect superficially dissimilar facts or ideas in order to develop new and deeper understandings (4).

Given the broad scope and diverse content of current civics courses, it is perhaps impossible to expect that this content could be ordered into a carefully unified whole. Moreover, since civics textbooks are committed to the overriding ideal of promoting good citizenship, they are under pressure to extend their scope even further because good citizenship concerns most subjects in some way. Nevertheless the fragmentation that results from trying to accomplish too much is a persistent barrier to effective instruction.

THE PERPETUATION OF MISCONCEPTIONS

Civics textbooks either avoid or gloss over subjects, and they misuse or omit important social science concepts. As a result these texts tend to perpetuate a number of misconceptions about American society. This tendency imposes a grave limitation on the practice of critical inquiry, for clear thinking can hardly take place in an atmosphere of ignorance and distortion. Discussions of racial problems are representative of the inaccuracies in textbooks. Not one of the examined textbooks discusses the Negro civil rights movement thoroughly, and only six books (6, 9, 14, 18, 22, 34) so much as mention that Negroes have suffered injustices in America.

Only two books (6, 9) discuss forthrightly and in detail several social problems faced by Negroes. Each textbook devotes parts of several pages to Negro efforts to gain equal educational, employment, and voting opportunities. This fair and straightforward treatment of racial problems may be seen in the following comments about Negro voting rights in the South:

> Some southern states have registration systems which prevent Negroes from voting. In these states federal investigations have shown that few Negroes get the opportunity to vote. (Dimond and Pflieger, 9, p. 276.)

> . . . a few southern states have used the literacy test as a device to keep Negroes from voting. The system used has been unfair because it has not been applied in the same manner to whites and Negroes. (*Ibid.*, p. 304.)

By contrast most texts avoid the issue of Negro voting rights with misleading statements in which the word "Negro" is left out:

> In some places people are purposely prevented from voting. A person may be "challenged" by election officials and required to prove that he meets the residence requirements or to take a literacy test or to show his poll tax receipts. The literacy test is sometimes exceptionally difficult, so that the person fails to pass the test and is refused a ballot. In general, however, the tendency is toward greater interest in getting people to vote. (Warren, Leinenweber, and Andersen, 38, p. 55.)

Another book (26) blandly says, "Some of our citizens in certain parts of our country still do not enjoy an equal opportunity for liberty and the pursuit of happiness." And still another text mis-represents the situation entirely by saying that:

> Because the Negroes had been kept uneducated as slaves and thus were without experience in politics, many states feared that they would abuse the privilege of the ballot. Therefore they worked out simple tests which kept many Negroes from voting. For example, many states required that voters take a literacy test or prove they could read and write, because so many former slaves were illiterate. Today, however, such requirements are not as restrictive as they were in 1900. Most Negroes, like most white people, are now able to read and write. (Steen and Faulk, 36, p. 94.)

Nowhere does the text mention racial bias as a reason for depriving many literate Negroes of their voting rights or the role of federal coercive legislation in restoring these rights.

In the typical text other issues—legislative reapportionment, urban renewal, various federal aid and welfare programs, unemployment and hard-core poverty, crime and juvenile delinquency, and the relation of the United States to the United Nations—are dealt with just as poorly. Most of these are discussed briefly and blandly or not at all.

The textbook accounts of the organization and function of local, state, and national governments illustrate the lack of key social science concepts. These accounts include dreary descriptions of the powers and duties of departments, officials, and levels of government, the step-by-step details of how a bill becomes a law (sometimes repeated three times—once each for local, state, and national governments), and interesting but frequently trivial descriptions of how the President or a congressman typically spends a busy day. Seldom are such important concepts as consensus, compromise, power, sovereignty, authority, freedom, social class, status, role, mores, or institution employed to interpret satisfactorily the process of political decision-making: why some bills become laws while others are tabled or voted down; why individuals vote for particular candidates for public office; why people join and/or support certain political organizations or pressure groups; why legislatures are becoming less important in the formulation of public policy.

Political scientist Francis J. Sorauf (35) reported that social characteristics account for differences in individual political behavior, yet this important idea is ignored in textbook discussions of government and politics. This is revealed by the meager utilization of concepts from the behavioral sciences. Status, role, and mores are not discussed in the texts; institution is briefly defined in only two books (18, 22) and social class is discussed in detail in only one book (9) and discussed sketchily in another (14). But even the detailed discussion of social class is confined to one small section of the textbook, and the concept is not related to governmental functions or political processes. The sparse use of ideas that are so basic to the research of most major political scientists indicates the considerable extent to which the scholarship of civics textbooks lags behind the main thrust of social science research.

Traditional political science concepts—such as freedom, sovereignty, consensus, compromise, and totalitarianism—that pertain basically to the relationships between state and citizen should have special significance for civics. Yet these basic ideas receive adequate treatment only infrequently in the textbooks examined.

None of the textbooks discuss consensus, a crucial element in the policy-making of democratic societies. It is likewise difficult to imagine effective discussions of federal-state government relations or international relations without systematic reference to sovereignty, but only one book (22) defines this key idea. The "Great Compromise" of the Constitutional Convention is always included, but the use of compromise as a political device is scarcely mentioned in discussions of contemporary governmental functions. And only two books (14, 26) discuss totalitarianism, viewed by most Americans as the major threat to democracy in the twentieth century.

The word "freedom" pervades the textbooks—it is, after all, a shibboleth of American society—but the many value-laden meanings of this basic idea are never examined carefully. In civics textbooks "freedom" apparently functions mainly as a precept, not as a concept, and it is primarily used as a device for moralistic prescriptions about democratic behavior. Only four textbooks (14, 22, 26, 31) have separate sections devoted to a discussion of freedom. The others discuss this basic idea briefly—for example, in relation to the Bill of Rights or the "free enterprise" economic system. Moreover, civics textbooks perpetuate many misconceptions about freedom. For example, the following comments may foster chauvinism and a misunderstanding of the practices of freedom around the world:

> No other people on earth enjoy as many rights and privileges as Americans.   (Steen and Faulk, 36, p. 68.)

Americans may well be proud of the fact that their country stands as the great champion of freedom and democracy in world affairs. Countries which favor liberty are friends of the United States. Those countries which favor communism and other forms of dictatorship consider the United States their greatest enemy. It is a great thing for a free people to be known as the champions of freedom. (*Ibid.*, p. 249.)

The authors of these statements are apparently not aware of the extensive rights and privileges enjoyed in many industrially advanced democratic states such as France, Switzerland, Sweden, Denmark, Norway, the Netherlands, Great Britain, Canada, Australia, and New Zealand. They also neglect to mention the particular distaste for freedom and democracy manifested by some of our anticommunist but autocratic allies in the cold war struggle, such as Spain, Portugal, Saudi Arabia, and several Latin American military dictatorships.

The meaning of freedom as it applies to social and economic conditions is often distorted:

Any man may rise to his best. (Rienow, 31, p. 17.)

You may choose any kind of work and aim for any job. (*Ibid.*, p. 19.)

The chance to get ahead is part and parcel of a free society. We do have social classes of a sort. There are economic differences between groups. But the social and the economic barriers can be overcome. People are not forced to stay forever within one class or at one economic level. . . . Of all the modern industrial nations ours comes the closest to being a classless society. (Gross and Devereaux, 14, pp. 20–21.)

These statements falsely represent hopes based on the "American dream" as facts derived from careful observation. According to this dream any poor boy can make good if only he is thrifty, hard working, and clever. But although certain conditions in America lend hope to this dream, opposing conditions make the achievement of this goal difficult for a sizable minority trapped in a vicious circle of ignorance, poverty, and prejudice. Recently the plight of this minority was compassionately exposed by Michael Harrington (15) in *The Other America: Poverty in the United States* and by Ben H. Bagdikian's *In the Midst of Plenty: A New Report on the Poor in America* (2). These books show clearly that many Americans cannot overcome the economic and social barriers that block the full realization of their potentialities. Furthermore, studies by W. Lloyd Warner (37) and other eminent sociologists have disproved the notion that we live in a virtually classless society.

The statements quoted above also illustrate another weakness in textbook explications of freedom—the presupposition that freedom consists mainly of the absence of external constraints. This limited conception overlooks the necessity for coupling freedom *from* with freedom *to*; not only political rights but effective opportunities are essential for the fullest development of freedom. This broader view of freedom corresponds to the views of Herbert J. Muller (24), who said in his highly lauded *Freedom in the Western World* that political oppression has not been the only major barrier to freedom; poverty and ignorance have been equally important limitations on the "condition of being able to choose and carry out purposes."

THE INCULCATION OF VALUES

Shallow treatment of controversial subjects is related to the tendency of civics textbooks to inculcate values through moralizing prescriptions. Instead of presenting detailed discussions of controversial subjects and indicating a variety of conflicting viewpoints on these issues, textbooks too often tell pupils what to believe and how to behave. Nothing could be more damaging to the encouragement of critical inquiry, because these preachments preclude the formulation of normative judgments based on careful appraisal of prevailing conditions and anticipated consequences.

The textbooks are infused with precepts about the attitudes and beliefs every good citizen should have:

> Other people's opinions on school or community problems may differ from ours, but we should give them the right to express their views. (Smith and Bruntz, 34, p. 230.)

> The effective citizen knows that it is impossible to live alone and be completely independent of others. He knows that he can and must rely on others. And he knows who those others are. He belongs to organizations that offer effective ways of meeting his important wants and needs. (Krug, Quillen, and Bernd, 18, p. 388.)

> Very likely it is best that people of different races should not be forced to live where the differences between them might cause unpleasantness; but every American citizen of every color should have

the opportunity to make the most of himself, and people of different races should work hand in hand for the good of all. (McCrocklin, 22, p. 204.)

Obviously the values prescribed by civics textbooks are worthy traditional norms of our society that children should know about. But to require uncritical acceptance of these norms is both an inefficient and an inconsistent way to achieve democratic ends. It is inefficient because learning is more thorough and long lasting when it results from self-discovery. Psychologists have long contended that mere sermonizing does not fundamentally alter values or behavior. Uncritical acceptance is inconsistent with democratic ends because it undercuts the basic democratic right of reasonable dissent from established ideas. For example, in regard to segregation in housing a good case can be made *against* the traditional precept that individuals should be free to rent or sell houses to whomever they please. This matter remains controversial, and the textbooks should not choke off rational inquiry into such issues with exhortations about what to believe. Also, philosophers of American democracy from Thomas Paine to John Dewey have stressed that improvement of society results only from the continuing critical appraisal of all standards and beliefs.

Prescription has a place in textbooks, however. One way to teach certain details is simply to impart instructions about what practices are most acceptable and efficient. Details about good grooming or proper study habits or how to find materials in a library are probably best prescribed. But fundamental values require continuous critical appraisal if they are to continue to serve us well.

THE PRACTICE OF CRITICAL INQUIRY

In general the examined textbooks failed to provide sufficient guidance about the procedures for conducting inquiry. All the texts mention inquiry methods, and two of them (6, 9) present detailed discussions of critical thinking, but none require the pupil to practice critical inquiry methods persistently and precisely. The superficial treatment of controversial issues, the omission of key social science concepts, and the attempts to inculcate values seem to be evidence of indifference toward the need for critical inquiry. Further evidence is found in the end-of-chapter exercises, which guide teachers and pupils in the use of the textbook. These exercises contain some questions and suggested activities that could stimulate critical inquiry, but even the books with exercises that best or most extensively stimulate inquiry do not give central emphasis to critical thinking. The assumption of text authors and publishers appears to be that before pupils can think critically they must absorb in an encyclopedic manner essential facts and a few pertinent precepts to ensure proper interpretation and application of these facts. For example, one textbook (9) states at the end of a typically descriptive issue-skimming unit about federal government that "this unit has provided the essential background for understanding the national government." And one teacher's manual (32) prefaces directions on how to use the end-of-chapter questions and activities with the comment that "once students have mastered essential information and understood important ideas, they need an opportunity to develop clearer understanding and new insights through discussion and investigation." But the textbooks themselves often preclude effective thinking about "essential" facts and ideas by presenting only the "right" facts and prescribing the "correct" values.

Case studies, which are included in three textbooks (9, 14, 38), appear to be the best end-of-chapter exercises. One book (9) presents six detailed cases, one at the end of each unit, that illustrate the basic ideas of the preceding chapters and pose issues that call for the implementation of previously learned facts and ideas. This book also contains shorter case problems that are presented in the "Learning Through Discussion" section following each chapter. For instance:

> The mayor of City Y has just vetoed a proposal passed by the common council to build two municipal swimming pools. The people of the city are divided on this issue. Some say the mayor is right. Others say that he is wrong and they will vote him out of office at the next election. What facts would you want to know before you join either side of this issue? (Dimond and Pflieger, 9, pp. 117–18.)

The "History Illustrates This Chapter" section of another book (38) presents documents that illuminate the topics of each chapter and occasionally pose controversial issues. The final chapter of another text (14) is devoted fully to ten brief cases that call for the use of understanding gained from the book. Some of these case studies include questions that crisply direct critical inquiry. For example, these questions follow a case about Senate filibustering:

> 1. What are the important issues in the arguments about the filibusters?

2. What is your stand on these issues?
3. What facts do you use to defend your stand?
4. What can you or other citizens do about the stand you take?

(Dimond and Pflieger, 9, p. 269.)

Unfortunately, these case studies are limited to only a few pages in each book and frequently appear to be peripheral to other concerns.

All the textbooks contain some thought-provoking questions or activities, but mixed among them are far too many time-consuming exercises that require the mere recall of facts or the compilation of lists. Such is the "Problems For Thinkers" section of one book (38), which includes this activity: "Make a list of the Presidents of the United States with the dates of their administrations and the party to which each belonged. Underline the names of those who became President at the death of the elected President." Another example of copy work is this: "Make a chart showing the qualifications needed to be a) a United States Senator and b) a United States Representative" (14). Nor is critical inquiry required to "memorize the Preamble of the Constitution. Recite it to the class or a group within the class" (27). And it takes very little reflection to answer questions such as, "What are three important functions of banks?" (30) or "What two powers does the Senate have which the House does not have?" (6). Such activities appear more congenial to nineteenth-century teaching practices than to the ideas of modern scholars.

These criticisms do not mean that questions asking for purely factual responses are not important. Certainly critical inquiry cannot be practiced without facts, but questions requiring factual answers should be utilized as a means to the formulation or appraisal of generalizations and fundamental social issues.

Finally some civics textbooks contain a number of exercises that pose issues and require inquiry, but the issues themselves are banal and uninspiring. For example, "Resolved, that summer is the best season of the year in which to live on a farm" (22) and "Should a lawn be placed at the front of the house or the back?" (22). It takes more than these to motivate meaningful inquiry.

Antiseptic textbooks, which distort reality and perpetuate social myths in naïve attempts to cultivate exemplary civic behavior, plainly violate their *raison d'être*—the development of good citizens. The good citizen in a democracy must be more than an obedient follower; he must be an active participant in the improvement of society. This requires the possession of conceptual tools that have been sharpened through continuous application to the study of crucial issues. Thus if civics courses are to be challenging and meaningful, if they are even to approximate their most cherished objectives, then the entrails of the American experience must not be hidden behind a pristine exterior of misguided patriotism.

Strategies for Improving Civics

Junior high school civics has been under severe attack during the past decade because of the inconsistency between the frequently splendid objectives of instruction and the woefully insufficient means employed to achieve them. Some critics contend that the objectives of civics instruction cannot be achieved and therefore the course should be abolished. Martin Mayer (21) contended that it is "universally despised" and that most political scientists would prefer to teach civics concepts in history courses. Other critics (13, 17) would transform civics into a rigorous study of political science and would replace the label "civics," which denotes citizenship education, with such course titles as government, political science, comparative political systems, or world politics. One of these latter critics (16) would restrict this formal study of government and politics to the senior high school grades.

The quality and intensity of these attacks threaten the existence of junior high school civics. There is already a trend toward replacing ninth-grade civics with courses in world history or world geography, and many schools now restrict the formal study of government to the twelfth grade (5, 33). If civics is to maintain its position in junior high school curricula, it will certainly have to be substantially reconstructed. But until the time when curriculum designers either remake or remove junior high school civics courses, there is much that can be done with existing materials to improve civics instruction.

Existing textbooks can be used profitably for inquiry-oriented teaching, since they are encyclopedic compendiums of information. Furthermore, some of them include useful prescriptions about study habits, discussion rules, and inquiry techniques. Instead of constituting the entire course of instruction, however, textbook content should be used selectively. One way to do this is to concentrate upon only certain topics in a typical textbook. The teacher emphasizes the relationships among these topics, directs the practice of scientific methods of inquiry, and uses the textbook along with several other sources of information.

The strategy for emphasizing selected topics most easily adaptable to current texts is the "springboard" technique, in which textbook generalizations are examined as a jumping-off point for depth studies.

> Government regulates business to the advantages of both the businessman and the customer who buys his products. Such regulation should be kept to a minimum and used only when necessary. (Rienow, 31, p. 287.)

> In no country in the world has the church had more influence in government than in the United States where we have religious freedom and separation of church and state. (Painter and Bixler, 26, p. 37.)

> Being a member of the United Nations is an important part of the foreign policy of the United States. (Clark *et al.*, 6, p. 362.)

> Many who are interested in good government think that in our zeal for democracy we have had the people elect more officers than they can choose intelligently. (McCrocklin, 22, p. 138.)

Let us consider the first quotation. This normative statement is not adequately clarified in the textbook and is in need of further examination. The teacher can initiate critical inquiry by asking for opinions about the adequacy of this statement. This speculative discussion may generate different, even conflicting, points of view and may also raise questions concerning basic contemporary issues: Why is governmental regulation of economic affairs necessary? By what criteria can the necessary amount of government regulation be determined? These questions would delineate a depth study of the government's role in economic affairs in which speculation about the textbook generalization would be checked against many sources. This depth study would require rigorous practice of the critical inquiry methods of analysis, synthesis, and hypothesis. Relationships must be sought among fragments of relevant information. These data must be categorized and further analyzed before formulating plausible explanations or hypotheses. Further research by the students should lead to evaluation and refinement of the basic hypothesis and a better understanding of the relationship between government and the economy.

The teacher's role in this process is to direct students to suitable sources of information and to develop and guide their use of inquiry methods so that they arrive at a satisfactory conclusion to their inquiry. This exercise may culminate in discussions in which research findings are pooled and evaluated. At this time earlier speculations about the adequacy of the textbook generalizations are confirmed, refined, or rejected in favor of more accurate explanations. Throughout these evaluative discussions pupils should be required to substantiate their ideas thoroughly and precisely, and in addition the teacher should take an active role in helping the class to make satisfactory judgments about the quality of generalizations offered in answer to the problem under investigation.

Questions appearing at the end of textbook chapters can also be used as springboards. The following questions involving both issues and values cannot be answered from typical textbook sources, which avoid detailed or accurate discussions of these complicated problems.

Should the electoral college be abolished? (Rienow, 31, p. 209.)

Which of the protections that are granted to an accused person make it more difficult for police and prosecutors to catch and convict criminals? Would you change any of these rights? Why or why not? (Smith and Bruntz, 34, p. 231.)

Why should the United States be concerned about the threat of communism to other countries? (Warren, Leinenweber, and Andersen, 38, p. 470.)

Would it result in better government if all lobbying activities were prohibited? (Painter and Bixler, 26, p. 499.)

Do you think that the TVA has justified the vast expenditure of public funds to carry out the project? Would you favor the extension of such projects by the federal government? (*Ibid.,* pp. 540–41.)

Another procedure for employing textbooks in inquiry-centered learning is to confront students with a provocative situation that elicits speculation about an issue. The pupils are then referred to a variety of sources (at least to several different textbooks) to check their speculations against the ideas of scholars. Case studies, brief problem-posing movies, reports of surveys such as those reported by the Gallup poll, controversial newspaper articles, and role-playing activities organized around issues can all stimulate inquiry. Sometimes simply asking a few exciting questions or presenting an explosive statement best generates the enthusiasm required for fruitful critical inquiry.

Speculation about provocative issues can function as hypotheses that direct subsequent inquiry. Several textbooks are convenient handbooks of organized facts and explanations that can be used in examining the hypotheses. Conflicting or inadequate textbook accounts can provoke still further speculation and inquiry that lead the student to a wider range of sources. As in the previously discussed strategy, the role of the teacher is to devise a perplexing situation that can challenge the student and motivate inquiry. The teacher should avoid pronouncements and final answers that impede inquiry, but he must provide continuous direction in the practice of inquiry methods.

The skillful teacher, by using textbooks selectively to facilitate critical inquiry, can minimize the typical weaknesses of the civics course. Fragmentation of course content may be limited by concentrating upon a few closely related topics rather than skimming over all the diffused information appearing in a typical textbook. Misconceptions may be decreased when textbook ideas are examined critically and compared with ideas from several other sources. Value judgments will be more meaningful and reliable when the assumptions upon which they are based and the modes of behavior to which they may lead are appraised carefully.

New Directions For Civics

Civics may eventually find its place in the junior high school curriculum (1) as part of a one- or two-year sequence of study in basic social science, (2) as part of a two- or three-year American studies sequence, or (3) as a distinct course in the analysis of public controversy. Each program would consist of interdisciplinary studies that combine several social sciences, history, and literature. This reconstructed civics course might focus upon man's reaction to the persistent problem of maintaining social control and reconciling individual freedom with necessary authority. Conflicting responses to this persistent social problem have generated many explosive issues. Study of the basic concepts related to these issues can serve to integrate the content of civics. Included among these basic concepts are those that explain how social scientists conduct research; for if pupils are to appraise public controversy effectively, then they must be familiar with the kinds of questions social scientists and philosophers ask and the methods by which they answer them.

The primary purpose of this remodeled civics instruction is the development of decision-making ability. At least one authority (12) has said that practice in decision-making should be the heart of social studies programs. Perhaps the most promising new citizenship education program (25) is organized around the analysis of public controversy in order to develop proficiency in appraising values and making rational judgments about issues.

Appraisal of public controversy concerning the state–citizen relationship might well be the essence of civics instruction, since students tend to be more highly motivated when exploring how and why events actually happen than when passively accepting bland descriptions of events. Students respond better to depth studies that involve issues than to sketchy and one-sided interpretations of events that indoctrinate more than they educate. Lawrence Metcalf (23) contended that the purpose of the social studies is to provide students with opportunities to inquire critically into the "closed areas" of American society, such as sex, religion, race, and social class. David Easton and Robert Hess (11) reported that it is crucial to emphasize issues in social studies during the pre-high school years because children appear to form their basic political beliefs from ages three to thirteen. Easton and Hess claimed that formal instruction about politics in high school seems to have little influence on previously held political values. The implications of their research are obvious and ominous: instruction in civics during the junior high school grades appears to be the last chance seriously to influence bedrock political values.

Another study that indicated the urgent need to stress critical inquiry into controversial subjects during the adolescent years was conducted by Remmers and Franklin (29). On the basis of responses to questionnaires from over 2,000 American teenagers, they concluded that a significantly large number of young people fail to understand clearly the important guarantees of the First Amendment to the Constitution—especially as they pertain to minority groups. They suggested that a prime reason for this misunderstanding is the shallow treatment of controversial subjects in social studies courses.

These proposals for reconstructed civics instruction call for multiple instructional materials. Textbooks certainly would continue to play an important role but would be reserved for use as factual handbooks—a traditional role for which today's textbooks are well suited. There always will be a need for this service. But inquiry-oriented instruction also requires books of case studies, documents, and in-depth descriptions of various relevant topics. Novels such as *The Ox-Bow Incident* by Walter Van Tilburg Clark, *Lord of the Flies* by William Golding, and *Animal Farm* by George Orwell also have a central place in the study of basic governmental issues. Textbook publishers, curriculum leaders, and teachers should no longer consider such materials mere supplements to textbooks but should regard them as crucial to social studies instruction.

Another innovation that might better serve the needs of inquiry-oriented instruction is the preparation of packets of loose materials, which can serve either as confrontation devices for the stimulation of inquiry or as readily available and well-organized documentary sources for the conduct of depth studies. Each packet would contain materials on a particular issue, and there would be several related series of these packets. The packets might include the tabulated results of social science research studies, surveys, statistical data, excerpts from legal documents, portions of newspaper articles and editorials, and newspaper cartoons.

Conclusion

M. Frank Redding (28) claimed in a recent essay that textbook publishers have always been "solid, conservative, and cautious" because to have been otherwise would have been ethically unthinkable and financially catastrophic. Redding went on to suggest that textbook publishers have always followed the market, and, when educators have adamantly demanded significant changes, the publishers have eventually moved in the direction of these changes. There are many signs today that publishers are starting to remodel their products in response to market research and stinging criticisms. The most recently published civics textbooks (6, 9, 14, 34) show significant improvement over earlier editions, and some of the criticisms leveled against civics textbooks in earlier studies by Krug (19) and

Marcus (20) are less applicable to these newer books. There is good reason to believe that when teachers and administrators indicate through their curriculum practices that they require vastly improved teaching resources designed to facilitate critical inquiry, publishers will move to comply with these demands.

Selected Bibliography

1. BABCOCK, CHESTER D., *Teacher's Manual for Civics in Action,* Harr Wagner, San Francisco, 1966.
2. BAGDIKIAN, BEN H., *In the Midst of Plenty: A New Report on the Poor in America,* The New American Library, New York, 1964.
3. BROWN, AROLD W., *The Improvement of Civics Instruction in Junior and Senior High Schools,* Standard Printing Company, Ypsilanti, Mich., 1929.
4. BRUNER, JEROME S., *The Process of Education,* Harvard University Press, Cambridge, Mass., 1963.
5. CARR, EDWIN P., *The Social Studies,* The Center for Applied Research in Education, New York, 1965.
6. CLARK, NADINE I., *et al., Civics for Americans,* Teacher's Annotated Edition, Macmillan, New York, 1965.
7. CRONBACH, LEE J. (ed.), *Text Materials in Modern Education,* University of Illinois Press, Urbana, 1955.
8. CUMMINGS, HOWARD H., "The Social Studies in the Secondary School Today," *Social Studies in the Senior High School,* Willis D. Moreland (ed.), National Council for the Social Studies, Curriculum Series No. 7, Washington, D.C., 1965.
9. DIMOND, STANLEY E., AND PFLIEGER, ELMER F., *Civics for Citizens,* Lippincott, Philadelphia, 1965.
10. ———, Teacher's Manual, *Civics for Citizens,* Annotated, Lippincott, Philadelphia, 1965, T1–T8.
11. EASTON, DAVID, AND HESS, ROBERT, "The Child's Political World," *Midwest Journal of Political Science,* 6 (Aug., 1962), 229–46.
12. ENGLE, SHIRLEY H., "Decision-Making: The Heart of Social Studies Instruction," *Social Education,* 24 (Nov., 1960), 301–04.
13. FENTON, EDWIN, AND GOOD, JOHN M., "A Social Studies Curriculum for Able Students," *Social Education,* 29 (Apr., 1965), 216–18.
14. GROSS, RICHARD E., AND DEVEREAUX, VANZA, *Civics in Action,* Teacher's Edition, Harr Wagner, San Francisco, 1966.
15. HARRINGTON, MICHAEL, *The Other America: Poverty in the United States,* Penguin Books, New York, 1963.

16. KELLER, CHARLES R., "History and the Social Sciences: A New Approach," Talk given at the annual meeting of the Inland Empire Education Association, Spokane, Wash., Apr. 3, 4, 1963.

17. KIRKPATRICK, EVRON M., AND JEANE J., "Political Science," *High School Social Studies Perspectives*, Herold C. Hunt (ed.), Houghton Mifflin, Boston, 1962.

18. KRUG, EDWARD A., QUILLEN, I. JAMES, AND BERND, JOHN M., *Living in Our Communities*, Scott, Foresman, Chicago, 1963.

19. KRUG, MARK M., " 'Safe' Textbooks and Citizenship Education," *School Review*, 68 (Winter, 1960), 463–80.

20. MARCUS, LLOYD, *The Treatment of Minorities in Secondary School Textbooks*, Anti-Defamation League of B'nai B'rith, New York, 1961.

21. MAYER, MARTIN, *Where, When, and Why: Social Studies in American Schools*, Harper & Row, New York, 1962.

22. McCROCKLIN, JAMES H., *Building Citizenship*, Allyn and Bacon, Boston, 1962.

23. METCALF, LAWRENCE E., "Some Guidelines for Changing Social Education," *Social Education*, 27 (Apr., 1963), 197–201.

24. MULLER, HERBERT J., *Freedom in the Western World*, Harper & Row, New York, 1963.

25. OLIVER, DONALD W., AND SHAVER, JAMES P., *Teaching Public Issues in the High School*, Houghton Mifflin, Boston, 1966.

26. PAINTER, FRED B., AND BIXLER, HAROLD H., *Citizenship in Action*, Charles Scribner's Sons, New York, 1962.

27. POSEY, ROLLIN BENNETT, *Civics for Young Americans*, Harper & Row, New York, 1965.

28. REDDING, M. FRANK, *Revolution in the Textbook Publishing Industry*, The Department of Audio-Visual Instruction, National Education Association, Washington, D.C., 1963.

29. REMMERS, H. H., AND FRANKLIN, R. D., "Sweet Land of Liberty," *Phi Delta Kappan*, 44 (Oct., 1962), 22–27.

30. RICHARDS, W. MARVIN, ISELY, BLISS, AND RICHARDS, JOHN M., *We the People*, Benefic Press, Chicago, 1964.

31. RIENOW, ROBERT, *The Citizen and His Government*, Houghton Mifflin, Boston, 1963.

32. ——, *Teacher's Guide for the Citizen and His Government*, Houghton Mifflin, Boston, 1963.

33. SMITH, FREDERICK R., "The Curriculum," *New Challenges in the Social Studies*, Byron G. Massialas and Frederick R. Smith (eds.), Wadsworth, Belmont, Calif., 1965.

34. SMITH, HARRIET FULLEN, AND BRUNTZ, GEORGE G., *Your Life as a Citizen*, Revised Annotated Edition, Ginn, Boston, 1965.

35. SORAUF, FRANCIS J., *Political Science: An Informal Overview*, Charles E. Merrill Books, Columbus, Ohio, 1965.

36. STEEN, RALPH W., AND FAULK, ODIE B., *Government by the People,* Steck Company, Austin, Tex., 1964.

37. WARNER, W. LLOYD, *American Life: Dream and Reality,* The University of Chicago Press, Chicago, 1962.

38. WARREN, HARRIS G., LEINENWEBER, HARRY D., AND ANDERSEN, RUTH O. M., *Our Democracy at Work,* Prentice-Hall, Englewood Cliffs, N.J., 1963.

PART 3

The Senior High School

CHAPTER 7

American History

Potential for Inquiry but Little Fulfillment

JOHN R. PALMER

While many elaborate attempts have been made to define history, it appears that what gets into history books are those events in the past that are now perceived as having affected large numbers of people. Accounts of wars and diplomacy, of revolutions and the more peaceful forms of political strife, of the deeds of kings, presidents, and their ministers and opponents—these have formed the bulk of historical writing. Even when historians have introduced into their works commentary concerning climate, terrain, economic conditions, and the like, they appear to be guided by the belief that these factors affected the lives of many people in some significant manner.

The crucial question here, of course, is whether or not such accounts of past events are of value in the process of inquiry as defined in the introduction to this volume. Can written history contribute to the identification or testing of hypotheses concerning social reality? I find it difficult to imagine carrying out these two central tasks of inquiry without resorting to historical materials. Although history as it is usually written may not be sufficient, it certainly is necessary. A reading of history should both generate hypo-

theses and provide data to test their validity. But there are many histories, that is, there are many ways that one can treat past events, and
certain emphases seem to be more promising than others in furthering the process of inquiry.

Like the social scientist the historian can analyze the complex
of factors involved in human interaction, but because he is an historian, he must also appraise larger interrelationships and attempt
a general synthesis. The analysis of interrelations goes on in all
social science, but the attempt to make a general synthesis of the
major factors at work in a given conjuncture of events is particularly
pertinent to historical studies. It is true that monographic studies
in history may isolate particular factors for intensive analysis, but
the conscientious historian, even when engaged in monographic research, never forgets the final goal of comprehensive synthesis.
Furthermore, the historian not only strives for an understanding
of the total situation *as it is* at any given point in time but also
explains how that situation *came to be.* From the historical point
of view an event is always the result of the interplay of dynamic
forces operating through preceding events and probably continuing
to operate through succeeding events. The significance of an event
lies in its relation to a past and a future.

Establishing the truth of an individual fact or even of a whole
series of facts is not history. History deals with whole situations, not
isolated facts; it deals with causes and effects, not just chronological
sequences. It would be quite possible to write an account of the
Battle of Jutland describing with a high degree of accuracy every
movement of every ship that took part in the engagement, but such
an account would not be a history of the battle, and no one would
be particularly anxious to read it. One needs to know why the battle
took place, why the Germans scored their initial successes, why the
British failed to cut off the German retreat, what effects the battle
had on the course of the war, how a modern naval battle differs
from one in the past, and what modifications of accepted strategy,
tactics, and naval construction were suggested by the battle. These
questions can be answered only by amassing facts to create a general
impression and by linking these groups of facts to establish a sequence of causes and effects.

This gathering and linking of facts is not only essential to history but is also one of the primary ways in which the human mind
deals with any past experience. Yet the linking of facts is the area

of greatest danger in all historical writing, since facts can be amassed in such a way as to produce a misleading impression, even though each fact may be true. Mistakes may also be made in trying to establish sequences of causes and effects. The causes of any historical event are always complicated and often obscure. There is a great temptation to oversimplify or to seize on surface explanations that merely state the problem in new terms.

Historians and the history they write can and should make a significant contribution to the understanding of the society in which we live. Otherwise history has little place in the school curriculum. The appropriate role for history in educating the young has become a subject of much debate in the last decade. Robert Lynd (11) complained as long ago as 1939 that historical scholarship tended to be a "self-justifying procedure carried on for its own sake in a general mood of disinterested curiosity." Lynd recognized the need for some historical knowledge and analysis but was not at all certain that much of the history being written and taught was of any value. Very recently the attack on history has been considerably sharpened by a fairly large and influential group of educators (3, 13), with the result that one can no longer take history's role in the general education of the child for granted. The traditional assumptions that all children need as much history as they can get and that teachers should teach the subject as historians write it are no longer accepted without reservation. In many social studies curriculum proposals history completely loses its identity as a separate discipline and becomes at most a handmaiden to the other social studies.

An examination of the criticisms of history makes it quite clear that no one really intends to eliminate the subject matter contained in written history from the curriculum of the high schools. The form and manner in which it is presented to the students, however, may be radically different from that found in the chronologically or topically arranged high school history textbooks now in common use. Historical material is included in almost all recent curriculum proposals, but it has undergone a very considerable transformation. Most of the criticism of history is lodged against a certain type of historian, a certain way of teaching history, and a certain type of history textbook. A recent critical work by Billington and a team of American and English historians (2) claimed that even some of our most respected historians become dull, prone to error and bias, and fact-oriented when they write for the young.

Some historians, of course, persist in the view developed late in the last century that written history explains little, reveals nothing than can be useful in the present or future, and consists only of a narrative of past events. It is this group and the teachers who take their cues from it that provide the critics with much of their ammunition. As long as some textbook writers and history teachers persist in emphasizing such information as the length of the Nile River, the salary of a United States Senator, or the date of the Ostend Manifesto, it is not difficult to raise doubts about the place of history in the curriculum.

But there are other historians and history teachers who agree with Thomas Cochran (6) that "History, if it is to hold its high place in the field of learning, must suggest policies for meeting current problems." Such an assumption has broad implications for the way history should be written and studied. Three of the most recent social studies methods textbooks (7, 12, 13), while departing considerably from the conventional ways of handling history, all recognize the necessity of including historical knowledge and historical approaches in social education. In a sense these books are searching for a means of implementing the spirit of the "New History" sponsored by James Harvey Robinson, Carl Becker, and others a half century ago. Emphasizing a concern for the present and the future and going far beyond what happened to the reasons why it happened and its possible significance for present problems, this approach is reflected in considerable measure in written history and in the classrooms of the country. It is this type of history that by its content, its organization, and its orientation lends itself most readily to classroom inquiry.

The Nature of Historical Inquiry

Inquiry into the past, in contrast to accounts of past happenings as interesting stories, begins with a problem, question, or hypothesis to be tested. A residue of the Ranke tradition in its transplanted American form remains among professional historians—that of gathering the "facts" and letting them speak for themselves.[1] Cer-

[1]For a recent assessment of Ranke's influence on history writing in the United States and the manner in which his views were distorted by many scholars, see Georg G. Iggers, "The Image of Ranke in American and German Historical Thought," *History and Theory*, II (1962), pp. 17–33.

tainly products of this point of view are poor examples of historical inquiry. They tell what happened but make few interpretations and come to few conclusions. As the knowledge explosion continues to accelerate, it becomes increasingly difficult to justify the inclusion of knowledge for its own sake in the school curriculum. It is naïve to suppose that an immature youngster will be able to so organize and analyze an extensively documented and detailed account of past happenings as to generate the insights that the historian himself was unable or unwilling to supply.

A critical element in historical methodology for the historian as well as the student, then, is a question generated by an historical or contemporary situation. It is necessary but not sufficient merely to know what happened; significance and implication must be supplied by the context within which the exploration into the past is undertaken.

Historical inquiry cannot begin from total ignorance of the past or present, because one needs knowledge and experience to recognize problems or issues. This does not mean that many years must be spent in studying history before one knows enough to engage in historical inquiry. Questions generated by experience or knowledge of the contemporary world are as pertinent as those that develop from a knowledge of the past. Students acquire far more of their social education outside social studies classes than in. With this background it takes only a little reading and discussion of historical events to generate questions concerning other times and places. While the motivational aspects have been debated by psychologists and teachers, it seems safe to say that historical inquiry can begin either in the present or the past. The question of why the civilization of ancient Egypt developed along the Nile is no more or less historical than the question of why crimes of violence are more common in the United States today than in most countries. Both questions have an historical dimension, but neither is exclusively historical.

While historical inquiry may be assumed rather than made explicit, it requires a frame of reference to guide the process. This framework will influence the questions selected for study, the manner in which the inquiry is conducted, and the conclusions reached. The variety and number of possible conceptual schema depend mainly on the sophistication and creativity of the investigator. Notions regarding the structure of historical situations and their dynamics will enter into most such conceptual schema. Structure suggests the need for determining for a particular place and time the significant economic, social, cultural, political, and ethical arrangements that order society and the life of the individual. Dynamics implies change and process, the configuration of forces working within the society to propel it into an unknown future. Both structure and process go far beyond historical narration and require liberal use of such sciences of culture as anthropology, sociology, psychology, and economics.

Every historical account involves an interrelationship of processes that are preeminently the concern of the several social sciences as distinct from history. A particular historical situation is to some extent unique, but the processes at work within that situation are similar to those found in other times and places. These general aspects of an historical situation are best understood in terms of the sciences of human culture and behavior.

To recapitulate, we have determined so far that at least three elements are essential to historical inquiry—a problem, a theoretical framework for dealing with the problem, and the relevant knowledge from history and the social sciences. Other considerations are also pertinent. The process of inquiry obviously demands a particular set of skills and attitudes on the part of participants. For example, both teacher and student must be willing to entertain a wide variety of beliefs and ideas, and they must be skilled at assessing the soundness of an argument and the reliability of a source of information. It is not necessary or appropriate in this context to list all the attributes and skills that may contribute to critical inquiry, but it is well to recognize the importance of preparing students to participate in such an intellectual process. Our concern here is with textbooks, and the books used in the process of inquiry are as much participants as the students and teachers. We should expect the textbook, then, to clearly present the conceptual frame within which selection and analysis of data have been carried out. Are we permitted a look inside the mind of the writer so that we can more adequately assess what he has written? If he is to participate in our inquiry, this is quite essential and no more than we would demand of each other. Does the writer demonstrate his willingness to engage in the process of inquiry by organizing his material in terms of the significant problems he himself finds in the past or present? If not, the material may be somewhat useful to us in dealing with the questions we generate, but it will convey a mood and organization that contribute little to our purposes. Has the writer made extensive use of social science materials in handling historical events? Explanation, the consideration of cause–effect relationships, and the examination of societal function and process demand that the historian employ the generalized knowledge developed in those social science disciplines that focus on institutional and human development. Without this knowledge he must interpret and attempt to understand the past solely on the basis of his own very parochial personal experiences.

Analysis of Textbooks in High School American History

It is very likely that no high school American history textbook currently available from a commercial publisher was written to stimulate the processes of inquiry in the history classroom. In fact, the criteria of textbook evaluation developed in the previous section might be totally rejected by the authors of the books reviewed or might be accepted only as a part of what they attempted to incorporate in their volumes. Nevertheless, if one proposes to focus on inquiry in the teaching of history, it is necessary to evaluate the materials now available in terms of their usefulness for that purpose.

American history is the most commonly offered secondary school social studies course, and a wide variety of textbooks is available. Obviously some selection had to be made for this study. My objective was not to find the one book that best met the criteria or to establish a rating list but rather to determine the problems and possibilities presented by typical high school American history textbooks in terms of inquiry teaching. I therefore chose five well-established textbooks (5, 8, 9, 15, 16) on the basis of national distribution and recent sales estimates.

My review technique was quite simple. The following four criteria were established: (1) Does the material focus on historical and/or contemporary problems? (2) Is the theoretical framework used by the author in selecting, organizing, and analyzing his material clearly set forth? (3) Are analysis and interpretation stressed rather than description and narration? (4) Is there wide use of social science knowledge and theory? I then read the five textbooks, making qualitative judgments and rough quantitative estimates as I proceeded. At least one conclusion—that American history textbooks are today very large and heavy—seems beyond dispute.

It is well to recognize at the outset that a factual statement can be the stimulus for historical exploration and inquiry. For example, "Early in 1775, more than a year before the colonists declared their independence, the old colonial governments began to crumble" (15). Or a picture showing people crowded outside a bank that has its doors locked can serve just as well. (See 8, page 675.) Under the proper questioning, students may become curious about the causes of these events, the alternative explanations that can be given, and their possible consequences. Viewed in this fashion it is difficult to think of any statement, picture, graph, or experience that could not, in the hands of an imaginative teacher, be a starting point for inquiry. Obviously every American history textbook provides this sort of material. In reading and evaluating these five textbooks, however, I tried to determine whether these books actually provide a positive impetus to inquiry by satisfying the four criteria that seem to be relevant. Do they include and arrange material so that inquiry processes as described in Chapter 1 of this volume are not only fostered but seem to be an integral part of the study of American history?

EMPHASIS ON HISTORICAL OR CONTEMPORARY PROBLEMS

In the textbooks themselves, as distinguished from teaching aids, there is very little direct attention given to the problems either of the past or of the present in the books reviewed. The basic structure of almost all high school American history textbooks today consists of arranging topics in a roughly chronological sequence. Subject matter is organized under descriptive topic headings, such as "Erecting the Frame of Government," "Organizing the Forces of Labor," and "The United States Rejects World Leadership," rather than in terms of the crucial issues of a period or the relevance of the past to contemporary problems. It seems fair to say that primary attention is on what happened, and the prevailing style is narrative. These conclusions will hardly startle anyone who is well acquainted with written history.

There is some indication, however, that at least one team of authors intended to write a book that would foster inquiry, rather than a narrative history. The following is quoted from the pages added to the Teacher's Edition:

The emphasis should be placed on thinking about issues, looking for cause-and-effect relationships, drawing conclusions from verified data, and assessing the comparative worth of interpretations provided by various historians. To contribute to such goals, a textbook must be much more than a compendium of facts. (Wade, Wilder, and Wade, 16, p. 10.)

This excellent statement of certain aspects of inquiry is illustrated by the following questions in the introductory materials added to the Teacher's Edition: "Was slavery profitable?" and "What were Senator Douglas's motives?" Both issues are developed to some extent in the textbook, and the reader is provided with a variety of evidence that could promote analysis and thought. It was somewhat discouraging to find on more careful examination of the volume, however, that the first such problem ("Did mercantilism hurt or help the colonies?") appears on page 60 and the second ("Was slavery profitable?") on page 329. This hardly seems to place an "emphasis . . . on thinking about issues."

Most of the texts examined, while making no general claim to be thought provoking, did in a very few places state and develop a significant issue in a most helpful fashion. There was no discernible pattern to these infrequent attempts, so they may represent areas of particular concern to the authors. Todd and Curti's *Rise of the American Nation* (15) closes with an excellent section entitled "The American people reexamine their goals," in which critical contemporary issues are brought to light and briefly examined. Six full pages are devoted to the issue of loyalty investigations by the Congress in *United States History* by Gavian, Hamm, and Freidel (8). In addition they discuss in a sophisticated manner the very difficult question of the control of individuals in our society who believe in different ideologies and the problem of the growth and spread of communism and its impact in the United States. Chapter Twelve, "The South: The Plantation" in Graff and Krout's *The Adventure of the American People* (9) contains thirteen pages of material focused on the issue of whether or not the institution of slavery and the cotton economy were beneficial to the South in the decades immediately before the Civil War. Although certain economic and ethical aspects are treated quite superficially, the material is organized so as to provoke thought and discussion. Such examples illustrate what can be done, but they are rare. Many other such points of controversy are implied but not developed sufficiently to assist the reader in understanding what is involved.

None of the books reviewed makes a direct attempt to relate the past to the present or use the past to clarify contemporary problems. Despite the continual insistence by historians that one needs to know the past to understand the present, almost no attempt is made by these authors to help the reader make that leap. The idea that such a relationship exists becomes apparent in the abundant study questions that all the books provide. But it is unfair to ask students the questions without assisting them in developing the answers. Either the student must resort to guessing, or he must do the research that the historian should have done. Questions such as these may well have been designed to get the student to draw relationships between the past and present:

> Which of our present democratic practices can be traced to colonial ideas?   (Todd and Curti, 15, p. 89.)

> Compare the power of labor unions during the period 1865–1900 with the power of labor unions today.   (*Ibid.*, p. 501.)

> Compare the motives of explorers in the fifteenth and sixteenth centuries with those of explorers in the nineteenth and twentieth centuries.   (Gavian, Hamm, and Freidel, 8, p. 32.)

It should be pointed out that some of these questions call for comparisons that do not directly explore how the past influences the present or how our behavior can be guided by the past.

The end-of-chapter teaching aids are quite elaborate and usually have been prepared by someone other than the authors. A large proportion of the suggested questions and activities, despite the use of such headings as "What Do You Think?" or "For Discussion," require only the recall of information supplied in the text. For example, an item such as "what were the chief articles of trade brought from the East" does not lead anywhere unless a teacher follows it up with a series of additional questions that are not supplied in the textbook.

However, many questions or suggested activities have considerable potential:

> Is an opposition party necessary in a democracy?   (Wade, Wilder, and Wade, 16, p. 179.)

When western farmers balked at paying the tax on whiskey, the government mobilized 13,000 men to enforce the law. In what ways was this situation comparable (or not comparable) to the colonists' refusal to pay the Stamp Tax? (*Ibid.,* p. 179.)

(a) Why is the TVA frequently referred to as a profoundly important "social experiment"? (b) Outline the advantages and disadvantages of organizing the country under the control of several regional authorities similar to the TVA. (Gavian, Hamm, and Freidel, 8, p. 706.)

But again it must be stressed that the material presented in the texts is only of limited value in grappling with such issues. For this reason teachers treat many of the fundamental social questions of the past and present as peripheral material rather than as the heart of the course (or do not consider these issues at all), because to do otherwise would require the gathering of materials and ideas from many additional sources.

USE OF ANALYSIS AND INTERPRETATION

None of the textbooks reviewed is limited to an account of what happened. While there is a considerable amount of rather simple narration, much of the material is organized in a cause–event–consequence pattern. Yet this pattern is handled so as to give one the feeling that he is reading a narrative. The analyses, the interpretations, the explanatory hypotheses, the conflicting viewpoints that one could consider with respect to a given cause–event–consequence sequence are largely absent. All three elements of the sequence are presented as a purely factual account rather than an interpretation. It is as if the authors have given us *the* history of the United States rather than *a* history. Analysis and interpretation imply a process and attitude of probing, questioning, and weighing alternatives. With rare exceptions, these aspects of the historian's work do not appear. Unfortunately these are the very things that would tend to stimulate inquiry on the part of the reader. If he is presented with only one "correct" interpretation, he is less likely to ponder an issue than if he is presented with the shortcomings of an interpretation or with two or more conflicting interpretations.

In this regard it appears that one feature of the volume by Graff and Krout (9) has considerable potential. Each chapter is introduced by a statement of about a page in length quoted from a contemporary figure. Generally these are quite biased and represent one viewpoint relative to the chapter topic. Included are selections from a jingoist speech by Albert Beveridge, a proslavery statement by William Harper, and John L. O'Sullivan's impassioned plea for manifest destiny. These lend themselves to analysis although it must obviously be done by the teacher or students since the authors have not done so. In the same book Frederick Jackson Turner's frontier thesis is presented in brief and analyzed in terms of its current acceptability, and the presidency of Franklin Roosevelt is evaluated in a most informative manner.

The forthright judgments and interpretations that are sprinkled throughout the last half of Gavian, Hamm, and Freidel (8) are refreshing and certainly constitute potential spurs to inquiry. It seems likely that they are the work of Professor Freidel, a specialist in twentieth-century American history, who recently revised the original volume prepared by Gavian and Hamm. Rather than merely defining the direct primary and recall and indicating how they enhance our democratic life, the book appraises frankly the meager impact they have had. It also presents a brief history of attempts to curb freedom of speech and the press and takes a firm stand against such curbs even in times of national emergency. The failure of prohibition is analyzed in sufficient depth to make it possible to generalize and form hypotheses concerning the relationship between legislation and social custom. In each case the authors make their own position and the reasoning behind it quite clear. The authors' distinctive interpretation of the Neutrality Act of 1937 and its consequences, for example, invites the reader to question or even disagree.

> This new law swept away the old principle of freedom of the seas for neutral trade. Thus it gave up the very rights for which we had fought in 1917. More important, it stopped the most powerful nation in the world, the United States, from contributing to collective security. As President Roosevelt said later, "Our arms embargo played right into the hands of aggressive nations." (Gavian, Hamm, and Freidel, 8, p. 713.)

High school social studies textbooks have frequently been condemned (1, 10, 14) for their consistent avoidance of controversy and analysis. Reviewers have complained that the significant issues of our national life, which continually challenge our capacities for adjustment, compromise, and innovation, are either ignored or pre-

sented in the most bland way possible to avoid offending special interest groups, particularly racial, religious, and sectional minorities.
These complaints do seem to be well founded, but it is necessary to
point out that books vary and all of those read in this study took up
the cudgel of interpretation and judgment in at least a few places.

Authors cite lack of space as the standard retort to the above
criticisms. This argument is not very convincing to anyone who has
read a few of these high school textbooks. Most are made up of more
than 800 very large pages. About half of this space, however, is devoted to pictures, charts, maps, and end-of-chapter exercises. Certainly some of these contribute to inquiry, but undoubtedly much
could be eliminated in the interest of more analysis and interpretation, particularly if it is true that the processes of inquiry are inherently more interesting for most students than reading a narrative
history.

EVIDENCE OF A THEORETICAL FRAMEWORK

Historians in the United States have long been reluctant to talk
about their theory of history or their basic assumptions in carrying
on their scholarly tasks. The exceptions to this pattern have included
some of our most prominent historians, such as Charles Beard and
James Harvey Robinson, as well as certain contemporary figures,
such as H. Stuart Hughes, Louis Gottschalk, and David Potter. Often
the most one can do is to identify an individual as an economic historian, an intellectual historian, a political historian, and so forth.
But regardless of this tendency of historians to hide their assumptions under a bushel, it is obvious that when one sees himself as an
historian rather than a compiler of chronicles he deals with his material in terms of certain hypotheses about the nature of reality and
human behavior. It is essential if we are to understand and evaluate
his writing that we know what these are. We are aided, too, if we
know what his purpose is in writing about the past. Is it an interesting story to be read and enjoyed, a guide for our own social
behavior, a vehicle for developing certain attitudes such as patriotism, or what?

When we are examining an assertion made by a participant in
a discussion, we can question him as to what assumptions he has
made and what empirical support he has for his position. Such procedures are essential in inquiry. The historical monograph typically

has as its primary focus one interpretation or one hypothesis supported by a mass of evidence that reveals the scholar's bases of interpretation and selection of data. Unfortunately the textbook writer feels compelled to eliminate almost everything but the conclusion reached, and as a consequence it is very difficult to determine why he makes the assertions he does and to decide whether we can agree with him.

In general, the textbooks reviewed reveal the reluctance of historians to indicate their assumptions or purposes; two books, however, make brief attempts to do so. In a section entitled "History and Historians," Wade, Wilder, and Wade (16) devote a few paragraphs to historiography, emphasizing the tentative nature of historical "facts" and interpretation. This discussion is certainly instructive but might well be passed over by students because it is found in the preface rather than in the main body of the book. The authors state that "in writing *A History of the United States* [they] have tried not only to provide the most widely accepted interpretations of great events but also to suggest various interpretations that deserve consideration and to make clear why these views merit attention." It is very difficult, however, to find instances of this technique in the text. The declared purpose of the volume is "to prepare each student to apply the lessons of history to his own experience." Yet extensive research on transfer indicates that there is little hope of accomplishing such an objective unless parallels between the past and his experiences are explicitly drawn for the student. This text, like the others used in this study, simply fails to do this, although it undoubtedly presents material that *could* be related to the student's own life. The intriguing question raised by the authors' statement of purpose is *how* can a youngster learn to relate past to present. Historians and others generally seem to assume that in some magical way it just happens. But transfer of this sort is difficult to demonstrate logically, psychologically, or empirically.

Somewhat more direct but no more promising for our purposes is the assertion by Graff and Krout (9) that their textbook is a narrative history. They make no claims to analysis or comparative interpretations. Because they are writing for young people, they "have aimed to inspire as well as instruct." The recent study by Billington and others (2), however, reaffirms the conclusion reached in several earlier studies that "inspirational" material tends to be inaccurate and biased, making it unworthy for use in the schools. Such material perpetuates myths that only increase the student's social and cultural astigmatism.

Graff and Krout (9) also assume that knowledge of the past is essential for understanding the present. This is best accomplished by reading "stories of every place and period." The use of the word "stories" implies that understanding occurs as a result of reading narrative accounts of past events, in much the same manner that one learns from reading a good short story or novel. This assumes that history is a humanistic study rather than a social science. Some historians would be pleased to have it that way; others would not. Inquiry-centered teaching is more consistent with viewing history as a social science.

As nearly as could be determined, the other authors had not a word to say about what they were doing or why. In view of the inadequate theoretical frameworks of all five textbooks, I widened the search in an attempt to locate at least one high school history textbook that met this criterion satisfactorily. Typical of such books is *The World Story* by Bruun and Haines (4), a recent textbook written for high school world history courses. The entire first chapter and the last several pages of the book are devoted to setting the task for the student and presenting some of the authors' assumptions. The following excerpts indicate the nature of this material:

> The term *history* has various meanings. . . . history in one sense can mean everything that has happened. . . . Fortunately the word *history* can also mean "the branch of knowledge that records and explains past events as steps in human progress." This sets more definite boundaries within which to work. The *period* for study is shortened to the few thousand years since human beings advanced from savagery to civilization. The *subject matter* is reduced to the information *available* on past steps in human progress. (Bruun and Haines, 4, p. 17.)

> A history text . . . is somewhat like your schoolroom globe, which shows you the continents and countries of the world represented in a reduced scale on a small globe. (*Ibid.*)

> The two most general and most striking trends in world history during the last five thousand years have been (1) the gradual linking up of widely scattered peoples, cultures, and continents, and (2) the advances in knowledge, in technology, and in world population. These trends are related, and neither could have developed rapidly had it not been stimulated by the other. (*Ibid.*, p. 18.)

Other topics dealt with include the historian's task, the value of history, the nature of civilization, the generalizations that are fundamental to an understanding of history, the sources of historical information, and the nature of the history textbook. In the last few pages of the book the student is reminded of the authors' opening statements, and certain points are reexamined in light of the material presented in the book. One cannot be certain that the framework set forth by Bruun and Haines would be effective in conveying to students what we want them to know, but there is much material in the book that appears to be useful for that purpose.

USE OF SOCIAL SCIENCE KNOWLEDGE

Historians, social scientists, and philosophers continue to debate about whether history is a social science or is qualitatively different from the other studies of human society. As indicated previously, the processes of historical inquiry—explanation, analysis and interpretation, and the testing of assumptions and hypotheses—require extensive use of concepts, methodologies, and generalizations developed within the other social sciences. Without them historical explanation and analysis tend to be superficial and to rely heavily on the folklore or "common sense" of the society rather than verified knowledge.

The relevance of social science knowledge to the study of the past is abundantly clear in the American history textbooks examined. It is difficult to find a page of text that does not illustrate concepts or generalizations from the other social sciences. The following account of the development of commerce and industry in sixteenth-century England is typical:

> Businessmen had money to invest. They looked around for opportunities to make more money. They were willing to risk their capital by taking shares in joint-stock companies formed to carry on foreign trade. By 1600 a number of trading companies were in operation. Each one had a charter from the crown giving it a monopoly of trade in some part of the world. (Gavian, Hamm, and Freidel, 8, p. 28.)

This description of events in the English economy can readily be learned by the student. However, unless he knows some economics (as well as more of the history of England during the period), he will not understand its implications. Such a passage could well serve to generate questions useful in the process of inquiry, but a wide variety of outside resource materials would be needed in order to undertake the process profitably, since the text does not explicitly state the significant issues involved or provide most of the knowledge needed to deal with them.

As any high school history teacher knows, American history textbooks usually contain chapters on the rise of industry and the growth of urban culture; chapters on the development of our political system; dictionary definitions of pool, trust, holding company, recall, and referendum; and many excellent graphic presentations of changes in demography, crop production, and so forth. Yet they include little explicit social, political, or economic analysis that is distinct from historical description.

However, there are certain exceptions to this observation, which illustrate the benefits of including more social science knowledge. The following is a rare example of a direct reference to economic theory:

> To understand why farmers thought this would help, we should keep in mind that the value of money changes according to the quantity in circulation. Increase the quantity in relation to the amount of goods and services available, and the dollar drops in value. Prices therefore go up. . . . We may express the relationship in an equation:
>
> $$\text{Prices} = \frac{\text{Quantity of money in circulation}}{\text{Quantity of goods and services}}$$
>
> (Gavian, Hamm, and Freidel, 8, p. 485.)

Although our economy is no longer quite so simple, this brief bit of economic theory is potentially a very useful analytical tool.

Of the authors being considered, Todd and Curti (15) are most sympathetic to the notion that history is in reality the study of society in all its complexity. Throughout their book one finds key developments in technology illustrated in detail. Thirteen of the chapters carry the subtitle "Changing Ways of American Life," indicating that much of the book deals with aspects of society other than political history. While the chapters include conventional descriptive material, much attention is given to the explanation of cultural changes. For example, in Chapter Twenty-four the plight of the farmer in the late 1800's is analyzed in considerably more detail than one usually finds in history textbooks. But even in such cases, and there are many in the book, the generalizations and theories upon which the explanation depends are not stated. It seems to be at this point that most practicing historians draw the line between history and the social sciences. In their analysis of historical events Todd and Curti make use of much of the information considered to be part of sociology, economics, and geography. But because such social science knowledge is not explicitly discussed in the text, the student can neither learn it directly from the book nor have it at his disposal to apply in the process of inquiry. This information will have to come from the teacher, from supplementary materials, or from other courses. At this time we lack evidence on whether it is better for the student's total learning process within the social studies curriculum if he acquires his social science knowledge from outside sources or from history textbooks. But since our goal is to evaluate the adequacy of textbooks as aids in inquiry, the significant point is that such knowledge seems to be essential for social inquiry and is lacking in the textbooks reviewed.

Conclusion

There are many possible objectives for American history courses. We have assumed that a worthy and feasible goal is the promotion of inquiry, as defined in this volume. If the textbooks used in them are to be of maximum value in promoting and conducting inquiry, they must focus on historical or contemporary issues, emphasize interpretation and analysis, clearly indicate the theoretical assumptions of the authors, and include at least the fundamental social science concepts, generalizations, and theories needed to analyze and understand the historical events under consideration.

As would be expected, individual books vary with respect to how well they satisfy these criteria. The overall judgment must be that they are of limited value to the teacher interested in promoting inquiry. Most significant is the fact that the authors generally tell the reader what happened rather than probing beneath the surface of events to help him fathom why a particular course of events took place and not something else.

At the same time, this analysis demonstrates that it is entirely possible to produce a textbook for high school American history that satisfies at least three of the four criteria. There are excellent examples in present books of the kind of text material that would promote inquiry in the classroom. The hardest criterion to satisfy is the inclusion of a theoretical framework indicating the critical assumptions of the author. However, I did discover at least one textbook that successfully meets this criterion. Moreover, it is likely that if an author took the other three criteria seriously, he would continually reveal his assumptions and biases in the process of treating historical events more analytically.

Selected Bibliography

1. ALEXANDER, ALBERT, "The Gray Flannel Cover on the American History Textbook," *Social Education*, 24(Jan., 1960), 11–14.

2. BILLINGTON, RAY ALLEN, et al., *The Historian's Contribution to Anglo-American Misunderstanding*, Hobbs, Dormand, New York, 1966.

3. BOLSTER, ARTHUR S., JR., "History, Historians, and the Secondary School Curriculum," *Harvard Educational Review*, 31 (Winter, 1962), 39–65.

4. BRUUN, GEOFFREY, AND HAINES, MILLICENT, *The World Story*, Heath, Boston, 1963.

5. CANFIELD, LEON H., AND WILDER, HOWARD B., *The Making of Modern America*, Teacher's Edition, Houghton Mifflin, Boston, 1966.

6. COCHRAN, THOMAS C., *The Inner Revolution: Essays on the Social Sciences in History*, Harper & Row, New York, 1964.

7. FENTON, EDWIN, *Teaching the New Social Studies in Secondary Schools: An Inductive Approach*, Holt, Rinehart and Winston, New York, 1966.

8. GAVIAN, RUTH W., HAMM, WILLIAM R., AND FREIDEL, FRANK, *United States History*, Revised Edition, Heath, Boston, 1965.

9. GRAFF, HENRY F., AND KROUT, JOHN A., *The Adventure of the American People*, Rand McNally, Chicago, 1965.

10. KRUG, MARK M., " 'Safe' Textbooks and Citizenship Education," *School Review*, 68 (Winter, 1960), 463–80.

11. LYND, ROBERT S., *Knowledge for What?* Princeton University Press, Princeton, N.J., 1939.

12. MASSIALAS, BYRON G., AND COX, C. BENJAMIN, *Inquiry in Social Studies*, McGraw-Hill, New York, 1966.

13. OLIVER, DONALD W., AND SHAVER, JAMES P., *Teaching Public Issues in the High School*, Houghton Mifflin, Boston, 1966.

14. PATTERSON, FRANKLIN, "Social Science and the New Curriculum," *American Behavioral Scientist*, 6 (Nov., 1962), 28–32.

15. TODD, LEWIS PAUL, AND CURTI, MERLE, *Rise of the American Nation*, Second Edition, Harcourt, Brace & World, New York, 1966.

16. WADE, RICHARD C., WILDER, HOWARD B., AND WADE, LOUISE C., *A History of the United States*, Teacher's Edition, Houghton Mifflin, Boston, 1966.

CHAPTER 8

Economics

Progress in Its Teaching

LAWRENCE E. METCALF
WILLIAM D. RADER

Heightened Interest in High School Economics

In recent years professional economists have become interested in the high school and its efforts to teach economics. Although the majority of economists continue to believe that economics ought not to be taught in high school at all, a growing number who have rejected this belief are actively engaged in efforts to improve high school and college offerings in economics. Much of the effort at both levels is motivated by the simple desire to recruit into economics some of the more able students. But there is also a genuine aim of raising the level of economic understanding among the public at large.

Interest in the high school program has taken four forms. First, economists have tried to define in some detail the content of economics. Second, they have recommended a teaching method that relies upon analysis, rather than expository descriptions, to develop student understanding of economics. Third, economists have studied textbooks and other instructional materials to determine the extent to which such materials present sound economic content. Finally, they have developed a test of economic understandings.

THE TASK FORCE REPORT

The definition of content that has received the most support from economists is to be found in a national task force report entitled *Economic Education in the Schools* (3), written by a group of economists and educators. Although it has been criticized for following too closely the contours of the college introductory course, the report nevertheless recommends content that is significantly different from what is usually covered in high school. The report suggests an emphasis on concepts and theory without neglecting factual data or the history and development of institutions. Both micro- and macroanalysis are strongly endorsed along with study of economic controversies. The report strongly condemns the kind of consumer education that fails to point up the effects of consumer choices upon the economy as a whole. A general preference for analysis over description in course content runs throughout the report.

The content recommended in the report is divided into four major parts. Part one deals with the fact of scarcity, the nature of an economic system, and its four functions: deciding what to produce, in what quantities, by what combinations of resources, and for whose consumption. Major attention is given to the free market as a theoretical model. Discussion of the effects upon a free market of monopolies and oligopolies on the one hand and of public policy on the other is also considered essential.

Part two focuses on the problems of economic growth and stability in mature and underdeveloped economies. High school students should learn what these concepts mean and how we measure both. They should learn how economic growth affects the general standard of living and how instability affects different people. Discussion of the forces that determine national income and total products is also recommended as well as the role of fiscal and monetary policies in fostering growth and stability.

Part three of the report recommends that students be taught how income is distributed. Is the common belief that the rich are fit and the poor unfit a valid explanation of why some people have more income than others, who gets how much income and why? How do labor unions affect wages? Is income more equally distributed now than in the past? And how does the distribution of income affect the economy as a whole? It is recommended that special attention be given to the farm problem in this context. This problem confronts students with a conflict between economic freedom and efficiency on the one hand and economic justice on the other.

The final section recommends a study of comparative economic systems. High school students should study as objectively as possible such systems as communism, socialism, and capitalism and thus examine their prejudices. A distinction is to be made between pure systems, which exist only in textbooks, and actual ones. All actual systems exemplify a mixed economy, but the mix varies from one existing system to another.

This, then, is the content that most economists now recommend. It is regarded by many educators and most economists as teachable in high school and as essential to the general education of citizens. Economic content would be taught partly through courses in history, government, and problems of American democracy, but a required high school course in economics is also considered necessary. This would mean that teachers whose preparation did not include formal exposure to economics as a discipline would undoubtedly have to receive in-service instruction in this field.

ECONOMISTS REVIEW TEXTBOOKS

In an education system that includes more than 20,000 high schools it is not easy to determine what actually occurs in secondary-grade classrooms. Direct observation in addition to posing the problem of sampling runs against the problems of financing such research and dealing with the inhibitions and role-playing of teachers who find themselves the subject of professional observation. Economists have tried to solve this problem by making a study of high school textbooks. This approach assumes that most teachers are still textbook-oriented in their classroom operations and that the widely used textbooks accurately reflect the content of economics that is taught. A committee of the American Economic Association (17) proceeded on these assumptions, and its findings are now available in a famous report.

A study was made of selected high school textbooks in economics, social problems, and United States history. For each course eight textbooks were studied. Four were "leading" textbooks, as determined by sales volume, and four were selected without reference to volume of sales. A total of twenty-four books were analyzed. The committee making this study used the report of the national task force as its content guide. On the basis of this conception of content the following criteria were established by the committee:

1. The principal objective of high school education in economics should be good citizenship, not the preparation of students for a college major in economics.

2. Economics is a social science and emphasis should be placed on the interdependence of decision-makers and the operation of economic systems, not on the solution of problems of the individual.

3. The economic understanding sought should concern vital matters, not trivia; and the coverage of these should be balanced, including (as examples) macro- and microeconomics, the generation of change in a system as well as its static operation, and international as well as domestic problems.

4. The approach to economic matters should be essentially analytical, though larded heavily with factual and descriptive material on economic institutions and their development.

5. The nature of value judgments should be explained; whenever relevant they should be identified; and the role they play in shaping economic systems, policies, and controversies should be clearly stated. Controversial issues should not be avoided but used to stimulate interest and to distinguish between facts, value judgments, and impartial analysis as these apply to vital matters.

6. Factual and analytical errors should be kept to a minimum.
(Special Textbook Study Committee, 17, p. viii.)

The committee concluded that high school students whose knowledge of economics was confined to the content of the textbooks reviewed would be "quite unprepared to cope understandingly with most problems of economic public policy." This judgment was supported by abundant evidence that many significant topics were omitted, while others received unwarranted attention, that routine description took the place of analysis, that value judgments were rarely identified or examined, and that errors of fact and analysis frequently marred a presentation.

In a particularly stringent conclusion the committee noted:

The real offense against understanding committed by these books, however, is that the endless cataloguing of facts is often regarded as an end in itself. Can a student be said to understand the operation of an economy when he knows the routine operations of banks but nothing about the role of money, credit, and interest; when he knows legislation acts but nothing about their purposes, effects, and limitations; when he knows about miles of track but nothing about the impact of changes in transportation on relative prices and resource allocation? In short when he knows trivial institutional detail but little of its significance for the structure and functioning of the economic system? The facts are that these texts do not employ simplifying assumptions or discuss their usefulness in stimulating clear thinking; they do not pose or develop hypotheses and test them with evidence; few chains of reasoning are presented and these often stop short of meaningful conclusions. "What" is detailed; "why" is ignored. (*Ibid.,* p. xi.)

This was the textbook situation around 1960. This study was followed by two studies of supplementary instructional material. It was assumed that even textbook-oriented teachers would make occasional use of such material and that it would be beneficial to such teachers to identify the more useful material. A fair appraisal of the content situation must include a reference to these two reports.

STUDY MATERIALS FOR ECONOMIC EDUCATION

In October, 1961, the first report on supplementary material was issued by the Materials Evaluation Committee (19). Chaired by Lewis Wagner, the committee examined materials available to supplement textbooks. Of the nearly 7,000 items examined, 97 were recommended as satisfying the criteria that the committee established. These basic criteria were: "(1) Were the materials genuinely concerned with economic matters? (2) Were they analytical in nature? and (3) Were they appropriate for high school use?"

The committee also considered questions concerning how and where the selected materials might be used. Some were designated as suitable for general use; others were suggested as useful for advanced or specialized treatment for certain students or for background reading, committee study, directed student research, or individual student reports. The Study Materials report was divided into four parts, categorizing suitable materials under these headings: production and its control through markets; distribution of income; inflation, recession, and stabilization policies; and special areas of study that included agriculture, public finance, economic security, international economics, economic growth, economic systems, and historical approach to economic matters.

In October, 1963, the report of the Second Materials Evaluation Committee was issued. It added sixty-five new titles to the original list of ninety-seven. Both these reports are now contained in the previously cited report (19).

The chief conclusion that one can draw from these two reports is that a teacher could strengthen his content by making wise use of supplementary material. The 162 items recommended by the committee represented in its judgment the best available; many other items were judged to be good, although they were not mentioned in the final report. It is clear that the content made available by this kind of material is vastly superior to the textbooks available at that time. There is considerable reason to doubt, however, that a typical social studies teacher, undertrained in economics, could be expected to choose wisely from the mountains of available material. More than likely, he would through ignorance or error use some very inferior material, much of it guilty of special pleading.

THE COMMITTEE FOR MEASUREMENT OF ECONOMIC UNDERSTANDING

Another committee was established in 1962 for the purpose of assisting school systems with the task of measuring the accomplishment of objectives in economic education. The Committee for Measurement of Economic Understanding was appointed by the Joint Council on Economic Education. Its chairman was John M. Stalnaker, and its task was to prepare two forms of a test of economic understanding for students in secondary schools and colleges. The report of the national task force furnished the guidelines for the fifty questions constituting each form of the test (20). Three members of the national task force, including its chairman, George L. Bach, served on the measurement committee. All the test items were directly related to the recommendations of the task force report.

Impact of Task Force Report

In 1966 two economists at the University of Virginia reviewed nine economics textbooks, eight of which had been published or revised since the task force report (21). It was their conclusion that the new editions did not appear to be a significant improvement over earlier editions, although some changes had been made. They did not state their objections in detail, but in general they found macroanalysis was not as well developed as microanalysis. In addition they observed that "the amount of time available for teaching economic theory and analysis is further reduced by the custom of including 'consumer economics' in these textbooks."

The authors of this chapter have not made an exhaustive survey of textbooks, but that the task force has had some impact appears to be the case. We examined three textbooks (5, 8, 16), using the following list of concepts from the task force (3) as our base:

aggregate demand
antitrust laws
balance of payments
balance of trade
balance sheet
bank deposits
business cycle
capital formation
closed shops
collective bargaining
corporate income tax
corporations
demand, supply, price
depression, inflation
diminishing returns
division of labor
economic growth
economic security
efficiency
equation of exchange
exchange
factors of production
farm problem
featherbedding
Federal Reserve System
fiscal policy
government budget
government expenditures

gross national product
income from productive services
interdependence
international specialization
investment
labor unions
market, competition, profit
money
money and real income
money costs
money creation
monopoly
national income
old-age insurance
opportunity cost
other economic systems
payroll tax
per capita product
personal distribution of income
personal income tax
price level
private security measures
productivity
profit and loss statement
property tax
public debt
public utility
real wages, money wages

sales tax	strikes, picketing
saving	tariffs
scarcity	taxes and resource allocation
social security	underdeveloped areas
specialization	unemployment insurance

Our investigation has revealed that nearly all of the concepts and major institutions are included in the three textbooks we examined. This is a marked improvement over the findings of the Special Textbook Study Committee of the American Economic Association, as reported earlier in this chapter, and many of the concepts are analytical in nature. There are two important concepts in the report, however, that are not discussed in the books examined.

The first of these is the equation of exchange. This concept interrelates the supply of money, its velocity of circulation, the level of output, and the price level through an equation $(MV = PQ)$, where M is the supply of money, V is its velocity of circulation, Q is the level of output, and P is the price level. Understanding this equation will help a student to understand that there is a connection between the amount of money and the level of spending. He will also be assisted in understanding that changes in spending can lead either to increases in output, to rises in prices, or to both at the same time.

OPPORTUNITY COST

The second of these is the concept of opportunity cost. It was considered so important that two full paragraphs in the brief task force report were devoted to a discussion of it.

In economics itself, the central problem is economizing—making the best use of the scarce productive resources available to us to satisfy our many wants—for resources to satisfy our wants are limited in amount and therefore are not free for the asking. Hence we must *choose* among the possible alternative uses to which these scarce resources can be put—whether to save or to spend, whether to spend our incomes on one object or on another, whether to tax ourselves more in order to finance government services, or to tax less and leave more for private spending. One of the essential lessons of economics is that we cannot have our cake and eat it too.

Given this overriding element of scarcity, the core of most economic issues is the need to make intelligent choices among competing
alternatives. This process of choosing among alternatives does not
always involve, directly and obviously, the problem of coping with
the fact of scarcity. But indirectly and ultimately the problem is
always there. It is the essence of economics that we have to think
and plan and work to make what we have go as far as possible toward
satisfying the objectives we consider most important. (National
Task Force on Economic Education, 3, p. 14.)

None of the three textbooks we examined list "opportunity
cost" in their indexes, and none discuss the concept. The first page of
a more recently published text (10) quotes the task force report on
the fact of scarcity but fails to mention the "central" concept of
opportunity cost.

It is difficult to determine the rationale for excluding discussion
of this concept. Do textbook authors regard the concept as too difficult for high school students to learn? An elementary school economics project, on which one author of this chapter is working, has
demonstrated that the concept of opportunity cost can be taught in
unadulterated form to sixth-grade students (9). It should be pointed
out that the economic term itself is not introduced to students in
this program, but students can understand an economic concept
without learning the economist's language.

COMPARATIVE ADVANTAGE

The Social Studies Curriculum Center at Syracuse University (11)
recently published a list of thirty-four social science concepts considered appropriate for elementary and secondary programs in social
studies. Of the eighteen substantive concepts on the list, five may
be classified as economic concepts: comparative advantage, scarcity,
input and output, saving, and the modified market economy. All but
the first are included to some degree in economics textbooks. Comparative advantage, however, is discussed only briefly in a few books
and not at all in others. In defense of the textbooks, however, it
should be stated that the task force has not included this concept
in its list of minimum understandings. And James Calderwood's
excellent explanation and further development of the task force list
of basic concepts (2) include a reference to absolute advantage but
contain no discussion of comparative advantage. The following quo-

tation presents what we consider a satisfactory definition of comparative advantage:

> The condition which exists when one nation or region can produce each of two products at less cost than some other nation or region and the relative saving in the case of one of these products is greater than in the case of the second. The nation or region thus favored is said to enjoy an absolute advantage in the case of both products over the nation or region not so favored and to enjoy a comparative advantage in the case of the product where the relative saving is greater. For example, nation A can produce both sugar and automobiles at less cost than can nation B. Nation A thus has an absolute advantage over nation B in the case of both of these products. But the relative saving of nation A over nation B in the production of automobiles is greater than the saving which nation A enjoys over nation B in the case of sugar. Hence nation A has a comparative as well as an absolute advantage over nation B in the production of automobiles. (Sloan and Zurcher, 15, pp. 69–70.)

In their discussion of the importance of this concept Price, Smith, and Hickman wrote:

> It is impossible for any individual, political party, or nation to dictate life to such an extent as to assure total acquiescence to all its desires by all outside forces. Compromise, adjustment, and resolution of conflicts by other means become an essential part of facing reality.
>
> When conflicts arise there often comes a time when advantages must be weighed. It even becomes advisable to permit an opponent to obtain advantages in resources, time, geographical position, morale, or public opinion in return for advantages considered of greater value in gaining a final objective.
>
> During the Second World War the Allies decided it was to their advantage to ship copper (indirectly) to Germany in return for desperately needed ball bearings. China was a major source for tungsten steel (required for armor plate and armor piercing shells) during the Korean War. On the basis of comparative advantage the British sold trucks to the Chinese in return for shipments of tungsten.
>
> Comparative advantage extends from the child deciding whether to trade a sand bucket for a sand shovel while constructing a castle on the beach to decisions regarding the exchange of prisoners of war. Without an understanding of this concept, a citizen is ill equipped to face a world in which no one ever does achieve "total victory." Students should understand this concept in order to appreciate the

need for long-range consideration of goals and methods. (Price, Smith, and Hickman, 11, p. 11.)

The basic nature of this concept is also documented by two economists, Alchian and Allen (1), who have written that *the economic principle of specialization depends upon comparative advantage,* which is a name for differences in the marginal cost of production.

The following passage is one of the most complete textbook descriptions of the concept; all others fall considerably short of this:

> Often one country has an *absolute advantage* over many others in the production of some things. Its production costs in man-hours and other inputs are clearly lower. India, for example, can produce tea more cheaply than Canada could. Climate and the presence of natural resources are more favorable in some cases than in others. International trade flows in response to such differences in production costs.
>
> More complicated factors creating what is called *comparative advantage* also influence the flows of trade. The people in one country may be able to produce several things more cheaply than the people in other lands. Nevertheless importing one or more of those things may be wise. Why? A nation's own productive resources can then be concentrated on producing the goods or services in which it has the *greatest* advantage.
>
> Suppose that a surgeon were a better typist than anyone he could hire. Would he be wise to do his own typing? Obviously not. He can use his time more productively as a surgeon. Similarly a whole economy, like the surgeon, will prosper best by concentrating its efforts where they are *most* productive. It will then export some of the output and import things which others produce even if it might have produced some of this output with fewer man-hours or other inputs. (Goodman and Harriss, 5, pp. 394–95.)

The above quotation is from a chapter on international trade. It represents a fairly adequate treatment of the concept. But we wish to reiterate that most of the books we surveyed did not treat the concept with this degree of clarity and completeness.

Since the publication of the task force report, then, there has been a slight improvement in the content of economics textbooks. The emphasis on analysis has increased, although descriptive chapters still remain in most texts. The major stumbling block to continued improvement appears to be the inclusion of consumer economics topics. A typical example of this is a chapter on the importance of credit in a leading text. Five questions are posed at the beginning of the chapter:

What makes a person a good credit risk?

Can you sometimes make a profit in business by borrowing?

Does the availability of credit help or hurt the average person?

Do you always have to pay more if you buy on the installment plan?

Does mass production depend on easy credit?

(Smith, 16, p. 237.)

Most texts still find it necessary to include a chapter on the forms and functions of business, discussing such topics as owning a business, proprietorships and partnerships, and the importance of small business (see, for example, 8). Students are introduced to an organizational chart of a typical large corporation, balance sheets, the advantages and disadvantages of partnerships, and the differences between stocks and bonds. Factual information such as this fills many pages in economics textbooks. The case for its removal may be made in term of opportunity cost: a textbook designed for a one-semester course can have only a limited number of pages. Thus the cost of factual or descriptive information is the economic analysis that cannot be included because of it.

One of the best-written and most analytic of the texts (10) was published as a consequence of the task force report. The first chapter places economics in perspective as one of the social sciences. It briefly but clearly discusses the use of the scientific method in solving problems and developing new knowledge. The book includes eight case analyses, inviting students to think about the interpretation of statistics and graphs, price-fixing, fiscal policy, and foreign trade. However, the book treats comparative advantage all too briefly, as the following complete quotation should make clear:

> From the illustration just used it does not follow that the profits of Swiss watchmaking firms are as high as those of American washing-machine manufacturers. But it would be safe to assume that the Swiss —due to the availability of highly skilled watchmakers and their long tradition of excellence in this craft—are making a better income by producing watches than they would if they turned to manufacturing washing machines instead. This is an illustration of what is known

as the law of comparative advantage.   (Mortenson, Krider, and Sampson, 10, pp. 406–07.)

ECONOMICS AS FIXED CONTENT

The body of economic content is now very well developed, and all of the textbooks examined are organized logically around a defensible economic framework. But a major shortcoming of all the texts is that they present the economic concepts as if they were fixed and unchanging. For example, all the books examined discuss the classical concept of utility. This late-nineteenth-century concept has caused economists difficulty, for they do not know how to measure it. However, a new theory about improvements in well-being has evolved— namely, indifference curve analysis, which permits economists to plot indifference curves on graphs. By hypothesizing that an individual will have certain goods preferences and will prefer a combination of goods that lies on a higher indifference curve to a combination that lies on a lower curve, economists can analyze the demand for products more precisely. Yet no high school economics textbook we have examined even mentions to students that economists have complemented classical utility theory with indifference curve analysis. We are not arguing for a full treatment of this concept in textbooks, but we do think that students should not be misled into thinking that economists' theory of utility is complete by referring only to classical theory.

The textbooks seldom encourage students to question or to inquire. They present the discipline of economics as if inquiry were complete and economists were agreed on most, if not all, issues. But students need only read newspapers and periodicals regularly to be aware that economists do indeed differ with each other.

While nearly all of the examined books list a few outside references, none take full advantage of the growing collection of paperbacks relevant to economics. High school teachers should know of two principal sources. The first is *Paperbound Books in Economics* (14),[1] which lists books in fourteen subject categories ranging from agricultural economics to theory. The second book is entitled *Suggestions for a Basic Economics Library* (7).[2] It has a broader scope

[1]This book is available for $.50 from the New York State Council on Economic Education, the State University of New York at Albany.
[2]This book is available for $.75 from the Joint Council on Economic Education, 1212 Avenue of the Americas, New York City.

than *Paperbound Books*, listing clothbound books, reference works, and relevant periodicals. A copy of this publication should be part of every high school social science curriculum collection.

New Programs in Economics

With the financial assistance of the United States Office of Education two economics courses have been developed and tried out. The first course, designed by Professor Meno Lovenstein, teaches economics at the ninth-grade level. Under his direction the Ohio State Social Studies Curriculum Center has produced student and teacher materials which are discussed in a recent report of the Lincoln Filene Center of Tufts University (12). These materials were field-tested in the state of Ohio and are in the process of revision.

A second course at the twelfth-grade level (Econ 12) was developed at San Jose State College (13). The principal investigators, Suzanne Wiggins and John Sperling, intended that the one-semester course be taught by average social studies teachers to students at all levels of achievement and of scholastic ability.

The principal investigators call Econ 12 "a teaching system." It consists of three parts:

1. The Econ 12 course designed around specific behavioral and experimental objectives and including both teacher and student materials. Teacher materials include a lesson plan consisting of carefully worked out model lessons for the complete course.
2. Course evaluation instruments, for teacher and student, to determine the extent to which the course objectives have been achieved.
3. The teacher training program, which includes (1) a training course in the rationale and proper use of the Econ 12 course and (2) a teacher supervision procedure to aid teachers teaching the Econ 12 course for the first time.

(Office of Education Project, 13, p. 4.)

The Econ 12 teaching system includes both audio-visual and student materials. Overhead transparencies, filmstrips, and three films have been produced. Among the student materials are worksheets, programmed instruction booklets, a readings book, a short text, and tests and examinations.

The tentative course outline consists of three basic and four optional units. The basic units are listed and described below.

> Unit I (6 weeks) introduces the student to basic social relationships studied in economics and the framework of ideas economists use to study these relationships. (Office of Education Project, 13, p. 1.)

> Unit II (7–9 weeks) has as its purpose to describe how the American market system allocates scarce resources and distributes income and to investigate the extent to which the system works in conformity with our national goals. To accomplish this objective, it is necessary for students to understand the job prices perform in a purely competitive economy, the effect of concentration of market power on prices and on resource allocation, the role of government in regulating markets and industries in the United States, and the effect of market forces and government actions on income and wealth distribution. (*Ibid.*, p. 3.)

> Unit III (4–6 weeks) intends to provide the necessary theoretical framework and institutional facts to analyze the success of the American economy in achieving three fundamental goals: full employment, a steadily increasing standard of living, and increasing personal economic security. (*Ibid.*, p. 7.)

The Econ 12 teaching system is designed to be related to a structure of the discipline of economics and represents one of the most promising new economics courses currently under development. It has evolved its own set of behavioral objectives, defined as "statements of required student performance of some written task and the conditions under which students perform the task" (13).

This chapter would not be complete without including some discussion of the far-reaching curriculum development program of the Joint Council on Economic Education. The Developmental Economic Education Program (DEEP) has reached twenty-seven public and two parochial school systems in the United States. DEEP aims to introduce economic education into the social studies curriculum for the first through twelfth grades. Each participating school system has appointed a coordinator of economic education. Each school system will develop its own curriculum and its own teacher and student materials, and each will provide in-service training for teachers.

Conclusion

Economists more than any other scholarly group have had a plan, an organization, and the financial resources for an attack upon certain deficiencies in public school curriculum. It is clear from our cursory survey that their efforts have not been in vain. There is no doubt that textbooks have improved somewhat with respect to content and economic analysis. But much remains to be done. We do not yet have the content we need if inquiry is to be fostered and if students are not to waste their time on sheerly descriptive material.

In the next generation economics textbooks will probably become more analytical and more sophisticated. This must happen if economics is not to go the way of the American history course, presenting students with essentially the same story year after year in several successive grades. The discipline of economics is beginning to acquire a place in the elementary grades. Those who are skeptical need only visit progressive elementary schools throughout the nation. They will discover locally or nationally developed curricula that did not exist a few years ago, at a level of sophistication that is at least equal to the present level in many high school economics courses. The import of this trend is clear: curriculum coordinators, high school teachers, and textbook publishers must begin now to prepare materials that will take into account the new sophistication of students who have learned price theory and national income analysis in elementary grades. If high schools can catch up with elementary schools, the next step will be for colleges to catch up with the high schools.

Selected Bibliography

1. ALCHIAN, ARMEN A., AND ALLEN, WILLIAM R., *University Economics*, Wadsworth, Belmont, Calif., 1964.

2. CALDERWOOD, JAMES, *Teacher's Guide to Developmental Economic Education Program, Part One, Economic Ideas and Concepts*, Joint Council on Economic Education, New York, 1964.

3. ECONOMIC EDUCATION IN THE SCHOOLS, National Task Force on Economic Education, Committee for Economic Development, New York (Sept., 1961).

4. FRANKEL, M. L., *Economic Education*, The Center for Applied Research in Education, New York, 1965.

5. GOODMAN, KENNARD E., AND HARRISS, C. LOWELL, *Economics*, Ginn, Boston, 1963.

6. KOURMADAS, JOHN F., (ed.), "Economic Understanding," *The Bulletin of the National Association of Secondary School Principals*, 49 (Nov., 1965), 3–148.

7. LEAMER, LAWRENCE E., AND GUYTON, PERCY L., *Suggestions for a Basic Economics Library*, Joint Council on Economic Education, New York, 1965.

8. LINDHOLM, RICHARD W., AND DRISCOLL, PAUL, *Our American Economy*, Harcourt, Brace & World, New York, 1964.

9. METCALF, LAWRENCE E., "Teaching Economic Concepts in the Social Studies," *The Councilor*, 21 (Mar., 1960), 24–31.

10. MORTENSON, WILLIAM P., KRIDER, DONALD T., AND SAMPSON, ROY J., *Understanding Our Economy*, Houghton Mifflin, Boston, 1964.

11. PRICE, ROY A., SMITH, GERALD R., AND HICKMAN, WARREN L., *Major Concepts for the Social Studies*, The Social Studies Curriculum Center, Syracuse University, Syracuse, N.Y. (Nov., 1965).

12. NEW FRONTIERS IN ECONOMIC EDUCATION, a report on the Conference on Economic Education held by the Lincoln Filene Center at Tufts University, Medford, Mass. (Nov. 11 and 12, 1965).

13. A PROGRESS REPORT OF ECON 12, design and evaluation of a twelfth-grade course in the principles of economics, Office of Education Project H153 (May, 1966).

14. SAYRE, J. WOODROW, *Paperbound Books in Economics*, New York State Council on Economic Education, State University of New York, Albany, 1965.

15. SLOAN, HAROLD S., AND ZURCHER, ARNOLD J., *A Dictionary of Economics*, Barnes and Noble, New York, 1961.

16. SMITH, AUGUSTUS H., *Economics for Our Times*, McGraw-Hill, St. Louis, Mo., 1963.

17. SPECIAL TEXTBOOK STUDY COMMITTEE OF THE COMMITTEE ON ECONOMIC EDUCATION OF THE AMERICAN ECONOMIC ASSOCIATION, "Economics in the Schools," *American Economic Review*, 53, Part 2 (Mar., 1963), 1–27.

18. STIGLER, GEORGE J., "Elementary Economic Education," *American Economic Review*, 53 (May, 1963), 653–59.

19. STUDY MATERIALS FOR ECONOMIC EDUCATION IN THE SCHOOLS, report of Materials Evaluation Committees, Committee for Economic Development, 1963.

20. TEST OF ECONOMIC UNDERSTANDING, Committee for Measurement of Economic Understanding, Forms A and B, Science Research Associates, Chicago, 1963.

21. TULLOCK, GORDON, AND JOHNSON, ROBERT, "Economics," *The University Bookman*, 7 (Autumn, 1966), 15–23.

CHAPTER 9

American Government

We Are the Greatest!

BYRON G. MASSIALAS

Political science entered a new era after World War II. This era has been characterized by an emphasis on the behavioral approach in the study of government, an orientation that may be traced to Lasswell and Herring. Their work was seminal in the renaissance of political science because it pressed forward "empirical inquiries illuminating the concept of politics as interpersonal and intergroup power relations in society" (39). The new mood of the profession was clearly stated in the opening paragraph of Lasswell's famous book *Politics: Who Gets What, When, How* (37): "The study of politics is the study of influence and the influential. The science of politics states conditions; the philosophy of politics justifies prefer-ences. This book, restricted to political analysis, declares no prefer-ences. It states conditions." The new approach called for a radical departure from the institutional, legalistic, and philosophical ap-proach, in which common-sense and descriptive methods of research were often used. According to the new approach government was studied both as an institution and a process (involving attitudes, be-havior, resources, and strategies of men seeking to influence policy) through the use of explicit theoretical models and scientific investigative techniques. Kirkpatrick, a well-known political scientist, assessed the impact of behaviorism on traditional political science in this succinct statement:

> They (the behaviorists) called attention to the lack of recognition on the part of political scientists of the developments in the other sciences of man, particularly psychology, sociology, anthropology, psychiatry; they were unhappy about the bulging inventory of facts that had no relation to a comprehensive theory; they noted the extent to which untenable assumptions and premises influenced and distorted findings; they criticized the failure to make better use of statistics and the statistical method; they called attention to the amount of so-called political science that served no function except to bolster the value preferences of the author; they made explicit the low level of generalization of findings; they pointed to the incomparability of much of the data collected; they made clear the difficulty of using the data of political science as it existed for accurate prediction. (Kirkpatrick, 33, p. 3.)

Although the debate between the "traditionalists" and the "behaviorists" on the proper method for studying government still continues in one form or another (see, for example, 36 and 40), there is some evidence to suggest "a resurgence of a classical balance: speculations informed and controlled by a deep understanding of the hard empirical facts" (28). The result is "a stronger political science, chastised by the agonizing introspection, made more self-conscious about its methods of inquiry," and reunited toward the common goal of developing a systematic body of theory about the political world. But in their attempt to avoid subjective and uncritical moralizing about government and politics, some political scientists have tried to exclude from their discourse (inasmuch as this can be done consciously) the examination of values and value-based policy alternatives and have avoided taking a position on public issues. In the work previously cited Harold Lasswell came very close to positivism when he explicitly stated that the study of politics does not justify preferences.[1] The role of values in political science will be further discussed later.

Given the current state of this field, let us see how teaching ob-

---

[1]One could argue that Lasswell's statement is largely prescriptive and does imply a value preference. In a recent publication Lasswell seems to have experienced a change of heart, because he suggested that "political scientists should use their knowledge to help solve public problems." See Peter Woll, "Recent Developments in Political Science," *Social Education*, 30 (Mar., 1966), p. 168.

jectives have been influenced by the various orientations to political science.

The Teaching Goals of Political Science

A mature profession continually defines and redefines its teaching and research goals in the light of new developments in the field. Since the turn of the century there have been five studies conducted under the auspices of the American Political Science Association that were concerned with the teaching of government. The first report, published in the 1908 *Proceedings* of the Association, was primarily concerned with precollegiate instruction in civics, and it recommended that "civics be taught earlier in grade schools and more intensively in the secondary schools" (47). The 1916 report, entitled *The Teaching of Government*, "was both modern and prophetic." It emphasized "the need to effect a closer working relationship between social science teaching at college and high school levels, called attention to the desirability of making the subject a separate discipline, and [released] it from dependence on history departments." It also outlined the direction of the new curriculum (14). The most important breakthrough that resulted from this report was a declaration of independence by American political scientists, who until then were largely treated as an appendage to departments of history or economics.

The 1923 report, based on a survey of political science conducted by Charles Merriam, traced the development of the field through four stages: (1) the use of a priori and deductive reasoning until 1850; (2) an emphasis on the historical and comparative method from 1850 to 1900; (3) a tendency since 1900 to employ empirical techniques of investigation—observation, survey, and measurement; and (4) a corresponding tendency to incorporate social psychology in political science.[2] Furthermore, the report "emphasized the need for political scientists to team up with other social scientists in an attack on common problems" (14). Although the primary focus of this report was on research, it had substantial impact on the content and teaching of political science, giving them a behavioral focus.

[2]As will be pointed out later, some of what passes for political science, government, or civics in the American high schools has not gone beyond the stage of historical emphasis.

The fourth comprehensive report of the field was issued by the Reed Committee (55) as a *Supplement* to the *American Political Science Review* in 1930. The main recommendation of the committee was that it form a standing policy committee with subcommittees on research, political education, publication, and personnel. William Munro, who wrote one section of the report, called attention to the "elaborate disintegration of the subject" because specialized areas within political science were multiplying too fast to be integrated conceptually and organizationally. Charles Beard, another contributor to the report, made a plea to teachers of political science "to stimulate imagination, to encourage the remorseless use of the Socratic *elenchus*, to stretch the range of student interest, and to promote contemplation, meditation, and future-reaching speculation." Needless to say, this plea is as timely in the 1960's as it was in the 1930's.

The most recent report on the state of political science was issued in 1951 under the title *Goals for Political Science* (14). Based on questionnaires and interviews, it sought "to discover means of improving the teaching of political science." The committee discovered that among American political scientists the goal of training for intelligent citizenship was of predominant interest and was given primary emphasis; the main difficulty, however, was in defining effective citizenship and developing programs that would best attain it.[3] The committee defined intelligent and effective citizenship by depicting a model citizen "who is politically sophisticated, who is familiar with the structure and dynamics of his government, who is 'sold' on the attributes and values of democracy, and who is willing to take action individually or collectively to preserve and develop democracy." Furthermore, the committee placed emphasis on the skills of critical judgment and propaganda analysis. It also recognized that formal training in political science could not be effective without taking into consideration other segments of the culture that influence the decisions of citizens. Other parts of the report dealt with teaching international relations; education for the public service; the field of concentration, integration, and cooperation in the social sciences; the introductory political science course; a better liaison between high schools and colleges; graduate instruction; and

[3]While several attempts have been made to resolve the problem of defining effective citizenship and explaining how one attains it, very few studies have offered empirically reliable and theoretically meaningful clues. (See, for example, 2, 19, 25, and 27.)

modernization of teaching methods. Basically these sections recommended: (1) the integration of specialized areas within political science and avoidance of proliferation; (2) the building up of integrated social science courses, issues courses, or area studies programs; and (3) emphasis on citizenship education, critical thinking, and a familiarity with American and foreign political institutions in the beginning course. It is important to note that the report stressed that "the training of citizens is one of the major goals of American political science."

In addition to the formal reports there have been several conferences and studies resulting in books and articles on learning experiences, teaching goals, and methods in political science. Charles S. Hyneman (31), a past president of the American Political Science Association and a scholar on the role of the Supreme Court, expressed concern over the emphasis on facts and details in college courses and the lack of opportunities for the student to think out problems. While he acknowledged that enlargement of the "cargo of knowledge" is a part of instruction, he made a strong plea for critical inquiry in teaching government. Hyneman declared that student experience

> should be one of examining positions; of making an inventory of value holdings; of confirming, reshaping, and rejecting premises; of enlarging vision and sharpening focus, of throwing off old habits and fixing new habits of working and thinking; of developing know-how for getting evidence, evaluating evidence, and extending evidence by reasoning. (Hyneman, 31, pp. 218–19.)

He pointed to the importance of identifying value issues and social problems and devising strategies for dealing critically with them.

Social studies educators have expressed concerns similar to Hyneman's and have made strong cases for an inquiry-centered orientation in teaching social studies. Engle (22), for example, suggested that the mark of the good citizen is his ability to make intelligent decisions on the perennial problems of society. Decision-making, according to him, "requires more than mere knowledge of facts and principles; it requires a weighing in the balance, a synthesizing of all available information and values." Hunt and Metcalf (29) and Oliver and Shaver (52) expressed the same concern over content and instructional goals, and they proposed social studies programs that would focus on the "closed areas" of society, such as intergroup relations, social class, religion and morality, nationalism, patriotism, and national institutions and sex, courtship, and marriage. Furthermore, they pointed to the importance of openly examining and testing beliefs and ideas in the classroom. Capitalizing on the concepts and methods of the social and behavioral scientists and philosophers, Massialas and Cox (45) offered a social studies program and an instructional method that would maximize inquiry on the part of high school students.

Both the political scientists and the social studies educators are strongly interested in preparing students for "intelligent participation in the decision-making process." The political scientists, especially those of modern persuasion, want to identify and study the elements that shape the political world. While they accept effective citizenship as a defensible goal, they usually make the questionable assumption that cognitive understanding of political phenomena will change beliefs and values. Their primary concern is to identify and predict political behavior rather than to influence it or to offer programs for change. The social studies educators, however, are more concerned with instructional outcomes, and they have a broader base of operations because they can draw on the concepts and methods of the social and behavioral sciences as well as the practical experiences of individuals.

Research on the Teaching of Government

It is impossible in this limited space to review all the research literature on the teaching of government. Since this paper will attempt to assess the teaching of government by examining current textbooks and related materials, it will concentrate on the research about textbooks.

A report of the Anti-Defamation League of B'nai B'rith (43) in 1961 on the treatment of minorities in secondary school textbooks concluded that the texts they examined were presenting "a largely white, Protestant, Anglo-Saxon view of history and of the current social scene" and that the problems of minority groups in America were "still very largely neglected." The report was based on a study of forty-eight textbooks in American history, world history, and social problems and civics, and its findings were elaborately documented. On the treatment of Negroes the study concluded:

In most cases the 1954 Supreme Court decision on public school desegregation is presented without any consideration of the underlying
principles and of the subsequent ongoing attempts at compliance and
evasion. The achievements of living Negro Americans are mentioned
in very few books. Residential segregation by race is seldom discussed.
American Negroes are portrayed, for the most part, in the eras of
slavery and of Reconstruction. What comes through in most books is a
stereotype of a simple, childlike, superstitious people. (Marcus, 43,
p. 60.)

The study also discovered a lack of scientific information about
race and about the historic achievements of American Negroes. With
few exceptions the textbooks did not include photographs and other
illustrations of Negroes.

Another study of citizenship education (34), based on the examination of three popular civics textbooks, concluded that (1) textbooks, while readable and attractive, either do not discuss controversial social issues, such as segregation and racial discrimination in
housing and voting, or treat these topics with "detached objectivity"
and (2) the books do not encourage commitment to the democratic
way of life and system of government. The study included the comments of a foreign student who said that the textbook authors, their
scholarship notwithstanding, "failed to point even to one mistake or
blunder committed by the United States in all its history."

In a 1963 study Ballinger (4) found that, like government and
civics texts, social studies methods texts used in the preparation of
teachers naïvely assume that if students are presented with all the
facts they will automatically form appropriate value judgments.
Ballinger concluded after analyzing fourteen textbooks that "only
two gave any indication at all that controversial issues contain value-
related or value-centered problems and that special consideration or
analysis might be called for."

A sophisticated and comprehensive study of social studies textbooks was conducted by Shaver (57) and released in 1965. It dealt
with the relative emphasis in social studies texts on reflective thinking or intelligent decision-making and on human values. After examining ninety-three current secondary school textbooks in American
government, American problems, and citizenship or civics, the investigator drew some important conclusions:

1. While practically all the books make appeals to critical or

mature thinking, none give the reader a conceptual framework that would help to develop critical skills. Most of the material purported to encourage critical thinking is presented in an exhortative manner.

2. Statements about American democracy present an "incredibly naïve" picture of society that would lead the student either to be "unrealistically optimistic" about his social world or to wonder about the discrepancies between what textbooks describe and what newspapers and other communication media report. Textbooks tend to confuse the ideals of democracy with the realities of the political system; in several instances the reader is given the impression that the "ideals" are actually operant in daily life.

3. Textbooks generally fail to give the student an intellectual scheme for adjudicating intelligently the clash of values in society.

Analysis of Selected Current Textbooks

This section of the paper will explore further some of the observations made in the preceding section about the teaching of government, focusing on selected textbooks.

The review that follows assumes that intelligent decision-making is an acceptable goal of social studies instruction and that the process of inquiry—defined as the systematic exploration and validation of alternatives on matters of public and individual concern—provides the best means for attaining this goal. The more detailed dimensions of inquiry as stated in the introductory chapter provide the basic framework for this study.

In selecting review books I used two basic criteria: First, I chose textbooks that were readily available. Second, I chose texts that are widely used and are representative of the field. Thus at least three of the texts analyzed here are included in publishers' best-seller lists. In all, six texts (5, 7, 15, 26, 41, 46) were reviewed and analyzed. Of these texts one (5) is generally used in the upper grades of the junior high school or the lower levels of the high school, and another (15) is the product of one of the social studies projects at the Carnegie Institute of Technology. The material in the latter publication is largely experimental, and it is important to view it as such. The other texts are used in senior high school classes, usually at the junior or senior levels.

In reviewing the textbooks in question I did not use an elaborate taxonomic scheme, nor did I apply recent techniques of content analysis; instead I stressed the qualitative aspect of the material. This study attempts to generate hypotheses about the teaching of government rather than to arrive at definitive conclusions.

THE NEED FOR A CONCEPTUAL FRAMEWORK

A conceptual framework is a theoretical construct that performs the following functions: (1) it gives focus and direction to the investigation; (2) it defines the boundaries of the subject to be investigated; (3) it separates the relevant data from the irrelevant; (4) it generates productive hypotheses; and (5) it logically interrelates the concepts or methods of inquiry within a field of study.

A well-formulated framework for political analysis was recently offered by David Easton (17). He conceives of politics as a pattern of behavior, and he posits the model of a political system that coexists and overlaps with other systems—social, economic, cultural, etc. The political system is represented as an input-output model: the flow of *wants* (from the electorate) is converted into *demands* that enter the system as inputs and are in turn transformed into policies or outputs by the authorities and then leave the system, perhaps to start another cycle. This model assumes that the political system can be distinguished from other social systems on the basis of two essential variables—"the allocations of values for a society and the relative frequency of compliance with them" (18). Easton's model is useful for several reasons: (1) It has universal applicability, that is, his model applies to all political systems, modern or primitive, small or large, democratic or totalitarian, national or international. (2) It delimits the field of government by setting its parameters. (3) It suggests relationships between political inputs and outputs. (4) It suggests relationships between frequency and volume of demands on one hand and governmental stability on the other. (5) It relates the political attitudes of the electorate to the functioning of the political system. (Easton points to a relationship between socialization—the way "a society transmits many political orientations across the generation"—and the persistence of the political system. The crucial problem to be explored in this context is: How does a society generate support for the political system through its agents for socialization, one of which is the school?) (6) It indicates ways in which the political system interacts with the total environment and its various systems (and sub-systems), for example, ecological, biological, personality, and social systems.

Similar conceptual models for political analysis, varying in sophistication and explanatory power, are developed by several other political and social scientists, including Milbrath (49), who elaborated on a communications model of government; Almond and Verba (2), who developed the concept of the "civic culture," defined as a "pluralistic culture based on communication and persuasion, a culture of consensus and diversity, a culture that permitted change but moderated it"; and Apter (3), who analyzed political modernization in terms of two authority types—the "sacred collectivity" model and the "secular-libertarian" model.

Although no educator would expect authors of secondary school textbooks to employ such sophisticated conceptual models, it is reasonable to expect some delimiting concept of political behavior or at least an appropriate definition of government. But most texts make no conscious effort to delimit the field of study and to define government. When a definition is offered, it is either too broad or too vague to be useful. One text (46) defines government as "the agent through which the state exerts its will and accomplishes its ends. It consists of the machinery and the personnel through which the state is ruled (governed)." Another (26) defines it as "the agencies and means (usually organized) through which a group of people directs action, exerts power, and secures results." But although they offer nonprescriptive definitions of government, both texts emphasize certain ethical precepts that suggest the purpose of government. One book (46) says, "All government in the United States—from that of the nation to that of the smallest unit in any State—is government of the people, by the people, and for the people." And the same book adds that "especially in democratic countries, such as the United States, it [the government] has become the *servant* as well as the protector of the people." Abraham Lincoln is quoted with monotonous regularity in almost every text I examined as saying: "The legitimate object of government is to do for a community of people whatever they need to have done but cannot do at all, or cannot so well do, for themselves in their separate and individual capacities."

While the two formal definitions of government above imply some group political behavior, the textbooks include material primarily on formal governmental structure. Thus the Constitution and the Executive, Legislative, and Judicial branches of government are described at length. The emphasis is on the national level, but units on state and local government are included. The books' lack of conceptual framework, however, makes the chapter and part divisions and the selection of material arbitrary and contributes to the failure to interrelate the basic ingredients of political life. If there is an implicit framework influencing the selection of topics, it is mainly an historical and legalistic approach to government or politics as an institution rather than as a process. Furthermore, in some instances the object of government is confused with the object of *studying* government.

The failure to present a consistent notion of government is exemplified in one text (15). In a reading entitled "Decision-Making in Stoerpenberg Camp," it vividly describes the interaction of a small group of war prisoners as they try to make decisions and select their leader. The purpose of this reading is ostensibly to illustrate the political process in small groups, yet the book undermines this purpose when it states:

> In American society political activity occupies a comparatively small amount of time of a typical citizen. Occupied with a job, a family, a group of friends, and innumerable opportunities to go to movies, watch television, attend baseball games, or listen to a symphony orchestra, the attention of American citizens is often focused on these activities instead of on politics. Any American who considers entering politics must recognize that his time is a scarce resource.   (Curriculum Development Center, Project Social Studies, 15, p. 4.)

Unlike the reading about the Stoerpenberg war prisoners (which presents a concept of political activity espoused by Lasswell), the quotation suggests that politics is a formal activity and does not exist in the job, the family, or the peer group. Such a concept of political activity is demonstrated again when the authors suggest that "voting is the only political activity of many Americans." One may also question the assertion that a "comparatively small amount of time is given to politics." If politics entails the authoritative allocation of values, it can take place in small or large groups, in tribal or modern societies, and in governmental or extragovernmental agencies.

The uncertainty about the definition of government and its field of study is reflected in the reasons given by texts for studying government. One text declares that the course in American government should provide insight into the "relationship of an American citizen to his government." But this purpose, which one might call cognitive or analytical, is immediately followed by "melioristic" purposes, some of which are posed as questions:

> What should be the role of the American citizen in party politics? How can he help shape public opinion? How can he keep informed on issues? What is the appropriate role of each of the three branches of our national government? How can more effective cooperation between them be assured? (Ludlum *et al.*, 41, p. 1.)

The opening question calls for a value judgment on the part of the reader. But the answers to the questions that follow will not in fact tell how to implement this ideal role but will merely indicate what a citizen's role *can* be, given the realities of the political system. The authors raise "is" and "ought" questions without distinguishing between them.

Another text (26) identifies seven reasons why we should study government, the first being to "appreciate more fully the nature of American democracy and its superiority to communism, fascism, or dictatorships of any kind." Other reasons are to understand relationships and to be interested and participate in political action. Another text (7) includes in its argument for the study of government the goals of individual responsibility and intelligent participation in public affairs. Practically all of the texts agree on cognitive goals (understandings, skills, and concepts) as well as affective goals (appreciations, attitudes, and values) for the study of government. These goals are certainly worthwhile. The difficulty arises, however, when authors are unable to discriminate carefully between the two types of goals and the peculiar means for attaining each. As we shall see in another section, this lack of discrimination between cognitive and affective categories results in a narrative that purports to discuss an event or phenomenon objectively but often expresses a bias of the writer or a particular group in society.

ETHNOCENTRIC TENDENCIES IN TEXTBOOKS

My study generally confirms the finding of earlier surveys that social studies textbooks present an unrealistic and naïve picture of the American political system. In effect the following picture of America is given to the younger generation: (1) the government operates on the principle of the consent of the governed; (2) America is the best country to live in; (3) American citizens are the most rational voters; (4) the American form of government is the best and most appropriate for all societies at any stage of development; and (5) since America is both the most powerful and the most democratic state, it should be the world's keeper. In sum "We are the greatest"—to paraphrase Cassius Clay—is the philosophy that predominates in secondary school textbooks on government.

Let us offer some specific illustrations of this philosophy. One textbook, while discussing modern political systems, makes the following statement:

> One needs only to look at the great achievements and the standard of living of the American people to see the advantages of our economic system. . . . We believe that a well-regulated capitalism—a free choice, individual incentive, private enterprise system—is the best guarantee of the better life for all mankind. (McClenaghan, 46, p. 20.)

The book conveniently excludes any consideration of the economic development and social well-being of people in England and in the Scandinavian countries. Moreover, a picture following the discussion presents a rather gloomy view of English society—a group of people waiting in line in the rain to be treated by the National Health Service. The discussion and the picture suggest to the reader that socialized medicine leads to certain hardship.

Some books present an overidealized picture of democratic polities; the statements about what a democracy *is* are virtually indistinguishable from those about what it *ought* to be. The following statement provides a good example of what is frequently said about democracy. "Democracy provides the individual with greater security and personal satisfaction. In a democracy the dignity and worth of the individual are recognized. . . . All are equal before the law . . . and have the law's protection."

A democratic state is depicted as the great champion of the poor, the underprivileged, and the ethnic minorities as well as the savior of man everywhere. Any other system or ideology is a priori inferior or evil. Such discussions imply that, since by definition America is a democracy, it incorporates all the divine qualities attributed to democratic polities. Hence America emerges as the champion of universal humanity, morality, and rationality. Needless to say, many of the social problems that the American system is faced with—for example, discrimination against ethnic minorities, slums, crime, delinquency, alcoholism, and lack of medical care for the aged—are omitted or glossed over. The Pollyanna mentality is illustrated in this statement: "There are challenges to democracy today, and it is evident to all who read the newspapers and magazines that the challenges are serious ones. Our attention, then, should be upon the conditions that contribute to the success of democracy." The second sentence of the paragraph is a *non sequitur*, since the reader expects to see attention drawn to the "serious challenges." One could certainly raise the question "why not deal with the challenges (and failures) of democracy as well as with its strengths and successes." Can the exclusion of controversial social issues from disciplined discourse solve the crucial problems of our time?

Even the book by Ludlum *et al.* (41), which is generally more sophisticated and operates at a little higher level than the others in Bloom's taxonomy of cognitive tasks (6),[4] expresses explicitly or implicitly an unfounded image of American greatness. In explaining the reasons for increased military expenditures the text (like several others) presents the United States as the unselfish guardian of the world's peace and tranquility. It stated (41): "Because the nations of the world have not yet learned to live permanently at peace, the United States today must maintain large defense forces." This statement, reflecting the general tone of the book, implies that only the United States is a peace-loving country and that only Americans are motivated by altruistic and humanitarian purposes.

All the books I reviewed assume that the American system actually operates on the principle of consent of the governed. After quoting Abraham Lincoln one book states in its opening chapter:

> In these few words he [Lincoln] seems to catch the whole spirit of American government, the very foundation of our democratic system—faith that the people, taken together, are able to control their government. With this idea as a guide our nation has grown and prospered over nearly two centuries. . . . By clinging to this principle we shall continue to be great. (Ludlum *et al.*, 41, p. 2.)

Another book (5) makes the following claim about the role of public opinion: "In our nation government has been organized to

[4]According to Bloom cognitive skills may be ranked hierarchically: knowledge and comprehension of ideas and facts form the lower levels, and application, analysis, synthesis, and evaluation form the higher ones.

serve the people and to provide for the general welfare of all the citizens. We will learn very shortly that all levels of government are responsive to the wishes of the people."

Although the principle of consent of the governed is a genuine American ideal, it cannot and does not account for political and economic behavior in daily life. Yet the legalistic point of view used by most of the textbooks reviewed to describe American political life gives the reader an image of a benevolent government, the personnel of which is elected or appointed through orderly processes, and a political system that rests on a rational interpretation of the civil rights of citizens as guaranteed by the Constitution. The concept of government as the study of influence and the influential is underplayed or excluded altogether from the discussion. Very little indeed is said about community power structure as presented by recent important studies (1, 16, 30); about the electoral process and patterns of voting behavior based on empirical investigations rather than myths (12, 32); about the formation of political elites (20, 21, 37, 38, 44, 50, 59); about government and politics from the behavioral and comparative perspective (2, 13, 48, 54, 58); and about political socialization (2, 25, 27, 53).

Newmann's recent view of research on citizenship and consent of the governed (51) presents statistics that highlight the gap between research findings and textbook presentations. For example, research has shown that less than 20 per cent of the adult population take an active part in government affairs; no President has been elected by a popular majority of the total number of eligible voters; urban areas are badly underrepresented in state legislatures (although these areas constitute about 70 per cent of the population, they elect only 20 per cent of the legislators); most policy-makers at the national level of administration are appointed rather than elected; more than half of American industry is organized along "oligopolistic" lines, that is, 50 per cent of industry is owned by approximately two hundred corporations; and less than 1 per cent of the American people are informed and analytical about, interested and active in foreign affairs. Newmann pointed out the need to acknowledge contemporary social realities by redefining the concept of consent of the governed, which was derived from the eighteenth- and nineteenth-century idea of majority rule and the image of a participatory and politically active citizenry. According to him a better definition of "consent" would be "the opportunity of people to select the men to whom they delegate the power of government."

While it would be unreasonable to expect studies released in the past two or three years to be included in textbooks, it is very rare to find even earlier studies on these topics incorporated into text discussions. Some texts list a few of the behaviorally oriented studies in their bibliographies or in the teacher's editions but fail to consider these studies in the text discussion itself. For example, one text (41) devotes an entire chapter to voting but fails to consider the findings of Angus Campbell *et al.* in *The American Voter* (12), despite the fact that the book is recommended to the teacher. The chapter ends with a section entitled "Clinching the Main Ideas," which combines ethical prescriptions, wishful thinking, democratic ideals, and a few descriptive data. The five main ideas of the chapter on voting are (1) "voting is a process that makes possible peaceful change," (2) "voting promotes citizen participation in government," (3) "voting helps to promote equality," (4) "voting promotes obedience to government," and (5) "voting promotes the self-respect of every individual." This chapter leaves much to be desired. Although lofty principles and democratic ideals should be considered, it is just as important to consider the realities of voting—social and behavioral factors in voting, the influence of electoral campaigns, discriminatory practices, and so forth. Unless the realities of politics are presented, the reader will get a distorted view of the political system and his participation in it.

The ethnocentric bias of textbooks on American government and the tendency to equate American ideals with American political realities make for particularly misleading and inadequate discussions when the United States and capitalism are compared with the Soviet Union and communism. My findings generally support the results of a recent national survey of policy statements and recommended courses of study including units on communism. The survey (24) revealed that few states seem willing to allow an unbiased analysis of the subject. Most textbooks "contrast the darkest realities of communism in the Soviet Union with the noblest ideals of American democracy" and tend to use such pejorative words as *slavery, menace, evil, threat, deadly, deceitful,* and *dishonest* when they discuss the Soviet Union and communism. Most of the proposals and courses of study concentrate on the fallacies and failures of communism, and they ignore the analytical works written by communists.

One text opens a chapter called "The Challenge of Communism" with the following statement:

Communism has become a kind of bad word used to make us angry. While abusive language may relieve frustrated feelings, it is no substitute for knowledge and reason. Citizens of democracies are called upon to defend their freedoms with policies and programs, not angry shouts.

It is best to begin by facing the facts squarely. (Brown and Peltier, 7, p. 699.)

In spite of this plea the authors proceed to use emotive language and to make several innuendos when they refer to the Soviet Union and communism. They point to the "typical tricks" of communist propaganda and to the "brutal" methods of the Soviet Union, and they warn the reader that he would be "badly fooled" if he were to "take the Russians at their word." The authors have selected only data that demonstrate the strengths of democracy and the weaknesses of communism; there is no information given on economic and social changes in the Soviet Union. It is also interesting to note that no excerpts from communist sources are used. The authors briefly discuss Karl Marx and his ideas, but they take pains to point out his errors and his inability to make accurate predictions. They also exclude any discussion of the European social context in which the *Communist Manifesto* was prepared.

The end-of-chapter exercises reflect the general tone of the chapter. Many questions prejudge the answer; for example, three questions in the section "Problems and Projects" (7:20–21) state: "Write a short research paper on agreements with other nations that the Soviet Union has broken"; "Draw a chart contrasting the way of life in a democracy and in a totalitarian government today"; "The presence of a communist dictatorship in Cuba poses a threat to the peace of the Western Hemisphere. Organize a panel to discuss what United States policy toward Cuba should be." In the teacher's edition (7) of the book the authors suggest that the teacher "ask students to compile a list of Marx's errors."

Another book (46) after giving a brief and superficial summary of Marxist theory, proceeds to expose the fallacies of communism. As in the case of other texts the authors assume that their readers will accept their claims to knowledge on faith. Yet this assumption is contrary to scholarly tradition and the democratic concept of objectivity in assessing social policy and a given political ideology. In addition the procedure of comparing the American ideological and political system with alien systems in terms of "good" versus "evil" contradicts the objective of developing critical thinking abilities among students, an objective espoused by virtually all the authors. The "good versus evil" approach implies that the authors have a very low opinion of the ability of high school students to structure their own learning by formulating hypotheses about social affairs, exploring alternatives, gathering relevant data, and drawing warranted conclusions. Nor does this approach imply much faith in the democratic process of judging the strengths and weaknesses of a system in the open market of ideas. At the end of the chapter, evidently in order to make sure that the students have mastered the information presented, the authors direct the students to "list as many criticisms of communism as you can."

The "either-or" philosophy is evident in several other instances, especially in regard to international politics. For example, a two-page map entitled "Challenging the Free World" (46:26–27) places all the countries of the world in four camps: (1) the United States, (2) the rest of the free world, (3) the communist bloc, and (4) the uncommitted nations. The entire globe is characterized in terms of the struggle of the United States and democracy versus the Soviet Union and communism. A blue-colored box describes the basic political, economic, and social conditions that characterize the United States. A gray box lists the prevailing conditions in the Soviet Union, including the existence of a single party, uncontested elections, and a parliament operating in name only. Strangely enough, countries that have political and economic conditions similar to those of the Soviet Union (one-party rule, etc.), such as Haiti, Spain, Portugal, and Formosa, are classified as members of the "free world." "Free world" appears to be a category based on the degree of a nation's friendliness to the United States rather than on its degree of democracy. In another passage in the book the authors include Spain in the same category of states (modern dictatorships) as Nazi Germany, Red China, and the Soviet Union, thus showing certain inconsistencies and ambiguities in their criteria for labeling and classifying nations (46:18).

A much more sophisticated and objective treatment of Soviet political life and communist ideology is offered in a book of readings entitled *Comparative Political Systems: A Book of Readings for Inductive Teaching* (15). The main strength of the book lies in its identification of explicit categories for making fairly objective cross-national comparisons between the United States and the Soviet

Union. For example, the book includes readings on the demographic attributes of American and Soviet political leaders, including occupational status, ethnicity, and education. The reader is asked on the basis of the available statistical data to form hypotheses about the pattern of political recruitment in the Soviet Union and compare it with those of the United States and tsarist Russia. Here are two of the text's questions:

> What personal characteristics should a man have to succeed in Soviet politics? Are such characteristics different from those needed to succeed in the United States?

> What kinds of pressures affect a Soviet politician which did not affect officials in the tsarist government? (Curriculum Development Center, 15, p. 69.)

With a few exceptions the main purpose of this part of the book is explanatory rather than exhortative. This cannot be said, however, for parts of the book where ideological issues are discussed (see pages 137–51).

THE TREATMENT OF CONTROVERSIAL SOCIAL ISSUES

My review by and large confirms the findings of several analysts that social studies textbooks do not deal with social controversy responsibly. (1) Highly controversial issues (or what one educator has called "inflammatory issues"), such as laws governing homosexuality, prostitution, birth control information and aid, pornography, abortions, illegitimate children, interracial marriages, and drug addiction, are excluded from discussion in the textbooks. (2) When controversial issues are discussed, they are presented in an "antiseptic" context where, with a few exceptions, the authors refuse to take a stand on the issue and to support their stand on valid and publicly communicable grounds. (3) While several authors exhort the reader to apply the skills of critical thinking to the analysis of social issues and value cleavages, no model is given, either explicitly or implicitly, that would suggest defensible ways for satisfactorily adjudicating among incompatible values.

Most of the texts I reviewed include references to Negroes, their voting rights, educational discrimination, and their employment possibilities. However, the quality of treatment of the Negro in the context of American society varies from text to text. One text (46), discussing literacy tests as one of the requirements for suffrage in some states, merely notes in passing that "the literacy requirement can be—and in some places is—used to prevent certain groups from voting." The text discusses the "grandfather clause" without pointing out that its purpose was to restrict the burden of literacy tests and poll taxes to Negroes and thus in effect to disfranchise them. In a footnote the text states:

> A "grandfather clause" was added to the Louisiana constitution in 1895 and six other southern states soon followed suit. These clauses provided that any person, or his male descendants, who had voted in the state at some time prior to the adoption of the Fifteenth Amendment (1870) could become a legal voter without regard to a literacy or taxpaying qualification. The basic purpose was to enfranchise those whites who were otherwise disqualified. (McClenaghan, 46, p. 150.)

Another text devotes only one sentence to Negro voting privileges (7:82): "Not only the poll tax, but unfairly administered literacy tests and direct intimidation have been used to prevent Negroes from voting."

Two other texts (26 and 41), however, give more than a passing reference to the practices that prevent Negroes from voting, and they point to the federal legislation and Supreme Court decisions that have attempted to change such unfair practices. One of these texts traces historically the legal battle to enfranchise Negroes and concludes with a section on the 1965 Voting Rights Act. The section opens with the following statement:

> Another long step in legal procedure to eliminate racial barriers to voting was taken in the Voting Rights Act of August 1965. The action was directed at the use of literacy tests in barring Negroes from registering and voting in all elections, such tests being the principal device then used to bar Negroes from the polls. (Haefner, Bruce, and Carr, 26, pp. 87–88.)

The second text, revealing some of the conclusions about voting discrimination of the 1961 and 1963 reports of the United States Commission on Civil Rights, states (41:90): "In about 100 scattered counties in several southern states there has been evidence of discrimination against Negro voting." The text further points out that discrimination in these counties takes such forms as "economic pressure against Negroes who attempt to register, removal of Negroes from voting lists, and registration procedures which make it impossible for Negroes to vote."

Finally, one text, *Citizenship and Government in Modern America* (5), has an entire chapter on intergroup relations that emphasizes problems of Negroes. Two charts provide useful data on the status of Negroes and other nonwhites. One chart on the costs of discrimination between "white" and "nonwhite" indicates that (1) the life expectancy for nonwhites is 64.1 years as compared with 70.9 years for whites in the United States; (2) the rate of infant mortality is 41.4 per 1,000 live births for nonwhites and 22.3 for whites; (3) the rate of maternal deaths is 95.9 per 100,000 live births for nonwhites and 23.8 for whites; (4) the average nonwhite attends school for only 8.6 years, while the figure for whites is 11.8 years; and (5) 71.3 per cent of nonwhites as compared with 35.4 per cent of whites have an average income of less than $5,000, whereas only 5.1 per cent of nonwhites compared with 19.0 per cent of whites have an average income of over $10,000. These statistics make the inferior status of Negroes and other minorities quite apparent. Unfortunately no such explicit data are given in any of the other books. Nor do the books make a strong appeal to outlaw discriminatory practices in education, employment, housing, and political representation. Like the treatment of the Negro in United States history, which according to John Hope Franklin (23) is superficial and inadequate, the status of the Negro in the political life of the country is not adequately presented in textbooks on government. With very few exceptions the textbook treatment of the social issues confronting the country is reportorial rather than evaluative.

While the level of objectivity and analytical rigor varies from book to book, none of the texts I reviewed provide an explicit model for discussing controversial social issues. None of the textbooks explore how beliefs and values are formed, how they are changed, what constitutes defensibility of a value judgment, how values relate to policies, or how values can be fruitfully categorized (for example, relative versus absolute values, instrumental versus end values). Nor do the books reflect the research of sociologists, social psychologists, and philosophers in the resolution of value conflicts.

THE USES AND MISUSES OF PROBLEM-SOLVING

A basic requirement of problem-solving or the process of critical inquiry is the presentation of alternatives or the indication that claims to knowledge are subject to continuous revision. With one possible exception (15) none of the texts I reviewed suggest that other interpretations of the social phenomena or political events they describe are possible. We have already referred to the omission of "unpleasant" interpretations in the discussion of American democracy. But even on less controversial topics—such as American voting patterns, the social background of political executives and legislators, the process of getting a bill through Congress, and the role of pressure groups—most authors present their assertions as if they were all supported by reliable research data and as if all phenomena were subject to only one interpretation.

The concept of problem-solving or critical inquiry that most authors use is neither clear nor based on current research. One book (7), for example, emphasizes the importance of applying a problem-solving method to teaching and learning but makes an inaccurate analogy with decision-making in the government. Under a section entitled "The Problem-solving Method" the authors raise the following rhetorical question: "What better way is there to teach the workings of government than by illustrating the way government goes about solving problems that affect us all?" The text adds, "All legislation—federal, state, and local—is the outcome of the problem-solving process." The authors are assuming that the government acts rationally and that the student who reads about how the government makes decisions will be able to make rational decisions himself. Both assumptions are questionable. First, legislators and government executives often do not use the rational model of inquiry suggested by the text in question: identifying a problem, suggesting alternative solutions, collecting data and testing possible solutions, and arriving at a generalization. There are many extraneous factors —social, political, economic, and psychological—that influence decisions in government. Secondly, the context in which governmental decisions are made is different from that in which decisions about social and political phenomena are made by school students. Finally, knowing how an agency makes decisions does not necessarily help the student sharpen his inquiry skills in exploring and testing ideas about the operation of the political system. Research indicates that critical inquiry and problem-solving skills are developed only when the learner is directly exposed to intellectual problems and is given the opportunity to work out alternative solutions for himself.

The end-of-chapter questions and exercises contribute little to the inquiry orientation. Most of the questions ask for a restatement of a point made in the chapter or for the naming of persons, things, or functions. Questions abound on who presides in the Senate, what the functions of the Speaker are, or how a bill becomes a law (see, for instance, 46, page 215). A student can usually answer these questions by merely finding the exact passage in the chapter that describes the item in question. Not much thinking is involved in this matching process. Even so-called why questions (rather than who, what, or when questions) often require only a restatement of causes of a phenomenon or event that are listed in the text. For example, a book asking, "Why does government at times try to influence public opinion?" (41) probably assumes that the student will turn to pages 118–19 to find the reasons. Unfortunately quoting the author's explanation for a phenomenon cannot substitute for personally developing the grounds for a policy or establishing a causal relationship based on original research. The former is a low-level mental operation, whereas the latter calls for the application of high-level cognitive tasks (6).

Even materials that purport to stimulate inductive thinking, such as those produced by Project Social Studies at the Carnegie Institute of Technology (15) include many questions asking for the recall of information or the restatement of a trend or phenomenon. For example, the following questions relate to a table on the educational background of American political leaders:

1. What percentage of the population in 1940 had college education?

2. How many of the 431 United States Representatives counted in this survey had received college educations?

3. In which governmental positions are better educated people found? Why do you think this was the case?

> (Curriculum Development Center, 15, p. 41.)

Most of the questions above can be answered by merely looking at the table that appears on the same page. The same observation applies to other material in this collection of readings. Indeed very few, if any, of the ideas advanced by Bruner (9, 10, 11) or Schwab (56) about creative and analytic thinking or teaching as inquiry are reflected in the books and materials reviewed here. It will take a concerted effort among publishers, textbook writers, teachers, and researchers to bring materials up to date and to incorporate in them recent findings in psychology, social science, and education.

Ideas for Improving Textbooks

It is hoped that this review will help authors and publishers to prepare better textbook materials for government courses and that it will offer guidelines to help teachers evaluate new textbook materials and instructional methods. To overcome the deficiencies of existing materials, we recommend the following specific proposals:

1. Materials and textbooks should be organized around themes and concepts, for example, political socialization, political recruitment, legitimacy of governments, and political decision-making. Concepts, generalizations, and data should be interrelated within a broad framework. This organizational scheme should be reflected in the social studies curriculum.

2. Government courses should rely on a series of paperbacks and supplementary materials rather than a single textbook. Courses should be conceptually related to the total social studies program in the first through twelfth grades as well as to the total school curriculum.

3. The materials presented to the student should provide the springboards for exploration and discovery of ideas, perhaps through the use of a more specialized case-study approach. Concepts and generalizations should be presented not as the ultimate truth but as working hypotheses subject to further revision and confirmation.

4. Value issues and social conflicts should constitute legitimate areas of study and should be dealt with dispassionately and in the spirit of critical inquiry. Defensible models for adjudicating conflicting values and social issues should be carefully discussed and analyzed. The philosophical, psychological, and social dimensions of value problems should be carefully considered.

5. New findings and methods of investigation in the social and behavioral sciences should be incorporated into social studies instruction. Empirical data and case studies should constitute the raw material upon which reliable generalizations about the political and social systems are built.

6. Students should be given a realistic picture of the United States' strengths and weaknesses. While there is a place for ideals and ethical precepts in classroom discussion, these should not be presented as if they were social realities and behavioral principles governing human conduct. An honest and critical appraisal of America will strengthen the system rather than weaken it.

7. A defensible way to examine the United States government is to present it in a cross-cultural and comparative perspective. It is hoped that the new curriculum and materials will give as much emphasis to other political systems as they do to the United States. Research methods for the conduct of cross-national investigations should be explored in the classroom.

Conclusion

A review of the goals of teaching government and of the research in political science indicates that: (1) There is a strong commitment on the part of political scientists and educators to train students for citizenship. Recent studies suggest that "good citizenship" consists of information about and interest and participation in the civic culture. (2) There is consensus that the formal curriculum should help to acquaint high school and college students with critical inquiry methods in the exploration of ideas about man and society. (3) The current focus in political science is on the political behavior of man and his relation to the political system, as examined through theoretical and empirical studies.

How does the field of secondary school social studies measure up to these expressed goals?

1. Textbooks generally present an unrealistic picture of American society and government. Many social problems that exist today are not discussed. In statements about democracy and the good life textbooks often do not separate prescriptions from descriptions. Thus the persuasive usages of concepts are not distinguishable from the descriptive and explanatory ones. America is presented as the champion of freedom, good will, and rationality, while all other nations are depicted as aggressors or "second-raters."

2. Most of the texts overemphasize the historical development and legal structure of American government and underplay the behavioral and socioeconomic factors that affect political decision-making. Many authors assume naïvely that the political system functions in accordance with the fundamental laws of the land. Although discussions of the legal tradition and ideology of a country are important, examination of informal factors, such as peer-group influences, social class, education, and sex, is equally essential.

3. Controversial issues are not dealt with in an ethically and

intellectually responsible manner. Nowhere do authors outline a defensible model for dealing with social cleavages and value incompatibilities.

4. The recent attempts of political scientists to develop a theoretical framework for examining government and man's political behavior are not reflected in current textbooks. Consequently many of the books are at best "cookbooks" without a major focus or an explicit theme that would relate study units to one another.

5. Except for passages attacking competing ideologies such as communism and socialism, very little is said in five of the texts I reviewed about other systems of government and political life in foreign countries, and cross-cultural research is not considered.

6. Practically all the books assume that students are not capable of participating in inquiry without committing to memory myriad details about government. Questions and exercises emphasize the recall of information in the chapter and do not give students sufficient practice in developing working hypotheses, collecting and sifting data, and producing statements about relationships. Textbook authors give very little evidence that they have seriously considered such new ways of teaching as induction or discovery.

The proposals for text improvement made in the last section generally call for the employment of contemporary concepts and methods of research in the social and behavioral sciences and in philosophy as well as provision for the development of inquiry skills among students. Although there is much more to be said about future tasks for government courses, we believe that this essay provides a beginning to a badly needed national debate on social studies. Only when we begin to take stock of our accomplishments and failures in a rational way can we say that we have come of age.

Selected Bibliography

1. AGGER, ROBERT E., GOLDRICH, DANIEL, AND SWANSON, BERT E., *The Rulers and the Ruled*, Wiley, New York, 1964.

2. ALMOND, GABRIEL, AND VERBA, SIDNEY, *The Civic Culture: Political Attitudes and Democracy in Five Nations*, Princeton University Press, Princeton, N.J., 1963.

3. APTER, DAVID E., *The Politics of Modernization*, University of Chicago Press, Chicago, 1965.

4. BALLINGER, STANLEY E., "The Social Studies and Social Controversy," *School Review*, 71 (Spring, 1963), 97–111.

5. BARD, HARRY, MORELAND, WILLIS D., AND CLINE, THELMA, *Citizenship and Government in Modern America,* Holt, Rinehart and Winston, New York, 1966.

6. BLOOM, BENJAMIN S. (ed.), *Taxonomy of Educational Objectives: Handbook I—Cognitive Domain,* David McKay, New York, 1956.

7. BROWN, STUART GERRY, AND PELTIER, CHARLES L., *Government in Our Republic,* Revised Edition, Macmillan, New York, 1964.

8. ——, *Teacher's Annotated Edition with Teacher's Manual, Government in Our Republic,* Revised Edition, MacMillan, New York, 1964.

9. BRUNER, JEROME S., "The Act of Discovery," *Harvard Educational Review,* 31 (Winter, 1961), 21–32.

10. ——, *The Process of Education,* Harvard University Press, Cambridge, Mass., 1960.

11. ——, *Toward a Theory of Instruction,* The Belknap Press of Harvard University Press, Cambridge, Mass., 1966.

12. CAMPBELL, ANGUS, *et al., The American Voter,* abridged edition, Wiley, New York, 1964.

13. COLEMAN, JAMES S. (ed.), *Education and Political Development,* Princeton University Press, Princeton, N.J., 1965.

14. COMMITTEE FOR THE ADVANCEMENT OF TEACHING OF THE AMERICAN POLITICAL SCIENCE ASSOCIATION, *Goals for Political Science,* William Sloane Associates, New York, 1951.

15. CURRICULUM DEVELOPMENT CENTER, PROJECT SOCIAL STUDIES, *Comparative Political Systems: A Book of Readings for Inductive Teaching,* by John R. Coleman *et al.,* Project Supervisors, The Carnegie Institute of Technology and the Pittsburgh Public Schools, Pittsburgh, Pa., no date.

16. DAHL, ROBERT A., *Who Governs?* Yale University Press, New Haven, Conn., 1961.

17. EASTON, DAVID, *A Framework for Political Analysis,* Prentice-Hall, Englewood Cliffs, N.J., 1965.

18. ——, *A Systems Analysis of Political Life,* Wiley, New York, 1965.

19. EASTON, DAVID, AND DENNIS, JACK, "The Child's Image of Government," *The Annals of the American Academy of Political and Social Science,* 361 (Sept., 1965), 40–57.

20. ELDERSVELD, SAMUEL J., *Political Affiliation in Metropolitan Detroit,* University of Michigan, Bureau of Government, Ann Arbor, 1957.

21. ——, *Political Parties: A Behavioral Analysis,* Rand McNally, Chicago, 1964.

22. ENGLE, SHIRLEY H., "Decision-Making: The Heart of Social Studies Instruction," in B. G. Massialas and A. M. Kazamias (eds.), *Crucial Issues in the Teaching of Social Studies,* Prentice-Hall, Englewood Cliffs, N.J., 1964, pp. 28–34.

23. FRANKLIN, JOHN HOPE, "The Negro in United States History," *American Teacher,* 12 (Feb., 1966), 5, 6, 9.

24. GRAY, ROLAND F., "Teaching About Communism: A Survey of Objectives," *Social Education*, 28 (Feb., 1964), 71–72.

25. GREENSTEIN, FRED I., *Children and Politics*, Yale University Press, New Haven, Conn., 1965.

26. HAEFNER, JOHN H., BRUCE, HAROLD R., AND CARR, ROBERT K., *Our Living Government*, Scott, Foresman, Chicago, 1966.

27. HESS, ROBERT D., AND TORNEY, JUDITH V., *The Development of Basic Attitudes and Values Toward Government and Citizenship During the Elementary School Years, Part I*, Cooperative Research Project No. 1078, The University of Chicago, Chicago, 1965.

28. HORRIGAN, FREDERICK J., "Political Science," in *Social Studies in the High School*, Willis D. Moreland (ed.), National Council for the Social Studies, Curriculum Series Number Seven, Revised Edition, 1965, 23–26.

29. HUNT, MAURICE P., AND METCALF, LAWRENCE E., *Teaching High School Social Studies*, Harper, New York, 1955. ·

30. HUNTER, FLOYD, *Community Power Structure*, University of North Carolina Press, Chapel Hill, 1953.

31. HYNEMAN, CHARLES S., "Some Crucial Learning Experiences: A Personal View," in *Teaching Political Science*, Robert H. Connery (ed.), Duke University Press, Durham, N.C., 1965, 217–37.

32. JENNINGS, M. KENT, AND ZEIGLER, L. HARMON (eds.), *The Electoral Process*, Prentice-Hall, Englewood Cliffs, N.J., 1966.

33. KIRKPATRICK, EVRON, "The Impact of the Behavioral Approach on Traditional Political Science," in *Essays on the Behavioral Study of Politics*, Austin Ranney (ed.), University of Illinois Press, Urbana, 1962, 1–29.

34. KRUG, MARK M., " 'Safe' Textbooks and Citizenship Education," *School Review*, 68 (Winter, 1960), 463–80.

35. LaPALOMBARA, JOSEPH (ed.), *Bureaucracy and Political Development*, Princeton University Press, Princeton, N.J., 1963.

36. ——, "Decline of Ideology: A Dissent and an Interpretation," *American Political Science Review*, 60 (Mar., 1966), 5–18.

37. LASSWELL, HAROLD, *Politics: Who Gets What, When, How*, Meridian, New York, 1958.

38. LASSWELL, HAROLD D., LERNER, DANIEL, AND ROTHWELL, C. EASTON, *The Comparative Study of Elites*, Hoover Institute Studies, Series B: Elites, No. I, Stanford University Press, Stanford, Calif., 1952.

39. LEISERSON, AVERY, "The Behavioral Approach," in *Teaching Political Science*, Robert H. Connery (ed.), Duke University Press, Durham, N.C., 1965, pp. 51–71.

40. LIPSET, SEYMOUR MARTIN, "Some Further Comments on 'The End of Ideology'," *American Political Science Review*, 60 (Mar., 1966), 17–18.

41. LUDLUM, ROBERT P., et al., *American Government*, Houghton Mifflin, Boston, 1965.

42. LUDLUM, ROBERT P., *et al.*, *Teacher's Edition of American Government*, Houghton Mifflin, Boston, 1965.

43. MARCUS, LLOYD, *The Treatment of Minorities in Secondary School Textbooks*, Anti-Defamation League of B'nai B'rith, New York, 1961.

44. MARVICK, DWAINE (ed.), *Political Decision-Makers: Recruitment and Performance*, The Free Press, New York, 1961.

45. MASSIALAS, BYRON G., AND COX, C. BENJAMIN, *Inquiry in Social Studies*, McGraw-Hill, New York, 1966.

46. McCLENAGHAN, WILLIAM A., *Magruder's American Government*, Allyn and Bacon, Boston, 1966.

47. MEEKISON, J. PETER, "A Bibliographical Essay," in *Teaching Political Science*, Robert H. Connery (ed.), Duke University Press, Durham, N.C., 1965, pp. 266–80.

48. MERRITT, RICHARD L., AND ROKKAN, STEIN (eds.), *Comparing Nations*, Yale University Press, New Haven, Conn., 1966.

49. MILBRATH, LESTER W., *The Washington Lobbyists*, Rand McNally, Chicago, 1963.

50. MILLS, C. WRIGHT, *The Power Elite*, Oxford University Press, A Galaxy Book, New York, 1959.

51. NEWMANN, FRED M., "Consent of the Governed and Citizenship Education in Modern America," *School Review*, 71 (Winter, 1963), 404–24.

52. OLIVER, DONALD W., AND SHAVER, JAMES P., *Teaching Public Issues in the High School*, Houghton Mifflin, Boston, 1966.

53. "Political Socialization: Its Role in the Political Process," Special Issue of *The Annals of the American Academy of Political and Social Science*, 361 (Sept., 1965).

54. PYE, LUCIAN W., AND VERBA, SIDNEY (eds.), *Political Culture and Political Development*, Princeton University Press, Princeton, N.J., 1965.

55. REED COMMITTEE, *Supplement* to the *American Political Science Review*, 24 (1930), 1–199.

56. SCHWAB, JOSEPH J., "The Teaching of Science as Inquiry," in *The Teaching of Science* by Joseph J. Schwab and Paul E. Brandwein, Harvard University Press, Cambridge, Mass., 1962.

57. SHAVER, JAMES P., "Reflective Thinking, Values, and Social Studies Textbooks," *School Review*, 73 (Autumn, 1965), 226–57.

58. WARD, ROBERT E., AND RUSTOW, DANKWART A. (eds.), *Political Modernization in Japan and Turkey*, Princeton University Press, Princeton, N.J., 1965.

59. WARNER, W. LLOYD, *et al.*, *The American Federal Executive*, Yale University Press, New Haven, Conn., 1963.

CHAPTER 10

World History

The Growing Focus on World Cultures

PAUL D. HINES

Introduction

The teaching of world history in the secondary school today is both disappointing and encouraging. It is disappointing that the majority of curriculum guides and textbooks are based on the learning theories and demands of a society of forty years ago. Some of the more recently published curriculum materials, however, are based on modern learning theories and are therefore much more applicable to the inquiry-oriented teacher. Among the recently published volumes that provide insight into the teaching of world history are Massialas and Smith's *New Challenges in the Social Studies* (23), Michaelis and Johnston's *The Social Sciences: Foundation of the Social Studies* (26), Erling M. Hunt's *High School Social Studies Perspectives* (16), and *The Social Studies and the Social Sciences* (2), sponsored by the American Council of Learned Societies and the National Council for the Social Studies. A meticulous and useful survey of current trends in the teaching of world history may be found in *New Perspectives in World History*, edited by Shirley Engle (11).

My study differs from those above in its emphasis on the evaluation of world history textbooks now being used by secondary-school teachers. In addition, this study will examine the current world history course and the influence of historiographic trends on the teaching of history.

The Focus of History

The word "history" was derived from a Greek noun that meant learning. When used by Aristotle, "history" referred to a systematic account of natural phenomena. In time "history" came to describe accounts of phenomena arranged in chronological order. From this rather simple beginning, enough definitions of history developed to satisfy almost everyone. Thomas Carlyle wrote that "the history of what man has accomplished in this world is at bottom the History of the Great Men who have worked here" (8). Karl Marx proclaimed that "the history of all hitherto existing society is the history of class struggles" (15). E. H. Carr more recently wrote that history "is a continuous process of interaction between the historian and his facts, an unending dialogue between the present and the past (9)." A student may prefer the suggestion that history is something that never happened written by a man who was not present. The scholar, however, may prefer Henri Pirenne's more sophisticated definition of history as "the development of human societies in space and time" (25).

Since there is disagreement on the definition of history, historians have been unable to agree on its central focus. Should its emphasis be descriptive or analytical? The venerable champion of descriptive history is Leopold von Ranke. Actually Ranke received the credit (or blame) for numerous deeds and pronouncements of his successors who were connected with the Ranke school of history. Regardless of Ranke's true intentions, his more zealous supporters interpreted *wie es eigentlich gewesen* ("how it actually was") to refer to a narrow and episodic political history. The result of their influence in the secondary schools was an overemphasis on memorizing incidents and dates (40).

A number of scholars have championed the role of analysis and evaluation in history. R. H. Tawney and James F. Rhodes emphasized that the cause–effect relationships surrounding historical events are of primary importance (25). Carl Becker contended that the proper function of historical research was "to be forever correcting the common image of the past by bringing it to the test of reliable information" (25). James Harvey Robinson outlined a comprehensive role for history early in the twentieth century.

> The "New History" . . . will avail itself of all those discoveries that are being made about mankind by anthropologists, economists, psychologists, and sociologists. . . . History must not be regarded as a stationary object which can only progress by refining its methods and accumulating, criticizing, and assimilating new material, but it is bound to alter its ideals and aims with the general progress of society and the social sciences, and it will ultimately play an infinitely more important role in our intellectual life than it has hitherto done. (Robinson, 33, p. 24.)

While there have always been historians who advocated an analytical and interdisciplinary approach to history, the nature of the world history program indicates the overwhelming influence of the descriptive approach. All historians agree that the descriptive approach to history has some value; however, because this approach is unselective, it prevents concentration on the important developments of mankind. As currently conceived, this approach to history leaves little time for analysis or evaluation of concepts and generalizations encountered in the course. And this approach becomes increasingly difficult to handle as more history is created.

The World History Course

The chronological development of the secondary school world history course may be easily traced from 1898. In that year the Committee of Seven of the American Historical Association recommended a four-year sequence of subjects designed to improve understanding of Western culture: ancient history (ninth grade), medieval and modern history (tenth grade), English history (eleventh grade), and American history and civil government (twelfth grade). By 1916 these courses formed the social studies curriculum in most high schools (46).

The present world history course was shaped by the 1916 Report of the Commission on the Reorganization of Secondary Education issued by the National Education Association. This report recommended a two-year world history course, a course in citizenship for the ninth grade, American history for the eleventh grade, and problems in American democracy for the twelfth grade. Faced with the dilemma of accommodating five social studies courses in a four-year sequence, the administrators eventually instituted the one-year world history course, which still exists in most secondary school curricula (46).

The secondary world history course is normally offered in the tenth grade. Masia (22) found that 35 percent of the schools surveyed in the North Central Accrediting Region require the course, while 62 percent of the schools offer it as an elective. There is no indication of a trend toward converting the course into a two-year one. Only two states (Missouri and North Dakota) actually require world history in high school (28), although Pennsylvania now requires one semester of world cultures for graduation (27).

World history is one of the most criticized offerings in the social studies curriculum. Both students and teachers have indicated dissatisfaction with the current course. Three factors contribute to its inadequacy: the educational background of world history teachers, the selectivity of the course content, and the methods used to teach it. An Illinois study by Pohlmann and Wellman (32) reported that 21.4 percent of its sample of world history teachers failed to meet the state teaching requirements. In addition the sample reveals that 50 percent of the athletic coaches who also taught world history failed to satisfy state requirements. In a California survey Siemers (37) reported that 46 percent of the world history teachers in his sample did not have graduate or undergraduate majors in history or social studies. Since the teacher is the most important factor in implementing a successful course offering, the results of these studies are disappointing. The inadequate training of such high percentages of teachers in states with the academic reputations of Illinois and California implies that other states may be in similar or worse situations.

Of the California teachers surveyed (37) 92 percent follow a basic textbook. Seventy-five percent of the sample attempt to provide equal coverage for every topic usually included in the world history course. Those who do not attempt equal coverage concentrate on Europe, ancient and medieval, or ancient and modern history. Seventy-eight percent of the teachers favor a chronological approach, and over one-third use this method exclusively. The topical approach is used by only 30 percent, of which 8 percent follow this approach exclusively.

Lectures and class discussions are the primary teaching vehicles; 80 percent of the sample require weekly memorization of important dates. From 40 to 50 percent of the sample indicated that they supplement the basic text with newspapers, periodicals, and other textbooks. Nearly one-half of the sample reported that they do not consider group or committee work in evaluating students. It is interesting to note that none of the teachers in the sample suggested the introduction of current methodology into world history as a way to expand the pool of source materials and shift the emphases of world history courses (37).

The figures cited in the Siemers and the Pohlmann and Wellman studies indicate myriad problems connected with the secondary school world history course. An alarmingly small percentage of teachers are providing their students with a variety of resource materials. Moreover, the appeal of the chronological approach (in order to cover maximum ground in the course) reinforces the preference among teachers for equal topical coverage as well as for regular memorization quizzes, and these techniques in turn reinforce the preference for the chronological approach.

Textbook Evaluation

> My desire is . . . that mine adversary had written a book.
>
> Job 31:35.

It is far more difficult to write a textbook than to evaluate one, and there are many problems in producing an acceptable textbook in world history. Out of thousands of events, themes, personalities, and movements, the author must select those that provide an accurate and thorough account of man's story. If an important event is omitted, the scholarship is shoddy. If the author includes trivial facts, the textbook is too bulky. On a topic on which many conflicting and lengthy interpretations are available, the textbook writer must try to present the issue objectively and accurately in one short paragraph. Finally, the author must consider the vigilant pressure groups who survey textbooks in search for the word or paragraph that might indicate "subversion."

In spite of the attention the textbook writer gives his product, the textbook can be only as effective as the teacher using it. Nonetheless, the textbooks used in world history courses provide insight into what takes place in the classroom. Wesley and Wronski in *Teaching Social Studies in High Schools* (45) pointed out that "the textbook has probably exerted a more direct and extensive influence upon the social studies curriculum and upon teaching methods than any other single factor."

Since nearly every textbook publishing company has one or more books available for the secondary school world history market, it was not feasible to evaluate all the books for this course. After a preliminary evaluation of twenty basic textbooks and four readings books, nine textbooks and two readings books were selected for inclusion in this study. Upon evaluating a large number of world history textbooks, one soon realizes that most of the texts have similar strengths and weaknesses and follow essentially the same criteria for the selection of content. I therefore used three criteria in selecting books for discussion: I chose some books because they are widely used in secondary schools today; I chose other books because they differ significantly from their competitors; and I chose still other books because they provide a balance between the chronological and the area studies approaches.

To facilitate the evaluation procedure, a set of criteria has been suggested in Chapter 1. These criteria, which are based on modern learning theories, can be used both as a means of evaluating current social studies textbooks and as a guide for future texts. In my review of world history textbooks I have concentrated on four criteria that seem particularly applicable to the teaching of this subject: (1) treatment of the non-Western world, (2) evidence of a conceptual framework, (3) use of inquiry-oriented techniques, and (4) the adequacy of supplementary materials.

Two basic patterns of textbook organization were found in the sample. As expected, the great majority of the books are organized chronologically, while a few of the more recently published texts follow an area studies approach. The books using the chronological approach will be examined first.

CHRONOLOGICALLY ORGANIZED TEXTS

Some edition of Rogers, Adams, and Brown's *Story of Nations* (34) has been used in the secondary schools since 1934. The text moves chronologically from prehistoric man through the Reformation. From this point on, individual countries—Great Britain, France, Spain, Italy, etc.—are discussed in terms of their contributions to Western culture. In keeping with the chronological organization India and the Far East are not introduced until the last quarter of the book. In the section devoted to China six pages are allotted to an explanation of Taoism and Confucianism—the same amount of space allocated to China since the fall of the Manchu emperors. Although knowledge of Confucianism is of value in studying China, the emphasis might more profitably be placed on information that would better enable the student to understand the problems of modern China. China has not been a Confucian state since at least 1911.

Similar comments could be made about the treatment of Africa: for instance, the celebrated Livingstone-Stanley meeting is given far more space than is any sub-Saharan African leader, past or present. The coverage of Africa (except for Egypt) begins with a chapter called "Africa Emerged from Darkness Late in World History." Rather than examining and evaluating contemporary Africa, the text discusses Africa's contacts with the mainstream of Western culture. While intercultural contacts should be discussed, a society should be examined in the context of its own environment and the development of its own institutions. African history did not begin with the Portuguese explorations or with the advent of the nineteenth century.

The text presents an accurate account of facts but provides too few situations for the student to analyze and apply the facts studied. These questions, which followed a chapter on the Old Kingdom, illustrate the focus of much of the book:

1. Who was the first ruler of all Egypt?
2. What are the three great periods of ancient Egyptian history?
3. How long did the civilization of the Old Kingdom last?
(Rogers, Adams, and Brown, 34, p. 33.)

The answers to these questions seem to be viewed as ends in themselves rather than "springboards" that the student can use to gain new insight into history and the modern world. For example, by drawing on the study of several civilizations the following question would allow the student to analyze and integrate the historical data studied: "What causes a culture to enter a period of great advancement? Find supporting evidence in the Egyptian, Roman, Greek, and Persian civilizations. Do the Middle East, Africa, or the Far East possess any of these traits today?"

Another chronological textbook is Mazour and Peoples' *Men and Nations: A World History* (24). The authors introduced the text by discussing nine "great themes" in history. Here are random examples of these themes:

1. What has caused the decline and fall of great civilizations of the past?
2. How have science and invention contributed to civilization?
3. How has geography influenced history?

(Mazour and Peoples, 24, pp. 4–5.)

The authors indicated that these themes run concurrently throughout the book. Introductions to each unit point out which themes will be developed, and these themes are reinforced in the review sections at the end of each unit. The theory underlying this approach is valid, but unfortunately the great bulk of material presented does not seem to contribute to the student's understanding and application of the themes.

The Mazour-Peoples treatment of non-Western cultures is similar to that of the *Story of Nations*. The principal discussion of Africa and Asia falls within a unit entitled "Great Power Rivalries." As the title indicates, these non-Western areas are reviewed in terms of their importance to Western civilization rather than on the basis of their own cultural importance. The discussion of Latin America is even more inconsequential than the treatment given Africa or Asia. Of the 822 pages in the text, the primary coverage of Latin America is limited to nine pages, and even these reflect an ethnocentric Western bias.

Living World History (42) by T. Walter Wallbank and Arnold Schrier provides a third example of chronological organization. Time-line charts are included to help the student compare the events occurring at a given time in a number of world areas. The text also provides adequate coverage of the contributions to mankind by early civilizations in non-Western areas. But the treatment given these areas in more modern periods is not so complete. In the Chinese section, for example, there is no mention of the Taiping Rebellion or of the reforms in the Chinese government around 1900. A more complete coverage on the communist takeover of China would also have been desirable. One-half page is devoted to this topic—the same amount of space devoted to Shih Huang Ti of the Ch'in dynasty. The treatment of Latin America since the "wars of liberation" is also limited.

Geography and chronological history apparently form the organizational framework of the text, but its conceptual framework is difficult to determine. The authors did provide an introduction dealing with the definition and uses of history and the role of the historian; this section should give the student a better understanding of world history. The majority of the review questions in the text, however, are oriented to factual recall, as are the sections on time, places, people, and historical terms, as well as the majority of the questions in the fourth section entitled "Questions for Critical Thinking."

A number of supplementary materials are offered for *Living World History*, including overhead projection materials and an excellent readings book—Edwin Fenton's *Thirty-two Problems in World History* (14) (to be discussed later). On balance I would say that despite the emphasis on factual recall in *Living World History* its variety of supplementary materials and its strong coverage of Western civilization and the early stages of non-Western culture make this textbook a possible selection for a teacher interested in the inquiry approach.

Arthur Boak *et al.*, in *The History of Our World* (6) attempted to present a balanced view of Western and non-Western cultures. Non-Western cultures such as India and China are examined first as ancient civilizations and then later as underdeveloped countries establishing contacts with the imperialistic West. This treatment has its shortcomings in the discussion of recent Asian history. One subsection is entitled "China's Civilization Was Little Changed for Centuries." This popular picture of a static China ignores ideas and changes brought about by the Buddhists, Mongols, and various contacts with the West. In essence this approach compares the limited progress of the non-Western cultures during the nineteenth and twentieth centuries with the much greater economic and technological achievements of a Europe that emerged dramatically during that same time period. Incidents that influenced the Chinese internal situation, such as the Taiping Rebellion and the reforms of 1900, receive little or no attention. This treatment contrasts with the coverage given events that had immediate international implications, such as the Boxer Rebellion and the Opium War. Again, the non-Western areas are viewed largely in terms of their effect on the West.

The History of Our World incorporates several unique features that contribute to its usefulness as a text. A section called "Linking the Past and Present" is provided for many topics to help the student relate historical events to contemporary occurrences. To emphasize the importance of the individual in history, picture biographies of such personages as Bolivar, Churchill, and Gandhi are included. The text also focuses on the development of freedom, from early codes that established order to more recent documents dealing with concepts of personal and political freedom. Although the text is organized chronologically and attempts coverage of most traditional world history topics, approximately one-half of the content is devoted to history since 1815. Moreover, the annotated teacher's edition (6) provides a number of teaching suggestions and insights into history. *The History of Our World* contains the usual chronology of events, but the authors show ingenuity in their techniques and teaching suggestions that help make the text a possible selection for the inquiry-oriented teacher.

Jack Abramowitz's *World History Study Lessons* (1) is directed toward the slow student who has had difficulty with world history. A reading consultant reviewed the text to ensure that such a student could understand the vocabulary and yet still improve his vocabulary skills during the course. The textbook is divided into nine short paperback units, a technique designed to encourage the slow student who heretofore has been stymied by the initial contact with 800 pages of material. The nine units apply more to Western civilization than to world history. The units are (1) "The Ancient World and the Middle Ages," (2) "From the Middle Ages to Modern Times," (3) "The Rise of Democracy," (4) "The Industrial Revolution," (5) "The French Revolution and Napoleon," (6) "The Expansion of Democracy," (7) "Nationalism and Imperialism," (8) "From World War I to World War II," and (9) "The World Since 1945." This text has several favorable features, but its fact-oriented approach limits its usefulness as an inquiry approach.

The evaluation of chronologically organized textbooks is disappointing for several reasons. Although some of the texts examined show ingenuity and certain commendable features, chronological organization seems to encourage the descriptive approach to history, which emphasizes the listing of facts rather than their application.

The chronologically oriented texts are also inadequate in their treatment of the non-Western world. Disproportionately little space is allotted to the non-West, and this area is usually not discussed until late in the books. These texts tend to discuss the non-West in terms of its contribution to Western civilization rather than in terms of its own cultural importance, thus neglecting events of strictly internal importance in non-Western countries. Most of the chronological textbooks are in fact teaching European history or Western civilization instead of world history. A 1956 UNESCO study (41) reported that nations geographically remote or not considered part of Western civilization receive inadequate textbook coverage, and my study agrees with these findings. With the establishment of the United Nations and the increasing importance of non-Western societies in world ideological and economic confrontations, an ethnocentric Western bias in presenting world history is particularly harmful to student understanding of the contemporary world.

AREA STUDIES TEXTBOOKS

Although most world history textbooks are organized chronologically, the area studies approach is gaining impetus in some academic circles. This approach divides the world into geographic spheres of influence. The non-Western areas of the world receive far more in-depth coverage in the area studies books than in any of the chronologically oriented texts examined. Of the twenty basic textbooks reviewed, three use the area studies approach. All three have been published since 1960, an indication that textbook writers and publishers have only recently begun to realize that it is important for students in the United States to study and understand cultures outside the traditional Western framework.

Ethel Ewing's *Our Widening World* (12) is the first popular world history textbook to use the area studies method of organization. The text is divided into seven cultural areas: the Middle East, the Slavic countries, Western Europe, the Far East, India and Southeast Asia, Anglo-America, and Latin America. The final section is devoted to the world today. The text ends with a supplementary chapter on sub-Saharan Africa. The author secured area specialists to prepare specific chapters of the book, which draw upon materials and techniques from several disciplines, especially anthropology. Many chapters use a very interesting and effective story-telling technique of surveying the daily life of an individual from a particular time and culture.

Discussion of societies deals with six critical areas: (1) geography, (2) technology, (3) organizations for living together, (4) special achievements, (5) interrelations of all parts of the culture, (6) relations with other societies. Each of the seven cultural areas is examined in terms of its early past, its culture before contact with western Europe, and the society's present struggle to adapt to the twentieth century.

A "workshop" is provided at the end of each unit, and some of the discussion questions can serve as springboards for student inquiry. The following is one of the better questions:

> 5. It has been said that the strength of our country is in the character of its society, in the kind of trust it commands in the world, and in the quality of its leadership in the community of nations.
>
> If the strength of the Soviet Union is measured by these standards, would you say that it is impressively great? Give facts to account for your answer. Do you agree with the statement quoted above? Would you add to it? If so, what? (Ewing, 12, p. 393.)

While the Ewing text has a number of good features, I found little continuity among the units of the text. Furthermore, the coverage of Africa is superficial compared to that of the other units.

Another recent area studies contribution is Paul Thomas Welty's *Man's Cultural Heritage* (44). Of particular interest is his extensive coverage of the great literature of the cultures examined. The section on India includes discussions of the *Jataka Tales*, the *Ramayana*, the *Mahabharata*, the *Panchatantra*, and the *Sakuntala*. The annotated teacher's edition of the text provides numerous suggestions, but in some cases these encourage pedestrian activities, such as using an encyclopedia. The Welty text examines early man, Asia, the Middle East, Europe, the communist world, the two Americas, and Africa, thus providing a balanced presentation of Western and non-Western cultures.

A Global History of Man by Leften Stavrianos *et al.* (39) resulted from a project conducted by Stavrianos at Northwestern University with funds furnished by the Carnegie Foundation. The text is designed to provide exposure to the time concepts of history and to offer an in-depth analysis of many cultural areas. Part I (which represents about 5 percent of the book) identifies the geographic factors that have influenced the course of history. Part II (which represents about 25 percent of the book) surveys man's history. Beginning with an analysis of man prior to written history and a discussion of "race," the section surveys man in ancient civilizations (3700–1000 B.C.), in classical civilizations (100–500 A.D.), and in medieval civilizations (500–1500 A.D.). The last section of Part II covers the period from 1500 to the present, with an emphasis on the European influence throughout the world. Part III (which comprises about 65 percent of the book) examines seven cultural areas of the world—the United States, the Soviet Union, Latin America, the Middle East, India, China, and sub-Saharan Africa. Part IV (comprising about 5 percent of the book) discusses the forces uniting and dividing the modern world.

There are several advantages to the Stavrianos method of organization. Part I creates a frame of reference for the rest of the text. The traditional world history course is presented in abbreviated fashion in Part II, leaving the bulk of the text for an in-depth analysis of the major areas of the world. This technique provides superior coverage of the non-Western world without slighting the influence of Europe on world history. One disadvantage of this text, however, is its neglect of the Renaissance.

The major objectives of *A Global History of Man* are "to give an overview of the state of the world today and, by giving an explanation of the world's historical evolution, help the student to gain an understanding of his contemporary global environment." If properly utilized by a good teacher, the textbook and its accompanying materials—which include *Readings in World History* (38), a book designed to complement the text—would contribute to the attainment of these objectives. The text and readings book are designed for either a one- or a two-year course, but the voluminous amount of material in both books and the nature of the course would seem to make the two-year sequence more realistic.

The textbooks using the area studies approach contain more in-depth analysis of non-Western cultures than do the chronologically organized texts I examined. The area studies approach presents problems in content selection and textual continuity, but at least this group of texts attempts to depart from the traditional selection of material. Although not specifically designed for an inquiry approach, the organizational structure of these texts appears to lend itself to that orientation.

SUPPLEMENTARY MATERIALS

Teacher's Manuals

A number of textbook publishers provide teacher's manuals to accompany the basic textbooks. These manuals are frequently written by individuals who have little to do with the original volume but who are given guidelines on the length and content desired for the manual.

The *Teacher's Manual for Story of Nations* (35) devotes three pages to philosophy and organization, eleven pages to audio-visual materials, and five pages to a bibliography. Fifty-five pages contain the key to the chapter questions. Of the 182 pages of Boak *et al. Teacher's Guide and Key for the History of Our World* (7), 120 pages contain answers for chapter questions. John M. Peoples and Alice J. Scott's *Teacher's Manual for Men and Nations: A World History* (31) contains teaching suggestions and outlines for use with the text, although half the book is allotted to answers for chapter review.

The *Teacher's Resource Book for Living World History* (43) contains 144 pages of answers to chapter questions. The remainder of the 254-page booklet consists of chapter introductions, audio-visual materials, and a particularly informative supplementary bibliography emphasizing paperback books. One promising section of this resource book is entitled "Applying Research Skills to World History." The manual utilizes the concept of cultural diffusion to illustrate the use of research skills. In explaining the steps needed to achieve an understanding of this concept, the author provides an excellent demonstration of the inquiry approach. More illustrations of this type would be beneficial in teacher's manuals.

Ella Leppert's *Teacher's Manual for A Global History of Man and Readings in World History* (21) consists primarily of answers to "Reviewing the Essentials" from the main text. More teaching suggestions would have been helpful, since the textbook follows an atypical approach. Louis M. de Gryse's *Teacher's Manual for Ethel E. Ewing's Our Widening World* (10) contains a number of helpful teaching suggestions.

In general the teacher's manuals are disappointing. Their main function is apparently to serve as answer books, and teaching suggestions are often traditional. Most of the manuals contain additional bibliographies and audio-visual lists, but the opportunity to provide new ways to view the textbook content has generally been neglected.

Testing Materials

For purposes of illustration two examinations from Harry D. Berg and Howard R. Anderson's *Tests for the History of Our World* (4) will be discussed. One hundred and fourteen of the 124 examples are fact-recall questions. (The other ten questions are based on an interpretive paragraph.) Despite the high percentage of rote memory questions, the tests are typical or better than most examined. A number of testing booklets, including *Tests for Mazour and Peoples' Men and Nations: A World History* (29), contain map questions. Questions from Peter Klassen and Marvin Veronee's *Tests for Living World History* (19) and from others (29, 5) involve comparisons of civilizations. All the workbooks examined (5, 20, 30) provide opportunity for little more than listing or arranging facts.

The focus of testing materials avaliable in world history indicates a problem for the teacher interested in the inquiry approach. If I were studying for any of the texts examined, I would memorize dates, names, and events, rather than study for concepts, themes, or generalizations. New testing materials are needed before the use of inquiry becomes the pattern within the classroom.

Readings

Another teaching aid appearing with increased frequency in the teaching of world history is the readings book. *Readings in World History* (38) was edited by Stavrianos to accompany *A Global History of Man* (39). This book of readings provides primary and secondary accounts of events and themes related to the textbook content. Edwin Fenton's *Thirty-two Problems in World History* (14) is designed to accompany *Living World History* (42) but can be coordinated with most available texts. The problem areas selected by Fenton give the student an opportunity to use the tools of historical research as well as to examine relationships and causal factors. The author provides an introduction to each problem that not only explains and clarifies but also encourages the student to think for himself. Let us examine Fenton's technique.

Problem 24 is "The Meaning of Imperialism." Four documents are presented to assist the student in defining "imperialism." The first reading is from a book written by F. D. Lugard of the British

East Africa Company. Rudyard Kipling's "The White Man's Burden" and Albert Beveridge's address to the Senate in support of the resolution to retain control of the Philippines present other viewpoints of imperialism. The final selection expresses the views of Alfred T. Mahan, the naval historian. These thought-provoking questions assist the student:

> 1. What were the stated or implied motives of the authors represented in these readings? Do you see selfish and selfless motives combined? Do the four writers share the same point of view?
> 2. How do you think educated Africans and Asians would react to the attitudes expressed in these four documents? What bearing does this issue have on international politics in the mid-twentieth century?
> 3. If you use the word "imperialist" to describe a man living about 1900, what would you want the word to mean? Would you use the same word to describe present-day Russian expansion into Europe? Why or why not?
>
> (Fenton, 14, p. 170.)

The approach of *Thirty-two Problems in World History* should prove of value in involving students in the secondary world history classroom.

Promising New Materials and Projects

New materials are continually being made available to the secondary school teacher. The Indiana Department of Public Instruction's *World Civilizations* curriculum guide (17) makes a concerted effort to acquaint teachers with the use of generalizations as a teaching aid. This technique assists the instructor in teaching the student not only what the facts are but how to analyze them. The guide lists a number of generalizations in specific areas and suggests a structure for a one- or a two-year world history course. This fifty-two page curriculum guide provides an excellent teaching resource that should be examined by teachers of all states.

Other good examples of useful generalizations for teaching can be found in the materials produced by the State Curriculum Commission of the California State Department of Education. These have been published in a number of sources, including Michaelis and Johnston's *The Social Sciences: Foundations of the Social Studies* (26).

Anthropology once played a minor role in the social studies, but today there is an increasing awareness of its importance in the social studies curriculum. In the past textbook writers have frequently turned for data to the anthropologist as an area specialist, but the anthropologist feels that his discipline can offer concepts that students could apply throughout the social studies curriculum (36).

The Anthropology Curriculum Study Project (3), sponsored by the American Anthropological Association and supported by the National Science Foundation, is currently designing anthropological materials for assimilation into the secondary school curriculum. Two units applying to world history—"The Study of Early Man" and "The Great Transformation"—are in advanced stages of preparation. "The Study of Early Man" is being taught for the second year in schools cooperating with the project.

The materials designed for this Project are intended to make a significant impact on the secondary school curriculum. Three of the project's suggested world history units would take from twelve to fifteen weeks to complete when taught in sequence. The first unit centers on man as a hunter-gatherer. The second examines the cultural transformation caused by the advent of agriculture, while the third develops a model for analyzing historical societies in anthropological terms and applies this model to an analysis of classical Greece. The techniques employed in the Project's units are numerous and sophisticated. Readings, evidence cards, cartridge films, slide-tapes, overhead transparencies, and plastic cards are used in the latter part of "The Study of Early Man."

Although this anthropological material is new and must still be proven in the classroom, it has already had some impact on the teaching of secondary school world history.

Recommendations and Conclusion

Most of the textbooks reviewed, especially those following the chronological pattern, are not impressive when evaluated by the criteria of this volume. Chronologically organized books have played an important role in the development of the current social studies curriculum, but the current textbook must meet the demands of today's society, not those of 1916's. The area studies organization presents content in a usable and realistic framework. Its improved treatment of the non-Western world and its use of material from a number of disciplines deserve praise, but these texts too could be further improved by a greater concern for the involvement of the learner in the subject.

Much has been written of the coming revolution (or perhaps it has already arrived) in social studies. History has long been the queen, or at least the mainstay, of social studies. But unless the historians shift their attention from voluminous lecture notes to the problems of the secondary school social studies teacher, they may find that the queen has been deposed. The focus of world history must shift from teaching isolated facts to teaching the student to understand and utilize concepts and generalizations. The secondary school world history course of tomorrow will be increasingly interdisciplinary in nature, but it remains to be seen whether history will play the dominant role in its structure. If the current world history course moves toward a world cultures focus, the roles of cultural anthropology, cultural geography, sociology, and social psychology will become more prominent in the course. There are indications that the dominant force in social studies tomorrow will be history or anthropology. The leading role will be played by the discipline that can better coordinate the interdisciplinary approach, that is more receptive to change, and that better implements the inquiry approach in the curriculum.

A greater focus on interdisciplinary materials in secondary school world history will necessitate certain changes in textbooks. Teams of specialists in various disciplines will probably be needed to compile the content. In addition educators for methodology, secondary teachers to ensure appropriate interest and academic levels, and a communications expert to prepare transparencies, charts, and maps will also be needed to put together a more broadly based textbook.

The textbook of tomorrow may consist of a series of paperbacks, which can be kept up to date more easily than today's hardbound volume. Future textbooks may well include sections advancing theories that will enable a student to choose and defend alternative values; these books may also help students to construct the type of comparative model that Shirley Engle advocated in *New Perspectives in World History* (11). He suggested that "we should be using the story of man to construct in our minds a kind of picture or model or theory (or concept if you like that word) of human behavior and of the potential for improved behavior, in organized social groups, large and small." This sort of framework may improve continuity of course content, the lack of which apparently causes some difficulty in the area studies approach.

The imminent changes in secondary school world history courses have many implications for teacher education. The requirements for teaching world history should include greater preparation in anthropology, geography, sociology, psychology, philosophy, and logic. The social science disciplines in the colleges and universities should provide courses for teachers that demonstrate modern methods of good teaching, as well as up-to-date scholarship. Too often the organizational and methodological examples provided the future teacher in the college are extremely poor. Colleges and universities should also provide opportunities for future teachers to participate in such innovations as closed-circuit television, programmed instruction, team teaching, flexible scheduling, and inquiry-oriented approach. These innovations are discussed but are too rarely demonstrated and experienced.

Change will undoubtedly be the keynote for the secondary school world history course of the future. Much of the course, however, can be based on traditional objectives. In 1949 Edgar B. Wesley proposed a list of objectives that are still valid for a world history course today:

> 1. The first and most obvious purpose in studying world history, then, is to provide an overview of the contemporary world. . . .
> 2. The second objective of world history, closely related to the first, is to secure an introduction to world problems. . . .
> 3. A third purpose in studying world history is to recognize that culture is international. . . .
> 4. A fourth objective of teaching world history is to derive and apply generalizations. . . .
> 5. So a fifth purpose of studying world history is to understand the world of tomorrow.
>
> (West, 46, pp. 2–4.)

Unfortunately far too often the objective of the world history course has been merely to examine the period from 5000 B.C. to the present, emphasizing factual recall of such events as 476 A.D., 800, 1066, 1215, and 1492. The problems facing the world of 1966, however, require a secondary school history course to be increasingly interdisciplinary in nature and to involve the learner in the exploration of the significant issues facing the peoples of the world.

Selected Bibliography

1. ABRAMOWITZ, JACK, *World History Study Lessons,* Follett, Chicago, 1963.

2. AMERICAN COUNCIL OF LEARNED SOCIETIES AND THE NATIONAL COUNCIL FOR THE SOCIAL STUDIES, *The Social Studies and the Social Sciences,* Harcourt, Brace & World, New York, 1962.

3. ANTHROPOLOGY CURRICULUM STUDY PROJECT, *Anthropology Curriculum Study Newsletter,* (Fall, 1965).

4. BERG, HARRY D., AND ANDERSON, HOWARD R., *Tests for the History of Our World,* Houghton Mifflin, Boston, 1965.

5. ————, *Workbook and Tests for the History of Our World,* Houghton Mifflin, Boston, 1965.

6. BOAK, ARTHUR, *et al., The History of Our World,* Annotated, Houghton Mifflin, Boston, 1965.

7. ————, *Teacher's Guide and Key for the History of Our World,* Houghton Mifflin, Boston, 1965.

8. BRON, WALTER C., *English Essays,* Henry Holt, New York, 1905.

9. CARR, EDWARD HALLETT, *What Is History?* Knopf, New York, 1962.

10. DE GRYSE, LOUIS M., *Teacher's Manual for Ethel E. Ewing's Our Widening World,* Rand McNally, Chicago, 1961.

11. ENGLE, SHIRLEY H. (ed.), *New Perspectives in World History,* Thirty-fourth Yearbook of the National Council for the Social Studies, Washington, D.C., 1964.

12. EWING, ETHEL, *Our Widening World,* Rand McNally, Chicago, 1961.

13. ————, *Study Guide for Our Widening World,* Rand McNally, Chicago, 1961.

14. FENTON, EDWIN, *Thirty-two Problems in World History,* Scott, Foresman, Chicago, 1964.

15. GARDINER, PATRICK (ed.), *Theories of History,* The Free Press, Glencoe, Ill., 1959.

16. HUNT, ERLING M., *et al., High School Social Studies Perspectives,* Houghton Mifflin, Boston, 1962.

17. INDIANA STATE DEPARTMENT OF PUBLIC INSTRUCTION, Supervised by Edgar B. Smith and Ellen Parr, *World Civilizations: A Curriculum Guide,* Indiana Department of Public Instruction, Indianapolis, 1965.

18. KERSHNER, FREDERICK D., JR., "Social Science and History, Conflict or Coexistence?" *Teachers College Record,* 64 (Mar., 1963), 456–65.

19. KLASSEN, PETER J., AND VERONEE, MARVIN D., *Tests for Living World History,* Scott, Foresman, Chicago, 1964.

20. KOSS, HERMAN, *Workbook for Story of Nations,* Holt, Rinehart and Winston, New York, 1960.

21. LEPPERT, ELLA, *Teacher's Manual for a Global History of Man and Readings in World History,* Allyn and Bacon, Chicago, 1962.

22. MASIA, BERTRAM, "Profile of the Current Social Studies in North Central Association Schools," *The North Central Association Quarterly,* 38 (Fall, 1963), 205–13.

23. MASSIALAS, BYRON G., AND SMITH, FREDERICK R. (eds.), *New Challenges in the Social Studies,* Wadsworth, Belmont, Calif., 1965.

24. MAZOUR, ANATOLE G., AND PEOPLES, JOHN M., *Men and Nations: A World History,* Harcourt, Brace & World, New York, 1964.

25. MEYERHOFF, HANS (ed.), *The Philosophy of History: An Anthology,* Doubleday Anchor Books, Garden City, N.Y., 1959.

26. MICHAELIS, JOHN U., AND JOHNSTON, A. MONTGOMERY (eds.), *The Social Sciences: Foundation of the Social Studies,* Allyn and Bacon, Boston, 1965.

27. MILLER, STANLEY N., "The World Cultures Course," *Social Education,* 25 (May, 1961), 237–38.

28. NIER, CHARLES, "China: The Treatment by High School World History Textbooks, 1920–1964," unpublished master's thesis, Graduate School of Education, University of Chicago, 1965.

29. PEOPLES, JOHN M., *Tests for Mazour and Peoples' Men and Nations: A World History,* Harcourt, Brace & World, New York, 1959.

30. ————, *Workbook for Men and Nations: A World History,* Harcourt, Brace & World, New York, 1959.

31. PEOPLES, JOHN M., AND SCOTT, ALICE J., *Teacher's Manual for Men and Nations: A World History,* Harcourt, Brace & World, New York, 1964.

32. POHLMANN, VERNON C., AND WELLMAN, FREDERICK L., "Are High School Social Studies Teachers Adequately Prepared?" *Social Education,* 24 (Nov., 1960), 310–12.

33. ROBINSON, JAMES HARVEY, *The New History,* The Free Press, New York, 1965.

34. ROGERS, LESTER B., ADAMS, FAY, AND BROWN, WALKER, *Story of Nations,* Holt, Rinehart and Winston, New York, 1960.

35. ————, *Teacher's Manual and Answer Book for Story of Nations,* Holt, Rinehart and Winston, New York, 1960.

36. SADY, RACHEL REESE, "Anthropology and World History Texts," *Phi Delta Kappan,* 45 (Jan., 1964), 247–51.

37. SIEMERS, ALLAN, "World History: Practices and Problems," *Social Education,* 24 (Apr., 1960), 153–57.

38. STAVRIANOS, LEFTEN S., *et al., Readings in World History,* Allyn and Bacon, Chicago, 1962.

39. STAVRIANOS, LEFTEN S., *et al., A Global History of Man,* Allyn and Bacon, Chicago, 1965.

40. STERN, FRITZ (ed.), *The Varieties of History: From Voltaire to the Present,* Meridian Books, New York, 1957.

41. UNITED NATIONS ECONOMIC AND SOCIAL COUNCIL, *Treatment of Asia in Western Textbooks and Teaching Materials,* UNESCO, Paris, 1956.

42. WALLBANK, T. WALTER, AND SCHRIER, ARNOLD, *Living World History*, Scott, Foresman, Chicago, 1964.

43. ———, *Teacher's Resource Book for Living World History*, Scott, Foresman, Chicago, 1964.

44. WELTY, PAUL THOMAS, *Man's Cultural Heritage: A World History*, Annotated, Lippincott, Philadelphia, 1965.

45. WESLEY, EDGAR B., AND WRONSKI, STANLEY P., *Teaching Social Studies in High Schools*, Heath, Boston, 1958.

46. WEST, EDITH (ed.), *Improving the Teaching of World History*, Twentieth Yearbook of the National Council for the Social Studies, Washington, D.C., 1949.

CHAPTER 11

Psychology and Sociology

The Study of Human Behavior

EMILY S. GIRAULT

The Objectives of Studying Psychology and Sociology

Any consideration of the status of psychology or sociology in the high school curriculum and any review of instructional materials currently used in these courses must begin with the question "why teach sociology or psychology in the secondary school?" This question has been thoroughly debated in pedagogical literature. Some argue that the high school curriculum is already overburdened and the high school student cannot afford the time to study these disciplines as separate courses (14); others offer detailed elaborations of course objectives (4, 18) as rationale for the separate treatment of psychology and sociology.

The latter observers have tried to identify the benefits that the student would derive from a pursuit of these studies. Generally these objectives can be classified into three closely interwoven categories: (1) familiarity with how a behavioral scientist thinks and training in the use of his methods; (2) awareness of the way in which an individual in our society relates to and uses the social sciences; and (3) enriched understanding of oneself and his social milieu.

The first objective has been spelled out in a number of ways. MacLeod (in 14) has pointed out that basic to all learning in this area is training and experience in looking at the real world, in clarifying the phenomena that one is talking about. This training should include development of the skill of categorization, of the awareness of implications and unstated assumptions, and of a sensitivity to the possibility of multiple causation. Furthermore, MacLeod points out, students cannot learn too early that human relationships can be studied and that there are useful ways of dealing objectively with issues close to their own lives.

The second objective, that of understanding the individual's relationship to the social sciences, requires a growing understanding of the methods and products of the sociologist or the psychologist. While this appreciation may be meaningful to only a small fraction of high school students in choosing a career, it helps every member of our society to become a more able, intelligent consumer of the products of the social scientist. And indeed the latter process is the more apt objective of the secondary social science curriculum.

The third objective, an enriched understanding of oneself in society, is universally agreed upon by educators and social scientists alike. A companion aim is the student's enlivened appreciation of literature and the arts through the application of psychological and sociological insights to these media.[1]

High School Psychology

If we can assume that psychology textbooks reflect the content and emphasis of the course, then it is apparent that the high school psychology course is pressed into one of two molds: one emphasizing the life-adjustment problems of the students or one stressing psychology as a science and academic discipline. I found no textbook that achieved a satisfactory blend of these two emphases. Two texts (3 and 9) have been selected for review and comparison because of their current popular usage and because they express very well this apparent dilemma.

The foreword of one text (9) itemizes six general gains that the

[1]Lewis Coser's *Sociology Through Literature* (6), which underscores the humanistic tradition of sociology in college level classes, might serve as a helpful model for high school materials of this nature.

student can expect from the course: (1) an "understanding of inter-personal relationships on a worldwide basis"; (2) an "understanding of one's own behavior"; (3) an appreciation of psychology as a science, with subsumed objectives related to an understanding of scientific thought and method; (4) the avoidance of fallacious claims made by pseudopsychologists; (5) an increasing objectivity on the part of the student in viewing social problems; and (6) a conviction of the dignity and the brotherhood of man. Actually it seems that the authors have had to opt for either the life-adjustment approach or the scientific-emphasis tack.

While the Engle text does develop a few of the concepts basic to psychology, this development is done in a context of student-centered problems. The overarching generalization it sets forth is that human behavior is both patterned and varied. Much of the text is devoted to a treatment of mental health, love and marriage, and social problems such as delinquency and crime. Branca, on the other hand, gives minimal attention to the on-going problems of the high school student, and directs his reader to a more strict construction of psychology as a science.

The following example illustrates how an extreme effort to fulfill the life-adjustment function hinders the teaching of psychology. The author asks, "What are some of the basic elements of a pleasing personality?" Assuming the role of the how-to-win-friends advisor, he then cites six of these "elements": (1) "Sincerity," (2) "A Basic Guiding Philosophy," (3) "Unselfishness," (4) "A Tendency to Look for Good in People," (5) "Cheerfulness," and (6) "Control of Emotions and Moods." After presenting this somewhat sermonistic list, the author asks, "What are some techniques for helping others to like us?" A five-rule prescription follows. One must (1) help to build the self-respect of the other person, (2) be tactful, (3) be skilled in several forms of social recreation, (4) practice the common rules of etiquette, and (5) make the most of his personal appearance.

Such statements are hardly representative of the discipline of psychology. Does not the student deserve some form of supportive rationale or, preferably, research evidence for the statements? At least the author should provide a line of rational hypothesizing to aid the student in recognizing and practicing the format or style of scientific speculation. Our central objection, however, is that the didactic presentation of the material violates the basic tenets of the inquiry approach to learning as well as the scientific method of psychology.

The preface of the text suggests that "a study of psychology should give the student an appreciation for the ways in which the general methods of science can be applied to problems of behavior." Yet the textbook makes no effort to familiarize students with these methods. For instance, defining a "pleasing personality" and identifying "techniques for helping others to like us" can be the first steps in examining valid problems of behavior and may thus offer the student rich opportunities to gain experience in scientific methodology. If the text were to pose questions for analysis, instead of presenting lists to be memorized, students might well be pressed to define terms, to share hunches and speculations, and to shape these hunches into verifiable hypotheses. The next equally important phase would be that of seeking data in the real world of their classmates, peers, and the older and younger people with whom they associate; these data could then be analyzed for validation or invalidation of the students' hypotheses. The class would then reshape and tighten its generalizations in the light of its own research findings. Such an approach seems to promise more fruitful scientific and interpersonal experience than the sterile presentation of rules for winning popularity.

The strongest section of the Engle volume is the one dealing with personality theory. In this part the reader is not only given a review of personality theories but is led to consider the importance of theory in any science. The text discusses the explanatory and predictive functions of theory as well as the tentative nature of theoretical formulation. Of equal importance to the student's understanding of scientific thought and method is the skillful way in which the author interlaces concepts of statistical measurement and data analysis throughout this section and the way he clarifies the relationship of these concepts to an objective or "scientific" understanding of social phenomena.

The development of concepts other than that of personality, however, seems unnecessarily shallow. An example of this oversimplification is the treatment accorded perception—a process and area of investigation so central to an understanding of psychology that it may well be second in importance only to personality theory. The discussion of perception is introduced by asking the reader to consider a line drawing and then suggesting ways in which this drawing might be interpreted. The text goes on to state that "the only explanation [as to the differences of these perceptions] can be in terms of the previous experiences of the individuals." This is certainly an acceptable introduction, but one expects a more careful exploration of the ways in which psychologists have worked to reduce the vast range of human experiences to a group of manageable factors. The author does deal with sensory deprivation and subliminal perception, but in view of the increasingly rich research literature on perception, his treatment of this topic only in terms of its threshold aspects seems to give short shrift to an area of central importance. The author fails to discuss in sufficient detail a variety of variables—such as context, learning, set, and motivation—that have been shown in recent research to influence the perceptual process.

A sizable section of the Engle text is devoted to love and marriage. The section begins by presenting eight criteria for "romantic love," from "strong physical attraction" to perhaps "some quarreling." The text then considers the advantages and disadvantages of going steady. Among the disadvantages cited are "being out of circulation" and the painfulness of breaking up; the advantages mentioned are convenience and security. Again a perfect opportunity to encourage students to collect their own data is overlooked. What research team would have greater access to first-hand data about going steady than a group of adolescent investigators? Following the section on going steady, the author moves to a consideration of marriage and children and then devotes three pages to "sex instruction for children."

The fact that there is no open, honest treatment of sex as a concrete problem for the adolescent is disturbing to me. Textbooks show no recognition of the fact that the central questions for high school students are not "how shall I make sex education available to my children?" or "what are some of the serious problems between married people?" or even "at what age should I marry?" Far more central to the teenage students using this text is the question "how much sexual familiarity and involvement should characterize my relationships now?"

I am not suggesting that sex education must necessarily be part of the high school psychology class. But if the class is going to deal with the personal and social problems of the student (and the Engle text certainly makes this attempt), then it must make a realistic and honest appraisal of these problems. Much of the literature dealing with sex and much of the "teaching of sex" emphasizes the sexual behavior of groups outside the classroom and distant from the students: marriage and divorce problems, sexual relations among college students or among Scandinavians, or "bundling" in the Puritan society. We go to considerable trouble, it seems, to avoid the recognition that our students (like the Swedes and the Puritans) are pressured by sexual needs. And we do not point out that while these needs are valid—in the sense of their being universal—social and cultural arrangements attach exceedingly heavy costs to their premature satisfaction and make their satisfaction in an emotionally healthy way all but impossible during most of the adolescent years. We talk about a learner-centered or a problem-centered curriculum, but we evade the basic issue completely when it comes to sex education, and we offer little assistance to adolescent students who are wrestling with the pressures of emerging sexual needs.

As if in recognition of the fact that a growing proportion of our population faces a struggle with mental illness at some time in their lives, both psychology textbooks I reviewed include some material on this topic. The texts differ drastically, however, in their discussions of mental illness.

The Engle text, which is more obviously directed toward life-adjustment issues than the Branca text, is seriously deficient in its exposition on mental and emotional disorder. It begins with this statement: "In modern mental hospitals those being cared for are spoken of as patients. This idea of patients in a hospital is quite different from the popular notion of 'nuts' in a 'nuthouse.'" The tone of condescension and the oversimplified presentation continue throughout the section. The text is equally wanting in its discussion of the treatment of mental illness. Psychoanalysis is defined simply as "a method of treatment for mental disorders and a body of psychology theory." An explanation of the id-ego-superego model follows. This very brief section, which purports to enlighten the reader on the psychoanalytic approach, concludes: "psychoanalysts must be given credit for helping us to appreciate the importance of . . . childhood experiences upon . . . later life and for striving to understand and help their fellow men." The text does not, however, offer the student an understanding of various treatment approaches.

By contrast, Branca offers a valuable practical section on the psychotherapies. His text distinguishes among group therapy, psychodrama, hypnotherapy, client-centered therapy, and psychoanalysis in such a way that the student can begin to develop an understanding of their differences that will be useful to him in the adult world. The text also explains the different roles of members of the "treatment team"—the psychiatrist, the clinical psychologist, the psychoanalyst, and the psychiatric social worker.

Both texts are inadequate in their treatment of drugs. Engle's sole reference in the text to the use of drugs is this statement: "There are drugs that are helpful. For example, the tranquilizing drugs help to relieve the fears and anxieties of disturbed patients. When used judiciously such drugs are of definite therapeutic value." There is no mention of the effects of those natural and synthetic drugs that expand consciousness. The Branca text (3) also gives the drug problem only passing attention. Note the prescriptive, sermonizing tone of this comment: "[drugs are] the poisons that human beings have learned to introduce into their systems voluntarily, [and] there is no doubt that the ultimate result of their prolonged use is the destruction of the worth of the person."

All of the above material concerning mental illness, psychiatry, and the use of drugs leaves me with the sad impression that the volume is speaking to a youth no longer existent. The author seems oblivious to the pressures, the questions, and the issues that are paramount for today's high school student. There is no recognition, explicit or implicit, of the fact that the author is speaking at least in part to a generation of adolescents not at all concerned about whether to use the term "patient" or "nut" but rather about whether to smoke "pot" or "take a trip" on LSD.

Branca's text consistently emphasizes the discipline of psychology as a field of scientific investigation and devotes very little space to the life-adjustment approach. The preface promises that the volume will provide "a truly scientific text for the beginning student . . . by emphasizing the fact that human behavior is a legitimate subject for scientific study." The text begins with a better-than-average chapter relating psychology to other sciences. It then moves from a consideration of the individual as an organism to problems of learning and perception and then to a treatment of the interaction of persons and some aspects of social psychology. Finally, the text offers an unusually comprehensive chapter on personality and its measurement.

The Branca text puts decidedly more emphasis upon psychology as a developing discipline than does the Engle volume. Branca consistently gives his reader a sense of the newness of the field and an appreciation for the rather dramatic convolutions through which its theoretical structure has already passed. At no point does Branca make his reader feel that the text is oversimplifying its presentation or being condescending.

An adjunct to the author's approach to psychology as a developing field of study is the text's emphasis on the predictive aspects of the discipline. In both the text passages and the end of chapter exercises the author encourages his reader to make speculations using data offered in the text or collected by the student. A notable strength of the Branca text is its obvious effort to give the student up-to-date information concerning the current frontiers of psychology. Exemplary sections are those treating cybernetics, the general concept of the feedback loop, and information theory.

The final chapter constitutes Branca's one concession to the life-adjustment approach. Entitled "Choosing a Vocation," the chapter surveys the various professions available to a student with advanced training in psychology. Not only is this chapter potentially helpful to the student who wants a career based upon psychology, but it offers all students a helpful explanation of what a psychologist does. The book contributes significantly to the removal of a "mystique" about psychology and its various practitioners.

In some respects the Engle and the Branca texts are complementary and might be used in the same class. The Engle text is without doubt more suitable for a class emphasizing life adjustment or personal problems, and its reading level is simpler than is that of the Branca text. Branca, while devoting less attention to the problems of adolescent development, does offer a more sophisticated view of psychology—one that would provide a firmer base for possible continuation of this study at the college level.

The popularity of two such different texts is a useful indication of the current dichotomy in high school psychology courses. The basic question remains: Should psychology be included in the high school curriculum for the purpose of facilitating the self-understanding and personal adjustment of the student or for the purpose of increasing the student's general sophistication and insight in the social sciences? The current practice seems to be for psychology classes to choose one alternative, rather than to combine the two.

Sociology in the High School Curriculum

The literature on the teaching of sociology suggests that the course, and hence a text for it, should expose the student to (1) the concepts central to the discipline, (2) a sampling of the theoretical models that have guided sociologists in their conceptualizations, and (3) examples of significant sociological studies. Let us examine each of these goals in greater detail.

1. Sociology is concerned with the entire complex network of social relationships. This network may be roughly divided into three fields of analysis: a study of groups, a study of institutions, and an analysis of general social structure. Certainly any secondary school course in sociology should introduce the student to an understanding of the ways in which humans form definite groups, an appreciation of institutions as organized systems of practice and action, and an awareness of the overall structure and function of society.

2. The student should be helped to identify and clarify the theoretical models that form the basis of the discipline. Newcomb and Chesler (in 14) suggested the exploration of a few sample theories, such as the life-space (force-field) model or balance theory. It is hoped that the student will also gain some familiarity with the historic evolution of sociology, with the several causation theories that have successively served this discipline, and with some of the concepts with which sociologists frequently work, such as deviancy, anomie, and primary and secondary groups.

3. The sociology course should survey some exemplary or significant sociological studies. A class might consider a series of community studies such as those by Lynd, Warner, Hollingshead, and Dobriner,[2] or it might peruse studies of deviancy such as Sutherland's work on criminal behavior[3] and Cohen's[4] study of delinquent boys. The main objective, of course, would not be to review the studies as an end in itself or to supply evidence for generalizations and conclusions. The object would be to increase the student's familiarity with the *modus operandi* of a sociologist—to enable him to understand the data-gathering techniques used by sociologists, the

[2]Helen and Robert Lynd, *Middletown*, Harcourt, Brace & World, New York, 1929; and *Middletown in Transition*, Harcourt, Brace & World, New York, 1937. W. Lloyd Warner *et al.*, *Social Class in America*, Science Research Associates, New York, 1949. William M. Dobriner, *Class in Suburbia*, Prentice-Hall, Englewood Cliffs, N.J., 1963. August B. Hollingshead, *Elmtown's Youth*, Wiley, New York, 1949.
[3]Sutherland, Edwin H., "White Collar Criminality," *American Sociological Review*, 5 (Feb., 1940), 1–12. Sutherland, Edwin H. (ed.), *The Professional Thief*, The University of Chicago Press, Chicago, 1937.
[4]Cohen, Albert K., *Delinquent Boys: The Culture of the Gang*, The Free Press, Glencoe, Ill., 1955.

meaning of measurement and quantification, and some of the pitfalls of data analysis and interpretation. The student should have an opportunity to participate in the active design and pursuit of at least one original field problem during his study of sociology.

We have, then, three criteria upon which to base our consideration of instructional materials: (1) a review of central concepts, (2) a sampling of theory models, and (3) an explication of sociological methodology. When measured against these criteria, both texts selected for review here (5 and 17) are disappointing. Each volume makes a substantial contribution toward the satisfaction of the first two requirements. But both texts are seriously wanting in the presentation of research studies both to substantiate conclusions and to exemplify research designs.

One text (5) promises the student aid in "gaining concrete and definite knowledge of social problems and scientific ways of studying them." But a reading of the text reveals instead a number of conclusive statements not only lacking empirical support but couched in language that would make their validation virtually impossible. For example:

> One of the fine qualities about Americans is that we admit our faults as well as our strong points. (Cole and Montgomery, 5, p. 342.)

> No other country has more nearly approached the goals of true democracy than has our United States. As long as we hold these goals high in our own aims, our nation will not falter in its progress toward a better world. (*Ibid.*, p. 341.)

> No doubt many of the early settlers were inspired men. (*Ibid.*, p. 342.)

> Delinquency rates are high in families which are broken and in which there is separation, viciousness, suspicion, or lack of idealism. (*Ibid.*, p. 311.)

> [Social] classes in society are more or less inevitable. . . . It is important to keep the social classes open. (*Ibid.*, p. 365.)

While the text does note that the concepts of social class and social stratification are associated with such factors as wealth, occupation, and family, it does not elaborate on the relationship that research has demonstrated between social-class membership and the life-space of the individual, his behavior patterns, his motivation for achievement, and his physical and emotional health. A broad array of empirical studies is available on the implications of social-class membership, but none are used in this text.

Hering's study (12) indicated that this deficiency is typical of sociology textbooks and suggested that textbook authors are reticent about reporting research findings that students might interpret as personally relevant in a negative way.

> For example, all texts indicate that the United States has much less rigid stratification than do many societies and emphasize the possibilities of social mobilities. Problems such as delinquency and prejudice resulting in segregation are treated as something apart from the reader—a general problem not involving the students who are studying it. Students may therefore attach less significance to these problems than they might if more realistic information were available. (Hering, 12, p. 15.)

Cole and Montgomery (5) exemplify the tendency described by Hering in their chapter on relations with minority groups. It is incredible that a text published in 1963 dealing with minority group relations has no reference to the civil rights movement! One paragraph in particular stands out as a classic example of understatement:

> Minorities are often discriminated against in education. Better programs and facilities may be made available for dominant groups. In some private schools racial and religious minorities are not accepted in any large numbers, if at all. In 1961 out of 6,373 school districts in the South, 2,804 were accepting Negroes and whites in the same schools on the same basis. About 7.5% of Negro school children were in schools with whites.   (Cole and Montgomery, 5, p. 320.)

One wonders whether such treatment of issues so prominent on the current national scene is a result of ignorance on the part of authors and publisher or an effort to ensure the salability of the text in all parts of the country.

The preface to Landis (17) indicates that the book intends to "recognize the contributions which anthropology has made to an understanding of other peoples and, indeed, even to our own customs and social institutions." This book carries out its intent in a four-chapter sequence setting forth substantial material on culture, cultural change, and the effects of culture on personality. Units 3 and 4 treat some of the central concepts in sociology: the social self, primary and secondary groups, status and role, and social change.

Landis then moves to sections dealing with problems of marriage and the family, problems of government, problems of our economic system, and the conservation of human resources.

A fairly respectable section on "how the sociologist works" describes the control-group method and emphasizes the importance of comparison in scientific validation. More should have been said, however, about participant-observation, interviewing, and survey techniques, since these are the field research tools most accessible to the student.

The appendices of the Landis text include materials to assist the teacher, particularly one with minimal training in sociology. The suggested references for outside reading, which are directed at both teacher and students, are pertinent and generally available. The bibliographical listing should also be of use to a school librarian in coordinating the library inventory with the curricular offerings. The annotated section on films and filmstrips appears to be equally useful. An appendix listing generalizations from anthropology used in the text may well serve the teacher in identifying points of significant emphasis and in evaluating what the students have learned. A substantial glossary that repeats and refines definitions of terms used in the text helps to make the appendix one of the greatest strengths of the volume.

After consideration has been given to the central concepts of sociology and the techniques employed by sociologists that should be mastered by a student, the question of the "spirit" of sociology still remains. Is there such a thing as a sociological frame of reference that may in fact alter the way the student views his world?

In his slender volume Peter L. Berger (1) argues that sociology constitutes a particular way of looking at the world—a special frame of reference that gives to social reality parameters different from those seen by the viewer unschooled in sociological thinking. This sociological awareness is characterized by three general traits. The first is *skepticism*, a kind of "debunking" thought posture: to ask sociological questions one looks "beyond the commonly accepted or officially defined goals of human action . . . and presupposes a measure of suspicion about the way in which human events are officially interpreted by the authorities." "*Relativization*," the second trait, is characterized by "the awareness that one's own culture, including its basic values, is relative in time and space." The third trait has to do with one's view of himself: he begins with the recognition that his roles and status in society represent a social bestowing of identity, and this identity is supported by society. According to the sociological view the self is not a constant: "looked as sociologically, the self is no longer a solid, given entity that moves from one situation to another. It is rather a process."

The dimensions of sociological awareness identified above deserve careful attention on the part of educators who debate placement of sociology in the curriculum. For example, curricular support of relativism poses serious ethical questions. The possibility that our American way of life (including our form of government, our Judeo-Christian heritage, and our economic system) is not necessarily the ultimate and "best" solution for all peoples is given only infrequent and halting consideration in the social studies literature.

The handling of religion in the high school sociology texts reviewed in this chapter highlights this dilemma. No functional treatment of religion as a system of belief appears in Cole and Montgomery (5); there is no effort to present religion as serving an important explanatory function in a society or to point out the role of religion as a mediating factor between man and those elements in his environment he cannot explain. The only definitive statement is: "Religion is not easy to define. It has to do with supernatural powers that control the universe and the ways in which these are believed to influence men." Such a statement is of dubious service to a young generation coming to maturity at a time of dramatic scientific forays into outer space. There are in fact several ways in which religion can be defined sociologically; furthermore, to say that religion "has to do with supernatural powers that control the universe" is quite different from saying that religion has to do with a people's *belief* in supernatural powers.

The Landis volume (17) takes an even more perplexing and frustrating view of religion. The chapter entitled "Religion and Ethical Ideals" opens with the statement, "Man cannot live by reason alone. He must have faith." This mandate for survival (scarcely empirical in tone) is a theme running throughout the text.

Declarative statements of the following type give the reader pause:

> Communism has been presented to masses of the world's people as a substitute religion. But political philosophies supported by emotional loyalties do not answer man's endless queries of the how and why of human existence. This is the sphere of religious faith. (Landis, 17, p. 450.)

Attributing to God the origin of life and the universe, we try to discover the natural laws. We try to govern ourselves according to these laws rather than expect God to change them to suit us. (*Ibid.*, p. 451.)

Surely the biological and social sciences share in the task of seeking tentative answers to "man's endless queries of the how and why of human existence." It is indeed strange that the author of a sociology text should remove this task from the province of science and place it exclusively in "the sphere of religious faith."

Not only does the text seem to disallow the validity of a non-religious belief system, but in effect equates "religion" with "Christianity." Such an equation makes the text offensive to potential users who are non-Christian and, moreover, violates the author's expressed intention of using anthropological insight to strengthen understanding of others. A section entitled "Christianity's World Challenge" opens with the statement that the "Christian missionary movement has been a vital force in world affairs." The passage lauds the work of various medical, technical, and agricultural missionaries who have "helped primitive peoples in many lands to a better life and to a higher standard of conduct." The concluding sentence of the chapter reads, "Today the Christian church faces a world challenge unparalleled in history." Such blatant ethnocentrism grossly misrepresents sociology and anthropology. In addition it may indeed do irremedial damage to the development of a scientific perspective of society.

These deficiencies demonstrate that the age-old confounding of science and religion is with us yet and evidently plagues textbook authors and publishers alike. The treatment of religion described above seems to offer no gain whatever to the student: such a presentation certainly does no justice to sociology nor can it seriously be thought to serve the cause of religion. A high school text cannot be completely comprehensive in its coverage of a field; if the author and publisher find it impossible (or impolitic) to deal honestly with a topic such as religion within the framework of sociology, why deal with such a topic at all?

The Need for Inquiry-Oriented Student Projects

Instructional materials in psychology and sociology must meet a greater responsibility than that of most social studies textbooks because teachers are particularly dependent on psychology and sociology textbooks both for substantive content and for the design of student activities. Engle (8) pointed out in 1960 that, in terms of academic training, teachers are ill equipped to read a psychology or sociology textbook critically and to set it aside or introduce other material when necessary. His findings were corroborated by a study of Illinois social studies teachers in 1961 (Grupp, 10), which indicated that 82 percent of those teaching one or more classes in sociology had taken fewer than thirteen semester hours of sociology, and 32 percent of these teachers had taken fewer than eight hours of sociology. Furthermore, the fact that most teachers have been trained in history at the college level rather than psychology or sociology means they are apt to have had little, if any, personal experience with the research techniques characterizing the latter fields. They are in no position, therefore, to help students to formulate problems or to collect, analyze, and interpret data—processes that are essential to the development of critical inquiry in the students.

Unfortunately none of the texts reviewed in this chapter make a truly effective move toward involving the students in the process of inquiry. Branca (3), however, goes much further in this direction than any other author. Not one of the volumes is organized in such a way that the student will be *forced* to gather and analyze his own data. Nor does any book reviewed here consistently employ what might be called a pseudolaboratory approach, that is, the presentation of problems through classic research studies.

While the utilization of exemplary research studies can never replace the student's own research, such studies can familiarize the student with the research process. Following the presentation of the research problem, but before reading the entire study, the student could design a plan for data collection and analysis and compare his plan with the one actually used by the researchers. If he were given the research findings and analysis in a simplified form, the student could try to interpret these data and compare his interpretation with that of the original researchers. One important result of this approach would be that the student would begin to sense the tentativeness of answers and of interpretative conclusions.

Since these observations on the high school psychology and sociology courses are extremely depressing, one can only search for promising signs among the new programs in curriculum development. At this writing there is no large-scale curriculum project specifically for the development of a psychology course or of psychology materials. In the field of sociology, however, a most enterprising project is Sociological Resources for Secondary Schools (SRSS), which is sponsored by the American Sociological Association and funded by the National Science Foundation (7). The project, located in Ann Arbor, Michigan, and directed by Professor Robert Angell, is developing new secondary school sociological materials and units. SRSS assumes as its major premise that "the education of today's high school students can be improved by familiarizing them with the sociological perspective." This perspective is characterized as the "effort to construct broad generalizations about social patterns by gathering empirical data through careful and self-conscious techniques that are as unaffected by value judgments as possible."

The SRSS group is taking its first step toward this goal with the construction of a series of "episodes" around sociological concepts. The episodes, which maximize the student's opportunity to have first-hand encounters with data, may be used serially as the basic material for a semester's course or may be employed singly to bolster topical treatment in other social studies courses. The major thrust of the episodes will be toward the active involvement of students in the collection, classification, and interpretation of data. Efforts are being made to design material for students of all abilities. The most promising pedagogical statement of the project is this: "the goal of SRSS materials is not so much to tell students what the 'answers' are as to show them the process of arriving at answers." If the materials do in fact accomplish this goal, they will constitute an important change in the nature of the sociological textual materials as well as provide valuable models for future materials.

Conclusion

Initially we identified three reasons for teaching psychology and sociology in the secondary school. It might be helpful to use each reason as a criterion for assessing the present situation.

The first objective was to make the student conversant with how a sociologist or psychologist thinks. The representative materials reviewed here seem altogether deficient in furthering this goal. These materials not only underemphasize the dynamic nature of knowledge in the social sciences and the tentativeness of conclusions, but they violate the spirit of inquiry through their didactic presentation of content. The texts offer only minimal exposition of social science methodologies or the role of theory, hypothesis, and question-asking in the process of social inquiry. The fulfillment of this objective requires at least two additional components: the provision of case studies as research models and the specific, repeated opportunities for students to design and pursue their own research problems.

It should be made explicit here that learning *how* a social scientist thinks and *what* he thinks may imply totally different activities and lead to different (if not contradictory) outcomes. The texts do go much further in presenting what a social scientist thinks than how he does so: they do convey some of the current concepts and theories of psychology and sociology. It is futile, however, for textbooks to try to present this content as though it were a fixed body of data to be memorized by the student, rather than as material that is subject to constant revision and reorganization.

The psychology and sociology texts also fall short on the second objective: giving students an awareness of how an individual in our society relates to and uses the social sciences. Students should be helped to assume the role of a consumer of social science knowledge. Practice in this role requires that students be trained in the retrieval and application of social science knowledge to problems that are salient for the adolescent. Skills such as identifying problems and information sources, assessing the reliability of these sources, and determining the relevance of particular knowledge to the problem at hand are virtually ignored in the textual materials.

It is in connection with this second objective that the mishandling of controversial issues seems particularly serious. The mistreatment of topics such as sex, religion, drugs, and social class completely misrepresents the social science perspective. Furthermore, since such topics are generally closed to free and open discussion in our society, textbooks miss an admirable opportunity to refine the issues in the light of existing social science knowledge.

The texts come closer to realizing the third objective, an enriched understanding of oneself and one's social milieu. Again, however, the preceptive, "lecturing" tone of the volumes is troublesome. The pursuit and use of data gathered within the parameters of one's own life would seem to promote self-understanding far better than the traditional didactic approach to knowledge. Nor does the feeding of information and conclusions drawn from remote social situations help to develop a student's awareness that the social transactions in which he participates are valid objects of study and change.

The overall situation described here certainly invites proposals for change. The fact that social science teachers are trained by and large not as social scientists but as historians has serious implications. The teacher of a psychology or sociology course is apt to be only vaguely familiar with social science methodology and with the ways in which social science knowledge can be effectively used. The teacher's own inexperience in designing and pursuing a research problem almost guarantees that he will not be able to give his students this experience. This deficiency suggests the need for intensive in-service training programs, as well as for reconsideration of the preservice academic training of teachers.

Until these changes in teacher preparation can be accomplished, the major responsibility for course content must be met by the available textual materials. The representative materials surveyed above indicate that sociology and psychology texts are not equal to the task. The need for new and varied kinds of instructional materials is apparent.

A relatively new pattern for curriculum design has appeared with the recent activity of several scholarly societies. The American Sociological Association is sponsoring the development of a sociology curriculum; the American Anthropological Association sponsors the Anthropology Curriculum Study Project. (The American Historical Association has for some time been active in the development of bibliographies for teachers but is not now involved in curriculum design.) It is possible that such support and the apparent lack of support by professional psychologists will determine the growing inclusion of sociology and anthropology in the high school curriculum and the gradual exclusion of psychology.

We are still left with the problem of several courses competing for time in the student's already crowded schedule. A general course in social science has not been characteristic of the high school curriculum; social science courses for the high school student consist largely of history, political science, and economics. High school courses in psychology, sociology, and anthropology are almost universally elective; this means that many students leave the high school with no training in those social sciences that focus their attention on human behavior.

All of this seems to indicate a need for considering a unified social or behavioral science course—one that would draw together the concepts, methodologies, and points of view that characterize the behavioral sciences.

Selected Bibliography

1. BERGER, PETER L., *Invitation to Sociology: A Humanistic Perspective*, Anchor Books, Garden City, N.Y., 1963.

2. BOHLKE, ROBERT H., "The Teaching of Sociology in Secondary Schools: Problems and Prospects," *Social Forces*, 42 (Mar., 1964), 363–74.

3. BRANCA, ALBERT A., *Psychology, the Science of Behavior*, Allyn and Bacon, Boston, 1964.

4. COFFIELD, K. E., AND ENGLE, T. L., "High School Psychology: A History and Some Observations," *American Psychologist*, 15 (June, 1960), 350–53.

5. COLE, WILLIAM E., AND MONTGOMERY, CHARLES S., *High School Sociology*, Allyn and Bacon, Boston, 1963.

6. COSER, LEWIS A. (ed.), *Sociology Through Literature*, Prentice-Hall, Englewood Cliffs, N.J., 1963.

7. *Designers' Manual*, Sociological Resources for Secondary Schools, a Project of the American Sociological Association, Ann Arbor, Mich. (July, 1966).

8. ENGLE, T. L., "Preparation for Teaching Psychology in High School," *American Psychologist*, 15 (June, 1960), 353–55.

9. ———, *Psychology, Its Principles and Applications*, Harcourt, Brace & World, N.Y., 1964.

10. GRUPP, STANLEY E., "High School Sociology: A Challenge," *High School Journal*, 46 (Feb., 1963), 170–74.

11. ———, "The State of Teaching Sociology in High Schools," *Sociology and Social Research*, 45 (Apr., 1961), 327–31.

12. HERING, WILLIAM M., JR., "An Analysis of the Five Secondary School Textbooks in Sociology," Sociological Resources for Secondary Schools, University of Michigan, Ann Arbor, 1966.

13. HUNT, ERLING M., *High School Social Studies Perspectives*, Houghton Mifflin, Boston, 1962.

14. JUNG, CHARLES, et al., *Retrieving Social Science Knowledge for Secondary Curriculum Development*, Publication No. 109 of the Social Science Education Consortium, Purdue University, Lafayette, Ind., 1965.

15. KOLLER, M. R., "Sociology in the Curriculum," *Educational Leadership*, 22 (Feb., 1965), 310–12.

16. KOLLER, MARTIN R., AND COUSE, HAROLD C., *Modern Sociology*, Holt, Rinehart and Winston, New York, 1965.

17. LANDIS, PAUL H., *Sociology,* Ginn, Boston, 1964.

18. LUCAS, ANN E., "A Guide to Upgrade the High School Psychology Course," *Clearing House* (May, 1963), 523–28.

19. ROSE, CAROLINE B., *Sociology: The Study of Man in Society,* Merrill Books, Columbus, Ohio, 1965.

20. RUPE, M. J., "Psychology for Seniors," *National Association for Secondary School Principals Bulletin,* 45 (Sept., 1961), 105–08.

21. SCHALL, J. H., "Sociology in the High School Curriculum," *Social Education,* 29 (May, 1965), 296–98.

CHAPTER 12

Geography

Understanding Man in a Changing World

PETER V. GRECO

The earth is a complex of elements—physical, biotic, and societal. It consists of different kinds of landforms, diverse plant types, and contrasting social practices, all coexisting in different areas. Each element is the product of a process or series of processes that operates systematically in time.

The Systematic Sciences and Geography

The systematic sciences, such as geology, botany, and sociology, each study a particular category of elements and the processes that give rise to them. Characteristically the natural or social scientist classifies the elements that come within his purview and then explains how they have evolved through an intellectual construct that minimizes variation in time as well as variety in space. He calls this generalization a *process*. Thus the geologist explains the existence of a certain type of rocks that he labels *sedimentary* by a process called *deposition*; the botanist explains the occurrence of *thorny desert shrubs* in terms of lower *transpiration* rates; and the sociologist explains certain *predictable social behaviors* on the basis of *socialization* in a given society. In brief the systematic sciences are concerned with the generalized genetic aspects of categories of occurrences, which give them a distinctive form or function. Although the systematic sciences may occasionally explain categories of elements in particular periods or in specific areas, this is peripheral to their core concern.

By contrast geography is a spatial or chorological science. Like history, which studies the association of diverse elements in particular periods of time, geography studies the association of different elements within an area. The geographer's primary interest is how arrangements of elements on the face of the earth differentiate one area from another. He is confronted by the same complex reality that natural and social scientists observe. The physicist, however, uses laboratory controls to reduce irregularities in the physical processes he seeks to measure and describe, and the social scientist reduces the differences in the relative influence of elements that impinge upon his investigation of social processes by postulating the equivalence of these influences. The geographer, on the other hand, seeks to assess the modifications of process that differentiate areas *where other things are not equal.* In effect he extends the findings of the systematic scientist.

If we shift our focus from ends to means, however, we find that the geographer's way of differentiating areas is similar to the efforts of any other scientist. At the outset the geographer must describe the elements in a given area. Second, he must classify these elements. Third, if geography is to be more than a compendium of uncoordinated facts, the geographer must seek explanations for the associations that he discovers among elements.

TOPICAL GEOGRAPHY

Geographers approach areal differentiation by assuming that there is a certain order in nature and that men organize themselves rationally. In uncovering this presumed order in nature and/or society, topical geographers tend to concentrate on the areal relations of one kind of element or category of elements in different parts of the world. Thus one who identifies himself as a physical geographer might explain the areal covariation between temperature and rainfall; the biogeographer might focus on the intricate areal relationships between certain plants and animals; the political geographer might delineate the relationship between isolationist attitudes and physical accessibility; the economic geographer might explore the interconnections between the production of steel and its natural and cultural environments; and the cultural geographer might concentrate on the ties between certain agricultural practices and religious beliefs. Attracted as these geographers are to specific kinds of occurrences and the processes that interrelate them, they, like systematic scientists, follow topical bents. In fact many geographers are quite at home with the natural and social scientists whose interests they share and have applied the exhaustive knowledge of related disciplines to their inquiries.

REGIONAL GEOGRAPHY

Other geographers approach areal differentiation by focusing on the interrelated elements of a particular place to understand its distinctiveness better. But since all physical, biotic, and societal elements occur in specific places and since the areal differentiation of places presupposes the existence of varied elements within them, topical and regional geography are two sides of the same coin. Just as the inquiry of the topical geographer confers a uniqueness upon certain regions, so, conversely, will the regional geographer who investigates relationships within a locale be involved in the topical aspects of the region.

THE REGIONAL CONCEPT AND METHOD

Whether the geographer approaches his investigation topically or regionally, he uses the regional concept and method to structure indeterminate reality. The research interests of the geographer require him to locate certain classes of elements in a given area and to explain their association in terms of systematic processes. The result is the *region*—an area that shows a certain cohesiveness among its selected components. This cohesiveness gives the region its salient character as well as a certain homogeneity arising either from a spread of covarying features throughout or from a pattern of circulation. In the former instance the geographer creates formal regions, such as vegetation regions or regions of meat animal and grain production; in the latter case he constructs regions based principally on function, such as the regions that consist of a central place from

which influences or movements (economic, political, or social) radi-
ate to certain boundaries. Since, however, the formal region has a
specific location, it may also function as a central place or may
itself be situated within one or several functional regions. Conversely, since functional relationships assume a certain form, the
functional region may exemplify a formal region as well. Hence it
should be noted that just as the topical and regional biases of
geographers merely represent differences in emphasis, formal and
functional regions are often used together in the task of areal differentiation.

Geography in General Education

As an elective course offering, geography might well be organized as
a separate field of inquiry that bridges the natural sciences and the
social sciences with its own distinctive workways, as has been outlined
above. However, as soon as one asks what the place of geography is
in the general education of American youth, kindergarten through
senior high school, the incorporation of geography into the curriculum or its exclusion from it is determined by how it meets the
needs of society.

Presumably the social sciences should contribute to an understanding of man in a changing world. Furthermore, the problems
that issue from this interaction between man and nature and man
and man should be analyzed if the child is to come to terms with
his century. Understanding the complex world in which American
young people live is sterile when there is no concern for the clashes
of values that occur in societies and in the international community.
If geography is to help young Americans to come to understand
their world, it must confront them with social issues. Geography is
not only a natural science but a social science, and it will be less
than efficacious if it remains separate from social studies in general
education.

Geography in the Social Studies

THE ELEMENTARY LEVEL

Social studies focus on man's interaction with other men and attempt to assess the mainsprings of his behavior. On the elemen-

tary level the child's world is restricted and unsophisticated. The child, however, is keenly aware of the different social groups to which he belongs and is concerned daily with easing conflicts and encouraging relationships that are pleasing, so there is ample opportunity to have him come to know how and why life elements have evolved and how and why places have come to be different.

If the aim of geography is to have the primary grader appreciate how man organizes himself in space to realize his goals, inquiry could lead to an understanding of the commonplace, such as the physical organization of the household as a large-scale functional region that maximizes human efforts within the institutional structure of the family. And, since comparison of regions is the hallmark of geography, which seeks to infer higher levels of generalizations, comparative analysis of the organization of the one-room thatched house of the tropics or the Indian longhouse would be well worthwhile. In such a fashion the elementary school could serve comparative value-judging and other attitudinal aims of the social studies while providing practice in rational inquiry through the methods of the geographer. The elementary curriculum could continue to work for such ends through an organization based upon expanding environments (neighborhood, city, state, region) or upon topics of greater and greater sophistication (mineral production, agriculture, the city).

THE SECONDARY LEVEL

Whatever organization is used, however, the school will eventually offer the child a geography course that provides a world view. In the expanding environments sequence this would presumably constitute a program in area studies. A topical program would probably explore that most-difficult-to-understand constellation of values and attitudes that helps shape earth space and human behavior—the culture of a people. A high school course in area studies built around the geographer's notion of culture regions would be equal to the task.

At this point one could logically ask whether persistent concern with a few well-documented studies of other cultures would equal or surpass in value a course that considered the whole globe, using a broad regional emphasis. There is much to commend the former approach (25). Since it would follow inquiry more closely, it could be more scientific. Children would presumably be better able to immerse themselves in a culture that is depicted as including virtually all of the facets of a given way of life. And, since such a study would take longer to complete, the child's identification with his subject would probably be greater and his study therefore more rewarding, albeit restricted. However, if the *salient* character of broad culture regions were described through relatively specific propositions marshaled under propositions of wider scope, all shown to be interrelated, the result would also be scientific and comprehensive—although in a horizontal rather than a vertical way (24). And, while time restrictions would not permit the study of world cultures in similar depth, the study of broad integrations of nature and culture would provide a meaningful backdrop against which the persistent concerns of contemporary man could be assessed.

Geography and Area Studies

Man is an aspirational animal: he aspires to shared power in the political order, shared respect in the social order, and shared well-being in the economic order. As an animal he also seeks safety. As a result he tries to achieve some semblance of progress and security in his life. His quests for progress and security vary in combination because of the different physical endowments of his surroundings and the variations in his cultural milieus (through which the physical endowments have been interpreted). Varied though they are, however, the compelling nature of what some observers have called the Revolution of Rising Expectations cannot for long be avoided by even the most isolated community where security presently outweighs progress. The Revolution of Rising Expectations, then, will have an increasing influence upon human creative choice. The implications for all social sciences are legion.

Can geography provide a context that can suitably accommodate the broad concerns of all social science disciplines? The region, broadly conceived, provides such a matrix. Since geography is defined not by a specific subject matter but by the way it looks at things, the region can provide us with the "personality" of a place and its people and allow us to assess the present and future impact of the Revolution of Rising Expectations. This distinctive stamp of a place consists of elements, both physical and cultural, that can be cast in the form of interconnected propositions through geographic inquiry; these propositions can be examined to see how they might assist or hinder change.

If students are provided with materials through which they may confront the characteristics of places and peoples, generalize about them in the form of propositions, and validate and interlink those propositions, they can engage in geographic inquiry. Since validated propositions have implications for the changes man seeks, the student will also be solving problems and, in suggesting solutions, making decisions and value judgments. Presumably these activities will help to form attitudes based upon understanding, since the students themselves will be integrating the aspects of living to which they are exposed. Rational inquiry can thus be served, along with a concern for the vital three-dimensional aspirations of twentieth-century man.

Since one cannot examine all elements of places and human living, he must select from among unique occurrences. The criterion would be typicality, and, since combinations of essential characteristics would involve the ecological segment of the social sciences, the propositions that would emerge from student inquiry would be systematic and comprehensive and scientific. To use Redfield's words (24), they would strive toward an "architecture of description" and would be "related to each other by a sort of natural order" or "compendency."

Secondary School Geography: The Given Situation

Having examined what the role of geography might best be in the secondary curriculum, let us now analyze the basic patterns of organization for geography courses in secondary education.

TOPICALLY ORGANIZED COURSES

Formal course patterns in geographic education are either topical or regional or a combination of both. A topical organization customarily begins with physical elements and processes in earth space and then considers the elements and processes that are more completely cultural products. The sequence is followed for good reason:

> The geographical complex is the product of two sets of factors, one natural and the other cultural or human. Relief, soils, vegetation,

climate, and other natural qualities and agencies are generally self-evident. The cultural factors—tradition, economy, skills, historical accident, evolutionary change, and the like—are not so easily observed. (Kniffen, 16, p. 126.)

The topical course generally focuses first upon the distributions of certain classes of landforms on the earth and the processes that explain their occurrence. World climate patterns might be the next topic. Here the concern would be with the distribution of temperature, rainfall, winds, etc., and the processes that produce them. Each of these systems is then related to the natural vegetation or soils, which are inextricably tied to the interaction of regularly distributed climatic elements with the irregularly distributed surface features of the earth. The emphasis on world-wide patterns in the topical course, however, does not prevent the teacher from making a more penetrating examination of specific areas.

Thus, to illustrate the notion that the interposition of high mountains in the path of moisture-laden winds will bring heavy rainfall, he might examine any of the several specific locations that exemplify this so well. And, if he wished to show the interconnectedness of the elements of a biome, he could make a detailed examination of the boreal forest. Thus in Soviet Siberia he generally finds an area within which needle-leaf evergreens predominate. Broad expanses of low-lying land far enough removed from the modifying influence of warm-water bodies and cut off from moisture-laden winds are characterized by dryness and cold. In such an area shallow-rooted trees can survive atop a permanently frozen subsoil and tough, resinous needle leaves are able to withstand transpiration of the little available moisture. The soils do not benefit from much organic material and, indeed, are leached of nutrients by the acidic ground water produced by the needle-leaf forest litter. The humus-poor gray soils have few soil animals, are poorly structured because of extreme ranges in temperature, and are therefore generally impoverished.

When the teacher introduces the facets of human occupance into his study, the same boreal forest context will illustrate the cultural interconnections of man in such natural environs. And in this connection much of what Forde (5) has done on the Northern Tungus could be emphasized here. Thus we observe that the topically organized course commonly shifts from world patterns to more specific areas. The core concern of the course is a specific topic. If information is available on related topics, those related topics are also discussed. But since related information is not always available, the mosaics constructed by topical geography are seldom complete.

REGIONALLY ORGANIZED COURSES

The traditional regional geography course is characterized by its concern with specific areas of the world and, commonly, with countries or composites of them. Again there is ample reason for this emphasis. Areal differentiation may be based upon cultural or natural elements or both. Cultures include systems of values and political, social, and economic organization, the language men speak, the art they create, the material structures they build, the clothing they wear, the foods they eat—all in more or less intimate association with their land bases.

In many ways the sovereign state is the region best suited to accommodate such natural-cultural complexes. First, political authority exerts profound effects upon culture. Governments influence the value systems adhered to by men; social and economic organization is manipulated by the state; public schools maintain a common language or languages; material structures are planned and funded by central governments; and purchases of clothing and articles in the diet are conditioned by government involvement in the production of fibers and food. Second, one can study the structure and functions of the sovereign state that is homogeneous in terms of political authority and heterogeneous in other characteristics. Third, secondary students are at least vaguely familiar with the names and locations of political units and, moreover, statistical data are customarily organized by countries.

In order to increase comprehension, however, some geographers have suggested grouping countries together and studying larger areas.

It is often advantageous . . . to examine major world segments for the purpose of defining political regions of greater size but of lesser political homogeneity than that found in individual states. . . . The highest ranks of political organization may be identified on the basis of uniformity of particular political characteristics or of other cultural characteristics that are politically significant. Thus throughout nearly all of Latin America there is not only the obvious similarity of language among politically dominant groups but also similarity in certain inherited institutions of even greater importance for political organization, such as the role of the family, church, social classes, and army officers in the government or the use of Roman law. In each of these respects almost all of Latin America stands in marked contrast with Anglo-America. Against this background of similarity throughout Latin America, its division into many independent political units is to be compared with the patterns of population density and movement, racial composition, transport systems, and patterns of administrative organization inherited from colonial days. (James and Jones, 12, pp. 186–87.)

This regional orientation is reflected in the current geographic organization based on culture areas, which was initiated on the college level in the early 1950's and introduced with modifications for the high school by James in 1958 (23). The core concern of this emphasis is the illumination of areas as expressions of the attributes and limitations of a culture, generally as they relate to the earth's space. In shedding light on the characteristic attitudes and actions of human beings, the teacher utilizes the findings of systematic science and topical geography. However, the culture of a people is such a multifaceted configuration that observable spatial patterns and systematic explanations are frequently lacking for its elements. The teacher is thus obliged to make mental leaps across the field within which certain elements lie and to assert a compendent, science-like explanation for their occurrence together. Regional studies consequently take on a subjective artistic quality.

For this reason regional studies have been looked upon with less than full favor by those geographers who believe that, if geography is to advance human knowledge, certain topical emphases should be pursued (2). Nonetheless the educator who asks what kind of geography is most conducive to the achievement of general education objectives might well conclude that the culture area organization has more to offer than does a topical emphasis. But first one must examine the goals of geography courses in the secondary social studies curriculum.

A review of reported research on the emphases of secondary curricula by Smith (20) revealed stress on the following topics with implications for geography: (1) world geography; (2) international understanding and cultures, particularly as they relate to current events; (3) world affairs; (4) non-Western studies; and (5) current problems of society. One observes that these topics all concern cultures and contemporary social problems.

We live in a world of nationalistic political states at a time when man's capacity for self-destruction has become horribly efficient. International understanding has accordingly become an important educational goal. If geography courses compartmentalize man and earth into neat topical boxes, will the integration of people and places be achieved by the child? The attempt to study all earthly elements in the differentiation of areas has been considered futile and unmeaningful (21). But does the study of "all that is relevant to human occupance" (8) deserve the same judgment? Is not the study of a totality of environing factors (10) a more reasonable vehicle for understanding the myriad underpinnings of man's behavior than a topical course, which too often ends the child's investigation by crying "Halt! Your concern with such far-removed sets of elements is peripheral to our specific inquiry"? Is not the study of totalities, composed of inputs from the natural sciences, social sciences, and humanities, in the best liberal tradition in education? Might not the study of factors unrestricted by special topical concerns elicit student interest in and appreciation of the ways of others and perhaps even dispose the student to bring the same attitudes to confrontations with other periods and other places? And if a culture area is dimly lit by available information, might we not take courage from the prehistorian who re-creates a milieu from a fragment and solace from the fact that the child will repeatedly meet learning situations that are poorly constituted wholes?

Geographers have long maintained that topical and regional studies represent for practitioners in the discipline different points of departure and not a dichotomy. When geography in general education is drawn to new horizons, however—such as the illumination of cultures—quite obviously there are elements that are only barely "observable as they relate to the earth's space" (1). For example, the characteristic stricture placed upon inquiry in Russian-Soviet culture has only the most tenuous relationship to geographic patterns within the Russian-Soviet land mass. Yet who would aver that an obligatory course on Russian-Soviet culture should avoid discussion of these political characteristics? The flexibility of the culture area approach permits this facet of Russian-Soviet life to be examined as an extension of the characteristic omnipresence of the state in political and economic matters (which *can* be observed in the spatial patterns in the Russian-Soviet land mass). In a study of the Middle East is there any denial of the fact that a heady national-

ism has significance for the present and future development of
political states there? Is it feasible to suggest that such a characteristic be excluded from a geography course merely because this feature
has less to do with the expression of political loyalties or sympathies
within a state or states (which indeed have a spatial dimension) than
with the nearsightedness of Middle Eastern states in their relations
with other states? In effect those who propose a culture area organization envision a course that is significantly geographic but that
accommodates material remote from geography's principal concerns.

THE HIGH SCHOOL GEOGRAPHY PROJECT

At the forefront of change in geographic education today is the
High School Geography Project of the Association of American
Geographers. Initiated in 1961 under the joint sponsorship of the
Association and the National Council of Geographic Education, the
Project assembled the leading figures in American geography and
systematically recorded their views on the concepts and organizing
principles for a prospective senior high school geography course.
The result was the *Advisory Paper for Teachers Associated with the
High School Geography Project* (13), issued in August of 1962. Ten
high school teachers from different locales in the United States who
taught students of varying aptitudes and interests agreed to develop
courses addressed to the objectives on content, skills, and attitudes
recorded in the *Advisory Paper*. For the guidance of the teachers five
learning units were suggested: (1) restrictive environments, (2) a
politically defined area, (3) a culturally defined area, (4) cities, and
(5) agriculture.

The degree of latitude allowed each teacher resulted in diverse
ideas and materials in the trial year, some aspects of which are
recorded in *Selected Classroom Experiences: High School Geography
Project* (17). The trial year culminated in a *Response Paper* (14),
which critically summarized the variety of undertakings as applications of what geographers thought their discipline should concern.

In 1964 the Project developed a course outline (6) around the
theme of human settlement, and certain units are now in various
stages of completion with a few already being tried in schools. The
outline is designed for either a whole course or for parts of a course
or courses in high school. As of January, 1966, the working draft
outline called for inclusion of the following units: "Introduction,"

"Urban Geography: Intracity Analysis," "Urban Geography: Intercity Analysis," "Manufacturing and Mining as Settlement-forming Activities," "Agriculture," "Culture Change," "The Habitat," "Fresh Water Resources," "Political Units and Political Processes," and "The Frontiers of Geography."

The Project's effort will certainly have an impact upon schools across the country, which are caught up in the ferment of curricular reform. One should ask, therefore, whether the present outline as a full-fledged course can serve what Smith (20) reports to be the persistent concerns of the schools.

First, the fact that the sequence of units almost inverts the traditional topical outline is of no great concern: its organizers point out well that the urban landscape is probably more familiar to contemporary youth than the farm and that in a technologically advanced society physical factors of earth space tend to be less significant for children. However, the generalized nature of unit specifications makes it difficult to analyze the outline further. Outlines by nature suggest only certain directions, especially when they are issued as guides for elaboration. Most of the time, analysis of them can consist only of questions and tentative conclusions:

1. The emphasis of Unit 9, "Political Units and Political Processes," is on "how political processes operate within and become part of the earth/man relationship." Will "political processes" be construed broadly enough to include the political quests of men that do not become political issues? If not, the unit will apparently omit consideration of the many important cleavages that rend political communities in the contemporary world.

2. "An understanding of world linkages and trade" (interdependence) is cited as a goal of instruction in Unit 3, "Intercity Analysis." Should this unit encourage children to speculate about what *ought to be*? In Unit 4, "Manufacturing and Mining," non-industrialized producers of raw materials are treated as adjuncts to the unit's focus on industrialized areas of the world. Will there be—should there be—a mandate for the teacher and students to ask what constitutes economic justice in commercial trade? The geographer might well reveal the "rich-land, poor-land" theme. Should the classroom consider whether foreign assistance should be 1 percent of the United States gross national product?

3. The outline suggests the notion of cultural change (Unit 6), and the word "cultures" appears several times in the outline. Will

there, however, be a concern with cultures as totalities, as "integrations of dispositions to behave" (25), so that the child will be able to predict what the development of certain culture areas is likely to be? Will the topical outline permit such a future-oriented course? Will diffusion of "ideas, beliefs, customs, or whole culture complexes" (Unit 6) include the diffusion of Western economic, political, and social ideas that have so great a significance for the ideologies in the world today?

These questions are of paramount importance. The criteria for preparing a course to initiate tyros into the substance and method of the discipline differ somewhat from those for preparing a course for inclusion in a general education program. And the Project is not unaware of this difference; its forthcoming publication of a book of course outlines on regional geography, social problems, political geography, historical geography, and world patterns and processes will be important for the schools to consider along with the *Settlement Theme* outline as they decide which aspects of good geography will constitute good general education for their youth.

High School Geography Textbooks

The final section of the chapter analyzes the geography textbook as the basic determinant of classroom concerns. At the outset the uneven quality of the nine books that were reviewed should be noted. Accordingly this discussion tries to single out textual elements that are praiseworthy and to suggest what texts *should be* by noting what seems to be less useful in the teaching of geography in social studies. Obviously texts are not comparable in all respects. Furthermore, spotty achievements do not merit praise to the same degree as consistently valuable contributions in certain areas. Therefore, in order to analyze the books comparatively, this section will examine their strengths and weaknesses in regard to four aspects of what has been called the creative encounter: questing, speculating, evaluating, and constructing.

QUESTING

Questing "is the conscious and deliberate pursuit of knowledge, exemplified by the student's independently initiated search for the problematic and his disposition toward wonder" (4). Certain formal and substantive elements of the textbook contribute to this component.

Formal Elements

WORD SYMBOLS   Just as student motivation in classroom discourse depends in large measure upon the vitality of the subject, so in a textbook the degree of *élan* with which it is written makes it more or less attractive, more or less a springboard for inquiry. This characteristic of expository material has little to do with the claims for texts that appear in so many prefaces and forewords; nor is this facet of a good text greatly diminished by the occasional misuse of words like the omnipresent "Sahara Desert." We refer instead to the quality of the prose—the concise, the insightful, the well-turned phrase. Consider the following abstract from Holt's *World Geography and You*:

> The Middle East is mostly a region of deserts, mountains, and arid valleys. In the north are the mountains; in the south, the deserts. But between these is an area which in ancient times was fertile, populated, and highly civilized. It is here that many believe the *Garden of Eden*, mentioned in the Bible, to have been. This was the site of the ancient civilizations of the Babylonians, Hebrews, Assyrians, and Persians. Although it is a barren area today, we are told that in ancient times it was a fertile region. Extending from the east coast of the Mediterranean Sea to the Persian Gulf, it was shaped like a crescent moon and included the valleys of the Tigris and Euphrates rivers. Gradually this *Fertile Crescent* became an arid region. Today it is a desolate area, populated by tribes of nomads searching for grass and water for their livestock. Modern engineers say that it could again become a land of "milk and honey" if it were properly irrigated and developed.   (Holt, 7, pp. 292–93.)

The style is repetitive and uneven. In addition to the paragraph's barrenness of substance, the writing is empty, flat. There are few verbal delights to urge on the reader. In contrast observe the following passage from Bradley's *World Geography*:

> The little flowering plants of the desert solve the problem of aridity by sleeping through most of the year. When the rains come, they suddenly spring into life. During the few weeks when the ground is relatively moist they do what similar plants in wetter lands take months to do. During these few weeks they may cover the somber face

of the desert for hundreds of square miles with the smile of their
bloom. (Bradley, 3, p. 103.)

The style is attractive, revealing, and eminently readable. Also
worthy of mention for discussing their subject with a fine expository
style are Israel, Roemer, and Durand's *World Geography Today* (9)
and Jones and Murphy's *Geography and World Affairs* (15). The
former is written with considerable power (see, for example, the
sections on the British Isles and the former Belgian Congo); the
latter's simple, intelligent, cogent, and insightful style is exemplified
in the section on culture and values. For attractive and insightful
but more sober expression, the reviewer should consult James and
Davis's, *The Wide World* (11) and Kohn and Drummond's *The
World Today* (18).

GRAPHIC SYMBOLS   The use of maps, pictures, diagrams, and draw-
ings is complementary to the basically expository nature of high
school texts. Such graphic aids should therefore possess a certain
appeal without sacrificing precision and should constitute an integral part of the text. James and Davis (11) exemplify this well with
a wide variety of maps from several sources.

Unfortunately the products map is still with us. In their quest
to vary map materials authors or publishers customarily fill base
maps with eye-catching pictorial symbols. Like the popular Replogle
globe, which depicts the sparsely populated Amazon basin as containing scores of settlements, products maps invariably mislead the
user by locating the pictorial symbols imprecisely and by not indicating the quantities produced. Thus Holt and Bradley fill certain
maps with noncomparable, imprecise symbols, which appeal to the
eye, perhaps, but do not edify the reader.

Complementary materials must form a certain unity with the
text. Usually texts will either coordinate word symbols with graphic
media or, better, will introduce in either the verbal or graphic media
other elements that will have implications for what has already been
broached. This technique is well exemplified, for instance, in Van
Cleef and Finney's *Global Geography* (27), where comparative analysis of well-designed maps coheres with verbally asserted areal relations. Ties of this sort solidify the textual base for questing. More
often, however, maps and text discussions do not support each other.
(For example, see 7, pp. 24 and 308–09; and 3, pp. 8–9 and 460.)

One of the striking characteristics of contemporary texts is their wide use of pictures, frequently in full color. This feature is a good one if it motivates and offers insights to the reader. The skillfully rendered pictures in Bradley are not only esthetically pleasing, they are conducive to student inquiry. However, there is reason to believe that the choice of pictures in textbooks is at times not based on anything more than visual appeal. Thus the pictures in Israel, Roemer, and Durand (9) could compete with any text for color, variety, and well-composed captions, but, unfortunately, like the illuminations of a medieval text they demand little visual analysis from the student because they seldom require or even permit the abstraction of significant elements. A more serious problem in textbooks is that an illustration is clearly inconsistent with the text (7:316, 318) or is presented with a generalization that it actually contradicts (7:333).

Cartoons have not been widely used in textbook design. Teachers who are disposed to their use will find Jones and Murphy's efforts worthy of their attention.

CONCEPTUAL FRAMEWORK   Although the quality of exposition and graphic materials are important in the formal design of a textbook, the conceptual framework of the book is even more significant. The majority of the texts reviewed follow a regional orientation, usually with a few introductory chapters of topical concern. In this group, which includes Kolevzon and Heine (19), Holt (7), and Israel, Roemer, and Durand (9), the dominant emphasis is on providing a broad but meaningful physicocultural sweep, and the organizations of these books are satisfactory for realizing this goal.

The reader should examine James and Davis (11) and Kohn and Drummond (18), however, for the most distinctive renditions of the focus on the culture area. The theoretical base for this organization was detailed by James in 1958 (23), implemented by him (with Davis) in *The Wide World* in 1959, and followed by Kohn and Drummond in a later textbook: broad areas are examined in terms of associated salient characteristics of habitat and culture that have profound importance for understanding the world today. The teacher of social studies who is drawn to a book with such a contemporary focus and worldwide scope will find that no small part is devoted to economic, social, and political concerns of America in a revolutionary world.

In addition to the novel organizational scheme followed by

James and Davis throughout most of their textbook, the introductory chapters attempt something unique—namely, to trace the development of certain elementary notions and methods through time. This technique is in marked contrast to the usual introductions, which follow topical lines. James and Davis relate the history of geographic thought to the text in a practical way: for example, when they discuss Aristotelian theory, they cite its effects upon early geographic inquiry. Each term is explained; the authors tell the reader what an astrolabe is, how it worked, and why it was so significant an invention. In sum the rationale behind this part of *The Wide World* is that students will better understand latitude and longitude or patterns of prevailing winds, etc., if they can observe how ideas about them grew out of human inquiry through time. The result is a sophisticated text that will be well received by the able student.

Kohn and Drummond's introductory chapters are organized similarly to those of other texts with a regional emphasis. In the regional accounts themselves, however, they offer a view of the culture region as a whole and then concentrate on the political states that constitute it. This technique has the virtue of giving a broad regional sweep as well as a glimpse of the spatial patterns and related concerns of the individual state. James and Davis, by comparison, spend less effort on preliminary characterizations of culture regions, choosing instead to interrelate the salient features of earth space within sovereign states. What they lose in a general regional sweep they gain in a specificity that still avoids the trivial.

The texts by Jones and Murphy (15) and Bradley (3) also have designs that are dominantly regional, but unlike the foregoing texts their emphasis is not on culture regions. Jones and Murphy's regional delineations are sovereign states. Within these states they consider a wide range of cultural phenomena that are politically relevant while they instill a healthy respect for politics. Thus the reader will observe in *Geography and World Affairs* more than the usual space given to such elements as constituent republics and governmental organization within political states. Bradley's work is dominated by an emphasis on climate, to which other physical and biotic elements are related. The book's main thrust is toward the understanding of the cultural facets of man's existence in physically and biotically defined areas. The space given to the study of political states is small by comparison.

The last two texts follow a definite topical orientation. Although Van Cleef and Finney's preface (27) asserts that the notion of geography as a social science has merit, the dominant emphasis of the work is expressed in the following:

> The trade center in a sense is a mark of progress for an entire region. It means that the people are taking advantage of their natural resources and of their geographic location. They are putting forth every effort to make useful products out of nature's gifts and exchanging them for those produced by other peoples who have still other kinds of commodities available. We might say that the maximum achievements of man and his major industrial and commercial efforts are concentrated in trade centers.   (Van Cleef and Finney, 27, p. 52.)

Clearly this is a text in economic geography. Accordingly the reader will find no discussion of the social and political implications of, say, the Suez Canal; he will notice that the salient character of Latin America includes nothing significant about its economic, social, and political institutions. Although the book is substantively sound and well engineered, the teacher will find it deficient for a general education course in social studies.

Pounds and Cooper's *World Geography: Economic, Political, Regional* (22) is essentially an economic geography text concerned principally with the United States. It admits a lack of concern, however, for the physical processes that underlie the patterns of economic undertakings, and it demeans regional geography: "In regional geography we must be content to *describe* what is there; in economic geography we must describe and *explain*." And what is the quality of explanation provided?

> Where are iron and steel made?
> The iron and steel industry of the Soviet Union is located in three important areas with a number of lesser centers. These centers are shown on the map. . . . One lies in European Russia just to the north of the Black Sea. This is the Donets region, so called from the river that flows through it. It is the oldest center.   (Pounds and Cooper, 22, p. 176.)

This is descriptive geography. However, good geography of any kind must consist of more than a medley of details about a given place. The essence of a region is its distinctiveness, and in order for an area to be distinctive the traits that make it unique must be interrelated. But the above discussion of the Donets Basin and a later one in the text leave the reader at a loss to know why the Donbas has loomed large in Soviet industrial production. Pounds and Cooper allude to the thick seams of coal suitable for coking in close proximity to iron ore deposits. Should not the text also mention the nearby manganese deposits, the association of limestone with coal and chernozem soils, the level land surface over which rails could be built easily, the abundance of water for industrial use and human needs, the rich agricultural base that with mechanization permitted a few people to feed an industrial labor force whose ranks were subsequently swelled by surplus farm labor, and so on? If this were done, the authors might find regional geography less threadbare.

One aspect of the conceptual framework of a textbook is the organization of ideas. Material that will induce questing by students must consist of seminal data or questions. These may be very open structured or only moderately so. Very open-structured materials might present sets of unconnected but connectable ideas in order to elicit student inquiry into the relations that will link them. Examples of this kind of structuring are difficult to find in textbooks. Such material might well resemble the investigation of a set of maps in a detective novel. The inquirer (in this case the textbook author) would first note certain percepts—points, lines, and areas—on the maps and call attention to them in the text. Then he would try to translate his observations into concepts. Finally, the author would assert some causal or conditional link that related concepts in propositional form. Students would have the information necessary to follow his inductive processes and could either accept his conclusions or disagree with them. Or a textbook might simulate the thought processes of an inquiring traveler who tries to find organizing principles in the places he visits and describes. Examples of this kind of description can be found in the writings of Herodotus, who reported accurately on the geology of Egypt and provided good explanations for the phenomena he observed, but in a factual account of the Nile flow offered reasons that were plausible to him but incorrect.

The "open-structured" organization that can be found even in better texts, however, allows for student analysis only on peripheral matters. The following extract from James and Davis illustrates how authors supply all the vital connections to interrelate data. The material in brackets indicates the sort of tangential analysis left for students:

Shortly before the middle of the nineteenth century an entirely new method of transportation, the steam-powered locomotive, appeared. But railroad routes could not follow the "natural lines of travel" [explained in the preceding paragraph] developed by the Indians, because the steam engine could not climb steep slopes or make sharp turns. [Why?] On the other hand it was not difficult to build railroad grades across swampy places. [Why?] Railroad bridges could be built across rivers, even where both banks were swampy. [How?] And the railroads could pass through tunnels and through cuts in the hills. As a result the railroads often followed quite different routes from the main roads. Many towns located along the old lines of travel could not be reached by the railroads. [Examples?] Therefore new towns sprang up at railroad junctions. [Examples?] The whole meaning of surface features changed as new "natural lines of travel" appeared. (James and Davis, 11, p. 164.)

The authors telescope the impact of technological change on the landscape by presenting a series of generalizations based on unmentioned but well-known facts; they thus provide a significant geographical understanding that can be applied to the reader's study of other landscapes in other times. Furthermore, they clearly imply which observations in the field or from maps led to such generalizations.

Both kinds of open-structured organization can engender enthusiasm for the creative encounter. The former appeals to the secure, outgoing student who finds living the challenge edifying. The latter appeals to the less secure student who may tomorrow be able to make new applications of the generalizations he has read.

A knowledge of the end products of geographic inquiry as well as some notion of how they came to be seem equally essential. It would thus appear that some combination of the two organizations should be achieved. This is presently done in the better texts by relating multidimensional ideas to core concerns or problems and then presenting open-structured materials as questions in the chapters or in the end-of-chapter exercises.

On the other hand, one too often finds a potpourri of uncoordinated detail masquerading as a scientific explanation of earth space. Consider, for example, the following compact and informative exposition:

The economic importance of London lies in its many-sided nature. Facing the southeast, London is well placed to do business with all the countries of Western Europe. The city is not only a center for the reshipment of goods to other parts of the world but a financial capital. No bank in the city has failed in the present century. Many finishing industries are also located in London. The machine, clothing, food processing, printing, furniture, leather, and electronics industries are examples. (Israel, Roemer, and Durand, 9, p. 63.)

But this is poor geography. "Many-sided nature" upon amplification turns out to be a series of uncoordinated elements rather than a multifaceted integration. Why is London "a financial capital"? What are the bases of these manufacturing industries? How have they developed in London in time? That this is not a technique for eliciting student inquiry is borne out by the busywork that fills the end-of-chapter exercises. When the evaluator repeatedly confronts descriptive, nonanalytical writing in texts, he can presume that the book alone will not generate desirable student response. A criterion for good internal organization of a text is that attention be paid to the how and why of phenomena. Without this, geography becomes encyclopedic and sterile; what, where, and when are not enough. It seems fitting that in a text that is at fault in this respect, one reads: "Midwestern farmers in Iowa, Kansas, Nebraska, Illinois, and other neighboring states raise millions of bushels of corn each ear [*sic*]" (7). Even the typesetter seems to have recognized that the "why" has been omitted as a matter of course.

Substantive Elements

Conditioning factors in questing also include the nature of the material that is selected for inclusion and its accuracy.

NATURE OF THE MATERIAL The materials of a text must support the author's overall conceptual framework. In general all the textbooks reviewed met this criterion—perhaps because texts on world geography tend to be so all-encompassing.

As for the use of controversial material, however, a reviewer is able to distinguish vapid, antiseptic texts from those that allow students to confront value-laden social conflicts, actual or potential. Consider the following:

As in Mexico before the revolution of 1910, people in the Andean countries are demanding political, social, and economic reform. Already there are groups working for equal voting privileges, for better educational opportunities, and for improved health programs. Groups are also working for modern farm practices, for a better division of the land, and for some control of the mineral resources. They want to see that the money received from the sale of minerals will not continue to enrich only a few wealthy families or some foreign mining companies.   (Jones and Murphy, 15, pp. 136–37.)

This kind of verve and candor, which may be found in the better texts, is in marked contrast to the policy of striking a compromise between exciting the student and paying heed to the status quo. Unfortunately, able teachers who regard lukewarm exposition with disfavor will find only a few texts that can spark a student-text dialogue by themselves. James and Davis (11), Jones and Murphy (15), and Kohn and Drummond (18) serve this end well.

The evaluator will also want to know if texts discuss a wide range of material and whether they present ideas of social import. Six of the textbooks reviewed meet both criteria to some extent, but Bradley (3) does not discuss a wide range of materials, and Pounds and Cooper (22) and Van Cleef and Finney (27) fall short on both criteria. Among those texts concerned with multifaceted social problems, one sometimes finds a commitment to the persistent quests of men in an obscure context, whereas the opportunity to highlight these same aspirations in an even more appropriate context is not pursued. Thus Israel, Roemer, and Durand (9) discuss the salient issues of contemporary Iraq well but reduce the role of Gandhi in modern India to that of a reformer of caste. One cannot fail to be impressed by the efforts of publishers to incorporate some important current issues—presumably for their currency alone—into textbooks. But even books that discuss current issues may omit less recent but classic cases. The texts that stand out for their commitment to persistent ideas of social import with a broad multidisciplinary bent are James and Davis (11), Jones and Murphy (15), and Kohn and Drummond (18).

Another dimension of the subject matter is the degree to which a multidisciplinary focus is applied to various times and places. The modern geographers' view that the meaning of the earth to man is a function of his attitudes, objectives, and technology predisposes the texts being reviewed to observe different cultural settings in different time periods, although texts tend to be concerned essentially with the present. Not unexpectedly the texts with an economic geographic bent show slight interest in broad cultural patterns. For example,

Brazil can look forward to a period of prosperity and expansion. It needs settlers who are prepared to face the hard life on a frontier cattle station or the labors of clearing scrub and savanna for cultivation. Brazil also needs capital and skill, which other countries, such as our own, are able to supply. (Pounds and Cooper, 22, pp. 363–64.)

Should not the get-rich-quick philosophy that has characterized Brazil's historical development be considered when one speaks of settlers? Might not the European and Japanese colonization schemes in Brazil be alluded to as precedents for attracting settlers to the interior? Or should American students conceive of prospective Brazilian settlement just as they have of the settlement of their own country—a kind of Westward Movement several thousand miles removed? Furthermore, is it beyond the pale even to suggest that Brazil might also need a social revolution? This textbook's glimpse into the future considers relatively few of the wide range of elements that make for a healthy economy and political viability.

ACCURACY OF THE MATERIAL The 1964 UNESCO interim report (26) on its textbook evaluation program revealed that in those books devoted to geography there were "an outstanding number of faulty and biased statements." We should note first that inaccuracies due to necessarily dated materials and such things as typesetting errors can be found in all texts.[1] In addition factual inaccuracies attributable to lack of knowledge need not concern us here, since the instructor who has been exposed to geography will detect these shortcomings and the instructor without experience in the field will not be edified by a list of specific errors. But there are certain kinds of inaccuracy against which the reader should be on his guard.

First, the reader should watch for internal contradictions. For example, a passage in one textbook (7) states: "cities that are 1,000 miles apart in an *east* or *west* direction are in different time zones and will therefore have a one-hour difference in time. If they are 2,000 miles apart, they will have a two-hour difference in time and so on." Yet earlier in the same paragraph the authors state: "each time zone is approximately 1,000 miles wide at the equator."

Textbooks often have contradictions between expository and graphic materials as well. Thus one reads the statement that Nile floods deposit rich water-borne silt on the floodplain, although

---

[1] The existence of bias in textbooks will be discussed later in this chapter.

within two pages two captions for pictures allude to dam construction that necessarily prevents this (9).

On other occasions statements are made that are contrary to common sense. Consider the following in light of our general knowledge of Egypt: "most homes in . . . Egypt are little more than roofs to keep off the rain" (7). Or consider the statement that, because of America's acquisition of overseas iron ores, "The cost of manufacturing steel must rise." Must costs necessarily rise? Moreover, one reads later: "Were it not for . . . imports of petroleum, the United States would be forced to use up its own reserves of oil more rapidly." The implication of these two excerpts is that conservation consists of using your neighbor's raw materials and that conservation or imports from overseas will necessarily increase consumer prices.

Ambiguities and vagueness also occur: "The United States also produces about four-fifths of the world's natural gas [and] 7 percent of its bauxite . . . . However, there are many minerals which must be imported, such as tin, asbestos, manganese, chromium, and nickel" (19). One cannot determine from the text whether production of 7 percent of the world's bauxite is considered a low figure or a significantly high one. The "however" implies the latter. In reality bauxite is one of the significant mineral *imports* of the United States.

So far as this criterion is concerned, James and Davis (11), Jones and Murphy (15), Kohn and Drummond (18), and Van Cleef and Finney (27) are consistently accurate and Bradley (3) not much less so.

SPECULATING

As we proceed through the three remaining components of critical thought, the reader will notice that less space is given to their discussion than has been given to questing. This is because texts customarily offer few opportunities for higher orders of creative inquiry. Since texts are not constructed to permit student discourse with them, they basically *tell*. Thus in evaluating how well a text attends to these higher processes, one can only guess at the response that the text would probably elicit from students.

Questing leads to formulating perceptive speculations or hypotheses. Speculating is the imaginative leap into the possible (4). Texts therefore should provide students with opportunities or encouragement to hypothesize. At best they suggest new ways to look at material, they play the gadfly and question traditional notions, they shock by contravening accepted values. Since intellectual ferment is presumably at odds with nationwide marketing, however, texts neglect this task in varying degrees. At one extreme one finds such end-of-chapter "Work Problems" as: "Ask five neighbors who were in World War II where they served and locate places in which they served" (7). Is the return on the time expended worth the student's effort? The same text presents interesting data on extremely wet and dry places in the world but does not use this information to elicit from the reader a knowledge of process that would explain these natural occurrences. Would not the pursuit of systematic inquiry be more fruitful than merely presenting the data for students to memorize? Without inquiry knowledge becomes a closed system to be disseminated and absorbed. How can students soar beyond the merely factual? Hopes rise when the reviewer sees this statement: "it is . . . possible that atomic power may replace . . . coal as a source of power." But this is followed immediately with: "However, coal will always be needed as an important material in the manufacture of steel" (7). The first sentence offers the imagination a suggestion (the possible uses of atomic energy), but the second sentence inhibits speculation with a time-bound observation. Is the world so much with us that we cannot envision changes? This consideration is particularly significant in this case, since technology is striving today to produce steel by using other fuels.

It is refreshing to notice in certain texts that whitewash is not applied as a matter of policy to all countries and all problems. For example, Israel, Roemer, and Durand's statements on Liberia (9) are commendable, although the section on contemporary Latin American society is not so severe as justice perhaps would require. Students know that bees sting and dogs bite; there is no harm in revealing some of the world's inequities in a textbook so that inquiry into them can lead to commitments on the part of our future citizenry. Our way of life requires it.

For the kind of encouragement and opportunities that may be commended, the reader is urged to look at the types of questions interspersed throughout Kohn and Drummond's text (18) as well as the "Using Maps," "Exploring Ideas," and "Extending Your Horizons" sections in James and Davis (11). The latter text perceptively links tasks that promote understandings and attitudes with a variety of techniques for skill development.

A text can also encourage speculating through an organization suitable for inductive thinking. Some attention has already been given to this. However, the reader can observe the advantages of composites of politically defined areas by comparing the pitfalls of Holt's Chapter 43 with, say, James and Davis's (11) or Kohn and Drummond's (18) analyses of the Mediterranean area. When one sees three lengthy—and discrete—references to capital within four pages of text (7), it becomes apparent that a topical organization within a broad areal approach does not allow inductive thought to proceed as readily as it does in the context of the political state. In the other two texts (11 and 18) the logical and interesting exposition of sets of interconnected phenomena enable the reader to make inferences about unobserved properties of these phenomena. This is speculative thinking.

EVALUATING

Evaluating is the third component of critical thinking. It begins with a formal examination of the logic of the propositions that form the hypothesis as well as the use of affective language in them. One then examines whether historical evidence affirms or denies the substance of the propositions as clarified.

Unfortunately there are exceedingly few instances where the student is asked to evaluate propositions in text materials. It is particularly rare in the expository material, where the textbook basically makes declarations. On occasion the end-of-chapter exercises will propose a statement for students to evaluate. These exercises can be quite well done. The student must analyze a proposition for its logic and meaning, and then he must refashion or add to the data provided by the text in order to determine the worth of the statement. For example, "It has been said that part of our foreign policy toward the countries south of the Sahara should be a recognition of their desire to be independent in world affairs. Would you defend this position? Explain" (15). To answer this question, the student must examine several questions: If foreign policy is construed as an instrument for furthering national interests, is it *logical* to recognize the desires of independent, largely nonviable states that oppose my country's views on certain international issues? What is the meaning of "desire to be independent in world affairs" as used in the statement? From what I have read in the preceding chapter, where does my commitment lie? What precedents are there to guide me in making a final judgment? What historical events might I investigate to help me to empathize with Africans? And so on.

From time to time, often unwittingly, authors provide excellent propositions for student evaluation. These are the statements that are presumably descriptive or analytical but are in reality value judgments disguised as facts.

> France has long been one of the great cultural centers of the world. The country abounds with universities, libraries, museums, and religious centers. Molière and Balzac are among the best loved of the world's great authors. Renoir and Rodin have produced painting and sculpture of lasting beauty. Debussy and Berlioz are only two of the many French composers. Among the scientists of France Louis Pasteur invented the process for eliminating harmful bacteria from milk, and the Curies discovered the element radium.
>
> We as Americans owe a debt to Frenchmen who, like Lafayette, helped us in our Revolution and who have fought bravely for the cause of freedom many times since then. The French Declaration of the Rights of Man [and Citizen] ranks with our Declaration of Independence as a great statement of the ideals of freedom. (Israel, Roemer, and Durand, 9, p. 75.)

How can this passage fail to indoctrinate students? If teachers use this material as a source for test items, students must swallow whole these "proofs" of French cultural contributions.

A map in Van Cleef and Finney (27) illustrates the effect of a different sort of hidden value judgment. The map is entitled "Distribution of Civilization" and has five categories ranging from "Very High" to "Very Low." The authors give no indication of the criteria they used in rating civilizations according to these categories. Yet the caption reads: "notice that the areas with the highest civilization are the highly industrialized areas. Notice also that the areas shown as high and very high in civilization are in the intermediate latitudes where climates provide the best working conditions." This is a relatively sophisticated method of asserting as fact what is really a value judgment. The caption implies that there is a scientific correlation between level of civilization and degree of industrialization, as well as between civilization and climate. But in fact the correlation is undoubtedly due to the fact that the authors defined "civilization" according to the characteristics of industrialized societies.

Another example of this problem is found in Bradley (3). He

states that "Russia's rulers today" are "unreasonable and unfriendly" because of an "ancient weakness"—"the lack of good outlets to the sea." Is this not too simplistic a view of history? Apart from the fact that the interpretation of Russian history as a drive to the sea has been debunked for a decade, should not students understand that the status quo is most desirable for the affluent, the influential? "Unreasonableness" and "unfriendliness" can be applied as easily to the rich, powerful, and cozy (who do not wish to change their status) as to the poor, weak, and afflicted (who seek improvement in their situation). How pertinent is Mark Twain's conception of the ethical man as the Christian who has four aces?

Bradley also states that "the strength of Russia lies in the brutal power of its dictatorial government . . . , [its] great wealth of natural resources . . . , [its] great armies . . . , [and] today it lies especially in its powerful rockets and nuclear bombs which it uses to threaten the rest of the world." He does not mention, however, that a significant part of the Soviet threat is a doctrine that promises social justice to millions of downtrodden, poverty-stricken people. Should not American children recognize that the Soviet challenge consists of more than just a harsh dictatorship and a crass materialism? Teachers know that communism and fascism are two different animals. Should not children be given an opportunity to evaluate the arguments of those who see an essentially democratic character in communism? Should they not recognize some of the aspirational appeal of a doctrine that lured many well-meaning people into communist ranks? We underestimate the Soviet Union if we do not examine the ideology that is certainly a principal thread in the fabric of Soviet life.

In sum, then, as far as text materials for evaluating are concerned, this component of critical thinking is relegated to the end-of-chapter activities, although value descriptions sometimes find their way into textbooks masquerading as factual statements. No direction is given to evaluation techniques aside from the bibliographical entries provided in most texts. In this regard the annotated bibliographies in Bradley are excellent.

CONSTRUCTING

Constructing is the fourth component of critical thinking. It is the process by which relationships are discovered among hitherto unconnected propositions. In this fashion newly acquired knowledge becomes integrated with the knowledge one already possesses.

Constructing rests on the other three components of critical thinking. If one is to assess how well a textbook encourages constructing, he must consider first whether it meets the needs of the student to whom it is directed and secondly whether its formal and substantive elements make the subject informative, interesting, and readable. In effect the whole package must be evaluated to determine to what extent it will be useful in a learning situation. The task involves more than basic arithmetic, because the elements must be weighed rather than counted and because no two evaluative scales will be exactly the same. According to the criteria suggested in this chapter for maximizing the role of geography in the secondary education curriculum, however, James and Davis (11), Jones and Murphy (15), and Kohn and Drummond (18) seem most desirable for classroom use.

Conclusion

The student should consider present textbooks as an array of more or less uncoordinated elements and propositions. He should be engaged in determining the validity of these propositions, separating the tenable from the untenable, and, under the aegis of a responsive teacher, he should reconstruct earth space in accordance with information from other disciplines, focusing on the salient problems that emerge after the material has been clarified and validated. Textbooks will presumably continue to be used in schools throughout the foreseeable future. Until the appearance of textbooks that elicit more complete student engagement, able teachers will have to fill the gap themselves.

Hopefully the day will soon come when open-structured texts are common. Since the information explosion adds daily to human knowledge, it will not be feasible to add factual detail to successive revisions of textbooks. Instead textbooks will be internally organized in two basic ways: First, details about certain places will be interconnected by explanations of physicocultural processes operating through time. A select fund of these geographical "sets" will make the reader aware of *what* the geographer can tell us about the earth and *how* he makes his discoveries. Second, there will be opportunities within each chapter for the student to engage in the same kind of discovery illustrated by the geographic sets. End-of-chapter activities will become in-chapter activities tied to the author's main thrust. They will involve the student in the task of establishing compendent relationships among propositions that depend upon the sets for data.

The sets and in-chapter activities would not be selected solely because they have become classic in geography. Selection would be based primarily upon their presumed efficacy in illuminating the persistent problems of mankind. An ongoing evaluation of the relative significance of mankind's problems in different regions of the world would sharpen the thrust of the text and permit the trimming of unrelated detail. Textbooks would become a source of light for the mind and cease to be a load on the memory.

Selected Bibliography

1. ACKERMAN, EDWARD A., "Regional Research: Emerging Concepts and Techniques in the Field of Geography," *Economic Geography*, 29 (July, 1953), 189–97.

2. AD HOC COMMITTEE ON GEOGRAPHY, National Academy of Sciences—National Research Council, *The Science of Geography*, Publication 1277, Washington, D.C., 1965.

3. BRADLEY, JOHN H., *World Geography*, Ginn, Boston, 1964.

4. EISNER, ELLIOTT W., "Critical Thinking," *Teachers College Record*, 66 (Apr., 1965), 624–34.

5. FORDE, C. DARYLL, *Habitat, Economy, and Society: A Geographical Introduction to Ethnology*, Dutton, New York, 1963.

6. HIGH SCHOOL GEOGRAPHY PROJECT OF THE ASSOCIATION OF AMERICAN GEOGRAPHERS, *Settlement Theme Course Outline*, draft (Jan. 24, 1966), Boulder, Colorado.

7. HOLT, SOL, *World Geography and You*, Van Nostrand, Princeton, N.J., 1964.

8. HOSELITZ, BERT F. (ed.), *A Reader's Guide to the Social Sciences*, The Free Press, Glencoe, Ill., 1959.

9. ISRAEL, SAUL, ROEMER, NORMA H., AND DURAND, LOYAL, JR., *World Geography Today*, Holt, Rinehart and Winston, New York, 1966.

10. JACKSON, W. A. DOUGLAS, "Whither Political Geography," *Annals of the Association of American Geographers*, 48 (June, 1958), 178–83.

11. JAMES, PRESTON E., AND DAVIS, NELDA, *The Wide World: A Geography*, Macmillan, New York, 1962.

12. JAMES, PRESTON E., AND JONES, CLARENCE F. (eds.), *American Geog-*

raphy: Inventory and Prospect, Syracuse University Press, Syracuse, N.Y., 1954.

13. JOINT COMMITTEE ON EDUCATION OF THE ASSOCIATION OF AMERICAN GEOGRAPHERS AND THE NATIONAL COUNCIL FOR GEOGRAPHIC EDUCATION, *Advisory Paper for Teachers Associated with the High School Geography Project,* University of California at Los Angeles (Aug., 1962).

14. ———, *Response Paper: Suggestions from Teachers Associated with the High School Geography Project,* University of California at Los Angeles (Aug., 1963).

15. JONES, STEPHEN B., AND MURPHY, MARION F., *Geography and World Affairs,* Rand McNally, Chicago, 1962.

16. KNIFFEN, FRED, "Geography and the Past," *Journal of Geography,* 50 (Mar., 1951), 126–29.

17. KOHN, CLYDE F. (ed.), *Selected Classroom Experiences: High School Geography Project,* Geographic Education Series No. 4, National Council for Geographic Education, 1964.

18. KOHN, CLYDE F., AND DRUMMOND, DOROTHY W., *The World Today: Its Patterns and Cultures,* McGraw-Hill, New York, 1963.

19. KOLEVZON, EDWARD R., AND HEINE, JOHN A., *Our World and Its Peoples,* Allyn and Bacon, Boston, 1964.

20. MASSIALAS, BYRON G., AND SMITH, FREDERICK R. (eds.), *New Challenges in the Social Studies,* Wadsworth, Belmont, Calif., 1965.

21. PLATT, ROBERT S., "Review of Regional Geography," *Annals of the Association of American Geographers,* 47 (June, 1957), 187–90.

22. POUNDS, NORMAN J. G., AND COOPER, EDWARD L., *World Geography: Economic, Political, Regional,* South-western, Cincinnati, Ohio, 1961.

23. PRICE, ROY A. (ed.), *New Viewpoints in the Social Sciences,* National Council for the Social Studies Yearbook No. 28, Washington, D.C., 1958.

24. REDFIELD, ROBERT, "Social Science in Our Society," *Phylon,* 11 (Mar., 1950), 31–41.

25. ———, "Study of Culture in General Education," *Social Education,* 11 (Oct., 1947), 259–64.

26. "Sources of Error: A Review of Geography Textbooks," *London Times Education Supplement,* 2567 (July 31, 1964), 174.

27. VAN CLEEF, EUGENE, AND FINNEY, JOHN C., *Global Geography,* Allyn and Bacon, Boston, 1963.

CHAPTER 13

Values and Controversy in Secondary Social Studies

A Critical Review of the Literature

MARK CHESLER

Introduction

The purpose of this chapter is to explore some value issues and problems in secondary social studies education as they are presented to teachers. My concern has not been to contribute new knowledge in this area but to review the contemporary state of affairs. I have therefore reviewed the articles written over the last six years in those social studies journals most available to teachers: *Social Education* and *The Social Studies.*

But after reviewing those journal articles that deal with problems of values and controversy in the classroom, I realized that very serious gaps exist in these materials. References to other materials are therefore sprinkled throughout this chapter. There are three major sections in this report: (1) a general review of discussions on the place of values and controversy in the classroom, with special attention devoted to the classroom treatment of communism and to the problem of indoctrination; (2) a review of commentaries on high school social studies textbooks, including a report on two texts that I examined; and (3) a discussion of the teacher's role in developing values and managing controversy in the classroom.

Whether to present controversies and values in the classroom and how to handle them are key issues in secondary social studies for several reasons: First, all knowledge and material in social studies is in some way controversial and value laden; therefore only value-conscious inquiry can help cut through these biases to understand social phenomena. Second, social studies scholars often postulate that one of their goals is to create an understanding and appreciation of the "democratic creed," or our American value system. And finally, social studies educators often claim that another goal is to help youngsters learn "desirable social behavior" and personal value systems.

In the American society, however, a wide variety of people and groups may make divergent individual and collective choices about the meaning of American goals, about their own values, and about the means for realizing goals based on these values. This moral pluralism, which is a central component of the American system, seems to make value conflicts inevitable. The essential questions are: What is the character of such conflict, and how do we deal with it? This chapter examines the suggestions that have been made for avoiding or dealing with these questions in the public school classroom.

Problems of Controversy and Values in the Classroom

When men care enough about an issue to differ, controversy occurs. When social studies enthusiasts commit themselves and their works to creating students who have "good human relationships" and "desirable socio-civic and personal behavior," we are at the threshold of important controversies and value issues (33). The general goals of social studies courses are agreeable to most people, but their particular form and meaning consistently generate controversy in our pluralistic society. Sometimes differences arise out of confrontations between opposing values or sets of values; at other times conflicts come about as a result of differing priorities or means for the same general values. For instance, the prime concern of some white Southerners is the maintenance of social order. For them justice is important but secondary. Negro protest movements are far more concerned with justice than order, although they would like both. This clash of priorities is not limited to the southern United States; it had its clearest exposition in the classical writing of Hobbes, Locke, and Rousseau. Even when goals are agreed upon, major differences can arise with respect to the means used to attain these goals. For example, Negro groups disagree on whether to seek social equality through accommodation, through integration, through black power, or through conflict. Each choice of means reflects a different value preference. One of the major problems in the consideration of controversy and values in social studies, or in the refusal to consider them, is the failure to recognize these particular realms of controversy and value clash.

Carey (5) felt that "our society believes in certain basic 'truths' and goals, which should be recognized and taught as such." According to this author, the truth includes what "ought to be" as well as "what is." He assumed that men can agree not only on the "facts" of social situations but on the "oughts" as well. Moreover, Carey assumed that there are "truths" that can be recognized. His own use of quotation marks suggests his probable discomfort with this position. Here are some of the goals that Carey felt represent value judgments agreed on in our society:

> Our society accepts, almost without question, that it is better for humans to live than to die and that pain and misery should be brought under control . . . [that] each human being has dignity and importance, that there should be equality of opportunity, and [that] the state exists to serve the man and not man to serve the state. (Carey, 5, p. 182.)

Several of these very general truths have only tangential relevance to the way we actually live in the United States. Inequality of opportunity is present and is subtly if not openly preached throughout the nation. Equality of opportunity is an American goal but certainly not a reality, and it is not even a goal that everyone shares on the behavioral level. We kill and die in Vietnam and elsewhere in flagrant contradiction to the first principle. Perhaps we believe that life is better than death for Americans but not necessarily for communists, Orientals, or Latin Americans. Another answer may be that we violate Carey's basic principles because of other values that we think are even more important, such as freedom or rolling back the communists. Why are some other principles omitted from Carey's list? The problems with teaching eternal truths are that (1) everyone disagrees about what they are or what they mean, except when stated at a very general level; (2) everyone puts different priorities on their relative values; and (3) these truths may not be relevant to the way people and groups actually behave.

Powell (22) held that it is quite appropriate to teach American values in the classroom and that the best way to teach is by teacher example. The critical theme in American values, he suggested, is that of service to one's fellow man, not service to self. Is that *the* key to the American system? First, Powell's statement is at such a high level of generality that one wonders what it means behaviorally or in specific circumstances. Second, if service to others is a meaningful value, one wonders what is uniquely American about it. Palmer (21) suggested that teachers can evaluate student behavior in terms of cultural mandates and human behavior, can show students the importance of thinking and working in a group, and can help them to evaluate our cultural heritage. These are presumed to be the relevant focuses of value inquiry. But no rationale is presented for the emphasis upon these as opposed to other focuses for value inquiry. Furthermore, Palmer failed both to give examples of cultural mandates and to explain what the terms mean in the classroom situation.

Willcockson (35) sought to understand why able students do not follow through on their class assignments. Her investigations quickly led to a concern for student values. She stated that "it is important that attitudes and values are learned not merely through catching them in hit or miss fashion but in a planned sequence of situations in which conscious understandings are developed." Certainly this is an agreeable statement, supporting the conclusions reached by Shaver in his discussion of reflective thinking (25). But the outcome of planned situations is, for Willcockson, the "gradual development of understandings toward the need for conformity to a common code of values." She suggested, furthermore, that students must progress from a "blanket acceptance" of values to a questioning posture. It is unclear, however, what degree of conformity she saw as necessary and what the common code is to which students are to conform. Each teacher is left to exercise his imagination on these matters.

Some other articles in these journals focus not upon general values to be taught but upon a process of inquiry into values. Gold-mark (8) suggested that teachers examine values in a scientific man-ner by identifying a problem, selecting the criteria for judgment, examining the values underlying choices, and then checking this through an inquiry process. She did not clarify what happens when a value can be checked no further, nor did she indicate whether there are distinctions between values as means and values as ends. The scientific method can be used in some value analyses, especially in verifying what we may call "means" values—values that are held to be good because they lead to a desirable state of affairs. Science and philosophy can help us test and confirm empirically or logically whether certain values do lead to their associated goals. These meth-ods are not so helpful, however, when we deal with "ends" values—values that are good only in themselves. It is interesting in this respect to consider Scriven's suggestion (24) that ultimate values probably do not exist as often as claimed, and in fact may not exist at all. Scriven argued, therefore, that we ought to submit ultimate claims to more rigorous empirical and logical tests.

Several authors concerned with the learning process, or "learn-ing to learn," stressed the importance of values and controversy. Engle (7), for instance, suggested dealing with value conflicts when he proposed teaching via the decision-making method. This tech-nique presents students with dilemmas or choices and requires them to suggest and select alternative explanations or courses of action. They must be able to defend their selection to others. This seems to be a very promising strategy, particularly when students are pre-sented with real choices and decisions. For example, how do you spend a limited amount of your own money, and how does that reflect your personal values? Or, as governor how would you spend a given amount of money, and how does that reflect your values, your conception of social needs, and the political pressure apparatus? Lieberman and Simon (13) seemed to concur with Engle in their argument for a curricular emphasis upon value clarification, on the search for an individualized value system. They made a serious attempt not to mediate or influence the student's choice of a par-ticular value system but did make a self-conscious attempt to aid stu-dents to see values as relevant, to inquire into their assumptions, to test them out behaviorally and compare them with their peers' values, and to continue to revise them in a search for identity and ethical meaning.

Massialas's concern (14, 16) was with the "discovery approach," or the "inquiry approach": here the goal is to force the student himself to engage in the act of discovery. Massialas argued that teaching facts or generalizations alone is fruitless because they are soon forgotten. What must be taught is a scheme for investigation, which is much more rewarding in the long run. The suggested procedure in the inquiry method is for the student to reach a conclusion himself through some approximation of a problem-solving method. This technique requires a nondirective teacher who encourages students to define their inquiry goals, to have an intuitive encounter with the subject, and then to test findings in some verifiable manner. Perhaps the student is given a bit of data and asked to analyze and interpret it; perhaps he is shown some persons interacting and is asked to explain what they are doing and why. A central question that must be resolved is whether the discovery should be real or just a replication of things we already know well. Of what avail is a student's joy of discovery if he learns it has been discovered before? Some students may then feel cheated. This seems to be the crucial failure of most discovery techniques in the physical sciences; the experiments are carefully controlled replications with predictable results. But to present students with unanswered questions for new discovery is truly exciting! There are many questions students may have about subject matter, classroom relations, or value preferences that could be explored in this manner.

Wass (34), like Lieberman and Simon (13), was particularly concerned with current events instruction. He suggested four alternatives that he felt have great promise for realizing the learning potential in current events. The first of these involves training youngsters to evaluate news, instead of merely knowing it. By examining the sources of bias in articles by columnists, editorials, and news accounts (such as when the account states, "according to informed sources") students would see news as controversial and would view reading the news as more complex and challenging. Second, Wass proposed that students engage in biographical studies of men who make the news. Third, he suggested that students conduct sociodramatic portrayals of news events and situations. Finally, he suggested that students be helped to combine their reading of current events with action projects. Such projects would include informing themselves and various publics of what they read, lobbying for some of their interests, or engaging in service programs, such as CARE.

For Wass and others action is both a way to define values behaviorally and a way to test them. We will see these assumptions reflected in several other articles as we move through the literature.

Ballinger (3), for example, suggested that an important aspect of controversy and value analysis is for students to become committed to some courses of action that represent and reinforce their value choices. He stated that it is impossible to see "how the student can become *vitally* interested in matters on which he is forbidden to take action."

Sobel and Cherkis (29) described a sample out-of-classroom activity in which students became junior peace corps workers. Students were involved in a variety of activities designed not only to study problems and clarify their values but to bring projects dealing with them to successful fruition. According to Sobel and Cherkis, students raised money for the United Nations, tutored elementary school youngsters, and "adopted" a girl in another country. These activities enhanced the youngsters' pride in self-action and also seemed to increase their interest in learning about foreign lands and regions.

Steinberg (31) suggested that students can learn about political science through the study of local and current politics. Students can follow up on field trips by working on local elections and campaigns or by working as assistant social workers or in other civic jobs. These experiences can then be brought back into the classroom. Such short work experiences after school, on weekends, or during certain school periods may be a very exciting future direction for social studies teaching methodology.

Simon and Harmin (27) pointed out the learning potential in such programs, arguing that merely studying controversy is an insufficient citizen or student activity. From their point of view learning is enhanced and citizenship roles are fulfilled when students are asked to make choices and take action on their values, opinions, and considered judgments. The authors provided examples of the types of action that are both meaningful and available to high school students: writing letters for or against a cause; sending money to an organization, an individual, or a cause; going to meetings; joining groups; signing petitions; engaging in demonstrations; confronting other students on an issue; and encouraging others to engage in one or more of these actions. These activities seem to be in the best psychosocial tradition, since they seek to connect beliefs with behavior and enhance learning partly by doing. In addition we well know the student's role as a passive observer of both the public and educational scenes. What an impetus to learning such activism could generate in students! These new postures would probably carry over to other aspects of student life as well.

ANTICOMMUNISM

General values and goals are often made specific when scholars and teachers concentrate upon a particular subject. Alilunas (2) and Leinwand (12) centered their attention on the courses named "Problems of Democracy" or a variation of the same. Both authors agreed that the purpose of such courses ought to be to enable the student to deal with the problems he will face in society. One of the topics typically dealt with in such courses is communism.

Steinberg (30) observed that the emphasis upon democracy in schools does not seem to include a concern for teaching about communism or anticommunism. At some point the teacher must stand clear of the official and stated policies of the social system and think critically himself. As Steinberg stated, "the goals of the teacher are not identical with the goals of the State Department, no matter how valid nor cogent are the latter's policies." Metcalf (17) came to essentially the same conclusion, suggesting that our approach to the teaching of communism is manifestly totalitarian.

Swearingen's main concern (32) seems to be to expose the evils of international communism and its plan for America's subversion in a way that will not permit students to forget its atrocities. He stated: "There are two tests that communism can never pass—truth . . . and comparison." The comparisons he suggested are ostensibly to be made between communist nations and the Western democracies, but, as Gray (9) pointed out, most of these comparisons are ill informed and fallacious. Gray reported that most state departments of education interested in teaching about communism are primarily concerned with demonstrating the evils, fallacies, and contradictions of communism:

> (1) [Communism is typically pictured as] a total evil in complete opposition to all democratic principles . . . . (2) There is a marked tendency to contrast the darkest realities of communism in the Soviet Union with the noblest ideals of American democracy . . . . They present a picture of an unswerving monolithic world Communist power dominated by the Soviet Union. (Gray, 9, p. 72.)

Moreover, these attempts concentrate on the failure of the Soviet system, use pejorative and emotional terms, and disregard differing views of communism by scholars in the field.

These views of communism and how to teach about it grow out of an ill-conceived notion of how to analyze controversies and social problems. If problems were considered unalterably bad and everyone agreed they must be eradicated, then it would make some sense to teach that all problems ought to be done away with "root and branch." But this is not necessarily the case. Another alternative is to see problems as things to be remedied but as endemic to the human situation. For instance, the relationship between man and the state is a problem that can be dealt with but never completely resolved unless we have anarchy or totalitarianism. Similarly, ideological conflict between competing social and political systems is a problem. Resolution and compromise can manage the problem, but annihilation or surrender are the only means of doing away with it. Furthermore, teaching approaches that ignore communism or recommend its annihilation betray a lack of concern for and faith in the free exchange of ideas and in controversial inquiry, and a primary emphasis on indoctrinating students with certain publicly approved values and ideologies.

INDOCTRINATION

The problem of indoctrination has been highlighted by the previous discussion of communism. But in other areas, too, many scholars are concerned with the uncritical promulgation of certain social values in the classroom. Miller (18) felt that indoctrination is often the case in schools: "when values are considered in our schools, too often the teaching is based upon compulsion rather than commitment." According to Miller not all Americans really agree with the values set forth in the Constitution. Perhaps we agree at a very general level, but we disagree at the level of means and of specific implementation. Metcalf (17) also pointed out the complexity of this problem and stated that the solution is not to ignore value issues but to discover how to teach without indoctrination. He argued that "no one, least of all our teachers, can tell the American people what their values are to be." The answer, he felt, is to teach *valuing*—that is, the process of developing, verifying, and acting out values. This approach is in marked contrast to attempts to teach ideological and behavioral conformity, whatever the rationale. The process of valuing would probably proceed according to some of the suggestions of Simon and Harmin (27), Massialas (14), and Massialas and Zevin (16), which we have already discussed.

Another perspective is offered by Carey (5). He suggested that we need not fear indoctrination because students will resist indoctrination and because indoctrination from one source will be matched by counterindoctrination from another source. Let us examine these two assumptions. First, there is little evidence to suggest that the variation in the views of teachers on matters of social controversy is so great that one can expect indoctrination to meet with counterindoctrination. Second, the passive and relatively noncreative roles of young people in most of our schools hardly support the notion that students will resist indoctrination. The best we can hope for is that students will resist silently—not accepting, but not openly resisting. If it were legitimate for them to disagree, and if they did resist openly, we would no longer be talking about indoctrination but about debate. Unfortunately, this seldom occurs, and private, silent resistance encourages the development of pluralistic ignorance. Students do not know how their peers feel, and in the absence of peer support only the public utterances of the indoctrinating teacher are legitimate. The student may often consider his silent opinions idiosyncratic and illegitimate.

Scovel (23) suggested the importance of making student opinions and reactions public: "only when students bring their ideas into the open can teachers hope to modify undesirable ones and to strengthen socially acceptable ones." In effect, making reactions public is Scovel's strategy for enabling the teacher to indoctrinate and manipulate more effectively. But publicity permits other things as well: the legitimation of differences, the presentation of a broader range of alternatives, the exploration of value conflicts, and perhaps even the voluntary reorganization of some principles.

The Treatment of Controversy and Values in Textbooks

It is unfortunate that very few articles discussing textbooks appear in the social studies journals; most discerning articles are written for scholars and appear in more academic journals. Thus teachers are seldom exposed to professional discussions and criticisms of texts and text materials.

Krug (11) pointed out that social studies textbooks consistently fail to present the United States as it is and to provide an opportunity for critical thinking. He stated that texts are guilty of "omitting or glossing over controversial issues and of avoiding a clear-cut commitment to fundamental democratic rights and the obligation to work for the betterment of our democratic society." The most common treatment of controversy is either to ignore it or to describe two or more positions on an issue "neutrally," with the implicit assumption that all positions are inherently equal within our democratic society. In a later article Krug (10) suggested that this bland approach does *not* mean that the textbook is neutral—far from it. Under the cover of impartiality clear value judgments do slip in, and this is most dangerous. Not to realize that impartiality is a logical and psychological impossibility blinds us to the real prejudices in seemingly fair presentations. For example, Krug felt that American history texts systematically overplay the cruelty of the North and the barbarism of Negroes and scalawags in the South during Reconstruction. Most texts take the position that the South eventually had no choice but to resist the imposition of rules by illiterate unwashed blacks. The solid achievements of southern Republicans and selected Negroes are systematically underplayed. This pair of articles suggests that those persons who argue for neutral textbooks may be guilty of two misconceptions. First, they fail to realize that neutrality often masks factual distortion and interpretive bias. Second, true neutrality would entail neutrality on fundamental moral issues, and I would argue that partisanship is a more appropriate student posture on moral dilemmas, although there may well be plural partisan responses to such issues.

Shaver (25) directly confronted another major issue alluded to earlier. The textbooks for American government courses that he examined do not seem to treat our society as a pluralistic system. They assume that there is a common web of values to which most people adhere. They "fail to treat systematically the problem of handling the inevitable clash of values as decisions are made in the society." Clearly many of these texts imply that clashes of values can be eradicated by being pragmatic or teaching the right values. While students are exhorted to think critically, no conceptual framework is presented to give them the skills necessary to do this highly complex and abstract task. Finally, American ideals are represented *not* as ideal forms of politics but as descriptions of reality. Shaver's discussion of civics texts follows much the same pattern. The government is dealt with as an umpire of sometimes competing interests, not as one of the competitors itself. Free speech and religion are first presented as absolutes and then as having encountered some restrictions in practice. Never are these inevitable restrictions treated as fundamental problems of a free and pluralistic society. Again, in discussions of critical and reflective thinking Shaver found that the emphasis "is on the factual basis for disputes," and the assumption is that by clearing up factual entanglements value problems will automatically disappear. The major point to be recognized is that value conflicts are inevitable in a pluralistic society. The only ways to avoid these conflicts are (1) to treat the society as nonpluralistic; (2) to treat values at such a high degree of generality that incompatibilities become obscured; or (3) to ignore values by treating them as epiphenomena of factual disagreements, prejudices, or pathologies. Textbooks that systematically overlook the problems of value conflict inadequately represent our plural moral system and discourage its continuation.

Alexander (1) found much the same situation in reviewing American history texts. His most damning criticisms are that (1) texts are dull and lifeless and bear striking resemblances to each other, (2) texts are critical of neither the past nor the present and therefore do not present the full face of America, and (3) texts consciously avoid controversy and artificially balance all issues. Palmer (21) noted that of the twenty-seven history texts he examined, only five attempted to explain the dynamics of change. Even those that attempted to do so generally failed to analyze a complex of social forces at work; instead they reverted to a unicausal and monolithic explanation of change.

Newmann (19) attacked the proposition, naïvely presented in most texts, that an important objective of civic education is to foster a belief in government "by the consent of the governed." "That is, we teach that consent of the governed is an ideal, a positive 'good' to strive for, and that our social system is superior in part because we do in fact enjoy consent of the governed." He examined this consent issue and presented much data from political and social studies suggesting that the conditions for a traditional consensual system have been eroded. The forces of elitism and corporate bureaucracy, the misrepresentation of geographic and ethnic minorities, and the general noninvolvement of people in political life all invalidate an active consent system. So Newmann suggested that instead we teach the proposition that each person, "by his consent, delegates much of his consent process to persons and techniques considered to be more able and/or more interested than he." So long as we have elections we will continue to have this delegated consent system. But the data contradict this "new" conception of consent just as clearly as they do the old. Low voter turnout, minimal citizen participation in party activity, and a narrowing of real alternatives suggest that mere existence of an opportunity for delegation does not mean that people take advantage of it. It is specious to argue that if a person does not vote he is nevertheless delegating his consent power to those who do. This may be a logical argument, but it clearly does not establish a democratic or representative consent system, as Newmann so well pointed out in his own discussion of traditional consent.

I reviewed some of these issues by personally examining two texts used for problems of democracy courses: Bohlman and Bohlman (4) and Dunwiddie and Kidger (6). Although the word "problems" is in the title of both books, neither makes a systematic effort to deal with social problems conceptually. Is a problem a pathology? Or is it a process? Are all problems bad? Or are some neutral or good? Who and what defines a problem? You? I? Critics? Competing interests? Unrealized aspirations? Is it appropriate to focus on social problems? Or on personal problems? Metcalf (17) spoke clearly about several of these issues when he commented that we teach problems as if they could be solved for good. On the contrary, problems must be continually solved and re-solved. Both texts discuss problems as an outgrowth of social change; in a sense both conceptualize a continuous process of reequilibration or readjustment to some harmoniously balanced social system. Dunwiddie and Kidger make a reference to problems as "basics"—as fundamental tasks that need to be done— but give them scant attention.

Both books describe a problem-solving sequence, and both sequences are essentially the same: one book tells the student to *define, gather, conclude,* and *act;* the other book suggests that he *define, discover, digest, decide,* and *do.* These statements suffer from three serious deficiencies. First, these problem-solving schemes do not include a final stage of either *evaluation* or *redefinition.* The absence of the final stage gives the impression that each problem can be solved and that action finishes our work—clearly an inadequate view of problem solving. Second, the final step of either scheme is grossly ignored throughout the texts. Although attention is paid to gathering information and although some hope is expressed that students will draw conclusions and digest alternatives, absolutely minimal attention is paid to action alternatives. If this step is a logical conclusion to the problem sequence, it must be dealt with. The text should raise questions such as: "What would you do about this?" "If you believe this, how do you demonstrate these beliefs in your actions?" Third, this problem-solving sequence is irrelevant to everything else in the books. It orients the student to a way of working that is implicitly denied by the remainder of both books. Bohlman and Bohlman, for instance, suggest that a good citizen votes, learns, informs others, and works in politics. How appropriate it would have been to apply problem-solving to this discussion. But here, as in the presentation of other text materials, the student is given no example to show that this sequence is meaningful, workable, or even visible.

The purpose of the chapters on communism is to "demonstrate the danger of communism through its study." Note that the "study" of communism is seen as instrumental to the purpose of opposing it effectively, and not as an intrinsic goal. Both texts present a brief, if somewhat vulgar, description of Marxist tenets. Then Bohlman and Bohlman note that their interpretation of the communist meaning of force "explains why communist talk of peaceful coexistence must be regarded warily by the Western democracies."

Both texts continue with brief synopses of Marx's "errors" and the revisions of his scientific socialism by Lenin, Stalin, and Khrushchev. There is very little discussion of the incredible industrial transformation of agrarian Russia. Bohlman and Bohlman do point out the great Soviet development, but neither text seriously examines the events of 1925–55 in Russia as problems of development rather than by-products of cruel leadership and a cruel ideology. One wonders whether the authors would have treated the American westward movement, American Negro slavery, or the toll of America's industrialization in anywhere near the same vein.

Both texts now turn to a consideration of "The Communist Challenge" (4) or "Why is Communism a Challenge?" (6). Both textbooks see the communists' major goal as imperialistic conquest, world domination, and territorial expansion. Bohlman and Bohlman report, moreover, that the United States has no aggressive designs. (Well even if not, this text certainly encourages youngsters to adopt a militant posture toward communism.) Both texts cite the 1949 revolution in China as an example of communist imperialistic goals in operation. Bohlman and Bohlman quite simply state that "in 1949 China fell to the communists." Neither text discusses the civil war that began in the 1920's, and neither discusses the corruption and loss of popular support of the Chiang Kai-shek regime in the 1940's.

Both texts then list the portions of the Smith Act, the McCarran-Walter Act, and the Landrum-Griffin Act that apply to the treatment of communists in the United States. No serious mention is made of the ways these provisions affect the civil liberties of Americans nor of the Supreme Court's concerns regarding the constitutionality of certain of these provisions.

These issues are controversial and still unresolved, and they should be treated as such. Textbooks should at least mention that there are alternative views of communism, of China's Revolution, and of the Smith Act. Anything short of this glorifies status-quo Americanism, and the price is another generation of closed-minded anticommunists.

It is also clear that such one-sided treatment of communism affects other issues as well. At the end of the chapter on race relations, for instance, Dunwiddie and Kidger ask: "Since three quarters of the world's population is nonwhite, how does that affect our relations with communism?" Thus almost all policy is eventually considered in terms of its relevance for anticommunism.

If we felt that teachers often went beyond such texts to supplementary materials or perhaps even used such texts for inquiry stimulation or propaganda analysis, we could rest comfortably. But as Steinberg (30) pointed out the greatest tragedy of textbooks is the misuse and overdependency on them by teachers.

The Teacher's Role and Methods

It is manifestly clear that teachers can expect little help from the social studies journals in classroom planning. Those articles that do deal with values consistently fail to spell out how the teacher can act on these concerns in the classroom (21, 22, 35).

Ballinger (3) searched through other sources discussing teacher skill development and preparation. In a review of a series of texts utilized for teacher education courses in social studies, Ballinger found that "almost no attention *at all* is paid to controversial issues in any form." When controversy is mentioned it is clear that the central concern is for the teacher to help the students "get the facts straight." I do not object to factual learning, but is this relevant to value analysis training? If it is, is this all that value training can consist of in the school?

Carey (5) and Snyder (28) were fairly direct, although general, about the teacher's role. From Carey's point of view "the teacher must preserve, perpetuate, and improve institutions of society." Why must he do this? And why did Carey assume that these three key terms are necessarily or even occasionally consistent with one another? Snyder argued for the use of a "democratic method of instruction" in social studies. In using this democratic method the teacher "couches the material in such a manner that the answer is not readily apparent [and] students work their way through to the solution." It is tragic that this manipulatory procedure should masquerade as a democratic method. The meaning of "democratic" is perverted by a teacher who presumes to have all the answers ahead of time and who leads students through an analytical process by the nose. With this sort of thinking it is no wonder that some students decide that politics and democracy are hoaxes that they cannot put their faith in. Snyder does suggest that alternative solutions might be found through the democratic method and that students could then look at the reasons this occurs and establish criteria for resolution or consensus. These aspects of the procedure are quite interesting, but can they truly be explored if the teacher already has the answer?

It is difficult for teachers to deal with values and controversy for a variety of reasons. Parents and community forces may, of course, object to seeing certain touchy issues brought to light. Moreover, many teachers do not care enough to explore issues clearly with their students. Sometimes, under the guise of not wanting to overinfluence their students, teachers may seek not to commit themselves on issues either. But it is my view and that of other authors discussed here that the teacher cannot be truly neutral and should not try to be. A teacher's choice of problems, texts, and classroom organization manifest his orientation to certain issues. In a number of semiconscious and conscious messages teachers inevitably present their own views. There are several dangers when these biases are masked as neutrality: (1) it is more difficult for students to dissent; (2) the student may learn that neutrality rather than partisanship is the model to follow; and (3) the student cannot identify the teacher's criteria or processes for coming to a conclusion or value choice. Massialas and Cox (15) presented a fruitful conception of the teacher as a fellow inquirer who adopts a role of "defensible partisanship."

Conclusion

For a variety of reasons it seems appropriate to try to teach young people some of the issues and problems involved in "valuing" instead of trying to ignore value clashes or to indoctrinate students with our personal values or our personal conceptions of societal values. How does one come to cherish certain principles? What does it mean to act upon these principles? Can we really believe in something if we do not act upon it consistently? What are the actual consequences for others and the effect on our own behavior of holding certain values? Teachers might appropriately involve students in trying to answer questions such as these. In this way, we might approach one goal of social studies courses: the reflective and self-conscious elucidation of the principles each individual believes in.

A second fruitful direction for social studies courses would be to explore problems of differences and conflicts in values. The United States is indeed a pluralistic moral entity in most matters. Therefore the discovery and management of such differences in values is an essential part of our heritage and future.

A final major problem is the development of strategies for classroom valuing. There are very few practical guidelines for teachers who desire to explore these issues in class. We have reviewed articles where such work has been urged, but few of these articles specify the teaching operations involved in such an innovation. These guidelines are necessary to specify and clarify new theory in this area and facilitate new practices.

Selected Bibliography

1. ALEXANDER, A., "The Gray Flannel Cover on the American History Text," *Social Education,* 24 (Jan., 1960), 11–15.

2. ALILUNAS, L., "Whither the Problems of Democracy Course?" *Social Education,* 28 (Jan., 1964), 11–14.

3. BALLINGER, S., "The Social Studies and Social Controversy," *School Review,* 71 (Apr., 1963), 97–111.

4. BOHLMAN, H., AND BOHLMAN, M., *Problems of Democracy,* Holt, Rinehart and Winston, New York, 1964.

5. CAREY, E., "Judgments in Economic Education," *Social Education,* 26 (Apr., 1962), 181–84.

6. DUNWIDDIE, W., AND KIDGER, H., *Problems of Democracy,* Ginn, Boston, 1962.

7. ENGLE, S., "Decision-making: The Heart of Social Studies Instruction," *Social Education,* 24 (Nov., 1960), 301–04.

8. GOLDMARK, B., "Another Look at Inquiry," *Social Education,* 29 (Oct., 1965), 349–51.

9. GRAY, B., "Teaching about Communism," *Social Education,* 28 (Feb., 1964), 71–72.

10. KRUG, M., "For a Fair Deal in the Teaching of Reconstruction," *Social Education,* 29 (Jan., 1965), 7–14.

11. ———, " 'Safe' Textbooks and Citizenship Education," *School Review,* 68 (Winter, 1960), 463–80.

12. LEINWAND, G., "A Course in Problems of American Democracy," *Social Education,* 27 (Feb., 1963), 81–82.

13. LIEBERMAN, P., AND SIMON, S., "Current Events and Values," *Social Education,* 29 (Dec., 1965), 532–33.

14. MASSIALAS, B., "Revising the Social Studies: An Inquiry-Centered Approach," *Social Education,* 27 (April, 1963), 185–89.

15. ———, AND COX, C., *Inquiry in Social Studies,* McGraw-Hill, New York, 1966.

16. ———, AND ZEVIN, J., "Teaching Social Studies Through Discovery," *Social Education,* 28 (Nov., 1964), 384–87.

17. METCALF, L., "Some Guidelines for Changing Social Studies Education," *Social Education,* 27 (April, 1963), 197–201.

18. MILLER, B., "The Quest for Values in a Changing World," *Social Education,* 29 (Feb., 1965), 69–73.

19. NEWMANN, F., "Consent of the Governed and Citizenship Education in Modern America," *School Review,* 71 (Winter, 1963), 404–24.

20. PALMER, J., "History Textbooks and Social Change," *Social Education,* 25 (March, 1961), 135–36.

21. PALMER, R., "Values, Value Systems, and the Good Life," *The Social Studies* (April, 1964), 129–31.

22. POWELL, T., "Teaching American Values," *Social Education,* 29 (May, 1965), 272–74.

23. SCOVEL, D., "The Bill of Rights in Iowa," *Social Education,* 26 (Dec., 1962), 448–50.

24. SCRIVEN, M., "Values in the Curriculum," *Social Science Education, Consortium Newsletter,* 2 (Apr., 1966), 1–3.

25. SHAVER, J., "Educational Research and Instructions for Critical Thinking," *Social Education,* 28 (Jan., 1962), 10–16.

26. ———, "Reflective Thinking, Values, and Social Studies Textbooks," *School Review,* 73 (Autumn, 1965), 226–57.

27. SIMON, S., AND HARMIN, M., "To Study Controversial Issues Is Not Enough," *The Social Studies,* 55 (Oct., 1964), 163–66.

28. SNYDER, E., "Democratic Social Studies at the Secondary Level," *The Social Studies,* 52 (Oct., 1961), 185–88.

29. SOBEL, S., AND CHERKIS, C., "A High School Peace Corps," *Social Education,* 27 (Oct., 1963), 310–12.

30. STEINBERG, SAMUEL, "Teaching History in a Rapidly Changing World," *Social Education,* 24 (Nov., 1960), 298–300.

31. STEINBERG, SONYA, "Pupils, Politics, and Politicians," *Social Education,* 24 (Oct., 1960), 251–54.

32. SWEARINGEN, R., "Teaching About Communism in the American Schools," *Social Education,* 28 (Feb., 1964), 68–70.

33. "The Role of the Social Studies," *Social Education,* 26 (Oct., 1962), 315–18.

34. WASS, P., "Improving Current Events Instruction," *Social Education,* 25 (Feb., 1961), 79–81.

35. WILLCOCKSON, M., "Why Children do Not Accept Responsibility," *Social Education,* 24 (Jan., 1960), 25–27.

36. ZELENY, L., AND GROSS, R., "Dyadic Role-Playing of Controversial Issues," *Social Education,* 24 (Dec., 1960), 354–58.

Correlates of the Social Studies Curriculum[*]

Grades 10-12

M. KENT JENNINGS

The social studies curriculum in the nation's schools continues to occupy the attention of scholars and lay people alike. In a time when curriculum revision is almost the rule rather than the exception, it is important to take repeated soundings on the shape of the curriculum in order to ascertain what movements are transpiring and what their concomitants are. As part of a larger survey study concerning the political socialization of high school seniors, information was collected about the social studies offerings available to the students, and it seems worthwhile to present the latter information independently.

We shall be talking about course offerings available to a national probability sample of high school *students*, rather than the offerings of a national probability sample of *schools*. In order to utilize an efficient sample of high school seniors and in order to use schools as well as students as units of analysis, 1,669 seniors in

* Support for this study came from the Danforth Foundation.

ninety-seven schools (public and nonpublic) were interviewed in the spring of 1965. The probability that a given school would be selected was proportionate to its size, while each senior within a selected school had an equal probability of being selected. It proved necessary to contact 111 schools in order to gain the cooperation of the final ninety-seven. Replacement schools were matched as nearly as possible with the few noncooperating schools.

Most studies of social studies curriculum trends and patterns have been based on random or interval samples of schools.[1] For purposes of characterizing schools or school systems this is an appropriate strategy.[2] However, since there are many more schools with senior classes under 100 than there are larger ones, greatly exaggerated weight is given to what prevails for students in small schools rather than to what prevails for all students. For example, unless appropriate weighting schemes are used, ten schools with an average senior class size of 100 would count for ten times as much as one school with a senior class of 1,000. Therefore it should be emphasized that we will be presenting the course offerings for a national sample of students.

As part of the collateral data used to explain the political socialization of the seniors, we obtained from the officials of the selected schools the titles of all social studies courses available from 1962 to 1965 in order to determine the social studies curriculum during the period when our sample of high school seniors was in the tenth through twelfth grades.

We shall make no distinction between required and elective courses. This is largely because the courses most frequently offered tend to be required in one form or another whenever they are found in the curriculum, and the courses appearing less frequently tend to be elective. Another reason is that, depending upon the type of program being pursued, a given course may be required for some stu-

---

[1]For reports of other studies see Scarvia B. Anderson *et al., Social Studies in Secondary Schools: A Survey of Courses and Practices,* Educational Testing Service, Princeton, N.J., 1964; Willis D. Moreland, "Curriculum Trends in the Social Studies," *Social Education,* 26 (Feb., 1962), 73–76, 102; Bertram A. Masia, "Profile of the Current Secondary Social Studies Curriculum in North Central Association Schools," *The North Central Association Quarterly,* 40 (Summer, 1963), 205–13; and Grace S. Wright, "Summary of Offerings and Enrollments in High School Subjects, 1960–61," (Preliminary Report) U.S. Office of Education (June, 1964).

[2]An excellent discussion of this sampling problem is presented in Leslie Kish's "Sampling Organizations and Groups of Unequal Sizes," *American Sociological Review,* 30 (Aug., 1965), 564–72.

dents but be optional for others; distinguishing between "required" and "elective" courses thus becomes difficult or meaningless in many schools.

Course Offerings in the Aggregate

Table 1 shows the proportion of seniors in schools where each of eleven subjects was offered during 1962 to 1965 (the years in which the seniors sampled were in the tenth through twelfth grades). To categorize social studies into eleven subjects we had to sacrifice some nuances. The nomenclature for such courses as American history, American government, world history, sociology, psychology, economics, and geography was rather uniform, but for other courses it was necessary to combine various titles under one name. For example, the course we called American problems consisted of the familar problems of democracy course (nearly half the courses on this subject carry that title) plus titles such as contemporary problems, social problems, and problems of American life. Specialized

TABLE 1   *Social Studies Offerings in the Tenth Through Twelfth Grades for a National Sample of High School Seniors*

COURSE	PERCENTAGE OF STUDENTS ATTENDING A SCHOOL OFFERING THE COURSE
American history	98
general world history	80
economics	65
American government	62
American problems	42
specialized world history	31
geography	30
sociology	30
psychology	16
international and comparative politics	13
personal problems	12
	$N = 2,048$[a]

[a]This is a weighted N used to correct for slightly inaccurate estimates of senior class size at the time the sampling frame was constructed. Weighted N's will be used for all succeeding tables. Total N's for any given classification may not always equal 2,048, due to rounding of weighted N's and occasional missing data.

world history included such courses as European history, Asian history, medieval history, non-Western history, and world cultures, which was more esoteric than the standard world history course. Under personal problems we included all courses oriented toward individual adjustment; under American problems we included those courses dealing with societal phenomena. International and comparative politics included courses so designated plus those called world affairs or world problems.

We recognize that a course title is not a foolproof guide to the content of the course. Sociology, for example, may be included in an American problems course. On the other hand the establishment of a specific course in sociology by a school would indicate a considerably greater emphasis on that subject than in the school where sociology is subsumed under another course title. While some precision is sacrificed by our not knowing the exact content of a course, we assume that no great violations have occurred because of our reliance primarily on course titles for grouping purposes. One partial validation for this assumption is the fact that courses with the same or similar designations tend to make use of the same group of textbooks.

Table 1 shows that there is a tremendous range in the relative prevalence of various courses. We may group courses into four general categories of prevalence. In the first are American history and world history, found in great abundance, with the former being virtually pervasive.[3] The second group consists of American government and economics, each taught in the schools of slightly over three-fifths of the students. A third group, offered to about three-tenths to two-fifths of the students, consists of sociology, specialized world history, geography,[4] and American problems. Finally, psychology, international and comparative politics, and personal problems are each offered to less than one-fifth of the students.

The old stand-bys—American and world history—very clearly continue to hold high priority in the curriculum. But the terrain is solidly occupied by other subjects as well. Given the trend toward incorporating more academic disciplines at the high school level, the status of economics, sociology, psychology, and international and

[3]Civics and junior high American history do not appear because they are predominantly ninth-grade courses.
[4]Since geography frequently appears as a ninth-grade course, the proportion is considerably lower than if the ninth-grade offerings had been included.

comparative politics will bear close scrutiny in the years to come. While the pattern set by the recommendations of the Committee on Social Studies in 1916—a sequence in the tenth through twelfth grades of European or world history, American history, and American social, economic, or political problems—is still in existence, the percentages in Table 1 would suggest a good deal of proliferation and innovation in other subjects.

SAMPLES OF SCHOOLS VERSUS SAMPLES OF STUDENTS

We noted earlier that most studies of the social studies curriculum have been based on samples of schools rather than of students. An intriguing question is whether findings about course offerings would differ depending upon whether samples of schools or samples of students were used. Because of procedural differences in the classification of the more esoteric subjects and because some doubt exists about the representativeness of the samples reported in other studies, we cannot make direct comparisons between our findings and previous ones. We can, however, adjust the percentages of students who are offered various courses in our sample to conform to a known distribution of seniors in different-sized high schools throughout the country. We can thus approximate what the distribution of course offerings would have been if the sampling units had been schools unadjusted for size. It was estimated that in 1964 and 1965 approximately 80 percent of the public school senior classes were under 100 in size.[5] (In our sample of students only 29 percent were in senior classes of that range.) By giving a weight of .80 to the percentages of students being offered each of the eleven social studies subjects in schools with senior classes under 100 and by assigning a weight of .20 to the corresponding percentages for students in schools with senior classes over 100, we can adjust the sample of students to represent a probability sample of schools.

Table 2 presents the distribution of subject offerings for students and for schools, along with the discrepancies between the two sets of

---

[5]A figure of 80 percent is reported for public schools in 1960 by John C. Flanagan *et al.*, *Project Talent: Studies of the American High School*, University of Pittsburgh, Pittsburgh, Pa., 1962, Chap. 2, p. 5. This figure is probably high for public schools in 1964, but since we lack more recent data on both public and nonpublic schools, we shall have to rely on the 80 percent figure as a reasonable approximation. Slight revision upward or downward would not appreciably affect the presentations.

TABLE 2   *Comparisons of Social Studies Course Offerings for the Tenth*
Through Twelfth Grades, Using Samples of Students Versus
Samples of Schools

COURSE	STUDENTS	SCHOOLS	DIFFERENCE[a]
American history	98%	98%	0%
general world history	80	89	+ 9
economics	65	49	− 16
American government	62	62	0
American problems	42	26	− 16
specialized world history	31	14	− 17
geography	30	29	− 1
sociology	30	31	+ 1
psychology	16	7	− 9
international and comparative politics	13	8	− 5
personal problems	12	11	− 1

[a]Signs indicate whether school unit percentages exceed or trail those for student units.

percentages. In five subjects—American history, American government, sociology, geography, and personal problems—virtually no differences result from changing the sample base. However, in the remaining six subjects—general world history, specialized world history, economics, American problems, international and comparative politics, and psychology—sampling schools rather than students would have produced visibly different results. With one exception—general world history—sampling by schools would have produced underestimates of the prevalence of social studies offerings. Nor are these underestimates trifling: the prevalence of specialized world history and psychology would have been underestimated by slightly more than 50 percent, American problems and international and comparative politics by nearly 40 percent, and economics by 25 percent.

Thus in general the social studies curriculum emerges as considerably more complete and varied when coverage is measured in terms of students instead of schools. In other words there is some variance in curriculum offerings according to the size of the school. Although this fact might seem obvious, the uniformity and rigidity of the social studies curriculum for the past several decades have probably minimized this variance—in contrast to the physical sciences, for example.

While the aggregate picture of course offerings is important, we are also interested in the characteristics associated with the presence or absence of various subjects. In the sections to follow we characterize the effect of three types of variables on the social studies curriculum—demographic features of the communities where the students live, structural features of the schools students attend, and the academic characteristics of these schools. Inasmuch as American history is ubiquitous in secondary schools and would therefore show no variation according to these variables, we will omit that subject from further discussion. Personal problems courses are also eliminated because they are at best tangential to the core of social studies.

Variables Affecting the Social Studies Curriculum

DEMOGRAPHIC FEATURES

Demographic characteristics are often associated with curriculum patterns. Table 3 shows the relationships between three demographic factors and the incidence of nine courses available to the students. First, a perusal of the percentages indicates that economics is the only subject not fluctuating considerably among the regions.[6] All other subjects exhibit a difference of at least 22 percent between the region with the highest incidence and that with the lowest. Even though the forces pushing the country toward a homogeneous system of education may be great, a great deal of regional variation in curriculum remains.

The most atypical profile is that of the Northeast region. There is a considerably greater emphasis than in the other regions on specialized world history and somewhat more on American problems but much less on American government and sociology and somewhat less on geography (above the ninth grade) and psychology. The Midwest is most prominent for its stress on geography and international and comparative politics. Most significant about the

---

[6]For sampling purposes and practical reasons we have been conservative in deciding what constitutes percentage differences of importance: differences of about 10 percent or more have been accepted as meaningful.

TABLE 3   *Availability of Social Studies Courses According to Three Community Characteristics*

	general world history	economics	American government	American problems	specialized world history	geography	sociology	psychology	international and comparative politics	N
	PERCENTAGE OF STUDENTS ATTENDING A SCHOOL OFFERING THE COURSE									
*Region*a										
Northeast	43%	66%	32%	56%	74%	16%	8%	6%	7%	*509*
Midwest	89	71	75	44	18	51	42	14	25	*629*
South	97	59	76	25	12	30	35	17	9	*562*
West	88	64	60	46	24	16	31	33	13	*348*
Size of Community										
0–4,000b	84%	51%	48%	28%	24%	22%	33%	9%	3%	*728*
5,000–30,000	91	61	82	51	27	40	27	16	21	*469*
31,000–100,000	72	82	59	48	45	31	35	31	13	*422*
100,000+	68	78	67	50	36	34	21	13	21	*429*
SMSA Classification										
12 Largest SMSA's	62%	67%	48%	73%	65%	23%	19%	14%	11%	*489*
Smaller SMSA's	83	79	74	27	24	40	40	23	20	*704*
Non-SMSA's	88	52	60	37	18	27	27	11	8	*856*

aRegional groupings follow Census Bureau classifications: the Northeast comprises New England and the Middle Atlantic states; the Midwest includes the East North Central and West North Central states; the South comprises the South Atlantic, East South Central, and West South Central states; and the West consists of the Mountain and Pacific states.
bIncludes schools in rural areas in addition to those in incorporated communities.

South is the low emphasis on American problems, while the West stands out for its strong showing of psychology.

The regional breakdown reveals a pattern that will recur in other tabulations—namely, that schools of certain characteristics may have a low incidence of a given course compensated for by a high incidence of a related course. One such example is the trade-off between the American government and American problems courses. Another illustration is that regions with a high incidence of specialized world history tend to be lower than other regions on incidence of general world history. Some schools do, of course, make available a much more varied and complete program than do others, as we shall see later. But schools without an extended repertory of social studies courses do have to make selections among competing alternatives, and such selections yield varying results. Moreover, in some instances legislative mandates leave few choices.[7]

Next let us consider community size. One interesting aspect here is that students attending schools in the largest communities (100,000 or more) do not necessarily have the greatest variety of courses (on the average) from which to select. Certainly no linear relationship exists between the size of the community and the likelihood that a particular course will be offered. Indeed eight of the nine subjects are most likely to be offered in either the 5,000–30,000 or the 31,000–100,000 categories of size.

On the other hand students in the smallest communities do enjoy the least probability of having a given course—with the exceptions of sociology and general world history—available to them. To this extent the widespread assumption that students in small communities are scholastically deprived is accurate. Beyond the threshold of the very small communities, however, the frequency of course offerings proves to be highly variable.

Another demographic classification utilized in Table 3 is that of the Standard Metropolitan Statistical Area (SMSA). An SMSA consists of a county containing at least one central city of 50,000 or more and contiguous counties that are essentially metropolitan and are socially and economically integrated with the central city. The sample of seniors was divided into those students who attend school in one of the twelve largest SMSA's, those who attend school in one of the smaller SMSA's, and those who attend school in areas that are not part of any SMSA.

In six of the nine course areas students in the smaller SMSA's more often attend a school offering such courses. Another salient feature of the course distributions is the greater emphasis placed on American problems and specialized world history in the very large SMSA's; conversely general world history and American government occur less frequently there. Finally, and perhaps contrary to popular

[7]See Franklin Patterson, "Citizenship and the High School: Representative Current Practices," in Franklin Patterson (ed.), *The Adolescent Citizen*, The Free Press, Glencoe, Ill., 1960, pp. 109–16; see also The Robert A. Taft Institute of Government, *Citizenship Education: A Survey for Citizenship Education Among the Fifty States*, New York, 1963.

belief, students in the non-SMSA's are by no means impoverished in the availability of social studies courses. They rank lowest on only four of the subjects, occupy the middle position on four others, and are first on one subject.

STRUCTURAL FEATURES OF SCHOOLS

Prominent structural features of the school itself may also be related to the nature of the curriculum. Three features are treated in Table 4—type of school, span of grades, and size of senior class. For present purposes nonpublic schools comprise both nonparochial and parochial types. Because the number of nonpublic students and schools covered in a sample of this size is quite small (219 and 11, respectively), extreme caution should be exercised in interpreting the relevant entries in Table 4. While differences between public and nonpublic schools are apparent, the magnitudes are modest. Of the

TABLE 4   *Availability of Social Studies Courses According to Three School Structural Characteristics*

	general world history	economics	American government	American problems	special world history	geography	sociology	psychology	international and comparative politics	N
Type of School										
Public	85%	66%	65%	41%	27%	31%	30%	17%	13%	1,828
Nonpublic	40	60	40	50	66	25	24	8	16	219
Span of Grades										
More than 9–12	77%	42%	60%	32%	32%	25%	18%	4%	3%	736
9–12	83	71	63	40	25	36	35	12	13	720
10–12	81	86	64	57	38	30	37	35	26	592
Size of Senior Class										
0–75	88%	38%	65%	14%	9%	27%	29%	0%	4%	502
76–200	73	60	53	41	36	24	31	14	13	465
201–475	81	75	66	51	38	38	32	23	14	610
476+	76	86	64	62	42	30	25	26	21	471

The header above the columns reads: PERCENTAGE OF STUDENTS ATTENDING A SCHOOL OFFERING THE COURSE nine courses only three—American government, general world history, and specialized world history—reveal differences of more than 9 percent. Public schools are more likely to offer the first two, and nonpublic schools are more likely to offer the third.

The span of grades in the school the seniors attend emerges as a far more discriminating school-level variable. Although slight irregularities exist in the figures, the clear pattern is one of more offerings with a fewer number of grades. In no case do students in schools with a span greater than the ninth through twelfth grades have the highest percentage. Except for nonpublic schools, those schools with more than four grades are typically less affluent and less cosmopolitan than schools with smaller grade spans.

Size of senior class constitutes the final structural feature. Here the picture is not quite so clear cut as with the grade-span measure. In American government, geography, sociology, and general world history small and irregular variations occur according to senior class size. Among the other five subjects, however, the larger the class size the more frequently the course will be offered. Differences are particularly apparent between the very small schools (0–75 seniors) and those in the next largest stratum (76–200). Above the threshold of around 75–100 students variations according to senior class size diminish considerably, and further increases do not necessarily bring increases in course titles, though they may result in qualitative differences if more resources are available.

SCHOOL ACADEMIC FEATURES

A final cluster of variables often related to curriculum practices measures the school's academic quality. Five variables are treated in Table 5. The results do not suggest any easily observed relationships between such factors and the pattern of social studies offerings.

We shall first examine the availability of courses according to the proportion of the senior class that was carrying a college preparatory program, as indicated in reports from the school officials. This proportion is one rough guide to academic emphasis in the school. Persons hypothesizing any direct relationships between the college preparatory proportions and the shape of the social studies curriculum will be disappointed by the data. In no way do students in schools of the highest stratum have a particularly distinctive set of offerings. Furthermore, only in the case of American government do

TABLE 5 · *Availability of Social Studies Courses According to Five School Academic Characteristics*

	PERCENTAGE OF STUDENTS ATTENDING A SCHOOL OFFERING THE COURSE									
	general world history	economics	American government	American problems	special world history	geography	sociology	psychology	international and comparative politics	N
Percentage of College Preparatory Students										
00–29	84%	50%	58%	30%	19%	33%	23%	0%	4%	*451*
30–49	77	62	65	49	35	36	32	23	11	*599*
50–59	84	79	50	60	46	30	36	26	23	*414*
60–98	76	70	71	32	27	23	27	15	15	*584*
Percentage of Student Dropouts										
00–04	64%	57%	55%	50%	44%	36%	28%	8%	14%	*778*
05–10	79	74	59	38	26	25	24	14	9	*674*
11+	100	66	75	36	20	29	38	28	17	*596*
Accelerated Curriculum										
Yes	77%	77%	55%	51%	42%	31%	29%	20%	20%	*1,145*
No	83	50	71	31	18	29	30	10	4	*903*
Social Studies Curriculum Guide										
Yes	75%	64%	53%	52%	40%	27%	26%	14%	10%	*1,225*
No	86	64	77	24	19	34	30	18	16	*780*
Recent Social Studies Evaluation										
Yes	79%	71%	58%	45%	34%	32%	34%	18%	15%	*1,366*
No	81	52	69	39	27	26	20	12	10	*668*

students in schools of the highest stratum surpass those in all other strata. Generally the second highest stratum (50–59 percent) shows the greatest frequency of courses offered. At the same time, though, students in schools with the lowest incidence of college "prepsters" (0–29 percent) do *tend* to have the lowest percentages of course offerings, although even here there are three irregularities (American government, geography, and general world history). Similar results are obtained when the students are grouped according to the proportion of graduates in their schools that enters a four-year college.

Proportions of student dropouts constitute another barometer of academic quality. No consistent patterns emerge here, but one cannot conclude that students in schools with the highest dropout rates (11 percent and above) have the most barren social studies array. In fact rates for American government, sociology, psychology, and general world history are highest in these schools. Schools with the lowest attrition rates prove especially likely to offer American problems and specialized world history courses.

During the post-Sputnik era accelerated curricula have blossomed in many schools. Such programs, while appearing most frequently for the physical and natural sciences, are now also being introduced in the humanities and social studies. The presence of an accelerated curriculum is often taken as evidence of an academic emphasis. Students in our sample attending schools with an advanced curriculum in any area were more likely to have five of the nine subjects available (see Table 5); the presence of an advanced curriculum made virtually no difference in the appearance of three other subjects—geography, sociology, and world history; and in only one subject—American government—did schools without an accelerated program exceed those having one. The propensity toward accelerated work in a given field such as social studies probably stems from similar, if not the same, sources as the tendency toward a greater variety of courses in that field.

In addition to the rather standard measures of academic quality considered thus far, two features have special relevance to social studies. While acquiring information about the social studies programs in the schools attended by our student sample, we inquired as to whether the school employed a formal curriculum guide for social studies. Provision of a guide may be considered a crude sign of greater resource investment in social studies. Slightly over three-fifths of the students attended schools where guides presumably indicated the shape and content of the social studies courses.

The presence of a guide does not always turn out to be a concomitant of differential course emphasis. In five of the subjects the presence or absence of a guide had little or no bearing on the appearance of the course. Schools with guides tended to offer specialized world history and American problems more frequently; schools without guides more often offered American government and general world history. Significantly, then, schools with guides put more emphasis on the newer subjects of American problems and specialized world history, whereas those without guides remained more committed to the traditional American government and general world history courses.

A second feature with unique relevance to the social studies curriculum is whether the school had recently undergone an evaluation of its social studies program from either internal or external sources. Approximately two-thirds of the students attended schools where such an evaluation had occurred. There was a very modest tendency for such schools to offer any given course (with the exceptions of American government and general world history) more frequently than did schools without recent evaluations. We do not know whether the evaluation resulted in the addition of courses or whether the schools with more offerings were also more likely to have evaluations.

The Relative Emphasis of the Curriculum

Up to this point we have discussed course offerings primarily in absolute percentages. This procedure has the advantage of revealing the offerings confronting absolute proportions of students during the tenth through twelfth grades in a variety of settings.[8] But, as we saw, the percentage distributions revealed only a modest number of clearly differentiated patterns of offerings according to the several variables examined. In part this may be a function of the large contingency tables, which obscure some meaningful relationships. What would be useful in such a situation are summary statistics showing overall relationships.

[8]For some purposes it may be more useful to read Tables 3–5 as one continuous table. For example, if one is interested in the relative frequency of a course offering across a broad range of variables, he can read Tables 3–5 vertically. These tables then tell us that sociology occurs most frequently for students living in smaller SMSA's, students in schools with 9–12 or 10–12 grade spans, and students in schools with a recent social studies evaluation. The course occurs least frequently for students in the Northeast, in the very large SMSA's and the non-SMSA's, in schools with a grade span greater than 9–12, and in schools where no recent evaluation has transpired. Such variables as size of community, type of schools, size of senior class, proportion of college preparatory students, percentage of student dropouts, accelerated curriculum, and the presence of a social studies curriculum guide have little effect on the frequency of the course's appearance.

Rank-order correlations offer a convenient way to observe the degree of similarity in the *relative* occurrence of course offerings according to any given pair of characteristics. To illustrate, we might note the rank order of the nine subjects in a given region and then compare this order with that of another region. A rank-order correlation will reveal the degree of similarity in these ranks. If the correlation is high we can say that the relative frequency of the subject is similar for students in the two regions. Note that this does not necessarily mean that the *absolute* frequency of the courses is similar in the two regions. Using rank-order correlations removes the effect of greater overall investment of resources in the social studies curriculum (that is, more courses) in one region than in another.

Table 6 contains eleven sets of rank-order correlation coefficients, using Spearman's *rho*. Each set is derived directly from the percentage distributions in Tables 3–5. All possible pairs within (but not across) each set of variables are represented. An overview of the coefficients in the table reveals that the relationships are all positive and, furthermore, predominantly in the upper ranges. While the range is from .24 (Northeast/South) to .97 (senior-class sizes of 76–200 paired with sizes of 201–475), some 76 percent actually fall in the .80 to .97 range. These are extraordinarily high coefficients, considering that 1.0 would be a perfect positive association and −1.0 a perfect negative association.[9] In the aggregate, then, we would conclude that regardless of demographic, structural, and academic characteristics, there is a remarkable similarity in the relative (rank-order) availability of social studies courses.

Despite the generally high associations several exceptions deserve mention. The variable showing the greatest range in association is that of region. Significantly the three pairs with the lowest coefficients all involve the Northeast. As we noted in the discussion of the absolute percentages, the Northeast stands out as the most distinctive region. These rank-order relationships indicate that the Northeast is also the most distinctive in terms of the relative attention it pays to the various subjects compared with other regions.

Mixed results prevail on the two remaining place characteristics. While the correlations according to community size vary quite modestly, considerably more variation occurs with respect to SMSA

[9]It should be noted that Spearman's *rho* usually yields somewhat higher coefficients than does Kendall's *tau*.

TABLE 6   *Rank-Order Correlations of Place and School Characteristics and Availabity of Social Studies Courses*[a]

	CORRELATION COEFFICIENT		CORRELATION COEFFICIENT
Region		*Size of Senior Class*	
Midwest/South	.88	76–200/201–475	.97
South/West	.80	201–475/476+	.96
Midwest/West	.67	76–200/201–475	.93
West/Northeast	.40	0–75/201–475	.84
Northeast/Midwest	.35	0–75/76–200	.83
Northeast/South	.24	0–75/476+	.70
Size of Community[b]		*Percentage of College Preparatory Students*	
0–4/31–100	.93	0–29/30–49	.95
31–100/100+	.92	50–59/60+	.95
5–30/100+	.91	30–49/60+	.94
0–4/5–30	.87	30–49/50–59	.90
5–30/31–100	.83	0–29/60+	.89
0–4/100+	.83	0–29/50–59	.80
SMSA Classification		*Percentage of Student Dropouts*	
Smaller SMSA's/Non-SMSA's	.93	0–4/5–10	.98
12 Largest SMSA's/Non-SMSA's	.61	5–10/11+	.82
Smaller SMSA's/12 Largest SMSA's	.48	0–4/11+	.78
Type of School		*Accelerated Curriculum*	
Public/Nonpublic	.54	Yes/No	.90
Span of Grades		*Social Studies Curriculum Guide*	
		Yes/No	.85
Over 9–12/9–12	.90	*Recent Social Studies Evaluation*	
Over 9–12/10–12	.90		
9–12/10–12	.83	Yes/No	.96

[a]Entries are the rank-order correlation coefficients (Spearman's *rho*) resulting from comparing the ranks for nine subjects of each given pair of characteristics.
[b]Figures for size of community are given in thousands.

classification. Here the twelve largest SMSA's distinguish themselves, inasmuch as relatively low coefficients are yielded when these SMSA's are paired with smaller ones and with non-SMSA's. This is due to the far greater emphasis in the largest SMSA's on specialized world history and American problems and the smaller emphasis on American government and general world history, mentioned earlier. Thus it would make a difference to the student whether he matriculated in one of the largest metropolitan areas or in a smaller one or a non-SMSA area.

Turning to the three school characteristics, we first observe that the correlation between public and nonpublic schools is relatively modest. As we stated earlier, the limited number of nonpublic students (and schools) in our sample calls for a very cautious interpretation of these results. However, other studies also indicate a different emphasis in nonpublic versus public schools.[10] This is particularly true with respect to the more classical emphasis in nonpublic schools as reflected in the abundance of history courses.

Surprisingly enough, a school's span of grades makes little difference in the relative frequency with which subjects appear. Although the absolute occurrence of some subjects is considerably less for students in schools where the grade span exceeds the 9–12 range (see Table 4) than for students in schools of smaller grade spans, the relative occurrence of the subjects is quite similar in all three grade–span categories. Minor variations among the three types are actually more prevalent in the 9–12/10–12 comparison.

Variations by size of senior class are somewhat more noticeable than those by grade span. An inspection of the pairings indicates that those involving the smallest class size (0–75 students) produce the lowest degrees of association. The smaller schools not only possess a somewhat more limited repertory of social studies courses (see Table 4) but also place a mildly different emphasis on their offerings than do larger schools.

Finally, we may consider the relative availability of various courses according to the academic quality of the schools the students were attending. Of the five characteristics dealt with, four—the presence of an accelerated curriculum, the use of a social studies curriculum guide, a recent social studies evaluation, and, surprisingly, the proportion of students in college preparatory programs—are essentially nondiscriminating. Only one characteristic, percentage

10See Anderson *et al., op. cit.,* p. 12.

of student dropouts, produced a comparison yielding a coefficient below .80; the overall dropout figures suggest that schools with the highest rates (11 percent and over) possess a slightly different emphasis on various courses than do schools with lower rates.

The Number of Course Offerings in the Curriculum

Implicit in much of the foregoing discussion is the fact that the sheer number of courses available, in addition to the particular types, varies a great deal from school to school. If we return to the original pool of eleven courses, which included American history and personal problems, we can now ask about the number of courses offered by each school in the eleven-course areas. This procedure will produce a slightly conservative estimate of offerings because a few schools have more than one course in a general subject area and because under our rules those schools will get credit for only one course in that area. Secondly, there are a small number of courses, primarily social science and social studies, that did not fall under any of the eleven subject titles employed. The school and place characteristics used previously will again be employed.

Overall, the average number of courses offered by schools in the eleven-course areas was 4.8. The standard deviation is a rather sizeable 1.5. All students except those in one school had a minimum of three courses available. Almost invariably these courses were American history, some form of world history, and either American government or American problems. This information lends added meaning to the mean number of courses available according to various school and place characteristics: the higher the mean number, the greater the variety of offerings beyond the basic trio of courses.

The number of course offerings according to the several variables is dealt with in Table 7. Some of the results have been anticipated by our discussion of specific course offerings. Thus we see that the Northeast region has a decidedly lower mean than the other sections and that the Midwest stands highest. Similarly students in very small communities and in non-SMSA's are presented with the least variety of courses. Comparing public and nonpublic schools produces only a minor difference, although when nonpublic schools are divided into parochial and nonparochial schools, the former

TABLE 7 *Mean Number of Social Studies Offerings in the Tenth Through Twelfth Grades for a National Sample of High School Seniors*[a]

Region		N	Size of Senior Class		N
Northeast	4.0	509	0–75	3.8	502
Midwest	5.4	629	76–200	4.5	465
South	4.7	562	201–475	5.4	610
West	5.0	348	476+	5.4	471
			Percentage of College		
Size of Community			*Preparatory Students*		
0–4,000	4.1	728	00–29	4.0	451
5,000–30,000	5.2	469	30–49	5.1	599
31,000–100,000	5.3	422	50–59	5.4	414
100,000+	5.0	429	60–98	4.7	584
			Percentage of		
SMSA Classification			*Student Dropouts*		
12 Largest SMSA's	4.8	489	00–04	4.6	778
Smaller SMSA's	5.3	704	05–10	4.7	674
Non-SMSA's	4.4	856	11+	5.2	596
Type of School			*Accelerated Curriculum*		
Public	4.8	1,828	Yes	5.1	1,145
Nonpublic	4.2	219	No	4.4	903
			Social Studies		
Span of Grades			*Curriculum Guide*		
More than 9–12	4.0	736	Yes	5.0	1,225
9–12	4.9	720	No	4.4	780
10–12	5.6	592	*Recent Social Studies*		
			Evaluation		
			Yes	4.7	1,366
			No	4.8	668

[a]These means are based on the extent to which each of eleven subject areas was represented by at least a one-semester course.

emerge with a mean of 4.8—exactly the same as the public schools—whereas the nonparochial schools have a much lower mean of 3.8.

Span of grades and size of the senior class emerge as two of the most distinctive factors affecting the variety of offerings.[11] The

[11]There is a positive correlation of .46 (using *eta* coefficients) between *decreasing* grade span and number of courses; the correlation between senior class size and number of courses is .43.

smaller the grade span and the larger the senior class, up to a certain threshold, the more diverse the curriculum. Once a senior class size of around 200 is reached, there is virtually no difference in the means. Considerable controversy exists over the optimal size and grade plans of schools. To some extent curriculum diversity is an important criterion of a good school. Our data suggest that a senior class size of at least 200 and a 10–12 grade span are factors closely associated with such curriculum diversity.

Two indicators of academic quality, proportion of college preparatory students and the dropout rate, show inconsistent relationships to the number of courses. It is significant, however, that students in schools with the lowest college preparatory proportions have a decidedly lower number of available courses. Students in schools of the next two strata average about one course more. But the tapering off in the mean number of courses for students in schools with the highest college preparatory proportions dispels the notion of a linear relationship between academic quality and social studies variety. Not surprisingly, schools with an accelerated curriculum and those having undergone a recent evaluation offer somewhat more courses. The incidence of a social studies curriculum guide accounts for little difference in mean scores.

Conclusion

Perhaps the best generalization to be made about social studies offerings to students in the tenth through twelfth grades is that generalizing is difficult. Irregular and nonlinear patterns abound. Strong, regularized patterns are most nearly approached in the regional, SMSA, span-of-grades, and accelerated-curriculum classifications. The lack of strong differences according to academic features is especially noteworthy. With the exceptions noted, the correlates of the social studies curriculum tend to be either unimposing or erratic according to various conventional measures.

Having said this, the question remains as to what other factors might be linked to varying curriculum profiles. It seems likely that a number of external factors affect the curriculum. One, certainly, is the legal requirements of state and local authorities. These requirements are not necessarily associated with any of the conventional modes of classification. Another set of factors consists of the discretionary choices on the part of curriculum committees, school principals, and the like. Decisions about where to invest one's teaching resources are undoubtedly affected by relevant reference groups and professional training, among other factors. These characteristics are not reflected in any systematic way in the conventional categories we have employed to analyze course offerings.

Three other points should be noted. First, the pattern of course offerings does not necessarily dictate the consumption pattern. However, preliminary analyses do indicate a very high rank-order correlation (.98) between availability and consumer patterns as a whole. Second, the presence of a course says little about its quality or precise content. For example, the fact that students living in a given region attend schools where a certain course is likely to be offered more frequently than for students in other regions does not necessarily mean that the civic skills and values of the former students are superior or different. Continual evaluation of the content and consequences of social studies materials should take high priority. Finally, as the shape of the social studies curriculum undergoes transformation, the opportunities for studying innovation and diffusion patterns should not go unheeded. A point of departure for research is the existing state of affairs, and this chapter represents an attempt to establish one such reference point.

CHAPTER 15

Conclusion

Social Studies, Present and Future

BYRON G. MASSIALAS
C. BENJAMIN COX

In Summary and Review

The authors of this text have undertaken three tasks. First, they have critically evaluated a number of social studies textbooks largely in terms of their possible contribution to the inquiry process. Second, they have tried to define inquiry as a mode of thought and teaching in the several disciplines and subject areas included in social studies. And, finally, they have related their explication of inquiry and the evaluations of textbook materials to the status of social studies in the United States.

Each of these undertakings is a large task. Together they represent a truly imposing one. But the authors found as they carried out their primary assignment of textbook analysis that neither of the other aspects could be ignored. They had to enunciate their conceptions of inquiry repeatedly in order to clarify their textbook criticisms. Furthermore, they discovered that each of these took on real meaning only when related to the social studies field as reflected in the literature and their own wide experiences in the schools.

We realize that this book has only begun the above undertakings. No comprehensive research exists on the present status of social studies teaching and curriculum to confirm the widely held suppositions and hints of its strengths and debilities. The need for such an investigation is clearly indicated, though it is obviously beyond the resources of any single group of investigators.

Moreover, new curriculum-project materials, new teaching strategies and tactics, new attempts at teacher education, and new commercial publications will undoubtedly change social studies teaching. The assessment of these effects will, of course, never be completed, and investigation will be continued by researchers far into the future. In addition new focuses of concern, such as the emphasis on values and issues in the personal and public sectors of society, suggest that eventual changes may be far reaching indeed. A general assessment of the status, materials, and methods of social studies no more than a few years hence will probably be very different from that of this volume.

Our appraisals of social studies textbooks have been both critical and complimentary. In every area there continue to be texts that fail to respond to any of the new departures in curriculum and methodology. One must suppose—or at least hope—that these are books that either reflect a misreading of the trends or that represent one last attempt to publish for a dwindling remnant of the market. But in nearly every area there are textbooks and other materials that reflect concerted efforts on the part of publishers and authors to incorporate some important new ideas about social studies.

At this point, however, one must acknowledge the balance of relationships that exists among textbook publishers, authors, and teachers. In some respects social studies publishing is a classical "buyers'" market, in which the teachers determine the kind of textbook to be produced. In other respects publishing in social studies operates as a "sellers'" market in which the publishers dictate the nature of the materials to be published. And in still other ways an "artists'" market prevails, in which the authors write what pleases them, imposing their private views and personalities on their textbooks. Obviously none of these markets is ever accommodated to the exclusion of the other two—though it might be interesting to classify texts in terms of which factor has predominated in their production. It appears that the most enlightened of house editors—those harrassed gentlemen who manage the production of books for publishers—make a fair accommodation of these three crucial factors. They interpret with considerable accuracy how receptive teachers will be to a certain new idea, restrict or prod creative authors to write along the conservative margin of the new idea, and thus produce a text that will both enlighten the reading public and make a decent profit for the company. While these editors perform an important economic service for the publishing houses, they also perform an educative service in the schools by helping to move classroom learning activities a notch or two toward a new focus.

Nonetheless the authors of the essays in this volume do feel that in general the educative function of public school texts is largely inadequate, uneven, and unintegrated. That is, textbooks play too conservative a role in school social studies. Where texts could, for example, be important tools in fomenting inquiry as the classroom mode, they tend instead to follow traditional patterns in structuring and presenting life experiences and social science and historical information. The occasional nods given to inquiry—largely in statements of purpose, exercises, questions, and projects—are generally unsupported by the information-giving sections of the texts. This discrepancy tends to give even the best texts an uneven and unintegrated appearance, with inquiry and noninquiry approaches vying, albeit unequally, for attention.

The authors also agree that practically any textbook or any material can be useful in an inquiry-oriented classroom. In a very real sense the amount of information and the manner of its presentation are less at issue than the use that is made of this information in classroom discussion or other activities. This should not suggest, however, that amount and presentation of information are unimportant considerations. A great amount of relevant information is a necessary element in the inquiry process. Where decisions and judgments are being made and hypotheses and generalizations are being supported or refuted, as is the case in inquiry, much more factual information is required than in traditional procedures. Suggestions for improving the presentation of information have been made throughout this volume and will be summarized later in this chapter. But the point to be made here is that if the teacher acquainted with inquiry procedures employs the appropriate means of critical evaluation, he can use practically any source of data—even an unreliable one—to consider a pertinent issue. And in addition the skilled teacher-inquirer can extract from almost any kind of historical or social science material or from direct observation usable facts, hypotheses, and value issues with which to work. The consensus of this book, however, is that even the veteran teacher-inquirer deserves more support from his textbooks. And for the novice in the classroom a textbook that only minimally reflects the inquiry mode leads to a desultory adoption of inquiry procedures in the classroom.

These authors also agree that a textbook alone—of whatever quality—seldom provides a sufficient base for teaching as inquiry. But they do not necessarily argue for the multiple-text idea. They feel that a variety of source materials will be needed in social studies inquiry. The textbook as a teaching aid, as a curriculum guide, as a general source book, or as a chronological chart may always have its place in the classroom. And after some changes the text could serve an additional function as the prompter and model of inquiry. But no single textbook or group of books in textbook format can provide the amount and variety of information needed in inquiry. Many kinds of specialized data—pictorial, graphic, and verbal—not ordinarily available in texts are needed for the thorough investigation of some issues.

Such outside sources are needed not only because of the limited amount of information that can be packed into a textbook but because of the age-old problem of bias in textbooks. Most of the authors point to the ethnocentrism, middle-class bias, Anglo-Saxon and white racial emphasis, Adam Smith economics, protestant Christianity, and sexual purity that prevail in school textbooks. Of course all kinds of material—with the possible exception of raw data—contain some biases. But when the teacher uses only one textbook or one source, he must rely on his own and his students' abilities to detect bias, or he must depend on the countervailing biases represented in his classroom to balance those of the text. This situation is not always destructive, of course. Some materials, including texts, are useful primarily because they do present a particular point of view, reveal a biased investigation, or illustrate a prejudice. Partly for this reason we were able to say earlier that even an unreliable source could be useful in the inquiring classroom.

Many texts, however, suffer from the opposite defect. Since textbook authors have long been very sensitive to the problem of bias, some have made special efforts to present "bias-free" books for classroom use. As a result these texts often seem less than honest, lacking in reality, and uninteresting. In an overly careful attempt to avoid bias the author produces a gray document with no explicit point of view or, more likely, with a changing and inconsistent viewpoint. The book that presents a consistent and well-articulated point of view—or bias, if you like—probably has the more usefulness in the inquiry-practicing classroom.

PRIMARY-GRADE SOCIAL STUDIES

In discussing social studies in the primary grades Joyce has identified the dominant pattern over the past forty years as the development of democratic skills and concepts in children through the cooperative exploration of their expanding world, especially through project-centered, inductive teaching. Critics of this approach have said that the world created in these primary-grade textbooks is generally antiseptic and unreal and, furthermore, that the approach insidiously encourages the child to value group morale to the detriment of his individualism. A few of the newer texts have responded to this criticism by producing more realistic—if not harsher—pictures of life. A special problem is presented by the evident ethnocentric and racial biases in the books. Many people feel that the accurate reflection of violent racial conflicts in the society is simply too harsh a reality for impressionistic seven-year-olds.

Primary books, perhaps in their maternal effort to overprotect the child, often deal with facts and concepts already mastered by him—for example, those about the home and family. In addition the dominant narrative approach has led to the superficial handling of topics. Some new materials, however, appear to be encouraging children to probe more deeply into their own social situations. The almost complete devotion to reading, writing, and arithmetic in the primary grades further militates against the intellectual treatment of social studies topics. But most recent attempts to counteract anti-intellectualism consist of moving middle-grade materials down into the primary curriculum. Heavy emphasis is on geography and history, long believed to be the hard intellectual core of social studies. A more vigorous reassessment of the field is likely to produce in the future several new syntheses of the social sciences that will prove more useful in primary social studies.

Joyce suggests that present inquiry materials tend to be deductive rather than inductive, with emphasis on predetermined concepts to be learned rather than on the conducting of inquiry itself. A few attempts are being made to prepare materials that will help pupils to conduct inquiry into situations in which they are personally involved. The best instructional material now available for primary-grade social studies, however, is a lively teacher, adequately prepared in the social sciences, who can involve her students in the investigation of significant aspects of society.

INTERMEDIATE-GRADE SOCIAL STUDIES

Rader has suggested that the middle-grade social studies classroom, responding to the pressing needs of a dynamic society, will eventually be very different from what it is now. Rather than emphasize passive receptivity among students, it will be a center of varied but coordinated activities associated with the process of inquiry.

At present, however, traditional curriculum emphases and non-supportive textbooks and materials make it difficult for all but the exceptional teacher to achieve a high inquiry potential. The present curriculum in the fourth, fifth, and sixth grades is marked by diversity, with considerable emphasis on the geography and history of the Western Hemisphere. Some schools give limited attention to Asia, Africa, and other parts of the non-West. In general history and geography are disproportionately represented in the middle grades. However, a few innovative programs, such as the Anthropology Curriculum Project at the University of Georgia, the work of the University of Michigan Social Science staff, and the Elementary School Economics Program of the University of Chicago, are beginning to produce materials that promise to broaden the possibilities for these grades.

Rader has stated that social studies textbook publishers have erroneously tried to follow criteria inappropriate to inquiry. Their striving for appealing, readable, handy books of medium difficulty and realism has inadvertently precluded the careful analysis of the social scientist. Furthermore, few elementary texts reflect any conceptual framework or related basic ideas around which a book or series could be developed. None illustrate the interrelationship of the social sciences. With painful consistency the books in each field avoid the development of relevant concepts from the other social sciences.

For the most part the upper-elementary texts do not encourage student questioning and thinking. Instead teachers are encouraged to ask the questions and children to supply the answers. Moreover, the answers are not presumed to emerge from a reflective consideration of societal problems but must be extracted from the conclusions and facts stated in the books.

Rader has proposed that a textbook could be designed to offer the harried elementary teacher increased support in promoting inquiry. Such a text would contain contemporary and historical, real and hypothetical problems and issues that would challenge pupils to ask questions and seek the information necessary to answer them. The book would contain relevant source materials translated into student language. And the book would demonstrate the process of scientific investigation and implement its practice.

JUNIOR HIGH SCHOOL AMERICAN HISTORY

Cox has suggested that the inquiry process in social studies has an historical dimension that legitimizes the study of history. But not all conceptions of history teaching are equally useful. The strict adherence to chronology, for example, may obviate the more productive inquiry procedures. If appropriately conceived, however, history can be a source of hypotheses about human relationships, can offer cases and evidence to test hypotheses about human relationships, and can provide a style of investigation appropriate to some types of inquiry.

Most junior high texts do not take advantage of these potential contributions of history to inquiry teaching. Hypotheses and generalizations that could alert the teacher to the focus of some material and could provide a powerful entry into the process of inquiry are ordinarily left out of history texts. The skilled inquirer, of course, may be able to operate effectively even without such aids, but the novice deserves more support. Moreover, these books do not often relate the information they present to a central idea or generalization. Instead facts and events are used to tell stories in a linear chronological fashion. The newer texts and materials, however, give evidence that the development of concepts and ideas is becoming more accepted as a goal in history teaching.

Cox has asserted that junior high school history texts use three main kinds of explanation: subsumptive, genetic, and causal. The first type, used only occasionally, classifies a particular event under a general principle. More often, however, textbooks explain an event either by tracing its genetic continuity with antecedent events or by identifying those factors or phenomena that caused the event in question. In junior high school texts none of these modes of explanation are carefully enough developed to be of much use.

A dogma of interpretation appears to embrace American history textbooks. Seldom can one find the presentation of a divergent idea. The teacher who can entertain divergent interpretations has a wider platform from which to launch inquiry, but only one or two of the new texts shows signs of departing from the traditional dogma. No text in this area makes a significant contribution to the development of skills used in testing an interpretation. If the teacher considers it important to develop skills of critical thinking and inquiry, then, he must, for the most part, teach these skills himself without support from the texts in junior high American history.

JUNIOR HIGH SCHOOL STATE HISTORY

Cousins has indicated that much confusion exists in social studies textbooks throughout the nation. This confusion, however, is related more to purposes than to content; for, despite touted local control and regional dissimilarities, social studies offerings are remarkably similar across the country. Practically every state, for example, offers state history in the seventh, eighth, or ninth grade. Yet no one has seriously questioned the contribution of state history to the important goals in education. State history is particularly vulnerable to the criticisms that social studies tends to be provincial, contributes little to social science literateness, and has little or no effect on social and political behavior.

In his investigation of the curricular requirements for state history, Cousins determined that each of the fifty states requires or recommends the teaching of its own history, though often local authorities may make decisions about the placement and length of the study. Considerably confused and imprecise judgment is evident at all levels, inasmuch as most decisions about state history are made in response to political rather than academic pressures.

The typical state history course or unit is organized chronologically, is frequently correlated with geography and government, and is likely to include an intensive study of the local community. State history textbooks tend to emphasize the importance of events within states so much that the nation as a whole appears less important than the individual state, and each state appears more important than its neighbors. State history courses split rather evenly into those emphasizing the exotic, romanticized, and sensational aspects of state history and those concerned with substantial contemporary problems. The famous and the heroic are always given places of importance.

The majority of state history texts do not exhibit any consistent framework or notion of history, though a few do give objective treatment to certain episodes. Cousins, however, has reaffirmed an idea stated earlier in this chapter—that sometimes highly biased passages present students with a more challenging confrontation than do very objective statements.

Perhaps only a third of state history texts, said Cousins, deal with issues in a manner that would make them adaptable to inquiry teaching. If the teacher is willing to use the text as a limited source of data, drawing on other sources for the statement of issues and problems and additional data, then the best of these books will have some value. But when used as course outlines, lesson guides, or exclusive sources of data, the books will be more detrimental than helpful in a social studies classroom.

Articles on the status of state history teaching revealed that teaching techniques in this field are reduced to a development of clever means to capture the interest of children. However, materials developed by the Anthropology Curriculum Study Project in Chicago for state history courses contrast favorably with the usual textbooks in this area. The anthropology materials develop generalizations about the family, political systems, the roles of men and women, education, and religion. Community resources might also be fruitfully employed to teach state history, providing their use is related to the major goals of the field.

Neither historians nor educators defend the state history course as it is now usually taught. A provincial, chronological approach that emphasizes memorization is more destructive of goals claimed for history and social studies than it is supportive. But if the materials now used in teaching state history can be adapted to the inquiry process in social studies, then state history will warrant some attention in the curriculum.

JUNIOR HIGH SCHOOL CIVICS

The wide variation in junior high school civics courses indicates that social studies educators have been uncertain about what they want the course to accomplish in the curriculum. The offerings tend to be loose and amorphous collections of content. This situation has partly grown out of the progressive attempts in the early 1900's to make civics instruction the keystone in the education of the effective citizen. These efforts aimed at expanding the narrow concern of civics courses with governmental structure to include wide experiences in civic behavior and content from several social sciences. The underlying goal was to bring social studies into a closer and more meaningful relationship with social reality. Perhaps the objective was too broad and too ambitious, for the present situation largely reflects ambiguity.

Smith and Patrick have identified two basic types of civics textbooks for the junior high school. One type concentrates mainly on the structure and function of democratic government and politics, particularly at the national level, taking most of its content from the academic area of government. The second type, while emphasizing the structure and function of government, relates governmental functions to the society at large and makes use of materials from all the social sciences. Such civics courses may include information on vocational and educational guidance or even health and personality-adjustment studies. Ordinarily the course is offered to ninth-grade students and, according to its scope of topics, is either one or two semesters in length.

Confusion about the course has been compounded by the attempt of authors to graft onto the traditional textbook chapters and units that reflect the new curriculum demands—namely that students be taught to think critically and that they inquire in the mode of the social scientist. But these adaptations remain only superficial stirrings at present. Texts in this area still do not effectively integrate the disparate content of the civics course, fail to represent reality, omit important concepts, and tend to moralize.

The misrepresentation or avoidance of crucial issues in most of the critical areas of our society—in an attempt either to protect the students from harsh reality or to avoid offending some elements of the society—is disastrous to inquiry procedures. Myths about society, government, politics, mobility, class, and many other facets of civic

instruction that have long been disproved by social research continue to be presented as fact by many civics books, while concepts
that enjoy more scientific support are completely ignored. Furthermore, preachments about correct value positions are consistently sub-
stituted for experience with the process of making and testing value
choices.

Nonetheless the present textbooks in civics can be used judiciously in inquiry. Teachers can seek out generalizations, concepts,
and value judgments in texts and help students subject these to
further inquiry. Also, teachers may use a situation or case described
or implied in the texts, experienced by them or their students, or
hypothetically created, as a provocative encounter in the classroom.
Student decisions and judgments on the posed dilemma can then be
checked against the ideas of scholars. Hypotheses generated by the
experience can then be further examined by inquiry procedures.
The most promising proposals for reconstructing civic education in
the junior high school focus on the improvement of decision-making
in the area of social control, the appraisal of the multi-faceted
public controversy over the state-citizen relationship, the use of the
research procedures of political science, and the consideration of
sociopolitical issues. While textbooks—even those now available—
may still be useful in implementing these proposals, outside materials of many kinds will be needed to support these inquiries
adequately.

HIGH SCHOOL AMERICAN HISTORY

Palmer has suggested that, in effect, the real criterion for choosing
which events to include in history books is whether they have involved or affected large numbers of people. He noted that history
is a necessary ingredient of inquiry, but he noted that some ways
of dealing with past events are more promising than others in
furthering inquiry. A reading of history should generate hypotheses
and provide data to test their validity. In general the historian is
a synthesist, rather than an analyst. He attempts to deal with whole
situations, placing them in causal relationship with other situations.
In doing so the greatest danger is that he will oversimplify these
linkages. He may, in fact, produce only superficial explanations that
do no more than restate the problem in new terms. If history cannot
make a significant contribution to the understanding of society, it

does not merit inclusion in the school curriculum. While no present proposals seriously recommend eliminating history from the school curriculum, many anticipate a changed role for the subject. Historical writing that purposely suggests policies for meeting current problems most effectively lends itself to classroom inquiry.

Historical inquiry, as envisioned by Palmer, always begins with an hypothesis. Rather than produce narrative accounts of the past for their own sake, historical methodology should generate questions to be answered by the historian and the student alike. To answer such questions, one must consider both the unique circumstances that surround events and the general processes that are at work. Four elements are essential to historical inquiry—a problem; a theoretical framework in which the problem can be examined; the relevant historical and social science knowledge; and a number of skills and attitudes, such as sifting and assessing information from documentary and secondary sources, developing an objective attitude of mind, and maintaining open-ended discussion.

Like others in this text Palmer has asserted that in the hands of the imaginative, inquiring teacher most history texts are usable as sources of data and hypotheses. However, no text reviewed is designed to stimulate inquiry activities; texts continue to emphasize the chronology of events and avoid focusing on either the problems of the past or the present. Some do develop certain controversial subjects in a thorough and thought-provoking manner, but such efforts serve principally as illustrations of what can be done with historical materials, for they are always isolated and sporadic. Furthermore the avowed goal of using a knowledge of the past to understand the present is actually aborted by high school United States history books. Students are enjoined by study questions to make the leap from past to present, but none of the textbook authors really help them do so. As a result end-of-chapter questions that do raise fundamental social issues often appear unrelated to the chapter content. Since nearly half a typical text consists of exercises and illustrations, Palmer has suggested that the ancient argument that there is simply not enough space to develop issues or present alternative points of view and interpretations is an empty rationalization.

Historians who write school textbooks rarely state their theory of history explicitly. Ordinarily they prepare a narrative purportedly devoid of theory, or they select a potpourri of the most popular current interpretations of various events, or they claim the precedence of humanistic ideals that are least useful in analytic inquiry. Palmer found only one text that makes any notable effort to state the assumptions and theoretical framework of the authors.

The debate continues as to whether history is a social science or is qualitatively unique in its study of society. In either case historical inquiry requires the use of concepts and methodologies from the social sciences. Lacking these, historical conclusions are reduced to superficial myth and folklore. While high school history books illustrate the relevance of social science knowledge in their portrayal of the past, they seldom make known their reliance on this information. If the social-scientific concepts and principles underlying the information in textbooks are not explained to students, the historical presentations in texts are likely to appear as pure narrative. Important questions may well be extracted from the narrative, but in most instances the methods of social, political, or economic analysis must be gained from other sources.

HIGH SCHOOL ECONOMICS

Metcalf and Rader have explored the extent to which economics courses and textbooks reflect the recommendations of the National Task Force on Economic Education about including certain economic concepts and laws. In particular they decried the fact that economics for secondary students has traditionally been conceived of as a course in consumer education with heavy emphasis on personal finance. This emphasis, while not in itself reprehensible, prevents the development of a more sophisticated appreciation and understanding of economic theory and analysis. Consumer education and the descriptive and historical treatment of economic institutions that have dominated this field in the secondary school have made it impossible to deal thoroughly with micro- and macroanalysis, economic controversies, and the conceptual-theoretical nature of the discipline itself. The basic concepts of scarcity, growth and stability, and distribution as well as the comparison of economic systems are strongly recommended for study but are presently neglected by secondary school courses and textbooks. This content, regarded as essential to the general education of citizens, could be taught through courses in history, government, social problems, and of course in required courses in economics.

Metcalf and Rader reported that in a recent study a committee of the American Economic Association examined economics and other social studies texts to determine whether their economic content dealt with decision-making about vital concepts in economic systems and economic analyses and value judgments. Their main concern was with the preparation of students for intelligent citizenship. The committee concluded that high school students who learned no more than what the books presented would be "quite unprepared to cope understandingly with most problems of economic public policy." A still more recent study revealed that economics texts have not yet been revised to reflect the task force's recommendation for increased analysis and decreased description and consumer economics.

Recent reports by the Materials Evaluation Committees of the American Economic Association identified 162 items as the best nontextbook materials available to the teacher. In addition the Committee for Measurement of Economic Education has developed a fifty-question test directly related to the Task Force Report.

Metcalf and Rader's general assessment of three current economics textbooks is in some disagreement with the conclusions of a recent review of books at the University of Virginia. While the latter report concluded that texts available in 1966 represented no significant improvement over earlier editions, Metcalf and Rader found that nearly all the concepts listed by the Task Force are included in the three texts they examined.

Metcalf and Rader also appraised these current economics texts on their treatment of two important economic concepts, opportunity cost and comparative advantage. They found that neither concept was adequately developed in any of the books. Furthermore, their analysis revealed that the continued inclusion of consumer economics topics in economics texts apparently prevents the appropriate development of economic theory and analysis. While analysis is increasingly emphasized, descriptive chapters remain in most texts.

A major shortcoming of the texts examined by Metcalf and Rader is their supposition of fixed and unchanging content. Although economics is constantly changing and economists are continually embroiled in controversy, secondary economics texts present economic laws and ideas as established facts. Thus students are not encouraged to inquire into what are really unsettled questions.

The most promising developments in secondary and elementary economics teaching are being made by curriculum centers funded by the United States Office of Education. The Ohio State Curriculum Center is now revising its ninth-grade course in economics, and a group of researchers at San Jose State College is developing an economics teaching system for the twelfth grade called "Econ 12." In addition, the Joint Council on Economic Education is continuing its work with the Developmental Economic Education Program, now operating in twenty-seven public and two parochial school systems in the United States.

HIGH SCHOOL AMERICAN GOVERNMENT

In his chapter Massialas reported that political science has undergone significant changes since World War II. In general it has moved toward a behavioral-empirical study of government and political life. Instructional goals in both secondary schools and colleges have reflected this scientific concern as well as a special interest in preparing students for intelligent citizenship. Social studies teachers in the secondary schools appear to be primarily concerned with education for citizenship, while political scientists concentrate on analyzing political behavior systematically.

Various past studies of texts in civics and other social studies subjects revealed that a white, Protestant, Anglo-Saxon view of history and society was dominant. Controversial issues were often neglected or excluded from the texts. Statements about American democracy were often made with incredible naïveté. Conceptual frameworks and strategies that could help the student deal with values were generally lacking. The skills of critical thinking were often lauded but seldom systematically developed. Massialas found that many of these earlier indictments of civics texts are still valid.

In making his analysis Massialas has assumed that intelligent decision-making is the prime goal of social studies instruction and that inquiry is the best means for attaining this goal. He found, however, that textbook authors are uncertain as to whether students should study government to achieve cognitive or affective goals, or both. Often texts fail to discriminate between these different kinds of goals. Civics or government texts not only fail to use conceptual models in defining and delimiting the field of examination, but they ordinarily offer no useful, consistent definition of government. This lack of framework makes the selection of topics arbitrary and the interrelation of the ingredients of political life difficult.

Social studies texts present an unrealistic and naïve picture of the United States based on the misrepresentation of American ideals as political reality. The texts proclaim that "we are the greatest." Discussions of other nations or of international issues are highly ethnocentric, and comparisons with other nations that would put the United States in a bad light are assiduously avoided. This bias is particularly pronounced in passages that compare the capitalist and communist systems. The strengths of capitalism are ordinarily pitted against the most glaring weaknesses of communism. Emotional, noncritical language predominates in such discussions, denying out of hand the ability of students to order their own learning and draw their own conclusions.

Textbook authors also avoid dealing with the controversial social issues of this country. They create a Pollyanna-like world by omitting discussion of these problems altogether or by discussing them without taking a position—such as on the question of full voting rights for minority groups—when doing so might offend influential segments of the society. None of the books offer students an explicit model for dealing with controversial issues. The authors either make hidden value judgments or at best assume that students will automatically form "correct" value judgments when given the facts of an issue.

Most of these texts fail to capitalize on the problem-solving potential in much of our social knowledge. Seldom are alternative interpretations incorporated into the reading material. The texts ignore even the more recent behavioral studies that offer radically different interpretations of such topics as voting, political elites, and political socialization. Text authors do not appear to understand the meaning of problem solving, the process of inquiry, or the use of discovery techniques in this process. The end-of-chapter exercises emphasize the memorization of facts. Very little is done to incorporate newer concepts of structure, inquiry, induction, and discovery. Seldom are students encouraged to order their own learning experiences. The Carnegie Institute of Technology instructional materials deviate from this pattern and present a way of incorporating political science behavioral data into the social studies curriculum. Although this is a welcome sign, Massialas believes that it will take a concerted effort among publishers, textbook writers, teachers, and researchers to overcome the many existing deficiencies in civics textbooks.

HIGH SCHOOL WORLD HISTORY

Hines reviewed the theories that have been influential in the writing and teaching of history. In the broadest sense theoretical schools divide into those emphasizing description and those emphasizing analysis in their approach to past human events. History as description has dominated the field, though there have recently been incursions by those who would concentrate on the analysis of events and emphasize interdisciplinary ties with the social sciences.

In the secondary school, world history has become a tenth-grade elective in the social studies curriculum. Many individual schools (but few states) require the course for graduation. Recent sampling surveys on the status of the world history course and the practices in teaching it tend to confirm its traditional characterization. Few teachers are sufficiently prepared in this vast area; the course is textbook dominated; chronology is the dominant pattern of presentation; and Europe tends to be emphasized unless an explicit effort is made to give equal coverage to several areas of the world.

Textbooks for the world history course follow either a chronological or an area-study pattern. Only a few of the more recent texts adhere to the latter pattern, which emphasizes interdisciplinary relationships. The remaining texts in world history illustrate many of the shortcomings of the purely chronological history against which the analytic historians have reacted. For the most part they are strongly oriented toward the Western world, making references to Asia, Africa, and Latin America only insofar as events and aspects of those areas of the world influence developments in Europe and ultimately the United States.

The best of the chronological texts present conceptual schemes—that is, basic themes that are to be examined in several historical contexts—around which the contents of the book are purportedly organized. But since these schemes seldom consistently determine the selection of material, the basic themes are often effectively buried in irrelevant material. Also, since the concepts tend to reflect the Western orientation of the book, cultural distortion results when they are applied to the non-West.

Three newer texts by Ewing, Stavrianos, and Welty incorporate an area-studies approach in which contiguous geographic areas rather than individual states serve as the basis of organization. These books contain more in-depth analyses of both Western and non-

Western cultures than do the chronologically organized books, though they have their own problems of content and continuity. They seem quite adaptable to inquiry teaching although not specifically designed for this approach. Workbooks accompanying the texts do not offer the teacher much help in this adaptation, however, for the workbooks are generally more descriptively oriented than the texts themselves. Similarly the tests prepared for use with the texts tend to encourage the memorization of dates, names, and events.

Special materials now available in world history—for example, Fenton's *Thirty-two Problems in World History,* the units prepared by the Anthropology Curriculum Study Project, and some recent state curriculum guides—offer the most promising help for the world history teacher who wishes to promote inquiry procedures. These materials attempt to increase the concern for the non-West, incorporate interdisciplinary concepts, and emphasize analytic rather than descriptive content. The world history course in the future may depend heavily on paperbacks and pamphlets that can be more easily kept up to date and can be related to theories or models developed by the teacher and class. The education of the future world history teacher will necessarily include a broader preparation in philosophy, logic, and the social sciences.

HIGH SCHOOL PSYCHOLOGY AND SOCIOLOGY

Girault has observed that the rationale for including the formal study of psychology and sociology in the school curriculum is threefold. First, through the study of these disciplines the student can learn to emulate the ways of thinking of the behavioral scientist as he examines his own social environment. Second, psychology and sociology courses can help the student become a more intelligent consumer of the products of social science research. And third, the student can enrich his insight and understanding of himself and society by studying these behavioral sciences.

Girault has argued that instructional material in psychology is ordinarily pressed into one of two molds. Some texts and secondary courses in psychology are heavily oriented toward life-adjustment problems of the student. Other texts and courses emphasize psychology as an academic discipline. None of the materials examined by Girault makes a satisfactory compromise between these polar emphases. Texts that follow the life-adjustment approach usually ignore the scientific basis of the discipline and tend to sermonize about such things as tact, recreation, etiquette, and personal appearance. Girault has suggested that life-adjustment topics could be used viably as springboards to psychological inquiry if students were guided toward examining textbook prescriptions and forming and testing their own hypotheses.

Texts emphasizing life adjustment also often treat legitimate psychological problems in a shallow manner. Topics such as mental illness, the use of drugs, sex, perception, and psychiatry are inadequately discussed or actually misrepresented in the context of modern life. On the other hand, discipline-oriented texts are so attuned to the academic competencies required for college work in psychology that they lack meaning for secondary students. Undoubtedly these latter texts present a more sophisticated view of the science, but they only sharpen the dilemma of how to make the study of psychology in the secondary school increase both the student's self-understanding and his insight into the social sciences.

Girault suggests that an adequate sociology text should discuss the central concepts of the discipline, some of the theoretical models that sociologists use to conceptualize their work, and examples of sociological studies. A sociology course based on such a text would involve students in the study of groups, institutions, and social structure—three main classifications in sociological analysis. Understanding of sociology as an evolving field would come from an examination of theories such as the life-space (force-field) model or balance theory. An understanding of the *modus operandi* of the sociologist would emerge from an examination of such studies as those of Lynd, Warner, Hollingshead, Dobriner, Sutherland, or Cohen, who researched social behavior in communities, among criminals, and among delinquent boys. Students should have the opportunity to design and pursue at least one original field problem themselves.

The texts examined by Girault make substantial contributions toward the review of concepts and theories but do not use available research studies to substantiate their conclusions. There is also evidence that textbook authors avoid confrontations in sensitive areas. One text discusses the problem of minority-group status without mention of the civil-rights movement. The topic of religion is typically dealt with almost completely outside the framework of sociology. Girault has suggested that honesty and consistency are called for in all such cases. First, all relevant facets of controversial issues should be explored, regardless of the social sensitivities of some potential readers. Second, if a subject cannot be treated in a manner consistent with the discipline, then it should be omitted from the text.

The teaching of both psychology and sociology suffers in still another way. Few teachers are adequately prepared in either area to supplement text material with their own knowledge in the field. As a result many teachers are heavily dependent on the text for both substantive content and student activities. Since few if any of these texts in these fields effectively involve students in the process of inquiry, courses often fail to elicit this kind of student involvement.

The most promising project in school sociology is the Sociological Resources for Secondary Schools, sponsored by the American Sociological Association and funded by the National Science Foundation. The project, located at Ann Arbor, Michigan, and directed by Professor Robert Angell, is now constructing a series of episodes around sociological concepts. SRSS intends to produce materials that actively involve students in the collection, classification, and interpretation of data. The goal of the project is to demonstrate how to seek answers rather than to give them.

HIGH SCHOOL GEOGRAPHY

Greco has defined geography as a spatial science that studies the association of different natural elements on the earth's surface. He distinguishes two types of geography—topical and regional. The topical geographer focuses on a given type of element or category of elements in different parts of the world. Thus there are many kinds of topical geographers—physical, biogeographic, political, economic, cultural, etc. The regional geographer, on the other hand, attempts to explore the interrelationships among several of these elements in order to characterize a specific area more completely. His purpose is to identify and describe existing formal or functional regions that exhibit a distinctive cohesiveness or homogeneity among their topical elements.

Geography can serve general education in both elementary and secondary schools by demonstrating comparatively how man everywhere organizes himself in space to maximize his goals. Area studies, emphasizing the cultural adaptations of man in various regions, can increase the students' understanding of man's quest for progress and security in many contexts. The region, in fact, can provide the conceptual matrix for accommodating the concerns of all the social sciences in the social studies curriculum. Geographic regions can provide the settings in which students may attack problems, analyze relationships, ascertain typicality, and engage in social inquiry.

Present courses in geography are topical, regional, or a combination of the two. In the topical course the treatment of physical elements ordinarily precedes consideration of the cultural. Regional courses focus either on political units or on groups of states that may be considered cultural areas. Unfortunately the study of a culture is so all encompassing that these courses often become subjective and artistic rather than objective and scientific. Nonetheless the regional approach, at least in theory, seems to serve the broad scope of the inquiry process better than a topical approach that necessarily limits investigation to predetermined aspects of an area. The High School Geography Project of the Association of American Geographers is presently producing materials that may suggest an appropriate combination of the two approaches.

Contemporary geography textbooks are of uneven quality. Textbooks differ in language style—some texts sound flat and uninteresting, while others are lively and readable—and in the quality of their graphic materials. Many textbooks are of only limited use in promoting inquiry because their internal organization consistently fails to show the interrelationships among described factors and avoids raising "how" and "why" questions. Only a few texts approach controversial topics with sufficient verve and candor to stimulate student questing. Most geography texts approach important issues with antiseptic care.

A textbook may also be judged on its potential for encouraging speculation or hypothesizing about new possibilities in man's world. Most texts deter student speculation by positing notions of closed systems. Moreover, too many geography texts present evaluative statements as fact, thus disallowing the student the right to make his own value judgments about the cultural world. Finally, texts may be judged according to their help in integrating student knowledge into new and meaningful constructs. On the basis of these four aspects of inquiry—questing, speculating, evaluating, and constructing—Greco judged only three major geography texts as adequate.

CONTROVERSY AND VALUES IN SOCIAL STUDIES

Chesler has reviewed the literature on the treatment of controversial issues in social studies, commentaries on social studies texts, and two representative texts in order to explore the teacher's role in managing value controversies in social studies classrooms. He has postulated that the preoccupation of social studies with value-laden material, with the understanding and appreciation of democracy, and with student attitudes and behavior makes the handling of conflict. and controversy a paramount concern.

Controversy arises in our society when men care enough about an issue to differ either on goals or on the means to reach them. At other times conflicts result from differing priorities of goals or means. Proposals for dealing with values in classroom settings range from the identification of common truths to the development of processes for adjudicating value issues. Such proposals often differentiate between "end" values and "means" values, though some philosophers suggest that ultimate or end values may not exist.

Many of the general proposals for teaching social studies—emphasizing decision-making, induction and discovery, and inquiry—involve strategies for dealing with the value dimension of problems. Most authors decry the fact that values and goals are often predetermined when teachers concentrate on certain subject matter. For example, some teachers assume that communism should be exposed as monolithic, subversive, and evil. Indoctrination is often the result in the classroom when teachers attempt to maneuver in sensitive value areas.

Textbooks in social studies regularly deal fallaciously with values. Under the cover of impartiality value prejudices are often included in textual discussions. In other instances textbook authors assume a consensus on values, thus obviating the possibility of students' confronting the clash of values that really occurs in our pluralistic society. Textbooks too frequently represent our plural moral system inadequately by assuming nonpluralism, treating values at too high a level of abstraction, or slighting them as epiphenomena of factual disagreements.

The role of the teacher in working with value problems is a sensitive one. If he takes too adamant a stand on an issue, he runs the danger of indoctrinating students or subverting the consideration of alternatives. If he feigns neutrality, he may subtly and unwittingly propagandize for one side or give his students the impression that bland impartiality is the appropriate stance of the citizen. Also, in an aura of studied neutrality, students may not find the needed guidance in identifying criteria or processes for making value choices. What the teacher needs are strategies that will allow the student to explore problems of differences and conflicts in values and force him toward the self-conscious, active assessment of his own beliefs. Chesler has suggested that in an atmosphere of defensible partisanship the teacher can join this enterprise as a fellow inquirer.

CORRELATES OF THE SOCIAL STUDIES CURRICULUM

Jennings has studied a national sample of 1,669 seniors in ninety-seven public and nonpublic schools to ascertain the availability of various social studies courses during the high school careers of these students. He categorized all courses into eleven basic social studies offerings, which were available to the students in the following order of frequency: American history, general world history, economics, American government, American problems, specialized world history, geography, sociology, psychology, international and comparative politics, and personal problems. American history was available to virtually all students in the sample, but less than one-fifth of them had had the opportunity to take a course in psychology, international and comparative politics, or personal problems.

By statistical manipulation Jennings tested whether there would be a difference between sampling schools and sampling the students themselves. In six subject areas differences of less than 10 percent resulted from sampling students rather than schools. However, the availability of the remaining five subjects—specialized world history, economics, American problems, international and comparative politics, and psychology—would have been underestimated by 25 to 50 percent if the traditional school sample had been used. The social studies curriculum appears more complete and varied when examined in terms of students than when examined in terms of schools.

Jennings also assessed the effect of three types of variables on the social studies curriculum—demographic features, structural features of schools, and the academic quality of schools. First, he examined various regions, communities of different sizes, and standard metropolitan statistical areas (SMSA's) for unique curriculum patterns.

The Midwest, Jennings concluded, is relatively strong on geography and international and comparative politics, while the Northeast emphasizes special world history and deemphasizes general world history, American government, sociology, and psychology.

Having considered the effect of community size Jennings determined that large cities do not necessarily have the best curricular offerings, but the smallest communities do, in fact, tend to be scholastically deprived. Going to school in a large SMSA presents no great advantage to the student in comparison to attending school in a non-SMSA, though American problems and specialized world history are courses more characteristic of the metropolitan than of rural counties.

Among the structural features of schools that affect school curriculum, the span of grades in the school is the most influential variable examined. The fewer the grades in the school, the more the social studies offerings. Other structural variables—such as public versus nonpublic schools and senior class size—are less informative, though, again, very small class size is associated with fewer offerings.

Various measures of academic quality—the percentage of college preparatory students, the student dropout rate, and the presence of an accelerated curriculum—show no consistent relationship to the availability of courses. Some factors do appear to be more associated with certain courses, however. American problems and specialized world history, for instance, are more likely to be offered by schools with low dropout rates. In a very modest way schools with accelerated programs, schools with curriculum guides, and schools having had a recent social studies evaluation tend either to display a greater variety of courses or to place more emphasis on newer courses.

Jennings also used rank-order correlations to compare the relative occurrence of course offerings according to pairs of categories for each variable. Overall, he discovered that regardless of demographic, structural, and academic characteristics there was a remarkable similarity in the relative availability of course offerings in social studies. Only the Northeast and the largest of the SMSA's differed significantly from the other areas in the availability or emphasis on courses. Seniors in the Midwest or in the large SMSA's had the greatest variety of courses. The greatest course diversity is found in large schools with small grade spans. Jennings' research appears to confirm the judgment that a senior class of 200 or more allows for a more diverse curriculum.

Social Studies in the Next Decade

Throughout this book the contributors have attempted to describe and critically evaluate the present status of social studies education. In the remaining pages we would like to offer some visionary and prescriptive material that will touch upon several aspects of social studies.

THE FOCUS: CRUCIAL ISSUES OF MAN AND SOCIETY

Other books have examined in detail the conditions of our society that precipitate conflict, which in its mildest form appears as disagreement in policy and in its extreme form, as mob violence and street fighting. (See 8, pp. 4–21, 153–58, and 179–98.) Recently a group of social and behavioral scientists who felt "a sense of international concern for the welfare of mankind" (10) has undertaken a study of human conflict—what it is, how it comes about, and how disciplines like anthropology or economics can contribute to its understanding and resolution. In addition, a small but articulate group of social studies educators has, after careful study, proposed ways in which the social studies teacher can deal rationally with social issues and human conflict in the classroom (5, 7, 8, 11).

Since social and human conflict is inescapable and since students are involved in it either as actors or as observers, responsibility rests with the school to provide the necessary concepts and tools to increase rationality in thought and action. The social studies classroom in particular becomes the laboratory in which students are trained to analyze value problems intelligently and to defend their own value positions on communicable grounds. Classroom participants learn or discover for themselves intellectual strategies that are applicable to the adjudication and validation of values. They learn, for example, that conflict in values implies uncompromised alternatives, that according to certain criteria some alternatives may be better than others, and that proposed solutions to the problem may be judged in terms of their consequences. They also learn that value incompatibilities may be resolved or minimized, provided the participants are willing to defend and negotiate their values in public and avoid the use of emotive language.

We believe that the primary social studies objective in the next decade should be to foster the conduct of inquiry into contemporary controversial social issues. While it is difficult to anticipate what the exact issues will be ten years hence, it is reasonable to assume that some present social issues will persist. For example:

1. *Inter-group relations.* The main issue here is the status of Negroes and other racial and ethnic minorities—their legal rights, education, housing, employment, political representation, and self-esteem, as well as intermarriages and relations with other groups.

2. *World citizenship.* The crucial issues here are proposals for world government, the elimination of the territorial boundaries of nation-states, the development of broader loyalties, nuclear disarmament, and the strengthening of international peace organizations such as the United Nations.

3. *Population control.* The pivotal issues here—such as birth control, legalized abortions, illegitimate children, and social welfare to unwed mothers—are closely connected with the economic and social conditions in a culture.

4. *Equitable distribution of income.* Poverty, unemployment, taxation, labor-management relations, and federal aid to states, local communities, and individuals are some unsettled questions.

5. *Ideological conflict.* Controversies stem from the differing assumptions and the clash of communist, capitalist, and socialist value systems; related issues are the concepts of coexistence and neutralism.

6. *Marriage and the family.* This area of controversy includes incest and other taboos, the sexual adjustment of husband and wife, premarital sexual relations, promiscuity, homosexuality, venereal diseases, marriage and divorce patterns, and prostitution.

We have by no means exhausted the list of critical social issues that will persist into the foreseeable future. The point is that the entire social studies program—the curriculum, the instructional process, textbooks, materials, audio-visual communication media, etc.—must focus on controversial issues and must provide appropriate models for dealing with them in a spirit of inquiry.

THE CURRICULUM

A social studies curriculum that will contribute to intelligent decision-making in the area of social issues will have to depart radically from the prevailing pattern of separate disciplines or subject areas, for example, history, geography, and government or civics. In Edgar Wesley's words, "The social studies are the social sciences simplified for pedagogical purposes" (13). Charles Keller agreed with this view of social studies when he claimed that "the social studies are . . . a federation of subjects each with its own discipline" (6). Furthermore, the present social studies program reflects a previous era of scholarship in which history reigned over all the other social and behavioral sciences. The current social studies program presents us with a perfect example of cultural gap—that is, a program that does not incorporate in a systematic way the concepts and methods of investigation of such fields as anthropology, economics, social psychology, and sociology. Finally, the social studies program of today is dysfunctional because, as we have discovered from our research, it neither focuses on nor deals reflectively with social controversy.

We realize that a change in curriculum without concomitant changes in the other aspects of the school milieu would not be very effective. The change must encompass all the dimensions of the educative process—the substantive, the procedural, and the environmental. In order to foster inquiry in social issues, the social studies curriculum should be reorganized on the following bases:

1. It must be truly interdisciplinary, drawing from history and geography but particularly from anthropology, economics, political science, social psychology, and sociology. The volume by Berelson and Steiner entitled *Human Behavior: An Inventory of Scientific Findings* (1) provides a very good example of the application of generalizations from the social and behavioral sciences to the examination and analysis of such concepts as learning and thinking, motivation, the family, social stratification, and culture.

2. It must be built around key social issues such as poverty and affluence in American society, civil rights and the Negro, marriage and the family, and civil disobedience. Starting with the first grade the social studies program should be based on selected issues treated in depth, followed by more complex analyses of the same issues at each grade level all the way through high school. This program of studies resembles Bruner's spiral curriculum, which proposes that certain basic topics or concepts be treated in progressively more sophisticated terms in the grades.

3. It must emphasize analytical concepts and generalizations that explain rather than merely narrate human conflict in societal contexts. For example, the concept of social change may explain why

societies in the past moved in a certain direction, what factors were pivotal in the change that occurred, and how social conflict or disorganization was avoided or fostered. On this concept Berelson and Steiner provide illuminating generalizations drawn from social science research literature:

> Social changes imposed on a society from outside are especially likely not to be accepted. Forced change from the outside tends to result in overt compliance but covert resistance.

> The more a social change threatens or appears to threaten the traditional values of the society, the greater the resistance to that change and the greater its attendant cost in social and personal disorganization.

> Social change is more likely to occur in heterogeneous societies than in homogeneous ones. (Berelson and Steiner, 1, pp. 614–15.)

4. It must incorporate models of exploration and validation of empirical and normative propositions. Such operations as the formulation of a hypothesis, the collection of data, the testing of the hypothesis, and the arriving at a conclusion supported by the evidence are indispensable in inquiry into empirical relations. Exploring alternative solutions to value problems, clarifying the meaning of expressed attitudes and values, and tracing logical consequences of proposed social policies are some important operations in the process of examining value judgments (8).

What are the implications of this shift in emphasis? First, descriptive material regarding the political development and military accomplishments of societies in the past—ancient Mesopotamia, Greece, Rome, Medieval Europe, etc.—will probably be omitted. So will much of the narrative surrounding the romantic adventures of the conquistadors and other epic figures who discovered and settled the New World. The Revolutionary War and the Civil War will not be fought over and over again unless they relate to the phenomenon of war as a social movement of considerable importance. Lists of Presidents and accompanying biographical notes will have to be put aside unless they have a direct relationship to an important social issue under examination.

Second, each offering in the curriculum will not be identified on the basis of a distinct field—for example, United States history or geography—but on the basis of an area of controversy—such as intrahuman family relations, pornography and its control, or communism. The rearrangement of the curriculum on the basis of social issues rather than traditional social studies fields will inescapably introduce a genuinely interdisciplinary orientation.

Third, since the basis for selecting concepts, generalizations, and methods of investigation is their relevance to the analytic study of social issues, it is possible that social and behavioral scientists will be increasingly motivated to study contemporary social problems. While we would not want scholars to become social engineers, we do hope that more scholars will move in the direction of C. P. Snow, Margaret Mead, Kenneth Boulding, Anatol Rappoport, David Riesman, Gunnar Myrdal, and others, who have greatly contributed to our understanding of crucial human problems. Elton McNeil has expressed his hope that "this effort will be the precursor of a growing refinement of theory and application of social science in the affairs of man." Perhaps this hope will soon be realized.

Fourth, the curriculum will have to be more flexible and open-ended. As new social issues appear, they will have to be incorporated into the program and replace those that have either been resolved or have lost their currency. Also, different states and communities in the United States may elect to emphasize those issues that relate directly to their local concerns. On the other hand certain problems common to all mankind could and should provide the basic referents for study for all students.

Finally, it is very possible (and desirable) that the new curriculum will draw substantively and methodologically on the field of philosophy. For one thing philosophy directly relates to human values—their meaning, justification, and adjudication. If social issues are to be studied analytically, philosophic concepts and methods will have to become part of the social studies curriculum. (See 8, Chapter 7, and 9, Chapter 4.)

INSTRUCTIONAL STRATEGIES

In order to foster the critical examination of social issues, the teacher will have to make major changes in his classroom role. The teacher must facilitate inquiry and be a fellow-inquirer. He can no longer pretend to have the right answers to both normative and empirical questions. He must believe that values are not taught but examined in the open market of ideas. The following general procedures are useful in the issue-centered classroom: (1) A value issue or a social problem is identified by the students or the teacher. (2) Each member of the group presents his own value position on the issue. (3) Individual value positions are grouped under broader value categories. (4) Each member is asked to explain how he came to hold a particular value. (5) Each student or group of students taking a similar stance is asked to defend his or its values on the issue. Defenses of a normative judgment will differ. Some students may defend a value on strictly personal grounds that cannot be communicated. Some may respond emotionally to the issue and use (intentionally or unintentionally) psychological tricks to support their value claims and discredit others. Some may appeal to an undisputed authority—such as the Bible or the Constitution—to legitimize their view. Some may use logic to examine their own values—their empirical or factual roots, their emotive or psychological bases, and their relation to other values.

While a group consensus on fundamental value incompatibilities is unlikely, value issues can be analyzed and clarified, alternative value postures and their consequences can be explored, and each member of the group can become more conscious of his own assumptions and biases about critical social problems. If nothing else, each participant can enlarge his perspective by recognizing that there are other value positions that purport to rest on valid grounds. Also, the participants can begin to see the major procedural differences between the validation of normative statements and that of empirical statements.

The teacher may rely on student presentation (solicited or unsolicited) of social issues of general concern, or he may devise classroom experiences that will bring about personal involvement in social issues. We found, for instance, that a newspaper article describing a case of "bad Samaritanism" (bystanders who refused to aid a man being robbed in the street) provided the springboard for a lengthy and rational examination of the issue in question. Similarly articles and books on such issues as the Vietnam War, interracial marriages in Brazil, city-bossism, and United States foreign policy toward Cuba have provided the basis for inquiry into social problems.

Simulation and games have also been productive teaching devices for training students to make rational decisions during critical periods. For example, a class on international relations may be taught the basic concepts of the field through simulating important political roles—such as prime minister, foreign secretary, minister of defense, or leader of the opposition party—and by having groups of students perform these roles for their country. In the process of conducting the business of the state, students learn the give and take of the political process, the risks involved in investing resources unwisely, and the intricate power relations among sovereign states. These games and simulated environments purport to give the participants direct insights into the social phenomenon or problem under study. (See Giffin (3), Guetzkow *et al.* (4), and Garvey and Seiler (2).) We expect that more of these devices will be used in the future in a more sophisticated way.

INSTRUCTIONAL MATERIALS

There is no single element in the educative process that militates so directly against the process of inquiry as the traditional social studies textbook. If the social studies classroom is to have some influence in sensitizing the younger generation to the problems of society and providing the intellectual means to cope with social issues, it must have certain materials to support this effort:

1. *Discovery episodes.* These include original documents, statistical tables, graphs, maps, art objects, poems, or musical records; their main function in the classroom is to stimulate students to explore and validate alternative solutions to social and personal problems. The discovery episodes serve as springboards into reflective thought about human affairs. For example, a statuette from ancient Sumer may be used as the discovery object that motivates students to raise such questions as: What culture could produce an art object of this kind? What was the social status of the person depicted in the statuette? What methods of inquiry can be used to identify the object and place it in its proper time-space context? Since it includes limited clues and is introduced in a gamelike atmosphere, the discovery episode encourages the student to develop defensible hypotheses and to figure out for himself the techniques and methods that will allow him to explore and confirm the hypotheses in a productive way. In the process of figuring out the answers to the questions posed by himself, the student develops sophisticated skills of social research. A collection of discovery episodes (including demographic charts, Chinese poetry, music from the Soviet Union, geography games, and a case of "bad Samaritanism") and student reaction

to them appears in a book by Massialas and Zevin entitled *Creative Encounters in the Classroom: Teaching and Learning through Discovery* (9).

2. *Monographs.* Short but scholarly treatises of selected social problems will present substantive material and demonstrate methods of investigation into social affairs that the inquiring student may use to conduct his own research. The Harbrace Casebooks in Political Science series presents a good example of this kind of material stressing legal and documentary research skills. One of the books in the series, *The Uses of Power: Seven Cases in American Politics* (14), offers seven cases, including one on the Congress entitled "Race, Religion, and the Rules Committee: The Kennedy Aid-to-Education Bills," one on the Supreme Court called "Bookies and 'Bugs' in California: Judicial Control of Police Practices," and one on regulatory agencies entitled "How to Get into TV: The Federal Communications Commission and Miami's Channel 10." Each case study represents original research, and it is fully documented.

3. *Reference materials.* Yearbooks, encyclopedias, books of readings, anthologies, almanacs, dictionaries, etc., will still be useful as convenient sources of data that will allow students to pursue some of the questions raised in the inquiry-centered classroom.

4. *Computer facilities.* Although elementary and secondary schools will probably not be using computers on a large scale in the near future, such facilities may well be used by students conducting field and survey research. The new focus on social problems will shift the emphasis from historical-documentary research to sociological, psychological, and philosophical research. Questionnaires, sampling techniques, data coding, key punching, and processing and tabulating of IBM cards will become commonplace. Research design and statistical techniques, as well as philosophic and linguistic analysis, will become central in the new program.

5. *Data banks.* It is conceivable that schools throughout the country will be linked by large information storage and retrieval centers. Thus any data required for research projects may be easily acquired by the teacher and the students.

6. *A-V Communication media.* Television and other media will be used more extensively in the classroom primarily to provide vivid and real pictures of the world, and they will emphasize social phenomena—a revolution in the Dominican Republic, food riots in India, the operation of a commune in China, a civil rights march in

Chicago, slum areas in New York and in London, an address on poverty and affluence by a United Nations official, etc.

The above list is not exhaustive, but it illustrates the fact that an inquiry-oriented approach requires the shift from a single textbook to multiple media.

THE EDUCATION OF SOCIAL STUDIES TEACHERS

We have been associated with teacher preparation programs for considerable time and have been dissatisfied with the prevailing practices. With few exceptions the major preparation of teachers is in history rather than in a social or behavioral science. Most teachers have very little, if any, experience with social-scientific or philosophic methods of investigation. What they know best is to narrate and sometimes dramatize for students what their college instructors and textbook authors consider to be important events in history. As David Potter said, and with good reason, historians have failed to deal adequately with generalization, and they have neglected the findings of scholars in the social and behavioral sciences. In Potter's words, "although history has constantly made all sorts of assumptions about the nature of man, it has never possessed any systematic method for checking these assumptions" (12).

While many of the ills in social studies can be attributed to the influence of the narrative school of historians or the "historians of the unique," educators have done their share to minimize the opportunity for inquiry into human and social problems. First, few if any teacher-preparation sequences can accurately be called "programs." Social studies teachers under the guidance of their college advisors become collectors of courses. The collection usually includes courses in general education, history, and, to a lesser extent, the social sciences and pedagogy. During their senior year prospective teachers take a course known as "student teaching." Nowhere in their formal college work do they get an opportunity to integrate knowledge and experience from their general education, their field of specialization, the social and psychological foundations of education, and their practice in teaching.

The course commonly known as "Methods in the Teaching of the Social Studies" does not help the teacher very much in dealing rationally with problems of man and society. Many methods courses are anti-intellectual; they concentrate on activities (such as lesson planning and conducting "effective" classroom discussions) that likely can be better learned through laboratory experience, student-teaching, or internship programs; and they do not offer a basic theoretical model to deal critically with human and social problems. Our observations of the available methods texts suggest that methods courses usually deal with the banal and the trivial—long lists of objectives, bibliographies, and "how-to-do" materials, activities, and techniques. One of the current best sellers in social studies methods is a text that lists basic principles of learning, aims for individual lessons, the factors in teaching various subjects, characteristics of effective social studies teachers, addresses of textbook publishers and United Nations agencies, etc., without much discussion or explanation. The book assumes that if the prospective teacher absorbs its "cookbook recipes," he will automatically be able to apply them to his teaching tasks. The author of this methods textbook is not concerned with the "why" of the proposed activities and classroom practices he proposes. Needless to say, the book is devoid of a conceptual framework that delimits the boundaries of the field, integrates the various elements in the educative process, and gives a theoretical base of operation to the practitioner.

It is no wonder that many proposals by Conant and others for strengthening teacher education programs either exclude the methods course altogether or relegate it to a secondary position. Unless the methods course becomes more rigorous in its intellectual content and changes its main focus, it will continue to maintain its low status in the academic community or will disappear altogether.

While there are grounds for looking at social studies pessimistically, there are some developments in progress that promise a brighter future for the profession. Let us then as teachers, educators, scholars, and publishers join hands in expediting our entry into a new and exciting era of teaching social studies as inquiry.

Selected Bibliography

1. BERELSON, BERNARD, AND STEINER, GARY A., *Human Behavior: An Inventory of Scientific Findings,* Harcourt, Brace & World, New York, 1962.

2. GARVEY, DALE M., AND SEILER, WILLIAM H., *A Study of Effectiveness of Different Methods of Teaching International Relations to High School Students,* Cooperative Research Project No. S-370, Kansas State Teachers College, Emporia (Feb. 28, 1966).

3. GIFFIN, SIDNEY F., *The Crisis Game: Simulating International Conflict*, Doubleday, New York, 1965.

4. GUETZKOW, HAROLD, *et al.*, *Simulation in International Relations: Developments for Research and Teaching*, Prentice-Hall, Englewood Cliffs, N.J., 1963.

5. HUNT, MAURICE P., AND METCALF, LAWRENCE E., *Teaching High School Social Studies*, Harper, New York, 1955.

6. KELLER, CHARLES R., "Needed: Revolution in the Social Studies," *Saturday Review* (Sept. 16, 1961), 60–62.

7. LUNSTRUM, JOHN P., "The Treatment of Controversial Issues in Social Studies Instruction," in *New Challenges in the Social Studies*, B. G. Massialas and F. R. Smith (eds.), Wadsworth, Belmont, Calif., 1965, pp. 121–53.

8. MASSIALAS, BYRON G., AND COX, C. BENJAMIN, *Inquiry in Social Studies*, McGraw-Hill, New York, 1966.

9. MASSIALAS, BYRON G., AND ZEVIN, JACK, *Creative Encounters in the Classroom: Teaching and Learning Through Discovery*, Wiley, New York, 1967.

10. MCNEIL, ELTON B. (ed.), *The Nature of Human Conflict*, Prentice-Hall, Englewood Cliffs, N.J., 1965.

11. OLIVER, DONALD W., AND SHAVER, JAMES P., *Teaching Public Issues in the High School*, Houghton Mifflin, Boston, 1966.

12. POTTER, DAVID M., *People of Plenty: Economic Abundance and the American Character*, The University of Chicago Press, Chicago, 1954.

13. WESLEY, EDGAR BRUCE, *Teaching the Social Studies*, Heath, Boston, 1942.

14. WESTIN, ALAN F. (ed.), *The Uses of Power: Seven Cases in American Politics*, Harcourt, Brace & World, New York, 1962.

Name Index

Subject Index